Arjun Appadurai is Goddard Professor of Media, (
at New York University. He is the author of many
Modernity at Large: Cultural Dimensions of Globalization, ...
Things: Commodities in Cultural Perspective; and *Fear of Small Numbers: An
Essay on the Geography of Anger.*

The Future as Cultural Fact

ESSAYS ON THE GLOBAL CONDITION

Arjun Appadurai

VERSO

London • New York

First published by Verso 2013
© Arjun Appadurai 2013
Chapter 1 appeared in an earlier form as the introduction to Arjun Appadurai, ed., *The Social Life of Things*, Cambridge: Cambridge University Press, 1986
Chapter 2 appeared in *Transcultural Studies* 1 (2010)
Chapter 3 appeared in H. L. Seneviratne, ed., *The Anthropologist and the Native: Essays for Gananath Obeyesekere*, London: Anthem Press, 2009
Chapter 7 appeared in *Public Culture* 12:3 (2000)
Chapter 8 appeared in *Public Culture* 14:1 (2002) and *Environment and Urbanization* 13:2 (2001)
Chapter 9 appeared in an earlier form in V. Rao and M. Walton, eds., *Culture and Public Actions,* Stanford: Stanford University Press, 2004
Chapter 12 appeared in an earlier form in *Public Culture* 23:3 (2011)

1 3 5 7 9 10 8 6 4 2

Verso
UK: 6 Meard Street, London W1F 0EG
US: 20 Jay Street, Suite 1010, Brooklyn, NY 11201
www.versobooks.com

Verso is the imprint of New Left Books

ISBN-13: 978-1-84467-982-9 (PBK)
ISBN-13: 978-1-84467-983-6 (HBK)

British Library Cataloguing in Publication Data
A catalogue record for this book is available from the British Library

Library of Congress Cataloging-in-Publication Data
A catalog record for this book is available from the Library of Congress

Typeset in Minion Pro by Hewer Text UK Ltd, Edinburgh
Printed in the US by Maple Vail

Contents

Acknowledgements   vii
Introduction   1

PART 1: MOVING GEOGRAPHIES

  1. Commodities and the Politics of Value   9
  2. How Histories Make Geographies:
     Circulation and Context in a Global Perspective   61
  3. The Morality of Refusal   71
  4. The Offending Part:
     Sacrifice and Ethnocide in the Era of Globalization   85
  5. In My Father's Nation:
     Reflections on Biography, Memory, Family   101

PART 2: THE VIEW FROM MUMBAI

  6. Housing and Hope   115
  7. Spectral Housing and Urban Cleansing:
     Notes on Millennial Mumbai   131
  8. Deep Democracy:
     Urban Governmentality and the Horizon of Politics   153
  9. The Capacity to Aspire: Culture and the Terms of Recognition 179
 10. Cosmopolitanism from Below:
     Some Ethical Lessons from the Slums of Mumbai   197

PART 3: MAKING THE FUTURE

 11. The Spirit of Weber   217
 12. The Ghost in the Financial Machine   233
 13. The Social Life of Design   253
 14. Research as a Human Right   269
 15. The Future as Cultural Fact   285

Bibliography   301
Index   317

Acknowledgements

A rolling book gathers a lot of moss, in the form of audiences, critical readers and friends. This book certainly has. In India, I owe a special debt to the community of housing activists centered on SPARC (Society for the Promotion of Area Resource Centers) and SDI (Shack/Slum Dwellers International), the global network of which it is a part. For more than a decade, key individuals in this movement opened my eyes, and their doors, so as to enable me to feel that I was a small part of this movement, a student of it and a supporter as well. Special in this context are: Joel Bolnick, Sundar Burra, Celine D'Cruz, A. Jockin, Sheela Patel, and David Satterthwaite. Sheela deserves special mention since our many conversations provided me with many deep insights on the struggles of these activists and demanded my best critical insights and my fullest imaginative capacities. The research work I did on this movement would not have been possible without a major grant from the Ford Foundation, which was due to the support of another remarkable scholar-activist, Srilatha Batliwala, who worked for Ford at that time.

My other window into India is the organization I helped to found in Mumbai, a non-profit research organization devoted to the interests of youth in the city of Mumbai, which is called PUKAR (Partners for Urban Knowledge Action and Research). In this context, my greatest debts are to Rahul Srivastava, the first director of PUKAR, whose own ideas about neighborhood-based documentation were the seed for PUKAR's activities in stimulating research projects among urban youth; and to its present director, Anita Patil-Deshmukh, whose remarkable vision, talents, and energies have taken PUKAR from a small, struggling organization to a widely known innovator in the lives of young adults in Mumbai. I also owe a debt to the trustees, advisors, staff, and youth fellows of PUKAR, who have given PUKAR its soul and deepened my own understanding of the potential of research for social transformation.

In New York, I had the privilege of getting feedback and encouragement from the following friends at the New School, where I taught for several years: Michael Cohen, Benjamin Lee, Arien Mack, Tim Marshall, Vyjayanthi Rao, Janet Roitman, Ann Stoler, and Joel Towers. At New York University, my present home, I have been the beneficiary of warm support from the Department of Media, Culture and Communication at the Steinhardt School and the Institute for Public Knowledge. At NYU, the following individuals are owed my thanks: Craig Calhoun, Manthia Diawara, Allen Feldman, Radha Hegde, Eric Klinenberg, David Ludden, Ritty Lukose, Nick Mirzoeff, Harvey Molotch, Arvind Rajagopal, Debraj Ray, and the members of the Cultures of Finance Group at the Institute for Public Knowledge have been especially generous to me.

I have also benefited from the ideas and questions of friends in many other parts of the world during the past decade. They include: Marc Abeles, Lisa Anderson, Christopher Bayly, Ulrich Beck, Regina Bendix, Ritu Birla, Bill Brown, Dipesh Chakrabarty, Jean and John Comaroff, Veena Das, Faisal Devji, Yehuda Elkana, Peter Geschiere, Andre Gingrich, Thomas Blom Hansen, Keith Hart, Achille Mbembe, Sheldon Pollock, Kenneth Prewitt, Vijayendra Rao, Regina Rœmhild, Bernd Scherer, Charles Taylor, Peter van der Veer, Steve Vertovec, Rudolf Wagner, and Michael Walton.

A recent visit to Harvard University as the Loeb Senior Fellow at the Graduate School of Design gave me fresh energy to complete this book in light of conversations with Homi and Jacqueline Bhabha, Sugata Bose, Michael Herzfeld, Arthur Kleinman, Rahul Mehrotra, Mohsen Mostafavi, and Amartya Sen.

Over the long haul, I owe much in my mode of thought to two late mentors from the University of Chicago, Bernard Cohn and Victor Turner, and to two exemplars who also encouraged me in person and by example during their lives: Clifford Geertz and Edward Said.

My deepest debts are to those closest to me. My wife, Gabika Bočkaj, has brought her sharp intellect and engaged love to bear on the completion of the long journey reflected on this book. My son, Alok, has been the living spark in my life for all of his thirty-four years. My late spouse and partner, Carol Breckenridge, should have lived to see this book in print, having touched and improved all the ideas in it in some manner.

Two young scholars have helped me in my recent years at New York University: the first is Robert Wosnitzer, who has offered me support in my teaching and research in untold ways. The other is Jennifer Telesca, who worked through each of these essays and helped to strengthen the book in myriad ways, large and small. They exemplify the best futures of the academy.

Arjun Appadurai
New York City
September 2012

Introduction

In 1996, I published a book under the title of *Modernity at Large: Cultural Dimensions of Globalization*. The present book is a sequel to that early effort to think anthropologically about the world that opened up after the fall of the Berlin Wall in 1989. In the years since, I have had occasion to learn from those critics of *Modernity at Large* who found it too celebratory, perhaps even breathless, about the new world of open borders, free markets, and young democracies that seemed to have entered world history. In part as atonement, I wrote a short book with the title *Fear of Small Numbers* (2006) to explore why the triumphant globalization of the late 1980s produced major ethnocidal movements in the 1990s and major civilizational wars—including the war against Islam—in the first decade of the twenty-first century. I tried in this later book to complement my interest in global flows with a focus on global bumps, borders, black holes, and quarks, diacritics of the new global order.

At the same time, over the last decade, I have regularly been going to Mumbai, where I have engaged with two—not wholly unconnected—projects. The first is an ongoing collaboration with the members of a remarkable movement of housing activists, which is the source of much of my discussion in part 2 of this book. They showed me what is possible, and the odds against it, in the worldwide effort to make the urban poor the shapers of a better destiny for themselves. They struggle against the slumification of Mumbai, the hard evaluative demands of their global funders, the suspicious eye of the state, and the criticisms of their fellow activists in the burgeoning civil society of urban India. But they also have assets—and dreams as well. These assets and dreams are being constantly turned into strategies that constitute my main evidence for what I call the politics of possibility—against the politics of probability—in the era of globalization. The lessons they have taught me about actually existing democracy, about critical cosmopolitanism, and about the capacity to aspire, are put before the reader in the middle part of this book. These lessons unfolded for me in the context of my growing understandings of crime, speculation, corruption, and the cinema in contemporary Mumbai. So the backdrop of the city and the foreground of housing activism cohabit in part 2, and amount to an ethnography of aspiration in a harsh global mega-city.

The second project is one I helped to initiate in Mumbai, starting with very few resources, in the year 2000. This project is a non-profit research collective called PUKAR (Partners for Urban Knowledge Action and Research), which is now just over a decade old. Its primary mission is to re-conceive research so that it can be made available as a technique to those who are on the margins of the current educational system, mostly young men and women who have used the tools of research to advance new urban agendas and visions as well as personal dreams for a better urban future. This experiment is the basis for chapter 14 of this book, which seeks to argue that research, more democratically conceived than it is today, should be a human right.

This journey is the animating force of the book. But to turn it into a credible narrative, as a culturally oriented social scientist, I had to reconstruct and reorganize my own journey over the past few decades. One requirement of this retro-engineering was to revisit my initial ideas about globalization, about flow, circulation, region, imagination, and nation. That backward look is the main burden of part 1 of this book. In this part, I revisit a much earlier moment when I had begun to think about circulation and the politics of value, and persuaded a group of colleagues to investigate "the social life of things" as they move across regimes of value, enable new commodity paths through diversions, and bridge worlds far apart in space and time through their own capacity to morph, without losing their cultural significance.[1] When the results of this inquiry appeared in print, I was not aware that it contained an unknowing glimpse of the world to come in the 1990s and since, in which new material flows would both shrink our geographies and expand our imaginations. The long essay I originally published in 1986 is reproduced in an abridged form as the lead-in to the present book, as it presents a broad picture of the heterogeneous journeys of our materialized sociality that seems relevant even now, linking our markets, our moralities, and our many modernities. The remaining chapters in part 1 take up other aspects of the uneven journeys of nation, sacrifice, memory, and violence in the journey from the colonial world to our present disjunctures of space, place, and loyalty. Violence appears prominently in these chapters as both a limit and as a fantasy, as the always seductive technology to help us distinguish our bodies, our nations, and ourselves even as globalization draws them into increasingly promiscuous alliances.

Likewise, the chapters in part 1 are a dialogue with my own journey through places, problems, and disciplines. Above all, two recurrent themes mark this journey. One is the effort to work through and from the archive of anthropology, returning to its centers and mining its peripheries. From my earliest graduate years, I saw culture as the great counterpoint to economy, and in much of my work over the last four decades I have sought to understand what this counterpoint is about. It informs my work about finance, about development, about cities, about media, and more. Above all, this is why the spirit of Max Weber haunts and animates this book. Weber's comparative studies of meaning, speculation, salvation, charisma, and much else remain for me the most heroic

1   A. Appadurai, *Modernity at Large: Cultural Dimensions of Globalization*, Minneapolis: University of Minnesota Press, 1996.

example of an honest engagement with the varieties of human experience and the concomitant variety of human institutions and innovations.

Hence it is that a reflection on my debt to Max Weber is the topic of the first chapter of the final part of this book, which seeks to lay the foundations for an anthropology of the future, by which I mean an anthropology that can assist in the victory of a politics of possibility over a politics of probability. I am certain that this goal can be arrived at by many paths, and this is also why I remain deeply interested in the work of many other theorists of globalization whose main preoccupations might seem very different from my own. As this last part of the book suggests, the future is ours to design, if we are attuned to the right risks, the right speculations, and the right understanding of the material world we both inherit and shape. And since, following Marx, we cannot design the future exactly as we please, it is vital to build a picture of the historical present that can help us find the right balance between utopia and despair. The chapters in this book are thus also part of an analytic diagnosis of our current global condition.

Like most of my peers, this sort of diagnostic effort has forced me to ponder two questions: the first is whether globalization has changed shape, force, or form in any significant way in the more than twenty years since the fall of the Berlin Wall, a period that might be seen as the age of high globalization. The second question is about our own disciplinary and critical optics, about those prejudices that make us value some problems more than others and that give greater weight to some parts of our humanity than to others. My own answer to these questions, substantially a product of unplanned twists and circumstantial turns rather than of a highly defined theoretical agenda, is to be found in the details of the chapters to come, since useful anthropological insights continue to be most nuanced when they are least general. Still, I have come to see a dominant drift in the process of globalization in the last two decades, to which I now turn.

As to the object of globalization, both theories and observations continue to proliferate. My own view is that a deep trend of the last twenty years, doubtless with its own longer history, is the broadening of risk-taking and risk-bearing as properties of human life that link distant societies, cross national and market boundaries, and connect both the institutions of power and the agencies of ordinary human beings worldwide. This trend has been noted by Ulrich Beck[2] and other scholars, who have developed a picture of "risk society" as a dominant global social form. There is no doubt that as statistical understandings of disease, catastrophe, welfare, and governance become increasingly dominated by quantifiable models of risk, governmentality worldwide increasingly takes on the character of a risk-management enterprise. What has been less widely

---

2   U. Beck, *Risk Society: Towards a New Modernity*, London: Sage Publications, 1992.

noted is the growth of risk-based orientations to everyday life among ordinary human beings in many different locations. Small loan and microcredit beneficiaries have begun to think about debt, investment, and loss in statistical terms. Increasing numbers of people engage in forms of market-based speculation, such as day trading, currency trading, and credit-based shopping. Astrological practices everywhere co-exist with more statistically-defined ideas about chance and uncertainty. Likewise, forms of gambling on the racetrack, poker, and the like increasingly operate in the milieu of marketized models of risk and uncertainty. The financial meltdown of 2007–2010 is the great tsunami that binds large global banks, national governments, small investors, shopkeepers, farmers, and traders in an intricate web of speculative practices and institutions that unite the most diverse classes and fractions of the world population. No catastrophe today falls outside the net of market manipulators, speculators, and hedge-fund managers. An unprecedented multiplicity of threads links these high-end risk-takers to the everyday bearers (and victims) of risk-based strategies in every society. And it is not only the world of virtual market devices (such as credit swaps and catastrophe bonds) that assists in building this web, but also the interlinked fluctuations in the markets for such global commodities as gold, bluefin tuna, tulips, rare earths, and many other commodities, which tie the fates of miners, fishermen, farmers, and small traders to the macro-risk management strategies of banks, states, and transnational corporations. The troubling managerial ethos produced by this global web of risk-making and risk-bearing groups characterizes what I call (in chapter 15) the ethics of probability. So, while the worldwide flow of goods, people, images, and ideologies still best defines the era of globalization, I would suggest that its emerging diacritic is the domination of techniques and mentalities oriented to manipulating or withstanding risk, understood as the statistical representation of any and all of life's uncertainties.

This worldwide shift has not left our own disciplinary and critical techniques and lenses untouched. The disciplines with which I am most concerned also reflect some of these world changes in their own changed priorities in the last two decades. Economics, which is my shadow interlocutor throughout this book, moved into the study of risk in the early part of the twentieth century, with the path-breaking work of Frank Knight.[3] Since then, risk has been a major topic in economic theory and is perhaps the central concept in the field of economics, which now constitutes a major sub-field of business economics. As I suggest in chapters 12 and 15, Frank Knight's original concern with risk and uncertainty was reduced to an exclusive preoccupation with risk, since it was more susceptible to numerical modeling. More importantly, the explosion in models of risk encouraged a cozy traffic between modeling risk and the

---

3   F. H. Knight, *Risk, Uncertainty and Profit*, Boston: Houghton Mifflin Co., 2009 (1921).

practical business of exploiting risk for purposes of profit in the financial markets. This loss of critical edge in much of mainstream economics is in no small part a cause of the reckless financial practices that underlay the recent global meltdown. So as economics, particularly business economics, has become largely the study of risk, at the same time the manipulation of economic models has itself become a major source of risk for the global markets and the global economy. This field of study within economics has become both the mirror and the engine of financial profiteering.

The situation is somewhat more cheerful in the fields of design and planning, as more design theorists and critics become concerned with sustainability and seek to incorporate risk into their design thinking. This is most noticeable in the field of architecture, as for example in the growing centrality of "green" standards for building design and construction. It is also becoming a more salient feature of many kinds of design involving infrastructure, as they have come to be more conscious of sustainability as a core value as regards transportation, manufacture, and consumer behavior as contributors to environmental degradation. This is a topic I address in chapter 13.

As for anthropology, the discipline that has provided the backbone for much of my own work, globalization has certainly become a growing focus of anthropological interest in the last two decades, as evidenced in studies of migration, mediation, medicine, science, and technology undertaken from an anthropological perspective. Still, there is an underlying pull in the core concepts of anthropology—such as culture, diversity, structure, meaning, and custom—toward earlier concerns with persistence, stability, and fixity in the cosmologies of different societies. This tendency has limited the anthropological contribution to the study of how different human societies organize the future as a cultural horizon. And although this tendency is beginning to be challenged in various recent anthropological calls for the study of "the good life" and of "happiness" as cultural visions, there is still a desperate need for some more basic reorientation in anthropology so as to encourage robust contributions to the study of the ways in which humans construct their cultural futures. In many ways, this need is in large part the justification for the arrangement of the chapters of this book and is the central preoccupation of its final chapter, which is also reflected in the title of the book.

In the end, as we are reminded forcefully by those who are most articulate about global warming, environmental degradation and the possibly short future of our species as the central architects of the future of nature, it is vital to collaboratively envisage and build a robust anthropology of the future. This requires a full-scale engagement with the variety of ideas of human welfare and of the good life that surround us today and that survive in our archives of the past. This search can no longer be content with analyzing the cabinet of curiosities that anthropology originally opened to our eyes. It needs a full-scale debate about the best ways to design humanity in what could well be its last chapter in the mysterious story of nature as a whole. In this sense, the anthropology of the future and the future of anthropology may well provide the best critical energies for one another.

Part I

MOVING GEOGRAPHIES

CHAPTER ONE

Commodities and the Politics of Value[1]

This chapter aims to propose an anthropological perspective on the circulation of commodities in social life. The gist of this perspective can be put in the following way. Economic exchange creates value. Value is embodied in commodities that are exchanged. Focusing on the things that are exchanged, rather than simply on the forms or functions of exchange, makes it possible to argue that what creates the link between exchange and value is *politics,* construed broadly. This argument, which is elaborated in the text of this chapter, justifies the conceit that commodities, like persons, have social lives.[2]

Commodities can provisionally be defined as objects of economic value. As to what we ought to mean by economic value, the most useful (though not quite standard) guide is Georg Simmel. In the first chapter of *The Philosophy of Money,*[3] Simmel provides a systematic account of how economic value is best defined. Value, for Simmel, is never an inherent property of objects, but is a judgment made about them by subjects. Yet the key to the comprehension of value, according to Simmel, lies in a region where "that subjectivity is only provisional and actually not very essential."[4]

In exploring this difficult realm, which is neither wholly subjective nor quite objective, in which value emerges and functions, Simmel suggests that objects are not difficult to acquire because they are valuable, "but we call those objects valuable that resist our desire to possess them."[5] What Simmel calls economic objects, in particular, exist in the space between pure desire and immediate enjoyment, with some distance between them and the person who desires them, which is a distance that can be overcome. This distance is overcome in and through economic exchange, in which the value of objects is determined reciprocally. That is, one's desire for an object is fulfilled by the

---

1   This chapter is based on my lengthy introduction to *The Social Life of Things* (1986). This version is intended to highlight those arguments from the original essay that anticipate concerns about circulation, mediation, and materiality, which have remained interests for me ever since and play a vital role in the present volume.

2   In starting with exchange, I am aware that I am bucking a trend in economic anthropology, which has tended to shift the focus of attention to *production* on the one hand, and *consumption* on the other. This trend was a justifiable response to what had previously been an excessive preoccupation with exchange and circulation. The commodity angle, however, promises to illuminate issues in the study of exchange that had begun to look either boring or incorrigibly mysterious.

3   G. Simmel, *The Philosophy of Money,* London: Routledge, 1978 (1907).

4   Ibid., 73.

5   Ibid., 67.

sacrifice of some other object, which is the focus of the desire of another. Such exchange of sacrifices is what economic life is all about, and the economy as a particular social form "consists not only in exchanging *values* but in the *exchange of values*."[6] Economic value, for Simmel, is generated by this sort of exchange of sacrifices.

Several arguments follow this analysis of economic value in Simmel's discussion. The first is that economic value is not just value in general, but a definite sum of value, which results from the commensuration of two intensities of demand. The form this commensuration takes is the exchange of sacrifice and gain. Thus, the economic object does not have an absolute value as a result of the demand for it, but the demand, as the basis of a real or imagined exchange, endows the object with value. It is exchange that sets the parameters of utility and scarcity, rather than the other way round, and exchange that is the source of value: "The difficulty of acquisition, the sacrifice offered in exchange, is the unique constitutive element of value, of which scarcity is only the external manifestation, its objectification in the form of quantity."[7] In a word, exchange is not a byproduct of the mutual valuation of objects, but its source.

These terse and brilliant observations set the stage for Simmel's analysis of what he regarded as the most complex instrument for the conduct of economic exchange—money—and its place in modern life. But Simmel's observations can be taken in quite another direction. This alternative direction, which is exemplified by the remainder of this chapter, entails exploring the conditions under which economic objects circulate in different *regimes of value* in space and time.

Contemporary Western common sense, building on various historical traditions in philosophy, law, and natural science, has a strong tendency to oppose "words" and "things." Though this was not always the case even in the West, as Marcel Mauss noted in his famous work *The Gift*, the powerful contemporary tendency is to regard the world of things as inert and mute, set in motion and annihilated, indeed knowable, only by persons and their words.[8] Yet in many historical societies, things have not been so divorced from the capacity of persons to act and the power of words to communicate.[9] That such a view of things had not disappeared even under the conditions of occidental industrial capitalism is one of the intuitions that underlay Marx's famous discussion, in *Capital*, of the "fetishism of commodities."

6   Ibid., 80.

7   Ibid., 100.

8   See also L. Dumont, *On Value (Radcliffe-Brown Lecture), Proceedings of the British Academy* (Vol. LXVI), London: Oxford University Press, 1980.

9   See I. Kopytoff, "The Cultural Biography of Things: Commoditization as Process," in A. Appadurai, ed., *The Social Life of Things: Commodities in Cultural Perspective*, Cambridge: Cambridge University Press, 1986.

Even if our own approach to things is necessarily conditioned by the view that things have no meanings apart from those that human transactions, attributions, and motivations endow them with, the anthropological problem is that this formal truth does not illuminate the concrete, historical circulation of things. For that we have to follow the things themselves, for their meanings are inscribed in their forms, their uses, their trajectories. It is only through the analysis of these trajectories that we can interpret the human transactions and calculations that enliven things. Thus, even though from a *theoretical* point of view human actors encode things with significance, from a *methodological* point of view it is the things-in-motion that illuminate their human and social context. No social analysis of things (whether the analyst is an economist, an art historian, or an anthropologist) can avoid a minimum level of what might be called methodological fetishism. This methodological fetishism, returning our attention to the things themselves, is in part a corrective to the tendency to excessively sociologize transactions in things, a tendency we owe to Mauss, as Firth has noted.[10]

Commodities, and things in general, are of independent interest to several kinds of anthropology. They constitute the first principles and the last resort of archeologists. They are the stuff of "material culture," which unites archeologists with several kinds of cultural anthropologists. As valuables, they are at the heart of economic anthropology, and, not least, as the medium of gifting, they are at the heart of exchange theory and social anthropology generally. The commodity perspective on things represents a valuable point of entry to the revived, semiotically oriented interest in material culture, remarked and exemplified in a special section of *RAIN*.[11] But commodities are not of fundamental interest only to anthropologists. They also constitute a topic of lively interest to social and economic historians, to art historians, and, lest we forget, to economists, though each discipline might constitute the problem differently. Commodities thus represent a subject on which anthropology may have something to offer to its neighboring disciplines, as well as one about which it has a good deal to learn from them.

The five sections of this chapter are devoted to the following tasks. The first, on the spirit of commodity, is a critical exercise in definition, whose argument is that commodities, properly understood, are not the monopoly of modern

---

10   R. Firth, "Magnitudes and Values in Kula Exchange," in J. W. Leach and E. Leach, eds., *The Kula: New Perspectives on Massim Exchange*, Cambridge: Cambridge University Press, 1983, 89. See Alfred Schmidt (A. Schmidt, *The Concept of Nature in Marx*, London: New Left Books, 1971) for a similar critique of the "idealist" tendency in Marxist studies, which promotes the view that "since Marx reduces all economic categories to relationships between human beings, the world is composed of relations and processes and not of bodily material things." Obviously, careless subscription to *this* point of view can lead to exaggerations of the "vulgar" variety.

11   D. Miller, ed., "Things Ain't What They Used to Be," special section of *RAIN* (Royal Anthropological Institute News), 1983, 59, 5–7.

industrial economies. The next, on paths and diversions, discusses the strategies (both individual and institutional) that make the creation of value a politically mediated process. The subsequent section, on desire and demand, links short- and long-term patterns in commodity circulation to show that consumption is subject to social control and political redefinition. The last substantive section, on the relationship between knowledge and commodities, is concerned with demonstrating that the politics of value is in many contexts a politics of knowledge. The concluding section brings the argument back to politics as the mediating level between exchange and value.

THE SPIRIT OF THE COMMODITY

Few will deny that a commodity is a thoroughly socialized thing. The definitional question is: in what does its sociality consist? The purist's answer, routinely attributed to Marx, is that a commodity is a product intended principally for exchange, and that such products emerge, by definition, in the institutional, psychological, and economic conditions of capitalism. Less purist definitions regard commodities as goods intended for exchange, regardless of the form of the exchange. The purist definition forecloses the question prematurely. The looser definitions threaten to equate commodity with gift and many other kinds of thing. In this section, through a critique of the Marxian understanding of the commodity, I shall suggest that commodities are things with a particular type of social potential, that they are distinguishable from "products," "objects," "goods," "artifacts," and other sorts of things—but only in certain respects and from a certain point of view. If my argument holds water, it will follow that it is definitionally useful to regard commodities as existing in a very wide variety of societies (though with a special intensity and salience in modern capitalist societies), and that there is an unexpected convergence between Marx and Simmel on the topic of commodities.

The most elaborate and thought-provoking discussion of the idea of the commodity appears in volume 1, part I, of Marx's *Capital,* though the idea was widespread in nineteenth-century discussions of political economy. Marx's own reanalysis of the concept of commodity was a central part of his critique of bourgeois political economy and a fulcrum for the transition from his own earlier thought[12] on capitalism to the full-fledged analysis of *Capital.* Today, the conceptual centrality of the idea of commodity has given way to the neoclassical, marginalist conception of "goods," and the word "commodity" is used in neoclassical economics only to refer to a special subclass of primary goods and no longer plays a central analytic role. This is, of course, not the case with

---

12   See especially K. Marx, *Grundrisse: Foundations of the Critique of Political Economy,* New York: Vintage Books, 1973.

Marxian approaches in economics and sociology, or with neo-Ricardian approaches (such as those of Piero Sraffa), where the analysis of the "commodity" still plays a central theoretical role.[13]

But in most modern analyses of economy (outside anthropology), the meaning of the term commodity has narrowed to reflect only one part of the heritage of Marx and the early political economists. That is, in most contemporary uses, commodities are special kinds of manufactured goods (or services) are associated only with capitalist modes of production and are thus to be found only where capitalism has penetrated. Thus, even in current debates about proto-industrialization,[14] the issue is not whether commodities are associated with capitalism, but whether certain organizational and technical forms associated with capitalism are solely of European origin. Commodities are generally seen as typical material representations of the capitalist mode of production, even if they are classified as petty and their capitalist context as incipient.

Yet it is clear that this is to draw on only one strand in Marx's own understanding of the nature of the commodity. The treatment of the commodity in the first hundred or so pages of *Capital* is arguably one of the most difficult, contradictory, and ambiguous parts of Marx's corpus. It begins with an extremely broad definition of commodity ("A commodity is, in the first place, an object outside us, a thing that by its properties satisfies human wants of some sort or another"). It then moves dialectically through a series of more parsimonious definitions, which permit the gradual elaboration of the basic Marxian approach to use value and exchange value, the problem of equivalence, the circulation and exchange of products, and the significance of money. It is the elaboration of this understanding of the relationship between the commodity form and the money form that allows Marx to make his famous distinction between two forms of circulation of commodities (Commodities-Money-Commodities and Money-Commodities-Money), the latter representing the general formula for capital. In the course of this analytic movement, commodities become intricately tied to *money*, an impersonal market, and exchange value. Even in the simple form of circulation (tied to use value), commodities are related through the commensuration capabilities of money. Today, in general, the link of commodities to postindustrial social, financial, and exchange forms is taken for granted, even by those who in other regards do not take Marx seriously.

---

13 P. Sraffa, *Production of Commodities by Means of Commodities*, Cambridge: Cambridge University Press, 1960; D. Seddon, ed., *Relations of Production: Marxist Approaches to Economic Anthropology*, London: Frank Cass, 1978.

14 See, for example, F. Perlin, "Proto-Industrialization and Pre-Colonial South Asia," *Past and Present*, 1983, 98(1), 30–95.

Yet in Marx's own writings, there is the basis for a much broader, more cross-culturally and historically useful approach to commodities, whose spirit is attenuated as soon as he becomes embroiled in the details of his analysis of nineteenth-century industrial capitalism. By this earlier formulation, in order to produce not mere products but commodities, a man must produce use values for others, social use values.[15] This idea was glossed by Engels in a parenthesis he inserted into Marx's text in the following interesting way: "To become a commodity a product must be transferred to another, whom it will serve as a use-value, by means of an exchange."[16] Though Engels was content with this elucidation, Marx proceeds to make a very complex (and ambiguous) series of distinctions between products and commodities, but for anthropological purposes, the key passage deserves quotation in full:

> Every product of labour is, in all states of society, a use-value; but it is only at a definite historical epoch in a society's development that such a product becomes a commodity, viz. at the epoch when the labour spent on the production of a useful article becomes expressed as one of the objective qualities of that article, i.e., as its value. It therefore follows that the elementary value form is also the primitive form under which a product of labour appears historically as a commodity, and that the gradual transformation of such products into commodities, proceeds *pari passu* with the development of the value-form.[17]

The difficulty of distinguishing the logical aspect of this argument from its historical aspect has been noted by Anne Chapman,[18] whose argument I will return to shortly. In the above passage from *Capital,* the shift from product to commodity is discussed historically. But the resolution is still highly schematic, and it is difficult to specify or test it in any clear way.

The point is that Marx was still imprisoned in two aspects of the mid-nineteenth-century episteme: one could see the economy only in reference to the problematics of production;[19] the other regarded the movement to commodity production as evolutionary, unidirectional, and historical. As a result, commodities either exist or do not exist, and they are *products* of a particular sort. Each of these assumptions requires modification.

Despite these epistemic limitations, in his famous discussion of the fetishism of commodities, Marx does note, as he does elsewhere in *Capital,* that the commodity does not emerge whole-cloth from the product under bourgeois

---

15 K. Marx, *Capital: A Critical Analysis of Capitalist Production,* Moscow: Progress Publishers, 1971, 48.

16 Ibid.

17 Ibid., 67.

18 A. Chapman, "Barter as a Universal Mode of Exchange," *L'Homme,* 1980, 20(3), 33–83.

19 J. Baudrillard, *The Mirror of Production,* St. Louis: Telos Press, 1975.

production, but makes its appearance "at an early date in history, though not in the same predominating and characteristic manner as nowadays."[20] Though it is outside the scope of this chapter to explore the difficulties of Marx's own thought on precapitalist, nonstate, nonmonetary economies, we might note that Marx left the door open for the existence of commodities, at least in a primitive form, in many sorts of society.

The definitional strategy I propose is a return to a version of Engels's emendation of Marx's broad definition involving the production of use value *for others*, which converges with Simmel's emphasis on exchange as the source of economic value. Let us start with the idea that a commodity is *any thing intended for exchange*. This gets us away from the exclusive preoccupation with the "product," "production," and the original or dominant intention of the "producer" and permits us to focus on the dynamics of exchange. For comparative purposes, then, the question becomes not "What is a commodity?" but rather "What sort of an exchange is commodity exchange?" Here, and as part of the effort to define commodities better, we need to deal with two kinds of exchange that are conventionally contrasted with commodity exchange. The first is barter (sometimes referred to as direct exchange), and the other is the exchange of gifts. Let us start with barter.

Barter as a form of exchange has been analyzed by Chapman[21] in an essay that, among other things, takes issue with Marx's own analysis of the relationship between direct exchange and commodity exchange. Combining aspects of several current definitions of barter (including Chapman's), I would suggest that barter is the exchange of objects for one another *without* reference to money and *with* maximum feasible reduction of social, cultural, political, or personal transaction costs. The former criterion distinguishes barter from commodity exchange in the strict Marxist sense, and the latter from gift exchange by virtually any definition.

Chapman is right that, insofar as Marx's theory of value is taken seriously, his treatment of barter poses insoluble theoretical and conceptual problems,[22] for Marx postulated that barter took the form of direct exchange of the product (x use value A = y use value B), as well as direct exchange of the commodity (x commodity A = y commodity B). But this Marxist view of barter, whatever problems it may pose for a Marxist theory of the origin of exchange value, has the virtue of fitting well with Chapman's most persuasive claim—that barter, as either a dominant or a subordinate form of exchange, exists in an extremely wide range of societies. Chapman criticizes Marx for inserting the commodity into barter and wishes to keep them quite separate, on the grounds that

20   Marx, *Capital*, 86.
21   Chapman, "Barter as Universal Mode of Exchange."
22   Ibid., 68–70.

commodities assume the use of money objects (and thus congealed labor value), and not just money as a unit of account or measure of equivalence. Commodity exchange, for Chapman, occurs only when a money object intervenes in exchange. Since barter, in her model, excludes such intervention, commodity exchange and barter are formally completely distinct, though they may coexist in some societies.[23]

In her critique of Marx, it seems to me, Chapman takes an unduly restricted view of the role of money in the circulation of commodities. Though Marx ran into difficulties in his own analysis of the relationship between barter and commodity exchange, he was right to see, as did Polanyi, that there was a *commonality of spirit* between barter and capitalist commodity exchange, a commonality tied (in this view) to the object-centered, relatively impersonal, asocial nature of each. In the various simple forms of barter, we see an effort to exchange things without the constraints of sociality on the one hand, and the complications of money on the other. Barter in the contemporary world is on the increase. International barter (Pepsico syrup for Russian vodka; Coca Cola for Korean toothpicks and Bulgarian forklifts are examples) has been developing into a complex alternative economy for many decades. In these latter situations, barter is a response to the growing number of barriers to international trade and finance, and has a specific role to play in the larger economy. Barter, as a form of trade, thus links the exchange of commodities in widely different social, technological, and institutional circumstances. Barter may thus be regarded as a special form of commodity exchange, one in which, for any variety of reasons, money plays either no role or a very indirect role (as a mere unit of account). By this definition of barter, it would be difficult to locate any human society in which commodity exchange is completely irrelevant. Barter appears to be the form of commodity exchange in which the circulation of things is most divorced from social, political, or cultural norms. Yet wherever evidence is available, the determination of what may be bartered, where, when, and by whom, as well as of what drives the demand for the goods of the "other," is a social affair. There is a deep tendency to regard this social regulation as a largely negative matter, so that barter in small-scale societies and in earlier periods is frequently regarded as having been restricted to the relation *between* communities rather than *within* communities. Barter is, in this model, held to be in inverse proportion to sociality, and foreign trade, by extension, is seen to have "preceded" internal trade.[24] But there are good empirical and methodological reasons to question this view.

The notion that trade in nonmonetized, preindustrial economies is generally regarded as antisocial from the point of view of face-to-face communities

23   Ibid., 67–8.
24   M. D. Sahlins, *Stone Age Economics*, New York: Aldine de Gruyter, 1972.

and thus was frequently restricted to dealings with strangers has as its close counterpart the view that the spirit of the gift and that of the commodity are deeply opposed. In this view, gift exchange and commodity exchange are fundamentally contrastive and mutually exclusive. Though there have been some important attempts to mute the exaggerated contrast between Marx and Mauss,[25] the tendency to see these two modalities of exchange as fundamentally opposed remains a marked feature of anthropological discourse.[26]

The exaggeration and reification of the contrast between gift and commodity in anthropological writing has many sources. Among them are the tendencies to romanticize small-scale societies, and to conflate use value (in Marx's sense) with *Gemeinschaft* (in Tönnies' sense); the tendency to forget that capitalist societies, too, operate according to cultural designs; the proclivity to marginalize and underplay the calculative, impersonal, and self-aggrandizing features of noncapitalist societies. These tendencies, in turn, are a product of an oversimplified view of the opposition between Mauss and Marx, which, as Keith Hart[27] has suggested, misses important aspects of the commonalities between them.

Gifts, and the spirit of reciprocity, sociability, and spontaneity in which they are typically exchanged, are usually starkly opposed to the profit-oriented, self-centered, and calculated spirit that fires the circulation of commodities. Further, where gifts link things to persons and embed the flow of things in the flow of social relations, commodities are held to represent the drive—largely free of moral or cultural constraints—of goods for one another, a drive mediated by money and not by sociality. My argument is designed to show that this is a simplified and overdrawn series of contrasts. For the present, though, let me propose one important quality that gift exchange and the circulation of commodities share.

My view of the spirit of gift exchange owes a good deal to Bourdieu,[28] who has extended a hitherto underplayed aspect of Mauss's analysis of the gift,[29] which stresses certain strategic parallels between gift exchange and more ostensibly "economic" practices. Bourdieu's argument, which stresses the temporal

25 K. Hart, "On Commoditization," in E. Goody, ed., *From Craft to Industry: The Ethnography of Protoindustrial Cloth Production,* Cambridge: Cambridge University Press, 1982; S. J. Tambiah, *The Buddhist Saints of the Forest and the Cult of Amulets: A Study in Charisma, Hagiography, Sectarianism, and Millennial Buddhism,* Cambridge: Cambridge University Press, 1984.

26 Dumont, *On Value*; L. Hyde, *The Gift: Imagination and the Erotic Life of Property,* New York: Random House, 1979; C. A. Gregory, *Gifts and Commodities,* London: Academic Press, 1982; Sahlins, *Stone Age Economics*; M.T. Taussig, *The Devil and Commodity Fetishism in South America,* Chapel Hill: University of North Carolina Press, 1980.

27 Hart, "On Commoditization."

28 P. Bourdieu, *Outline of a Theory of Practice,* R. Nice, trans., Cambridge: Cambridge University Press, 1977.

29 M. Mauss, *The Gift,* New York: W. W. Norton & Co., 1967, 70–3.

dynamics of gifting, makes a shrewd analysis of the common spirit that underlies both gift and commodity circulation:

> If it is true that the lapse of time interposed is what enables the gift or countergift to
> be seen and experienced as an inaugural act of generosity, without any past or
> future, i.e., without *calculation*, then it is clear that in reducing the polythetic to the
> monothetic, objectivism destroys the specificity of all practices which, like gift
> exchange, tend or pretend to put the law of self-interest into abeyance. A rational
> contract would telescope into an instant a transaction which gift exchange disguises,
> by stretching it out in time; and because of this, gift exchange is, if not the only
> mode of commodity circulation practiced, at least the only mode to be fully
> recognized, in societies which, because they deny "the true soil of their life," as
> Lukacs puts it, have an economy in itself and not for itself.[30]

This treatment of gift exchange as a particular form of the circulation of
commodities comes out of Bourdieu's critique not only of "objectivist" treat-
ments of social action, but of the sort of ethnocentrism, itself a historical
product of capitalism, that assumes a very restricted definition of economic
interest.[31] Bourdieu suggests that "practice never ceases to conform to economic
calculation even when it gives every appearance of disinterestedness by depart-
ing from the logic of interested calculation (in the narrow sense) and playing for
stakes that are non-material and not easily quantified."[32]

I take this suggestion to converge, though from a slightly different angle,
with the proposals of several authors,[33] all of which represent efforts to restore
the cultural dimension to societies that are too often represented simply as
economies writ large, and to restore the calculative dimension to societies that
are too often simply portrayed as solidarity writ small. Part of the difficulty with

---

30   Bourdieu, *Outline of a Theory of Practice*, 171.

31   The use of terms such as "interest" and "calculation," I realize, raises important problems
about the comparative study of valuation, exchange, trade, and gift. Although the danger of
exporting utilitarian models and assumptions (as well as their close kin, economism and Euro-
American individualism) is serious, it is equally tendentious to reserve for Western man the right to
be "interested" in the give and take of material life. What is called for, and does not now exist, except
in embryo (see H. Medick and D. Sabean, eds., *Interest and Emotion: Essays on the Study of Family
and Kinship*, Cambridge: Cambridge University Press, 1984), is a framework for the comparative
study of economies, in which the cultural variability of "self," "person," and "individual" (following
Geertz and Dumont) is allied to a comparative study of calculation (following Bourdieu) and of
interest (following Sahlins). Only after such a framework is developed will we be able to study the
motives, instruments, telos, and ethos of economic activity in a genuinely comparative way.

32   Bourdieu, *Outline of a Theory of Practice*, 111.

33   Tambiah, *The Buddhist Saints of the Forest and the Cult of Amulets*; J. Baudrillard, *Le
Système des Objets*, Paris: Gallimard, 1968; *The Mirror of Production*, St. Louis: Telos Press, 1975; *For
a Critique of the Political Economy of the Sign*, St. Louis: Telos Press, 1981; M. D. Sahlins, *Culture and
Practical Reason*, Chicago: University of Chicago Press, 1976; and M. Douglas and B. Isherwood,
The World of Goods: Towards an Anthropology of Consumption, New York: Basic, 1979.

a cross-cultural analysis of commodities is that, as with other matters in social life, anthropology is excessively dualistic: "us and them"; "materialist and religious"; "objectification of persons" versus "personification of things"; "market exchange" versus "reciprocity"; and so forth. These oppositions parody both poles and reduce human diversities artificially. One symptom of this problem has been an excessively positivist conception of the commodity, as being a certain *kind* of thing, thus restricting the debate to the matter of deciding *what kind* of thing it is. But, in trying to understand what is distinctive about commodity exchange, it does not make sense to distinguish it sharply either from barter on the one hand, or from the exchange of gifts on the other. As Simmel[34] suggests, it is important to see the calculative dimension in all these forms of exchange, even if they vary in the form and intensity of sociality associated with them. It remains now to characterize commodity exchange in a comparative and processual manner.

Let us approach commodities as things in a certain situation, a situation that can characterize many different kinds of thing, at different points in their social lives. This means looking at the commodity potential of all things rather than searching fruitlessly for the magic distinction between commodities and other sorts of things. It also means breaking significantly with the production-dominated Marxian view of the commodity and focusing on its *total* trajectory from production, through exchange/distribution, to consumption.

But how are we to define the commodity situation? I propose that *the commodity situation in the social life of any "thing" be defined as the situation in which its exchangeability (past, present, or future) for some other thing is its socially relevant feature.* Further, the commodity situation, defined this way, can be disaggregated into: (1) the commodity phase of the social life of any thing; (2) the commodity candidacy of any thing; and (3) the commodity context in which any thing may be placed. Each of these aspects of "commodity-hood" needs some explication.

The idea of the commodity phase in the social life of a thing is a summary way to capture the central insight of Kopytoff,[35] where certain things are seen as moving in *and* out of the commodity state. I shall have more to say on this biographical approach to things in the next section, but let us note for the moment that things can move in and out of the commodity state, that such movements can be slow or fast, reversible or terminal, normative or deviant.[36] Though the biographical aspect of some things (such as heirlooms, postage stamps, and antiques) may be more noticeable than that of some others (such as steel bars, salt, or sugar), this component is never completely irrelevant.

---

34   Simmel, *The Philosophy of Money*, 97–8.

35   Kopytoff, "The Cultural Biography of Things."

36   Simmel, *The Philosophy of Money*, 138, in a quite different context, anticipates the notion that things move in and out of the commodity state and notes its Aristotelian pedigree.

The commodity *candidacy* of things is less a temporal than a conceptual feature, and it refers to the standards and criteria (symbolic, classificatory, and moral) that define the exchangeability of things in any particular social and historical context. At first glance, this feature would appear to best be glossed as the *cultural* framework within which things are classified, and this is a central preoccupation of Kopytoff. Yet this gloss conceals a variety of complexities. It is true that in most stable societies, it would be possible to discover a taxonomic structure that defines the world of things, lumping some things together, discriminating between others, attaching meanings and values to these group-ings, and providing a basis for rules and practices governing the circulation of these objects. In regard to the economy (that is, to exchange), Paul Bohannan's[37] account of spheres of exchange among the Tiv is an obvious example of this type of framework for exchange. But there are two kinds of situations where the standards and criteria that govern exchange are so attenuated as to seem virtu-ally absent. The first is the case of transactions across cultural boundaries, where all that is agreed upon is price (whether monetary or not) and a minimum set of conventions regarding the transaction itself.[38] The other is the case of those intracultural exchanges where, despite a vast universe of shared understand-ings, a specific exchange is based on deeply divergent perceptions of the value of the objects being exchanged. The best examples of such intracultural value divergence are to be found in situations of extreme hardship (such as famine or warfare), when exchanges are made whose logic has little to do with the commensuration of sacrifices. Thus a Bengali male who abandons his wife to prostitution in exchange for a meal, or a Turkana woman who sells critical pieces of her personal jewelry for a week's food, are engaging in transactions that may be seen as legitimate in extreme circumstances, but could hardly be regarded as operating under a rich shared framework of valuation between buyer and seller. Another way to characterize such situations is to say that in such contexts, value and price have come almost completely unyoked.

Also, as Simmel has pointed out, from the point of view of the individual and his subjectivity, *all* exchanges might contain this type of discrepancy between the sacrifices of buyer and seller, discrepancies normally brushed aside because of the host of conventions about exchange that are complied with by both parties.[39] We may speak, thus, of the cultural framework that defines the commodity candidacy of things, but we must bear in mind that some exchange

37   P. Bohannan, "Some Principles of Exchange and Investment among the Tiv," *American Anthropologist*, 1955, 57(1), 60–70.

38   J. N. Gray, "Lamb Auctions on the Borders," *European Journal of Sociology*, 1984, 25(1), 59–82 is an excellent discussion, also influenced by Simmel, of the divergences of value that can shape the nature of exchange across cultural borders. His study of lamb auctions on the English-Scottish borderlands is also a rich ethnographic illustration of what I have called tournaments of value.

39   Simmel, *The Philosophy of Money*, 80.

situations, both intercultural and intracultural, are characterized by a shallower set of shared standards of value than others. I therefore prefer to use the term *regimes of value*, which does *not* imply that every act of commodity exchange presupposes a complete cultural sharing of assumptions, but rather that the degree of value coherence may be highly variable from situation to situation, and from commodity to commodity. A regime of value, in this sense, is consistent with both very high and very low sharing of standards by the parties to a particular commodity exchange. Such regimes of value account for the constant transcendence of cultural boundaries by the flow of commodities, where culture is understood as a bounded and localized system of meanings.

Finally, the commodity *context* refers to the variety of *social* arenas, within or between *cultural* units, that help link the commodity candidacy of a thing to the commodity phase of its career. Thus in many societies, marriage transactions might constitute the context in which women are most intensely, and most appropriately, regarded as exchange values. Dealings with strangers might provide contexts for the commoditization of things that are otherwise protected from commoditization. Auctions accentuate the commodity dimension of objects (such as paintings) in a manner that might well be regarded as deeply inappropriate in other contexts. Bazaar settings are likely to encourage commodity flows as domestic settings may not. The variety of such contexts, within and across societies, provides the link between the social environment of the commodity and its temporal and symbolic state. As I have already suggested, the commodity context, as a social matter, may bring together actors from quite different cultural systems who share only the most minimal understandings (from the conceptual point of view) about the objects in question and agree *only* about the terms of trade. The so-called silent trade phenomenon is the most obvious example of the minimal fit between the cultural and social dimensions of commodity exchange.[40]

Thus, commoditization lies at the complex intersection of temporal, cultural, and social factors. To the degree that some things in a society are frequently to be found in the commodity phase, to fit the requirements of commodity candidacy, and to appear in a commodity context, they are its quintessential commodities. To the degree that many or most things in a society sometimes meet these criteria, the society may be said to be highly commoditized. In modern capitalist societies, it can safely be said that more things are likely to experience a commodity phase in their own careers, more contexts to become legitimate commodity contexts, and the standards of commodity candidacy to embrace a large part of the world of things than in noncapitalist societies. Though Marx was therefore right in seeing modern industrial capitalism as entailing the most intensely commoditized type of society, the comparison of societies in regard to the degree of "commoditization" would be a most

---

40   J. A. Price, "The Silent Trade," *Research in Economic Anthropology,* 1980, 3, 75–96.

complex affair given the definitional approach to commodities taken here. By this definition the term "commodity" is used in the rest of this chapter to refer to things that, at a certain *phase* in their careers and in a particular *context*, meet the requirements of commodity candidacy. Keith Hart's[41] analysis of the importance of the growing hegemony of the commodity in the world would fit with the approach suggested here except that commoditization is here regarded as a differentiated process (affecting matters of phase context and categorization differentially) and the capitalist mode of commoditization is seen as interacting with myriad other indigenous social forms of commoditization.

Three additional sets of distinctions between commodities are worth making here (others appear later in this chapter). The first, which is a modified application of a distinction originally made by Jacques Maquet in 1971 in regard to aesthetic productions,[42] divides commodities into the following four types: (1) commodities by *destination*, that is, objects intended by their producers principally for exchange; (2) commodities by *metamorphosis*, things intended for other uses that are placed into the commodity state; (3) a special sharp case of commodities by metamorphosis are commodities by *diversion*, objects placed into a commodity state though originally specifically protected from it; and (4) *ex-commodities*, things retrieved either temporarily or permanently from the commodity state and placed in some other state. It also seems worthwhile to distinguish "singular" from "homogeneous" commodities in order to discriminate between commodities whose candidacy for the commodity state is precisely a matter of their class characteristics (a perfectly standardized steel bar indistinguishable in practical terms from any other steel bar) and those whose candidacy is precisely their uniqueness *within* some class (a Manet rather than a Picasso; one Manet rather than another). Closely related though not identical is the distinction between primary and secondary commodities; necessities and luxuries; and what I call mobile versus enclaved commodities. Nevertheless, all efforts at defining commodities are doomed to sterility unless they illuminate commodities in motion. This is the principal aim of the section that follows.

PATHS AND DIVERSIONS

Commodities are frequently represented as mechanical products of production regimes governed by the laws of supply and demand. By drawing on certain ethnographic examples I hope to show in this section that the flow of commodities in any given situation is a shifting compromise between socially regulated paths and competitively inspired diversions.

41   Hart, "On Commoditization."

42   I am indebted to Nelson H. H. Graburn (N. H. H. Graburn, *Ethnic and Tourist Arts*, Berkeley: University of California Press, 1976), whose use of Maquet's original terminology, in his classification of ethnic and tourist arts, inspired my own adaptation.

Commodities, as Kopytoff points out,[43] can usefully be regarded as having life histories. In this processual view, the commodity phase of the life history of an object does not exhaust its biography: it is culturally regulated, and its interpretation is open to individual manipulation to some degree. Further, as Kopytoff also points out, the question of what sorts of object may have what sorts of biography is more deeply a matter for social contest and individual taste in modern societies than in smaller-scale, nonmonetized, preindustrial ones. There is, in Kopytoff's model, a perennial and universal tug-of-war between the tendency of all economies to expand the jurisdiction of commoditization and of all cultures to restrict it. Individuals, in this view, can go with either tendency as it suits their interests or matches their sense of moral appropriateness, though in premodern societies the room for maneuver is usually not great. Of the many virtues of Kopytoff's model the most important, in my view, is that it proposes a general processual model of commoditization in which objects may be moved both into and out of the commodity state. I am less comfortable with the opposition between singularization and commoditization, since some of the most interesting cases (in what Kopytoff agrees are in the middle zone of his ideal-typical contrast) involve the more or less permanent commoditizing of singularities.

Two questions can be raised about this aspect of Kopytoff's argument. One would be that the very definition of what constitutes singularities as opposed to classes is a cultural question, just as there can be unique examples of homogeneous classes (the perfect steel bar) and classes of culturally valued singularities (such as works of art and designer-label clothing). On the other hand, a Marxist critique of this contrast would suggest that it is commoditization as a worldwide historical process that determines in very important ways the shifting relationship between singular and homogeneous things at any given moment in the life of a society. But the important point is that the commodity is not one kind of thing rather than another, but one phase in the life of some things. Here, Kopytoff and I are in full agreement.

This view of commodities and commoditization has several important implications, some of which are touched upon by Kopytoff while others will be addressed later in this chapter. But my immediate concern is with one important aspect of this temporal perspective on the commoditization of things, which concerns what I have called paths and diversions. I owe both these terms, and some measure of my understanding of the relationship between them, to Nancy Munn's contribution[44] in an important collection of papers on a phenomenon that is of great importance to the topic of this chapter, the celebrated kula system of the Western Pacific.[45]

---

43   Kopytoff, "The Cultural Biography of Things."
44   N. D. Munn, "Gawan Kula: Spatiotemporal Control and the Symbolism of Influence," in Leach and Leach, eds., *The Kula.*
45   E. Leach, "The Kula: An Alternative View," in Leach and Leach, eds., *The Kula.*

The kula is the best-documented example of a non-Western, preindustrial, nonmonetized, translocal exchange system, and with the publication of the collection by Jerry W. Leach and Edmund Leach, it becomes, arguably, the most thoughtfully and fruitfully analyzed one. Malinowski's classic account of this system[46] was partial and problematic, though it has laid the foundation for even the most sophisticated analyses. The implications of this rethinking of the kula phenomenon for the general concerns of this chapter are several.

The kula is an extremely complex regional system for the circulation of particular kinds of valuables, usually between men of substance, in the Massim group of islands off the eastern tip of New Guinea. The main objects that are exchanged for one another belong to two types: decorated necklaces (which circulate in one direction) and armshells (which circulate in the other). These valuables acquire very specific biographies as they move from place to place and hand to hand, just as the men who exchange them gain and lose reputation as they acquire, hold, and part with these valuables. The term *keda* (road, route, path, or track) is used in some Massim communities to describe the journey of these valuables from island to island. But keda also has a more diffuse set of meanings, referring to the more or less stable social, political, and reciprocal links between men that constitute these paths. In the most abstract way, keda refers to the path (created through the exchange of these valuables) to wealth, power, and reputation for the men who handle these valuables.[47]

Keda is thus a polysemic concept, in which the circulation of objects, the making of memories and reputations, and the pursuit of social distinction through strategies of partnership all come together. The delicate and complex links between men and things that are central to the politics of the keda are captured in the following extract from the perspective of the island of Vakuta:

> The successful keda consists of men who are able to maintain relatively stable keda partnerships through good oratorical and manipulative skills, and who operate as a team, interpreting one another's movements. Nevertheless, many keda collapse, regularly making it necessary for men to realign themselves. Some form completely different keda, while the remnants of a broken keda may want to form another keda by drawing in new men. Yet others may never kula again because of their inability to form another keda owing to a reputation for "bad" kula activity. In reality, the population of shell valuables in any one keda is migratory and the social composition of a keda transitory. A shell's accumulation of history is retarded by continual

---

46   B. Malinowski, *Argonauts of the Western Pacific*, London: Routledge, 1978 (1922).
47   S. Campbell, "Kula in Vakuta: The Mechanics of Keda," in Leach and Leach, eds., *The Kula*, 203–4.

movement between keda, while men's claims to immortality vanish as shells lose association with these men after being successfully attracted into another keda, thus taking on the identity of its new owners.[48]

The path taken by these valuables is thus both reflective and constitutive of social partnerships and struggles for preeminence. But a number of other things are worth noting about the circulation of these valuables. The first is that their exchange is not easily categorized as simple reciprocal exchange, far from the spirit of trade and commerce. Though monetary valuations are absent, both the nature of the objects and a variety of sources of flexibility in the system make it possible to have the sort of calculated exchange that I maintain is at the heart of the exchange of commodities. These complex nonmonetary modes of valuation allow partners to negotiate what Firth[49] calls "exchange by private treaty," a situation in which something like price is arrived at by some negotiated process other than the impersonal forces of supply and demand.[50] Thus, despite the presence of broad conventional exchange rates, a complex qualitative calculus exists[51] which permits the competitive negotiation of personal estimates of value in the light of both short- and long-term individual interest.[52] What Firth here calls "indebtedness engineering" is a variety of the sort of calculated exchange that, by my definition, blurs the line between commodity exchange and other, more sentimental, varieties. The most important difference between the exchange of these commodities and the exchange of commodities in modern industrial economies is that the increment being sought in kula-type systems is in reputation, name, or fame, with the critical form of capital for producing this profit being people rather than other factors of production.[53] Pricelessness is a luxury few commodities can afford.

Perhaps even more important than the calculative aspect of kula exchanges is the fact that these studies make it very difficult to regard the exchange of kula valuables as occurring only at the boundaries between communities, with more giftlike exchanges occurring within these communities.[54] The concept of *kitoum* provides the conceptual and technical link between the broader paths that the valuables take and the more intimate, regular, and problematic intra-island

48   Campbell, "Kula in Vakuta: The Mechanics of Keda."
49   Following R. Cassady, *Exchange by Private Treaty,* Austin: Bureau of Business Research, University of Texas at Austin, 1974.
50   R. Firth, "Magnitudes and Values in Kula Exchange," in Leach and Leach, eds., *The Kula,* 91.
51   Campbell, "Kula in Vakuta: The Mechanics of Keda," 245–6.
52   Firth, "Magnitudes and Values in Kula Exchange," 101.
53   A. J. Strathern, "The Kula in Comparative Perspective," 80; F. H. Damon, "What Moves the Kula: Opening and Closing Gifts on Woodlark Island," 339–40, in Leach and Leach, eds., *The Kula.*
54   Damon, "What Moves the Kula: Opening and Closing Gifts on Woodlark Island," 339.

exchanges.[55] Though the term *kitoum* is complex and in certain respects ambiguous, it seems clear that it represents the articulation between the kula and other exchange modalities in which men and women transact in their own communities. Kitoums are valuables that one can place into the kula system or legitimately withdraw from it in order to effect "conversions" (in Paul Bohannan's sense) between disparate levels of "conveyance."[56] In the use of kitoum we see the critical conceptual and instrumental links between the smaller and larger paths that constitute the total world of exchange in Massim. As Annette Weiner has shown, it is a mistake to isolate the grander interisland system of exchange from the more intimate, but (for men) more suffocating local transfers of objects that occur because of debt, death, and affinity.[57]

The kula system gives a dynamic and processual quality to Mauss's ideas regarding the mingling or exchange of qualities between men and things, as Munn[58] has noted with regard to kula exchange in Gawa: "Although men appear to be the agents in defining shell value, in fact, without shells, men cannot define their own value; in this respect, shells and men are reciprocally agents of each other's value definition." But, as Munn has observed, in the reciprocal construction of value, it is not only paths that play an important role, but diversions as well. The relations between paths and diversions are critical to the politics of value in the kula system, and proper orchestration of these relations is at the strategic heart of the system:

> Actually, diversion is implicated in the path system, since it is one of the means of making new paths. Possession of more than one path also points to the probability of further diversions from one established path to another, as men become subject to the interests and persuasiveness of more than one set of partners. . . . In fact, men of substance in kula have to develop some capacity to balance operations: diversions from one path must later be replaced in order to assuage cheated partners and keep the path from disappearing, or to keep themselves from being dropped from the path.[59]

These large-scale exchanges represent psychological efforts to transcend the more humble flows of things, but in the politics of reputation, gains in the larger arena have implications for the smaller ones and the idea of the kitoum assures that both conveyances and conversions have to be carefully managed for the

---

55 A. B. Weiner, "A World of Made is Not a World of Born: Doing Kula on Kiriwana," in Leach and Leach, eds., *The Kula*; Damon, "What Moves the Kula"; Campbell, "Kula in Vakuta"; Munn, "Gawan Kula."

56 Bohannan, "Some Principles of Exchange and Investment among the Tiv."

57 Weiner, "A World of Made Is Not a World of Born," 164–5.

58 Munn, "Gawan Kula," 283.

59 Ibid., 301.

greatest gains overall.[60] The kula may be regarded as the paradigm of what I propose to call *tournaments of value*.[61]

Tournaments of value are complex periodic events that are removed in some culturally well-defined way from the routines of economic life. Participation in them is likely to be both a privilege of those in power and an instrument of status contests between them. The currency of such tournaments is also likely to be set apart through well understood cultural diacritics. Finally, what is at issue in such tournaments is not just status, rank, fame, or reputation of actors, but the disposition of the central tokens of value in the society in question.[62] Finally, though such tournaments of value occur in special times and places, their forms and outcomes are always consequential for the more mundane realities of power and value in ordinary life. As in the kula, so in such tournaments of value generally, strategic skill is culturally measured by the success with which actors attempt diversions or subversions of culturally conventionalized paths for the flow of things.

The idea of tournaments of value is an attempt to create a general category, following up an observation by Edmund Leach[63] comparing the kula system to the art world in the modern West. Baudrillard's analysis of the art auction in the contemporary West allows one to widen and sharpen this analogy. Baudrillard notes that the art auction, with its ludic, ritual, and reciprocal aspects, stands apart from the ethos of conventional economic exchange, and that it "goes well beyond economic calculation and concerns all the processes of the transmutation of values, from one logic to another logic of value which may be noted in determinate places and institutions."[64] The following analysis by Baudrillard of the ethos of the art auction deserves quotation in full since it could so easily be an apt characterization of other examples of the tournament of value:

> Contrary to commercial operations, which institute a relation of economic *rivalry* between individuals on the footing of formal *equality*, with each one guiding his own calculation of individual appropriation, the auction, like the fete or the game, institutes a concrete community of exchange among peers. Whoever the vanquisher in the challenge, the essential function of the auction is the institution of a

---

60   Damon, "What Moves the Kula," 317–23.

61   In coining the phrase tournaments of value, I was stimulated by Marriott's use, in a very different context, of the conception of tournaments of rank (M. Marriot, "Caste-Ranking and Food Transactions: A Matrix Analysis," in M. B. Singer and B. S. Cohn, eds., *Structure and Change in Indian Society*, Chicago: Aldine, 1968).

62   In his discussion of world's fairs and expositions, Burton Benedict (B. Benedict, *The Anthropology of World's Fairs: San Francisco's Panama Pacific International Exposition of 1915*, London: Scolar Press, 1983, 6) has noted the elements of contest, competitive display, and status politics associated with these events.

63   Leach, "The Kula," 535.

64   Baudrillard, *For a Critique of the Political Economy of the Sign*, 121.

community of the privileged who define themselves as such by agonistic speculation upon a restricted corpus of signs. Competition of the aristocratic sort seals their *parity* (which has nothing to do with the formal equality of economic competition), and thus their collective caste privilege with respect to all others, from whom they are no longer separated merely by their purchasing power, but by the sumptuary and collective act of the production and exchange of sign values.[65]

In making a comparative analysis of such tournaments of value, it may be advisable not to follow Baudrillard's tendency to isolate them analytically from more mundane economic exchange, though the articulation of such value arenas with other economic arenas is likely to be highly variable. I shall have more to say on tournaments of value in the discussion of the relationship between knowledge and commodities later in this chapter.

The kula, at any rate, represents a very complex system for the intercalibration of the biographies of persons and things. It shows us the difficulty of separating gift and commodity exchange even in preindustrial, nonmonetary systems, and it reminds us of the dangers in correlating zones of social intimacy too rigidly with distinct forms of exchange. But perhaps most important, it is the most intricate example of the politics of tournaments of value, in which the actors manipulate the cultural definitions of path and the strategic potential of diversion, so that the movement of things enhances their own standing.

Diversions, however, are not to be found only as parts of individual strategies in competitive situations, but can be institutionalized in various ways that remove or protect objects from the relevant social commodity contexts. Royal monopolies are perhaps the best-known examples of such "enclaved commodities," as Kopytoff points out.[66] One of the most interesting and extensive discussions of this type of monopolistic restriction on the flow of commodities is that of Max Gluckman[67] in the context of royal property among the Lozi of Northern Rhodesia. In his discussion of the categories "gift," "tribute," and "kingly things," Gluckman shows how even in a low-surplus agricultural kingdom, the flow of commodities had very diverse and important implications. In his analysis of "kingly things," it becomes clear that the main function of these royal monopolies was to maintain sumptuary exclusivity (as in the royal monopoly of eland fly whisks), commercial advantage (as with elephant tusks), and the display of rank. Such royal restrictions of things from more promiscuous spheres of exchange is part of the way in which, in premodern chieftainships and empires, royalty could assure the material basis of sumptuary exclusivity. This type of process might be called decommoditization from above.

---

65   Ibid., 117.
66   Kopytoff, "The Cultural Biography of Things."
67   M. Gluckman, "Essays on Lozi Land and Royal Property," *Research in Economic Anthropology*, 1983, 5 (1), 1–94.

But the more complex case concerns entire zones of activity and production that are devoted to producing objects of value that cannot be commoditized by anybody. The zone of art and ritual in small-scale societies is one such enclaved zone, where the spirit of the commodity enters only under conditions of massive cultural change.[68]

Davenport's discussion of ritual objects in the Solomon Islands illuminates the commodity aspects of social life precisely because it illustrates one sort of moral and cosmological framework within which commoditization is restricted and hedged. In the funeral observances of this region, particularly the large-scale *murina*, much energy and expenditure are invested in making objects that play a central role in the ritual but are scrupulously placed in the category of "terminal" commodities,[69] that is, objects which, because of the context, purpose, and meaning of their production, make only *one* journey from production to consumption. After that, though they are sometimes used in casual domestic ways, they are never permitted to reenter the commodity state. What makes them thus decommoditized is a complex understanding of value (in which the aesthetic, the ritual, and the social come together), and a specific ritual biography. We may paraphrase Davenport's observations and note that what happens here, at the heart of a very complex and calculated set of investments, payments, and credits, is a special kind of transvaluation, in which objects are placed beyond the culturally demarcated zone of commoditization. This type of transvaluation can take different forms in different societies, but it is typical that objects which represent aesthetic elaboration and objects that serve as sacra are, in many societies, not permitted to occupy the commodity state (either temporally, socially, or definitionally) for very long. In the rigid commitment of traditional Solomon Islanders to placing their most aestheticized ritual products beyond the reach of commoditization, we see one variation of a widespread tendency.

A somewhat different example of the tension between sacra and commodity exchange is to be seen in Patrick Geary's analysis of the trade in relics in early medieval Europe.[70] The relics he describes are, of course, "found" and not "made," and the circulation of these relics reflects a very important aspect of the construction of community identity, local prestige, and central ecclesiastical control in Latin Europe in the early medieval period.

These relics belong to a particular economy of exchange and demand in which the life history of the particular relic is essential, not incidental, to its value. The verification of this history is also central to its value. Given the

---

68   W. H. Davenport, "Two Kinds of Value in the Eastern Solomon Islands," in Appadurai, ed., *The Social Life of Things*.

69   Kopytoff, "The Cultural Biography of Things."

70   P. Geary, "Sacred Commodities: The Circulation of Medieval Relics," in Appadurai, ed., *The Social Life of Things*.

general approach to the difference between gift and commodity that I have taken in this chapter, I would suggest that Geary may draw too sharp a contrast between them; indeed, his own material shows that gift, theft, and commerce were all modes for the movement of sacra, in a larger context of ecclesiastical control, local competition, and community rivalry. From this perspective, medieval relics seem less carefully protected from the hazards of commoditization than Davenport's ritual objects. Yet the implication remains that commercial modes for the acquisition of relics were less desirable than either gift *or* theft, not so much because of a direct moral antipathy to trade in relics, but rather because the other two modes were more emblematic of the value and efficacy of the object.

Thus these relics, too, fall into the category of objects whose commodity phase is ideally brief, whose movement is restricted, and which apparently are not "priced" in the way other things might be. Yet the force of demand is such as to make them circulate with considerable velocity and in much the same way as their more mundane counterparts. Thus, even in the case of "transvalued" objects, which take on the characteristics of enclaved, rather than mobile, commodities, there is considerable variation in the reasons for, and the nature of, such enclaving. Gluckman's "kingly things," Geary's relics, and Davenport's ritual objects are different kinds of enclaved commodities, objects whose commodity potential is carefully hedged. It may also be appropriate to note that a very important institutional way to restrict the zone of commodity exchange itself is the "port-of-trade" associated with many premodern kingdoms,[71] though such restrictions on trade in premodern politics may not have been as thoroughgoing as has sometimes been imagined.[72] The reasons for such hedging are quite variable, but in each case, the moral bases of the restriction have clear implications for framing and facilitating political, social, and commercial exchanges of a more mundane sort. Such enclaved commodities bear a family resemblance to another class of thing, frequently discussed in the anthropological literature as "primitive valuables," whose specialness is directly linked to commodity exchange.

Though commodities, by virtue of their exchange destinies and mutual commensurability, tend to dissolve the links between persons and things, such a tendency is always balanced by a countertendency, in all societies, to restrict, control, and channel exchange. In many primitive economies, primitive valuables display these socially restricted qualities. We owe to Mary Douglas[73] the insight that many such valuables resemble coupons and licenses

71 C. Geertz, "Ports of Trade in Nineteenth-Century Bali," *Research in Economic Anthropology*, 1980, 3, 109–22.

72 P. D. Curtin, *Cross-Cultural Trade in World History*, Cambridge: Cambridge University Press, 1984, 58.

73 M. Douglas, "Primitive Rationing: A Study in Controlled Exchange," in R. Firth, ed.,

in modern industrial economies. That is, although they resemble money, they are not generalized media for exchange but have the following characteristics: (1) the powers of acquisition that they represent are highly specific; (2) their distribution is controlled in various ways; (3) the conditions that govern their issue create a set of patron-client relationships; (4) their main function is to provide the necessary condition for entry to high-status positions, for maintaining rank, or for combining attacks on status; and (5) the social systems in which such coupons or licenses function is geared to eliminating or reducing competition in the interests of a fixed pattern of status.[74] Raffia cloth in Central Africa, wampum among the Indians of the eastern United States, shell money among the Yurok and the shell currency of Rossell Island and other parts of Oceania are examples of such "commodity coupons" (in Douglas's phrase), whose restricted flow is at the service of the reproduction of social and political systems. Things, in such contexts, remain devices for reproducing relations between persons.[75] Such commodity coupons represent a transformational midpoint between "pure" gifts and "pure" commerce. With the gift, they share a certain insensitivity to supply and demand, a high coding in terms of etiquette and appropriateness, and a tendency to follow socially set paths. With pure barter, their exchange shares the spirit of calculation, an openness to self-interest, and a preference for transactions with relative strangers.

In such restricted systems of commodity flow, where valuables play the role of coupons or licenses designed to protect status systems, we see the functional equivalent but the technical inversion of "fashion" in more complex societies. Where in the one case status systems are protected and reproduced by restricting equivalences and exchange in a *stable* universe of commodities, in a fashion system what is restricted and controlled is *taste* in an *ever-changing* universe of commodities, with the illusion of complete interchangeability and unrestricted access. Sumptuary laws constitute an intermediate consumption-regulating device, suited to societies devoted to stable status displays in exploding commodity contexts, such as India, China, and Europe in the premodern period. (These comparisons are pursued more precisely in the following section of this chapter.)[76]

Themes in Economic Anthropology, London: Tavistock, 1967.

74   Ibid., 69.

75   See also Dumont, *On Value*, 231.

76   G. Simmel, "Fashion," *American Journal of Sociology*, 1957, 62(6), 541–58 is a seminal discussion of the cultural logic of fashion. See also the reference to Bougle's analysis of consumption patterns in village India in Christopher Bayly (C. Bayly, "The Origins of Swadeshi (Home Industry): Cloth and Indian Society, 1700–1930," in Appadurai, ed., *The Social Life of Things*) and Max Weber (M. Weber, "Classes, Status Groups, and Parties," in W. G. Runciman, ed., *Max Weber: Selections in Translation*, Cambridge: Cambridge University Press, 1978 [1922]).

Such forms of restriction and the enclaved commodities they create some-times provide the context and targets of strategies of diversion. Diversion, that is, may sometimes involve the calculated and "interested" removal of things from an enclaved zone to one where exchange is less confined and more profit-able, in some short-term sense. Where enclaving is usually in the interests of groups, especially the politically and economically powerful groups in any soci-ety, diversion is frequently the recourse of the entrepreneurial individual. But whether it is groups or individuals who are involved in either kind of activity, the central contrast is that whereas enclaving seeks to protect certain things from commoditization, diversion frequently is aimed at drawing protected things into the zone of commoditization. Diversion, however, can also take the form of strategic shifts in path within a zone of commoditization.

In an extremely interesting discussion of British trade in Hawaii in the late eighteenth and early nineteenth centuries, Marshall Sahlins has shown how Hawaiian chiefs, in stretching traditional conceptions of *tabu* to cover new classes of trade goods (in keeping with their own cosmopolitical interests), succeeded in transforming the "divine finality" even of economic tabus into instruments of expedience.[77] Thus, what Sahlins calls "the pragmatics of trade" erodes and transforms the cultural bounds within which it is initially conceived. In a word, the politics of enclaving, far from being a guarantor of systemic stability, may constitute the Trojan horse of change.

The diversion of commodities from specified paths is always a sign of crea-tivity or crisis, whether aesthetic or economic. Such crises may take a variety of forms: economic hardship, in all manner of societies, drives families to part with heirlooms, antiques, and memorabilia and to commoditize them. This is as true of kula valuables as of more modern valuables. The other form of crisis in which commodities are diverted from their proper paths, of course, is warfare and the plunder that historically has accompanied it. In such plunder, and the spoils that it generates, we see the inverse of trade. The transfer of commodities in warfare always has a special symbolic intensity, exemplified in the tendency to frame more mundane plunder in the transfer of special arms, insignia, or body parts belonging to the enemy. In the high-toned plunder that sets the frame for more mundane pillage, we see the hostile analogue to the dual layer-ing of the mundane and more personalized circuits of exchange in other contexts (such as kula and gimwali in Melanesia). Theft, condemned in most human societies, is the humblest form of diversion of commodities from preor-dained paths.

But there are subtler examples of the diversion of commodities from their predestined paths. One whole area involves what has been dubbed

---

77 M. D. Sahlins, *Historical Metaphors and Mythical Realities: Structure in the Early History of the Sandwich Islands Kingdom,* Ann Arbor: University of Michigan Press, 1981, 44–5.

tourist art, in which objects produced for aesthetic, ceremonial, or sumptuary use in small, face-to-face communities are transformed culturally, economically, and socially by the tastes, markets, and ideologies of larger economies.[78] I shall have more to say on tourist art in the section of this chapter on knowledge and commodities. Another, related area is that of the history and nature of the major art and archeology collections of the Western world whose formation represents extremely complex blends of plunder, sale, and inheritance, combined with the Western taste for the things of the past and of the other.[79] In this traffic in artifacts, we can find today most of the critical cultural issues in the international flow of "authentic"[80] and "singular"[81] commodities. The current controversies between English and American museums and governments and various other countries raise all the moral and political delicacies that come into play when things get diverted, several times over, from their minimal, conventional paths and are transferred by a variety of modes that make their history of claims and counterclaims extremely difficult to adjudicate.

The diversion of commodities from their customary paths always carries a risky and morally ambiguous aura. Whenever what Bohannan[82] called conveyances give way to what he called conversions, the spirit of entrepreneurship and that of moral taint enter the picture simultaneously. In the case of the kula exchanges of Melanesia, movement of commodities across spheres, though somehow out of order, is also at the heart of the strategy of the skillful and successful kula player. Inappropriate conversions from one sphere of exchange to another are frequently fortified by recourse to the excuse of economic crisis, whether it be famine or bankruptcy. If such excuses are not available or credible, accusations of inappropriate and venal motives are likely to set in. Excellent examples of the political implications of diversion are to be found in the arena of illegal or quasilegal commodity exchanges, one case of which is discussed next.

Lee Cassanelli discusses the shift in the last fifty years in Northeastern Africa, in the political economy of a quasilegal commodity called *qat* (*catha edulis*).[83] Qat provides an excellent example of change in what may be referred

78   N. H. H. Graburn, *Ethnic and Tourist Arts*, Berkeley: University of California Press, 1976.

79   An excellent example of this process appears in H. Hencken, "How the Peabody Museum Acquired the Mecklenburg Collection," in *Symbols* (Vol. 2–3), Peabody Museum: Harvard University, 1981.

80   B. Spooner, "Weavers and Dealers: The Authenticity of an Oriental Carpet," in Appadurai, ed., *The Social Life of Things: Commodities in Cultural Perspective,* Cambridge: Cambridge University Press, 1986.

81   Kopytoff, "The Cultural Biography of Things."

82   Bohannan, "Some Principles of Exchange and Investment among the Tiv."

83   L. V. Cassanelli, "Qat: Changes in the Production and Consumption of a Quasilegal Commodity in Northeast Africa," in Appadurai, ed., *The Social Life of Things.*

to as a commodity ecumene,[84] that is, a transcultural network of relationships linking producers, distributors, and consumers of a particular commodity or set of commodities. What is particularly interesting, in this case, is the dramatic expansion of the scale of consumption (and of production) of qat which is clearly tied to changes in the technical infrastructure as well as the political economy of the region. Although the expansion of production appears consistent with conditions that fit with more universal patterns in the commercialization of agriculture, what is more intriguing is the expansion of demand and response of the state—especially in Somalia—to the explosion in both the production and the consumption of qat.

Of course, the best examples of the diversion of commodities from their original nexus are to be found in the domain of fashion, domestic display, and collecting in the modern West. In the high-tech look inspired by the Bauhaus, the functionality of factories, warehouses, and workplaces is diverted to household aesthetics. The uniforms of various occupations are turned into the vocabulary of costume. In the logic of found art, the everyday commodity is framed and aestheticized. These are all examples of what we might call commoditization by diversion, where value, in the art or fashion market, is accelerated or enhanced by placing objects and things in unlikely contexts. It is the aesthetics of decontextualization (itself driven by the quest for novelty) that is at the heart of the display, in highbrow Western homes, of the tools and artifacts of the "other": the Turkmen saddlebag, Masai spear, Dinka basket.[85] In these objects, we see not only the equation of the authentic with the exotic everyday object, but also the aesthetics of diversion. Such diversion is not only an instrument of decommoditization of the object, but also of the (potential) intensification of commoditization by the enhancement of value attendant upon its diversion. This enhancement of value through the diversion of commodities from their customary circuits underlies the plunder of enemy valuables in warfare, the purchase and display of "primitive" utilitarian objects, the framing of "found" objects, the making of collections of any sort.[86] In all of these examples, diversions of things combine the aesthetic impulse, the entrepreneurial link, and the touch of the morally shocking.

---

84   My use of the term "ecumene" is a rather idiosyncratic modification of Marshall Hodgson's use of it in *The Venture of Islam: Conscience and History in a World Civilization*, Chicago: University of Chicago Press, 1974.

85   Also compare to Alsop's notion (J. W. Alsop, *The Rare Art Traditions: The History of Art Collecting and its Linked Phenomena*, Princeton: Princeton University Press, 1982) that art collecting invariably "pries loose" the things that are collected from their former context of use and deprives them of significant social purpose.

86   It is worth noting that despite a superficial opposition between them, there is a deep affinity between trade and art, at least from the point of view of the material life of simpler societies. Both involve what might be called the *intensification of objecthood*, though in very different ways. Tourist art builds on this inner affinity.

Nevertheless, diversions are meaningful only in relation to the paths from which they stray. Indeed, in looking at the social life of commodities in any given society or period, part of the anthropological challenge is to define the relevant and customary paths, so that the logic of diversions can properly, and relationally, be understood. The relationship between paths and diversions is itself historical and dialectical, as Michael Thompson[87] has skillfully shown in regard to art objects in the modern West. Diversions that become predictable are on their way to becoming new paths, paths that will in turn inspire new diversions or returns to old paths. These historical relationships are rapid and easy to see in our own society, but less visible in societies where such shifts are more gradual.

Change in the cultural construction of commodities is to be sought in the shifting relationship of paths to diversions in the lives of commodities. The diversion of commodities from their customary paths brings in the new. But diversion is frequently a function of irregular desires and novel demands, and we turn therefore to consider the problem of desire and demand.

DESIRE AND DEMAND

Part of the reason why demand remains by and large a mystery is that we assume it has something to do with desire, on the one hand (by its nature assumed to be infinite and transcultural), and need on the other (by its nature assumed to be fixed). Following Baudrillard,[88] I suggest that we treat demand, hence consumption, as an aspect of the overall political economy of societies. Demand, that is, emerges as a function of a variety of social practices and classifications rather than a mysterious emanation of human needs, a mechanical response to social manipulation (as in one model of the effects of advertising in our own society), or the narrowing down of a universal and voracious desire for objects to whatever happens to be available.

The dilemmas of consumption among the Muria Gonds of central India are usefully analyzed by Alfred Gell, who makes many interesting and important points about the cultural complexities of consumption and the dilemmas of desire in small-scale societies undergoing rapid change.[89] After reading Gell's essay, it would be difficult to see the desire for goods as being bottomless or culture-free, and demand as being a natural and mechanical response to the availability of goods and the money with which to purchase them. Consumption among the Gonds is closely tied to collective displays, economic

87 M. Thompson, *Rubbish Theory: The Creation and Destruction of Value*, Oxford: Oxford University Press, 1979.

88 Baudrillard, *For a Critique of the Political Economy of the Sign.*

89 A. Gell, "Newcomers to the World of Goods: Consumption among the Muria Gonds," in Appadurai, ed., *The Social Life of Things.*

egalitarianism, and sociability. This poses a problem for those Muria who, as a consequence of shifts in the tribal economy over the last century or so, have acquired considerably more wealth than the rest of their communities. The result is a pattern of what, inverting Veblen, we might call "conspicuous parsimony," where simplicity in lifestyle and possessions is maintained against the growing pressures of increased income. When expenditures on commodities are made, they tend to revolve around traditionally acceptable commodity forms, such as brass pots, ceremonial finery, and houses, where collectively shared values are incarnated. This is not a world dominated by the ethos of limited good, as it might first appear, but one where there is no real interest in most of what the market has to offer. Group identity, sumptuary homogeneity, economic equality, and hedonistic sociality constitute a value framework within which most externally introduced goods are uninteresting or worrisome. The collective regulation of demand (and thus of consumption) is here part of a conscious strategy on the part of the wealthy to contain the potentially divisive implications of differentiation. The Muria example is a striking case of the social regulation of the desire for goods, even when the technical and logistical conditions for a consumer revolution have been met, as is the case with cloth in India, which is discussed next.

In a subtle and suggestive analysis of the changing moral and political economy of cloth in India since 1700, Christopher Bayly[90] demonstrates the links between politics, value, and demand in the social history of things. In Bayly's argument, the production, exchange, and consumption of cloth constitute the material of a "political discourse" (rather as qat does in Somalia) that ties together royal demand, local production structures and social solidarities, and the fabric of political legitimacy. It is the consumption side of this political discourse, and not just the brute logics of utility and price, that accounts for the deep penetration of English textiles into Indian markets in the nineteenth century. Finally, in the nationalist movement of the late nineteenth and early twentieth centuries, especially in Gandhi's rhetoric, the many strands of the political discourse on cloth are reconstituted and redeployed in what might be called a language of commodity resistance, in which older as well as more recent meanings of cloth are turned against the British imperium. Bayly's essay (which is, among other things, an extraordinarily rich application of the ideas of Werner Sombart), by taking the long view of the social life of a particular significant commodity, affords us two insights that are of considerable interest: first, that the customary consumption logics of small communities are intimately tied to larger regimes of value defined by large-scale polities; and second, that the link between processes of "singularization" and "commoditization" (to use

---

90   C. A. Bayly, "The Origins of Swadeshi (Home Industry): Cloth and Indian Society, 1700–1930," in Appadurai, ed., *The Social Life of Things*.

Kopytoff's terms) in the social lives of things is itself dialectical and subject (in the hands of men like Gandhi) to what Clifford Geertz would call deep play.

Demand is thus the economic expression of the political logic of consumption and thus its basis must be sought in that logic. Taking my lead from Veblen, Douglas and Isherwood,[91] and Baudrillard,[92] I suggest that consumption is eminently social, relational, and active rather than private, atomic, or passive. Douglas has the advantage over Baudrillard of not restricting her views of consumption as communication to contemporary capitalist society but extending it to other societies as well. Baudrillard, for his part, places the logic of consumption under the dominion of the social logics of both production and exchange, equally. In addition, Baudrillard makes an immensely effective critique of Marx and his fellow political economists in regard to the twin concepts of "need" and "utility," both of which the latter saw as rooted in a primitive, universal, and natural substrate of basic human requirements.

My own inclination is to push Baudrillard's deconstruction of "need" and "utility" (and his relocation of them in the larger sphere of production and exchange) one step further and extend this idea to noncapitalist societies as well. What does this view of consumption entail? It means looking at consumption (and the demand that makes it possible) as a focus not only for *sending* social messages (as Douglas has proposed), but for *receiving* them as well. Demand thus conceals two *different* relationships between consumption and production: on the one hand, demand is determined by social and economic forces; on the other hand, it can manipulate, within limits, these social and economic forces. The important point is that, from a historical point of view, these two aspects of demand can affect each other. Take *royal* demand, for example, as in Bayly's discussion of premodern India. Here royal *demand* is a message-sending or production-molding force, looked at from the internal point of view of eighteenth-century Indian society. That is, royal demand sets parameters for both taste and production within its relevant sphere of influence. But royal demand is also a message-receiving force, as is borne out in its relationship to contemporary European styles and products. Elite tastes, in general, have this "turnstile" function, selecting from exogenous possibilities and then providing models, as well as direct political controls, for internal tastes and production.

One mechanism that frequently translates political control into consumer demand is that of the "sumptuary laws" that characterize complex premodern societies, but also characterize small-scale, preindustrial, and preliterate societies. Wherever clothing, food, housing, body decoration, number of wives or

---

91   Douglas and Isherwood, *The World of Goods.*
92   Baudrillard, *Le Système des Objets; The Mirror of Production; For a Critique of the Political Economy of the Sign.*

slaves, or any other visible act of consumption is subject to external regulation, we can see that demand is subject to social definition and control. From this point of view, the plethora of "tabus" in primitive societies, which forbid particular kinds of marriage, food consumption, and interaction (as well as their cognate positive injunctions), can be seen as strict moral analogues to the more explicit, legalized sumptuary laws of more complex and literate societies. It is by virtue of this link that we can better understand the shrewd analogy that Douglas[93] drew between "primitive" and "modern" rationing systems.

What modern money is to primitive media of exchange, fashion is to primitive sumptuary regulations. There are clear morphological similarities between the two, but the term fashion suggests high velocity, rapid turnover, the illusion of total access and high convertibility, the assumption of a democracy of consumers and of objects of consumption. Primitive media of exchange, like primitive sumptuary laws and tabus, on the other hand, seem rigid, slow to move, weak in their capacity to commensurate, tied to hierarchy, discrimination, and rank in social life. But as Baudrillard[94] and Bourdieu[95] have shown so well, the establishments that control fashion and good taste in the contemporary West are no less effective in limiting social mobility, marking social rank and discrimination, and placing consumers in a game whose ever-shifting rules are determined by "taste makers" and their affiliated experts who dwell at the top of society.

Modern consumers are the victims of the velocity of fashion as surely as primitive consumers are the victims of the stability of sumptuary law. The demand for commodities is critically regulated by this variety of taste-making mechanisms, whose social origin is more clearly understood (both by consumers and by analysts) in our own society than in those distant from us. From the point of view of demand, the critical difference between modern capitalist societies and those based on simpler forms of technology and labor is *not* that we have a thoroughly commoditized economy whereas theirs is one in which subsistence is dominant and commodity exchange has made only limited inroads, but rather that the consumption demands of persons in our society are regulated by high-turnover criteria of "appropriateness" (fashion), in contrast to less frequent shifts in more directly regulated sumptuary or customary systems. In both cases, however, demand is a socially regulated and generated impulse, not an artifact of individual whims or needs.

Even in modern capitalist societies, of course, the media and the impulse to imitate (in Veblen's sense) are not the sole engines of consumer demand.

---

93   Douglas, "Primitive Rationing."
94   Baudrillard, *For a Critique of the Political Economy of the Sign.*
95   P. Bourdieu, *Distinction: A Social Critique of the Judgment of Taste*, Cambridge, MA: Harvard University Press, 1984.

Demand can be manipulated by direct political appeals, whether in the special form of appeals to boycott lettuce grown under bad labor conditions or in the generalized forms of protectionism, either "official" or "unofficial." Again, Bayly's treatment of Gandhi's manipulation of the meaning of indigenously produced cloth is an arch-example of the direct politicization of demand. Yet this large-scale manipulation of the demand for cloth in twentieth-century India was possible only because cloth had long been, at the local level, an instrument for the sending of finely tuned social messages. Thus we can state as a general rule that those commodities whose consumption is most intricately tied up with critical social messages are likely to be *least* responsive to crude shifts in supply or price, but most responsive to political manipulation at the societal level.

From the social point of view, and over the span of human history, the critical agents for the articulation of the supply and demand of commodities have been not only rulers but, of course, *traders*. Philip Curtin's monumental work on cross-cultural trade in the preindustrial world suggests that earlier models, such as Polanyi's, of administered trade may have overstated state control over complex premodern economies.[96] What is clear is that the relations between rulers and states varied enormously over space and time. Though studies like Curtin's are beginning to show patterns underlying this diversity, the demand component in these trade dynamics remains obscure. The very close historical links between rulers and traders (whether of complicity or antagonism) might partly stem from the fact that both parties are often claimants to the key role in the social regulation of demand. The politics of demand frequently lie at the root of the tension between merchants and political elites; whereas merchants tend to be the social representatives of unfettered equivalence, new commodities, and strange tastes, political elites tend to be the custodians of restricted exchange, fixed commodity systems, and established tastes and sumptuary customs. This antagonism between "foreign" goods and local sumptuary (and therefore political) structures is probably the fundamental reason for the often remarked tendency of primitive societies to restrict trade to a limited set of commodities and to dealings with strangers rather than with kinsmen or friends. The notion that trade violates the spirit of the gift may in complex societies be only a vaguely related byproduct of this more fundamental antagonism. In premodern societies, therefore, the demand for commodities sometimes reflects state-level dynamics *or*, as in the kula case, the hinge function of status competition between elite males in linking internal and external systems of exchange.

This may be an appropriate point at which to note that there are important differences between the *cultural biography* and the *social history* of things. The

---

96   Curtin, *Cross-Cultural Trade in World History*.

differences have to do with two kinds of temporality, two forms of class identity, and two levels of social scale. The cultural biography perspective, formulated by Kopytoff,[97] is appropriate to *specific* things, as they move through different hands, contexts, and uses, thus accumulating a specific biography or set of biographies. When we look at classes or types of thing, however, it is important to look at longer-term shifts (often in demand) and larger-scale dynamics that transcend the biographies of particular members of that class or type. Thus a particular relic may have a specific biography, but whole types of relic, and indeed the class of things called "relic" itself, may have a larger historical ebb and flow, in the course of which its meaning may shift significantly.

Colin Renfrew[98] raises a series of important methodological as well as theoretical questions about commodities seen over the long run. He reminds us that commodities are central to some very early and fundamental shifts in human social life, specifically the shift from relatively undifferentiated hunter-gatherer societies to more complex early state societies. In the first place, to look at such processes over the very long run is necessarily to be involved in inferential models linking production with consumption. In the second place, to examine production processes in early human history entails looking at technological change. Here Renfrew shows us very persuasively that the decisive factors in technological innovation (which is critical to the development of new commodities) are often social and political rather than simply technical. Once this is seen, it follows, as Renfrew makes clear, that considerations of value and demand become central to the understanding of what look, at first glance, like strictly technical leaps.

Thus, in analyzing the role of gold and copper at Varna, and of similar objects of "prime value" in other prehistoric situations in Europe, Renfrew removes us from the temptations of the reflectionist view (where valuables simply reflect the high status of the people who use them) to a more dynamic constructionist view, in which it is the use of high technology objects that is critical to shifts in status structure. What is thus to be explained are changing notions of value, which in turn imply new uses of technological discoveries and new forms of political control of the products of such innovations. Renfrew's complex argument illustrates the point that changes in the social role of objects of display (themselves based on control over materials of prime value) illuminate long-term shifts in value and demand. At the same time, his essay reminds us that the cultural role of commodities cannot ultimately be divorced from questions of technology, production, and trade. Yet, though the archeological problem serves to highlight the complexity and historical depth of the

---

97   Kopytoff, "The Cultural Biography of Things."
98   C. Renfrew, "Varna and the Emergence of Wealth in Prehistoric Europe," in Appadurai, ed., *The Social Life of Things.*

relationship between values, social differentiation, and technical change, the absence of more conventional written or oral documents does make the reconstruction of value change more difficult than the reconstruction of social or technical change. Renfrew has the virtue of going against the grain of what his evidence most comfortably supports.

The social history of things and their cultural biographies are not entirely separate matters, for it is the social history of things, over large periods of time and at broader social levels, that constrains the form, meaning, and structure of more short-term, specific, and intimate trajectories. It is also the case, though it is typically harder to document or predict, that many small shifts in the cultural biography of things may, over time, lead to shifts in the social history of things. Examples of these complex relations between small- and large-scale trajectories and short- and long-term patterns in the movement of things are not widespread in the literature, but we can begin to look at these relations with reference to the transformations of exchange systems under the impact of colonial rule,[99] and to the transformations of Western society that have led to the emergence of the souvenir, the collectible, and the memento.[100] The best general treatment of the relationship between demand, the circulation of valuables, and long-term shifts in commodity production appears in the work of Werner Sombart.[101]

To Sombart we owe the major historical insight that in the period from approximately 1300 to 1800 in Europe, which he regards as the nexus of early capitalism, the principal cause of the expansion of trade, industry, and finance capital was the demand for luxury goods, principally on the part of the *nouveaux riches*, the courts, and the aristocracy. He locates the source of this increased demand, in turn, in the new understanding of the sale of "free" love, sensual refinement, and the political economy of courtship during this period. This new source of demand meant that fashion became a driving force for the upper classes, satiated only by ever-increasing quantities and ever-differentiated qualities of articles for consumption. This intensification of demand, sexual and political in its origins, signaled the end of a seigneurial lifestyle at the same time as it stimulated nascent capitalist manufacture and trade.

Although Sombart's general approach to the social history of capitalism was, during and after his lifetime, legitimately criticized for a variety of empirical deficiencies and methodological idiosyncrasies, it remains a powerful (though subterranean) alternative to both the Marxian and the Weberian views

99   G. Dalton, "The Impact of Colonization on Aboriginal Economies in Stateless Societies," *Research in Economic Anthropology*, 1978, 1(1), 131-84; Strathern, "The Kula in Comparative Perspective."

100   S. Stewart, *On Longing: Narratives of the Miniature, the Gigantic, the Souvenir, the Collection*, Baltimore: Johns Hopkins University Press, 1984.

101   W. Sombart, *Luxury and Capitalism*, Ann Arbor: University of Michigan Press, 1967.

of the origins of occidental capitalism. In its focus on consumption and demand, it belongs to an oppositional and minority tradition, as Sombart was well aware. In this sense, Sombart is an early critic of what Jean Baudrillard calls the "mirror of production," in which much dominant theory of the political economy of the modern West has seen itself. In his emphasis on demand, in his key observations about the politics of fashion, in his placement of economic drives in the context of transformations of sexuality, and in his dialectical view of the relationship between luxury and necessity, Sombart anticipates subsequent semiotic approaches to economic behavior, such as those of Baudrillard, Bourdieu, and Kristeva.

Sombart's approach was revived in an extremely interesting study of the cultural background of early capitalism by Chandra Mukerji.[102] Mukerji's argument, which converges at several points with my own, is that far from being a *result* of the industrial/technological revolution of the nineteenth century, a materialist culture and a new consumption oriented to products and goods from all over the world was the *prerequisite* for the technological revolution of industrial capitalism. In this bold critique of the Weberian hypothesis about the role of Puritan asceticism in providing the cultural context for capitalist calculation, Mukerji follows Nef[103] and others. Her argument is a sophisticated historical account of the cultural backdrop of early capitalism in Europe. It provides fresh evidence and arguments for placing taste, demand, and fashion at the heart of a cultural account of the origins of occidental capitalism, and for the centrality of "things" to this ideology in Renaissance Europe.[104]

For our purposes, the importance of Sombart's model of the relationship between luxury and early capitalism lies less in the temporal and spatial specifics of his argument (which is a matter for historians of early modern Europe) than in the generalizability of the *logic* of his argument regarding the cultural basis of demand for at least some kinds of commodities, those that he calls luxuries.

I propose that we regard luxury goods not so much in contrast to necessities (a contrast filled with problems), but as goods whose principal use is *rhetorical* and *social*, goods that are simply incarnated signs. The necessity to which *they* respond is fundamentally political. Better still, since most luxury goods are used (though in special ways and at special cost), it might make more sense to regard luxury as a special "register" of consumption (by analogy to the linguistic model) than to regard them as a special class of thing. The signs of this register, in relation to commodities, are some or all of the following attributes:

102   C. Mukerji, *From Graven Images: Patterns of Modern Materialism*, New York: Columbia University Press, 1983.

103   J. U. Nef, *Cultural Foundations of Industrial Civilization,* New York: Harper, 1958.

104   See also R. Goldthwaite, "The Empire of Things: Consumer Culture in Italy," paper presented at Ethnohistory Workshop, University of Pennsylvania, November 10, 1983.

(1) restriction, either by price or by law, to elites; (2) complexity of acquisition, which may or may not be a function of real "scarcity"; (3) semiotic virtuosity, that is, the capacity to signal fairly complex social messages (as do pepper in cuisine, silk in dress, jewels in adornment, and relics in worship); (4) specialized knowledge as a prerequisite for their "appropriate" consumption, that is, regulation by fashion; and (5) a high degree of linkage of their consumption to body, person, and personality.

From the consumption point of view, aspects of this luxury register can accrue to any and all commodities to some extent, but some commodities, in certain contexts, come to exemplify the luxury register, and these can loosely be described as luxury goods. Looked at this way, all societies display some demand for luxury goods, and one could argue that it is only in Europe after 1800 (after the eclipse of the sumptuary laws) that this demand is freed from political regulation and left to the "free" play of the marketplace and of fashion. From this point of view, fashion and sumptuary regulation are opposite poles in the social regulation of demand, particularly for goods with high discriminatory value. In certain periods, the flow of luxury goods displays a powerful tension between these two pulls: the last centuries of the *ancien régime* in Europe, for example, shows a pull in both directions. The first decades of colonial contact almost everywhere also display this tension between new fashions and existing sumptuary regulations. Fashion, in these contexts, is the urge to imitate the new powers, and this urge is often integrated, for better or worse, with traditional sumptuary imperatives. This tension, at the level of demand and consumption, is of course linked to the tensions between indigenous and introduced production systems and goods, and indigenous and introduced media of exchange. An extremely interesting case study of the complex links between trade, fashion, sumptuary law, and technology is Mukerji's discussion of the calico connection between England and India in the seventeenth century.[105]

The second important matter to which Sombart directs our attention is the complexity of the links between luxury goods and more mundane commodities. In the case with which he is concerned, the links principally involve the production process. Thus, in early modern Europe, what Sombart regards as primary luxury goods have as their prerequisites secondary and tertiary production processes: the manufacture of silk looms supports silk-weaving centers, which in turn support the creation of luxury furnishings and clothing; the sawmill produces wood that is critical to the production of fine cabinets; when timber is exhausted, coal comes to be in great demand for the glass industry and other luxury industries; iron foundries provide the pipes critical for the fountains of Versailles.[106] To the degree that a growth in demand for primary luxury

---

105   Mukerji, *From Graven Images*, 166–209.
106   Sombart, *Luxury and Capitalism*, 145–66.

goods is critical to the expansion of production of second-order and third-order instruments, the demand for luxuries has system-wide economic implications. Such is the case for complex early modern economies.

But in economies of different scale, structure, and industrial organization, the connection between luxury goods and goods from other registers of use may involve not the ripples of a complex set of production milieux and forms but, critically, the domains of exchange and consumption. Thus, to return to the kula systems of Oceania, it is now clear that the "trade" in kula valuables is related in a complex social and strategic dialectic with inputs from, and drains into, other exchange registers, which may involve marriage, death, and inheritance, purchase and sale, and so forth.[107] The demand for the kinds of valuables we call luxuries and what I have called the luxury register of any particular flow of commodities is intimately connected with other, more everyday, high-turnover registers in the language of commodities in social life.

This may also be the appropriate juncture at which to make a general point about luxury commodities, which appear to constitute a sample that is bound to favor a cultural approach in a way that humbler, more mass-produced commodities might not. The fact is that the line between luxury and everyday commodities is not only a historically shifting one, but even at any given point in time what looks like a homogeneous, bulk item of extremely limited semantic range can become very different in the course of distribution and consumption. Perhaps the best example of a humble commodity whose history is filled with cultural idiosyncrasies is sugar, as is shown in very different ways by Sidney Mintz and Fernand Braudel.[108] The distinction between humble commodities and more exotic ones is thus not a difference in kind, but most often a difference in demand over time or, sometimes, a difference between loci of production and those of consumption. From the point of view of scale, style, and economic significance, Mukerji has made an eloquent argument, at least in the case of early modern Europe, for not drawing rigid boundaries between elite and mass consumption, luxury goods and humbler ones, consumer and capital goods, or the aesthetics of display as against the designs of primary production settings.[109]

Demand is thus neither a mechanical response to a structure and level of production nor a bottomless natural appetite. It is a complex social mechanism that mediates between short- and long-term patterns of commodity circulation. Short-term strategies of diversion (such as those discussed in the previous section) might entail small shifts in demand that can gradually transform commodity flows in the long run. Looked at from the point of

---

107   See especially Weiner, "A World of Made Is Not a World of Born."
108   S. W. Mintz, "Time, Sugar and Sweetness," *Marxist Perspectives*, 1979, 2(4), 56–73; F. Braudel, *The Wheels of Commerce*, New York: Harper & Row, 1979.
109   Mukerji, *From Graven Images*, chapter 1.

view of the reproduction of patterns of commodity flow (rather than their alteration), however, long-established patterns of demand act as constraints on any given set of commodity paths. One reason such paths are inherently shaky, especially when they involve transcultural flows of commodities, is that they rest on unstable distributions of knowledge, a subject to which we now turn.

KNOWLEDGE AND COMMODITIES

This section is concerned with the peculiarities of knowledge that accompany relatively complex, long-distance, intercultural flows of commodities, though even in more homogeneous, small-scale, and low-technology loci of commodity flow, there is always the potential for discrepancies in knowledge about commodities. But as distances increase, so the negotiation of the tension between knowledge and ignorance becomes a critical determinant of the flow of commodities.

Commodities represent very complex social forms and distributions of knowledge. In the first place, and crudely, such knowledge can be of two sorts: the knowledge (technical, social, aesthetic, and so forth) that goes into the production of the commodity; and the knowledge that goes into appropriately consuming the commodity. The production knowledge that is read into a commodity is quite different from the consumption knowledge that is read from the commodity. Of course, these two readings will diverge proportionately as the social, spatial, and temporal distance between producers and consumers increases. As we shall see, it may not be accurate to regard knowledge at the production locus of a commodity as exclusively technical or empirical and knowledge at the consumption end as exclusively evaluative or ideological. Knowledge at both poles has technical, mythological, and evaluative components, and the two poles are susceptible to mutual and dialectical interaction.

If we regard some commodities as having "life histories" or "careers" in a meaningful sense, then it becomes useful to look at the distribution of knowledge at various points in their careers. Such careers have the greatest uniformity at the production pole, for it is likely that at the moment of production, the commodity in question has had the least opportunity to accumulate an idiosyncratic biography or enjoy a peculiar career. Thus the production locus of commodities is likely to be dominated by culturally standardized recipes for fabrication. Thus factories, fields, forges, mines, workshops, and most other production loci are repositories, in the first place, of technical production knowledge of a highly standardized sort. Nevertheless, even here it is worth noting that the technical knowledge required for the production of primary commodities (grains, metals, fuels, oils) is much more likely to be standardized than the knowledge required for secondary or luxury commodities, where taste, judgment, and individual experience are likely to create sharp variations in production knowledge. Nevertheless, the thrust of commoditization at the production end is toward standardization of technical (how-to) knowledge. Of course, with all commodities, whether primary or not, technical knowledge is always deeply interpenetrated with cosmological, sociological, and ritual assumptions that are likely to be widely shared. Evans-Pritchard's Azande potters,[110] Taussig's Colombian peasant producers,[111] Nancy Munn's Gawan canoe makers,[112] Stephen Gudeman's Panamanian sugarcane producers,[113] all combine technological and cosmological layers in their production discourse. In most societies, such production knowledge is subject to some discontinuity in its social distribution, either by simple criteria of age or gender, by more complex criteria distinguishing artisan households, castes, or villages from the rest of society, or by even more complex divisions of labor setting apart entrepreneurs and workers, in role terms, from householders and consumers, as in most modern societies.

But there is another dimension of production knowledge and that is knowledge of the market, the consumer, the destination of the commodity. In small-scale, traditional societies, such knowledge is relatively direct and complete as regards internal consumption, but more erratic and incomplete as regards external demand. In precapitalist contexts, of course, the translation of external demands to local producers is the province of the trader and his agents, who provide logistical and price bridges between worlds of knowledge that may have minimal direct contact. Thus it is reasonable that traditional Borneo forest dwellers had relatively little idea of the uses to which the birds' nests they sold to intermediaries have played in Chinese medical and culinary practice. The paradigm of merchant bridges across large gaps in knowledge between producer and consumer characterizes the movement of most commodities throughout history, up to the present. Today these bridges persist either because of unclosable cultural gaps (as between opium producers in Asia and the Middle East and addicts and dealers in New York) or because of the infinitesimal specialization of commodity production or its inverse—the distance between a particular bulk commodity (such as, say, copper) and the hundreds of transformations it will undergo before reaching the consumer. We note that such large gaps in knowledge of the ultimate market by the producer are usually conducive to

---

110   E. E. Evans-Pritchard, *Witchcraft, Oracles and Magic among the Azande*, Oxford: Clarendon Press, 1967 (1937).

111   M. T. Taussig, *The Devil and Commodity Fetishism in South America*, Chapel Hill: University of North Carolina Press, 1980.

112   N. D. Munn, "The Spatiotemporal Transformations of Gawa Canoes," *Journal de la Société des Océanistes*, 1977, 33(54), 39–53.

113   S. Gudeman, "Rice and Sugar in Panama: Local Models of Change," paper presented at the Ethnohistory Workshop, University of Pennsylvania, October 6, 1984.

high profits in trade and to the relative deprivation of the producing country or class in relation to the consumers and the trader.[114]

Problems involving knowledge, information, and ignorance are not restricted to the production and consumption poles of the careers of commodities, but characterize the process of circulation and exchange itself. In a powerful cultural account of the Moroccan bazaar, Clifford Geertz has placed the search for reliable information at the heart of this institution and has shown how difficult it is for actors in this system to gain reliable information either about people or about things.[115] Much of the institutional structure and cultural form of the bazaar is double-edged, making reliable knowledge hard to get and also facilitating the search for it. It is tempting to conclude that such complex and culturally organized information mazes are a special feature of bazaar-style economies, and are absent in nonmarket, simple economies, as well as in advanced industrial ones. Yet, as Geertz himself suggests,[116] the bazaar as an analytical category may well apply to the used-car market (though not the new-car market) in contemporary industrial economies. We can put this point in a more general form: bazaar-style information searches are likely to characterize any exchanges setting where the quality and the appropriate valuation of goods are not standardized, though the reasons for the lack of standardization, for the volatility of prices, and for the unreliable quality of specific things of a certain type may vary enormously. Indeed, systems for the exchange of kula valuables, of used cars, and of oriental rugs, though they occur in very different institutional and cultural settings, may all involve bazaar-style information modified by destination, which are largely "fabricated," in Nancy Munn's sense, early in their careers.[117] These require more direct mechanisms for the satisfactory negotiation of price and the matching of consumer taste to producer skill, knowledge, and tradition. Perhaps the best examples of this kind of more direct communication involve the international commerce in ready-made clothes[118] and the tourist art trade in what Nelson Graburn[119] has called the fourth world.

Whenever there are discontinuities in the knowledge that accompanies the movement of commodities, problems involving authenticity and expertise enter the picture. Brian Spooner's essay on oriental carpets[120] is a provocative anthropological interpretation of a problem that brings together art history, economic

114   See Spooner, "Weavers and Dealers."
115   C. Geertz, "Suq: The Bazaar Economy in Sefrou," in C. Geertz, H. Geertz, and L. Rosen, eds., *Meaning and Order in Moroccan Society*, Cambridge: Cambridge University Press, 1979.
116   Ibid., 224.
117   Munn, "The Spatiotemporal Transformations of Gawa Canoes."
118   D. Swallow, "Production and Control in the Indian Garment Export Industry," in E. Goody, ed., *From Craft to Industry: The Ethnography of Proto-Industrial Cloth Production*, Cambridge: Cambridge University Press, 1982.
119   Graburn, *Ethnic and Tourist Arts*.
120   Spooner, "Weavers and Dealers."

history, and cultural analysis. Spooner's topic—the shifting terms of the relationship between producers and consumers of oriental carpets—brings into
focus a particularly striking example of a commodity linking two largely isolated
worlds of meaning and function. Traded originally through a series of Asian
and European entrepôts, each of which imposed economic and taste filters,
today oriental carpets involve a much more direct negotiation between Western
upper-middle-class tastes and Central Asian weaving organizations. But this
shift involves not simply changes in the context of the negotiation of price.
What is being negotiated, as Spooner pithily puts it, is authenticity. That is, as
the pace of mobility and the crowding at the top of Western society become
more marked, and as technology permits the multiplication of prestige objects,
there is an increasingly ironic dialogue between the need for ever-shifting criteria of authenticity in the West and the economic motives of the producers and
dealers. The world of dealers, further, becomes itself tied up with the politics of
connoisseurship and the formalization of rug lore in the West.

In a general way, we can suggest that with luxury commodities like oriental
rugs, as the distance between consumers and producers is shrunk, so the issue
of *exclusivity* gives way to the issue of *authenticity*. That is, under premodern
conditions, the long-distance movement of precious commodities entailed
costs that made the acquisition of them *in itself* a marker of exclusivity and an
instrument of sumptuary distinction. Where the control of such objects was not
directly subject to state regulation, it was indirectly regulated by the cost of
acquisition, so that they stayed within the hands of the few. As technology
changes, the reproduction of these objects on a mass basis becomes possible,
the dialogue between consumers and the original source becomes more direct,
and middle-class consumers become capable (legally and economically) of
vying for these objects. The only way to preserve the function of these commodities in the prestige economies of the modern West is to complicate the criteria
of authenticity. The very complicated competition and collaboration between
"experts" from the art world, dealers, producers, scholars, and consumers is
part of the political economy of taste in the contemporary West. This political
economy has perhaps best been explored in France, by Baudrillard and
Bourdieu.[121]

There is a particular set of issues concerning authenticity and expertise
that plagues the modern West, and this set, which revolves around the issues
of good taste, expert knowledge, "originality," and social distinction, is especially visible in the domain of art and art objects. In his famous essay on "The
Work of Art in the Age of Mechanical Reproduction," Walter Benjamin[122]

---

121   Baudrillard, *For a Critique of the Political Economy of the Sign;* Bourdieu, *Distinction.*
122   W. Benjamin, "The Work of Art in the Age of Mechanical Reproduction," in H. Arendt,
ed., *Illuminations*, New York: Harcourt, Brace & World, 1968.

recognized that the aura of an authentic work of art is tied up with its originality, and that this aura, which is the basis of its authenticity, is jeopardized by
modern reproductive technologies. In this sense, copies, forgeries, and fakes,
which have a long history, do not threaten the aura of the original but seek to
partake of it. In a footnote to this essay, Benjamin made the following shrewd
observation: "To be sure, at the time of its origin a medieval picture of the
Madonna could not yet be said to be 'authentic.' It became 'authentic' only
during the succeeding centuries and perhaps most strikingly so during the last
one."[123] In an essay on the concept of the "signature" in the modern art world,
Baudrillard[124] pushes this point further:

> Until the nineteenth century, the copy of an original work had its own value, it was
> a legitimate practice. In our own time the copy is illegitimate, inauthentic: it is no
> longer "art." Similarly, the concept of forgery has changed—or rather, it suddenly
> appears with the advent of modernity. Formerly painters regularly used collaborators
> or "negros": one specialized in trees, another in animals. The act of painting, and so
> the signature as well, did not bear the same mythological insistence upon
> authenticity—that moral imperative to which modern art is dedicated and by
> which it becomes modern—which has been evident ever since the relation to
> illustration and hence the very meaning of the artistic object changed with the act
> of painting itself.

With this in mind, it is possible to place the consumption side of the processes
that Spooner absolves in the context of what Baudrillard sees as the emergence
of the "object," that is, a thing that is no longer just a product or a commodity,
but essentially a sign in a system of signs of status. Objects, in Baudrillard's view,
emerge fully only in the twentieth century in the modern West, in the context
of the theoretical formulations of the Bauhaus,[125] though it has been shown that
the emergence of the object in European culture can be traced back at least to
the Renaissance.[126] Fashion is the cultural medium in which objects, in Baudrillard's sense, move.

Yet problems of authenticity, expertise, and the evaluation of commodities
are obviously not only twentieth-century phenomena. We have already
mentioned Patrick Geary's essay[127] on the trade in relics in Carolingian Europe.
Here there is a crucial problem with regard to authentication, and here too it is
tied to the fact that relics circulate over long periods of time, through many

---

123   Ibid., 243.
124   Baudrillard, *For a Critique of the Political Economy of the Sign,* 103.
125   Ibid., 185.
126   Mukerji, *From Graven Images.*
127   P. Geary, "Sacred Commodities: The Circulation of Medieval Relics," in Appadurai, ed.,
The Social Life of Things.

hands, and over large distances. Here too there is a concern with fakery, an obsession with origins. But the cultural regime for authentication is quite different from the modern one. Though there is a small body of technical procedures and clerical prerogatives involved in authentication, it is by and large a matter in which popular understandings about ritual efficacy and folk criteria of authenticity play a central role. Authenticity here is not the province of experts and esoteric criteria, but of popular and public kinds of verification and confirmation.

The problem of specialized knowledge and of authenticity takes yet another form in William Reddy's fascinating case study of the shifts in the organization of expert knowledge in the textile industry in France before and after the Revolution of 1789.[128] Focusing on two commercial dictionaries published in France, in the 1720s and in 1839, Reddy argues that though the French Revolution appeared to destroy a whole way of life overnight, this was not in fact the case. The vast edifice of everyday knowledge and practice changed slowly, uncertainly, and reluctantly. One example of this extended crisis—a period, that is, when knowledge, practice, and policy were notably out of step—was to be seen in the codified world of knowledge regarding the trade in textiles. In complex early modern systems of commodity flow, Reddy shows us that the relationship between technical knowledge, taste, and political regulation are very complex and slow to change. Ways of knowing, judging, trading, and buying are harder to change than ideologies about guilds, prices, or production. It took a very complex series of piecemeal and asynchronous shifts in politics, technology, and culture, stretching over a century, before a new epistemological framework emerged for classifying commercial products. In this new scheme, we might say that *goods* were reconceived as *products*, and the "gaze" (in Foucault's sense) of the consumer and the trader had given way to the "gaze" of the producer. Textiles, in the first third of the nineteenth century, came to be seen in what Baudrillard calls the "mirror of production." Authenticity, in this early industrial framework, is no longer a matter of connoisseurship, but of objectively given production methods. The expertise of the dealer and the financier gives way to the expertise of industrialized production. Reddy reminds us that the social history of things, even of humble things like cloth, reflects very complicated shifts in the organization of knowledge and modes of production. Such shifts have a cultural dimension that cannot be deduced from, or reduced to, changes in technology and economy.

One final example of the very complex relationship between authenticity, taste, and the politics of consumer-producer relations concerns what have been called ethnic or tourist arts. These have been subject to fairly close study by

---

128 W. M. Reddy, "The Structure of a Cultural Crisis: Thinking About Cloth in France Before and After the Revolution," in Appadurai, ed., *The Social Life of Things*.

anthropologists.[129] Though the phenomena discussed under these labels include a bewildering range of objects, as Graburn notes in his introductory essay, they constitute perhaps the best example of the diversities in taste, understanding, and use between producers and consumers. At the producer end, one sees traditions of fabrication (again, following Munn) changing in response to commercial and aesthetic impositions or temptations from larger-scale, and sometimes far-away, consumers. At the other end, one has souvenirs, mementos, curios, collections, exhibits, and the status contests, expertise, and commerce on which they rest. In between one has a series of commercial and aesthetic links, sometimes complex, multiple, and indirect, and sometimes overt, few, and direct. In both cases, tourist art constitutes a special commodity traffic in which the group identities of producers are tokens for the status politics of consumers.

Alfred Gell makes some astute observations on the kinds of complicated refractions in perception that can accompany the interaction of small traditional populations with larger-scale economies and cultural systems.[130] Reflecting on the Muria interest in brassware produced from outside their region, Gell notes that the Muria, a traditional people with no home-grown tradition of craft and prestige-good production, in fact show an interest in exotic goods from outside their own worlds in just the way we normally expect Westerners to do. In a similar vein, studies of exhibitions and museums by anthropologists and historians,[131] as well as by semioticians and literary theorists, extend and deepen our understanding of the role of objects of the "other" in creating the souvenir, the collection, the exhibit, and the trophy in the modern West.[132] In a more general way, it might be said that as the institutional and spatial journeys of commodities grow more complex, and the alienation of producers, traders, and consumers from one another increases, culturally formed mythologies about commodity flow are likely to emerge.

Culturally constructed stories and ideologies about commodity flows are commonplace in all societies. But such stories acquire especially intense, new, and striking qualities when the spatial, cognitive, or institutional distances between production, distribution, and consumption are great. Such distancing either can be institutionalized within a single complex economy or can be a function of new kinds of links between hitherto separated societies and economies. The institutionalized divorce (in knowledge, interest, and role) between

129   Graburn, *Ethnic and Tourist Arts*.

130   A. Gell, "Newcomers to the World of Goods: Consumption among the Muria Gonds," in Appadurai, ed., *The Social Life of Things*.

131   B. Benedict, *The Anthropology of World's Fairs: San Francisco's Panama Pacific International Exposition of 1915*, London: Scolar Press, 1983; C. Breckenridge, *The Subject of Objects: The Making of a Colonial High Culture*, unpublished paper, 1984.

132   Baudrillard, *Le Système des Objets; For a Critique of the Political Economy of the Sign*; Stewart, *On Longing: Narratives of the Miniature, the Gigantic, the Souvenir, the Collection*.

persons involved in various aspects of the flow of commodities generates specialized mythologies. I consider, in this section, three variations on such mythologies and the contexts in which they arise. (1) Mythologies produced by traders and speculators who are largely indifferent to both the production origins and the consumption destination of commodities, except insofar as they affect fluctuations in price. The best examples of this type are the commodity futures markets in complex capitalist economies, specifically the Chicago Grain Exchange in the early part of this century. (2) Mythologies produced by consumers (or potential consumers) alienated from the production and distribution process of key commodities. Here the best examples come from the cargo cults of Oceania. And (3) mythologies produced by workers in the production process who are completely divorced from the distribution and consumption logics of the commodities they produce.

The commodity sphere in the modern capitalist world-system appears at first glance to be a vast impersonal machine, governed by large scale movements of price, complex institutional interests, and a totally demystified, bureaucratic, and self-regulating character. Nothing, it appears, could be further from the values, mechanisms, and ethics of commodity flows in small-scale societies. Yet this impression is false.

It should by now be clear that capitalism represents not simply a techno-economic design, but a complex cultural system with a very special history in the modern West. This view, which has always had distinguished adherents in economic and social history,[133] has received additional support from anthropologists and sociologists of Euro-American culture.[134]

The study of the cultural design of capitalism in its American form has been undertaken with enormous vigor in the last decade, and historians, anthropologists, and sociologists are beginning to put together a rich picture of the culture of capitalism in the United States.[135] Though this larger context lies outside the scope of this discussion, it is quite clear that capitalism is itself an

---

133   M. Weber, *The Protestant Ethic and the Spirit of Capitalism*, T. Parsons, trans., New York: Charles Scribner's Sons, 1958; Sombart, *Luxury and Capitalism*; Nef, *Cultural Foundations of Industrial Civilization*; Braudel, *The Wheels of Commerce*; R. S. Lopez, *The Commercial Revolution of the Middle Ages, 950–1350*, Englewood Cliffs, NJ : Prentice-Hall, 1971; J. Thirsk, *Economic Policy and Projects*, Oxford: Clarendon Press, 1978.

134   Baudrillard, *For a Critique of the Political Economy of the Sign*; Bourdieu, *Distinction*; Douglas and Isherwood, *The World of Goods*; Mukerji, *From Graven Images*; Sahlins, *Culture and Practical Reason*.

135   R. Collins, *The Credential Society*, New York: Academic Press, 1979; P. Dimaggio, "Cultural Entrepreneurship in Nineteenth-Century Boston: The Creation of an Organizational Base for High Culture in America," *Media, Culture & Society*, 1982, 4(1), 33–50; T. J. J. Lears, *No Place of Grace: Antimodernism and the Transformation of American Culture, 1880–1920*, New York: Pantheon Books, 1981; G. Marcus, "Spending: The Hunts, Silver, and Dynastic Families in America," *European Journal of Sociology*, 1985, 26(2), 224–59; M. Schudson, *Advertising, the Uneasy Persuasion: Its Dubious Impact on American Society*, New York: Basic Books, 1984.

extremely complex cultural and historical formation, and in this formation commodities and their meanings have played a critical role. One example of the peculiar and striking cultural expressions of modern capitalism is the market in commodity futures in the United States, which developed in the middle of the nineteenth century and whose paradigmatic example is the Chicago Grain Exchange.

Trade in bulk commodities remains today an extremely important part of world trade and the world economic system,[136] and this large-scale commodity trade remains perhaps the central arena where the contradictions of international capitalism can be observed. Central among these contradictions is the one between the free-trade ideology of classical capitalism and the various forms of protectionism, cartels, and regulatory agreements that have evolved to restrict this freedom in the interests of various coalitions of producers.[137] Commodity futures markets represent the institutional arena where the risks that attend the national and international flows of these commodities are negotiated by hedging on the part of some and sheer speculation on the part of others.

Markets in commodity futures revolve around a large number of transactions involving contracts to buy and sell commodities at future dates. This trade in contracts is a paper trade, which rarely involves actual exchanges of the commodities themselves between traders. Like the stock market, these markets are speculative tournaments, in which the play of price, risk, and exchange appears to be *totally* divorced, for the spectator, from the entire process of production, distribution, sale, and consumption. One might say that speculating in commodity futures makes a dramatic separation between price and value, with the latter being of no concern at all. In this sense, the logic of trade in commodity futures is, following Marx, a kind of meta-fetishization, where not only does the commodity become a substitute for the social relations that lie behind it, but the movement of prices becomes an autonomous substitute for the flow of the commodities themselves.

Though this double degree of removal from the social relations of production and exchange makes commodity futures markets very different from other tournaments of value, such as those represented in the kula, there are some interesting and revealing parallels. In both cases, the tournament occurs in a special arena, insulated from practical economic life and subject to special rules. In both cases, what are exchanged are tokens of value that can be transformed into other media only by a complex set of steps and only in unusual circumstances. In both cases, there are specific ways in which the reproduction

---

136   See, for example, F. G. Adams and J. R. Behrman, *Commodity Exports and Economic Development*, Lexington, MA: Lexington Books, 1982.

137   C. Nappi, *Commodity Market Controls: A Historical Review*, Lexington, MA: Lexington Books, 1979.

of the larger economy is articulated with the structure of the tournament economy.

But perhaps most important, in both cases, there is an agonistic, romantic, individualistic, and game-like ethos that stands in contrast to the ethos of everyday economic behavior. The role of kula participation in the construction of fame and reputation for individuals in Oceania is very clear. But the same is the case with commodity futures markets. In the second half of the nineteenth century, the "wheat pit" (the Grain Exchange) in Chicago was obviously the scene of the making and breaking of individual reputations, of intense and obsessive competitions between specific individuals, and of hubristic efforts on the part of particular men to corner the market.[138] This agonistic, obsessive, and romantic ethos has not disappeared from the commodity markets, as we are reminded by the case of the Hunt brothers in regard to silver,[139] although the moral, institutional, and political framework that governs speculation in commodities has changed a good deal since the nineteenth century. Of course, there are many differences between the kula and the commodity futures market in scale, instrumentalities, context, and goals. But the similarities are real, and, as I suggested earlier, many societies create specialized arenas for tournaments of value in which specialized commodity tokens are traded, and such trade, through the economies of status, power, or wealth, affects more mundane commodity flows. The trade in relics, the market in commodity futures, the kula, the potlatch, and the Central Asian *buzkashi*[140] are all examples of such "tournaments of value." In each case, we need a fuller examination of the modes of articulation of these "tournament" economies with their more routine commodity contexts than is possible here.

The mythology of circulation generated in commodity markets (as well as, in other ways, in stock markets) is a mythology of rumor mixed with more reliable information: regarding commodity reserves, government regulations, seasonal shifts, consumer variables, intramarket developments (including the rumored intention or motives of other speculators), and so on. These constitute an endlessly shifting (and potentially infinite) scenario of variables that affect price. Though there have been consistent improvements in the technical basis for analyzing and successfully playing the commodities market, there remains the quasi-magical search for the formula (divinatory rather than efficacious) that will prove to be the fail-safe predictor of price shifts.[141] The structural basis

---

138   E. J. Dies, *The Wheat Pit*, Chicago: Argyle Press, 1925; *The Plunger: A Tale of the Wheat Pit*, New York: Covici-Friede, 1975.

139   Marcus, "Spending."

140   G. W. Azoy, *Buzkashi, Game and Power in Afghanistan*, Philadelphia: University of Pennsylvania Press, 1982.

141   M. J. Powers, *Getting Started in Commodity Futures Trading*, Columbia: Investor Publications, 1983, 47.

of this mythology of circulation of commodities is the fact that it plays *indefinitely* with the fluctuation of prices; that it seeks to exhaust an inexhaustible series of variables that affect price; and that its concern with commodities is purely *informational* and *semiotic* and is divorced from consumption altogether. The irrational desire to corner the market in some commodity, the counterintuitive search for magical formulas to predict price changes, the controlled collective hysteria, all these are the product of this complete conversion of commodities to signs,[142] which are themselves capable of yielding profit if manipulated properly. The primitive counterpart to this type of mythological and context-free construction of commodities is to be found in that anthropological staple, the cargo cults that multiplied in the stateless societies of the Pacific in this century.

Cargo cults are social movements of intense, millennial character centered on the symbolism of European goods. They have occurred mainly in the Pacific since early colonial contact, though they have precolonial antecedents and analogies in other societies. They have been subject to intensive analysis by anthropologists, who have looked at them as psychological, religious, economic, and political phenomena. Though there has been considerable variation in the anthropological interpretation of these movements, most observers agree that the emergence of cargo cults in early colonial Pacific societies has something to do with the transformation of production relations in this new context; the inability of natives to afford the new European goods they desired; the arrival of a new theological and cosmological system with missionaries; and the resulting ambivalence toward indigenous ritual forms. The result was a series of movements spread throughout Oceania (and later Melanesia) of uneven success, duration, and intensity, which both mimicked and protested European social and ritual forms and took either strongly oppositional or strongly revivalistic positions in regard to their own myths and rituals of prosperity and exchange. In the symbolism of many of these movements, an important role was played by the promise by the leader/prophet of the arrival of valued European goods by plane or by ship and their "showering" upon the true believers in the movement and in the prophet.

It is difficult to doubt the contention of Worsley[143] and others that the symbolism of the mysterious arrival of European goods has a lot to do with the distortion of indigenous exchange relations under colonial rule, the perception by the natives of the apparent contradiction between the wealth of Europeans (despite their lack of effort) and their own poverty (despite their arduous labor). It is no surprise, given their sudden subjection to a complex international

---

142 Baudrillard, *For a Critique of the Political Economy of the Sign.*
143 P. Worsley, *The Trumpet Shall Sound: A Study of "Cargo" Cults in Melanesia,* London: MacGibbon & Kee, 1957.

economical system of which they saw only few and mysterious aspects, that their response was occasionally to seek to replicate what they regarded as the magical mode of production of these goods.

When we look at the symbolism and ritual practice of these movements, it is possible to see that they constitute not just a myth about the origins of European commodities, but an attempt to ritually replicate what were perceived as the social modalities of European life. This is the significance of the use of European military forms, speech forms, titles, and so forth, in these movements. Though often ordered in indigenous patterns, the ritual practice of cargo cults was in many cases no less than a massive effort to mime those European social forms that seemed most conducive to the production of European goods. In a kind of reverse fetishism, what was replicated was what was seen as the most potent of European social and linguistic forms in an effort to increase the likelihood of the arrival of European commodities. But Glynn Cochrane[144] has reminded us that these cults were, however distorted, not pursuits of *all* European commodities, but only of those commodities that were seen as particularly conducive to the maintenance of status discontinuities in local societies. Cargo cults also represent a particular mythology of production of European finished goods by natives embroiled in the production of primary commodities for the world trade and an associated imitative and revitalistic ritual. The commodities involved in cargo, as with kula valuables, and other indigenous forms of specialized exchange, are seen as metonymic of a whole system of power, prosperity, and status. Cargo beliefs are an extreme example of the theories that are likely to proliferate when consumers are kept completely ignorant of the conditions of production and distribution of commodities and are unable to gain access to them freely. Such deprivation creates the mythologies of the alienated consumer, just as the commodity markets of modern capitalism spawn the mythologies of the alienated trader. We turn, finally, to the third variation, the mythologies of producers at the service of demand and distribution forces outside their control and beyond their universe of knowledge.

The rites of production in the tin mines of Bolivia[145] and their associated mythology, for example, are not a simple carryover of peasant rites of production. They reflect the tensions of a society in which commoditization has not yet become commonplace, where the fetishism of commodities, because of its incomplete hegemony, is regarded as evil and dangerous, and there is thus a paradoxical attempt to envelop the Devil in reciprocal rituals. This is not commodity fetishism in the classic Marxian sense (where products conceal and represent social relations), but a more literal fetishism, in which the commodity, itself iconicized as the Devil, is made the pivot of a set of ritual transactions

144   G. Cochrane, *Big Men and Cargo Cults,* Oxford: Clarendon, 1970.
145   Taussig, *The Devil and Commodity Fetishism in South America.*

designed to offset the cosmological and physical risks of mining. In this mythol-ogy of alienated producers/extractors, the impersonal and invisible sources of control (the state) and of demand (the world commodity market) are relocated in an icon of danger and greed, social metaphors for the commodity economy. Though Taussig's account tends, like Gregory's and many others, to overstate the contrast between gift and commodity economies, his is a persuasive account of the literal fetishism of commodities that seems to accompany primary commodity production for unknown and uncontrolled markets.

In each of the examples I have discussed, the commodity futures market, cargo cults, and mining mythology, mythological understandings of the circu-lation of commodities are generated because of the detachment, indifference, or ignorance of participants as regards all but a single aspect of the economic trajectory of the commodity. Enclaved in either the production, speculative trade, or consumption locus of the flow of commodities, technical knowledge tends to be quickly subordinated to more idiosyncratic subcultural theories about the origins and destinations of things. These are examples of the many forms that the fetishism of commodities can take when there are sharp discon-tinuities in the distribution of knowledge concerning their trajectories of circulation.

There is one final point to be made about the relationship between knowl-edge and commodities, and it is one which reminds us that the comparison of capitalistic societies with other kinds of societies is a complicated matter. In complex capitalistic societies, it is not only the case that knowledge is segmented (even fragmented) between producers, distributors, speculators, and consum-ers (and different subcategories of each). The fact is that knowledge *about* commodities is itself increasingly commoditized. Such commoditization of knowledge regarding commodities is of course part of a larger problem of the political economy of culture itself,[146] in which expertise, credentialism, and high-brow aestheticism[147] all play different roles. Thus, though even in the simplest economies there is a complex traffic in things, it is only with increased social, technical, and conceptual differentiation that what we call a *traffic in criteria* concerning things develop. That is, only in the latter situation does the buying and selling of expertise regarding the technical, social, or aesthetic appropriateness of commodities become widespread. Of course, such a traffic in commodity criteria is not confined to capitalist societies, but there seems to be considerable evidence that it is in such societies that such traffic is most dense.

In contemporary capitalist economies, further, it is difficult to separate the commoditization of goods from the commoditization of services. Indeed the

146   Collins, *The Credential Society.*
147   Bourdieu, *Distinction.*

routine pairing of goods and services is itself a heritage of neoclassical economics. This is not to say that services (sexual, occupational, ritual, or emotional) lie
wholly outside the domain of commoditization in noncapitalist societies. But it
is only in complex postindustrial economies that services are a dominant, even
definitive, feature of the world of commodity exchange.

But perhaps the best example of the relationship between knowledge and
the control of demand is provided by the role of advertising in contemporary
capitalist societies. Much has been written about this important topic, and in
the United States there are signs of a revived debate about the functional effectiveness of advertising. In a now classic study, Michael Schudson[148] has
questioned the neo-Marxist analyses of the manipulation of consumers by
advertising in America. He proposes that the textual and graphic images
produced by the advertising machine are better regarded as a species of "capitalist realism," a form of cultural representation of the virtues of the capitalist
lifestyle, rather than as techniques for seduction into specific acts of consumption. The adulation with which this argument has been greeted by the
advertising profession is a source of some circumstantial doubt about the argument itself. What is probably the case is that any decisive analysis of the effects
of advertising would have to proceed to see the images of advertising in tandem
with changing ideas about art, design, lifestyle, and distinction, in order to
unravel the role of this kind of "capitalist realism" in the social mobilization of
demand.[149]

Whatever the effectiveness of advertising in ensuring the success of any
particular product, it does seem true that contemporary modes of representation in advertising (particularly on television) share a certain strategy. The
strategy consists in taking what are often perfectly ordinary, mass-produced,
cheap, even shoddy, products and making them seem somehow (in Simmel's
sense) desirable-yet-reachable. Perfectly ordinary goods are placed in a sort of
pseudo-enclaved zone, *as if* they were not available to anyone who can pay the
price. The largely social images that create this illusion of exclusivity might be
glossed as the fetishism of the consumer rather than the commodity. The images
of sociality (belonging, sex appeal, power, distinction, health, camaraderie) that
underlie much advertising focus on the transformation of the consumer to the
point where the particular commodity being sold is almost an afterthought.
This double inversion of the relationship between people and things might be
regarded as the critical cultural move of advanced capitalism.

The relationship between knowledge and commodities has many dimensions that have not been discussed here. But the essential point for my purposes

148   Schudson, *Advertising, the Uneasy Persuasion.*
149   D. Hebdige, "Travelling Light: One Route into Material Culture," *RAIN* (Royal
Anthropological Institute News), 1983, 59, 11–13; Bourdieu, *Distinction.*

is this: as commodities travel greater distances (institutional, spatial, temporal), knowledge about them tends to become partial, contradictory, and differentiated. But such differentiation may itself (through the mechanisms of tournaments of value, authentication, or frustrated desire) lead to the intensification of demand. If we look at the world of commodities as a shifting series of local (culturally regulated) commodity paths, we can see that the politics of diversion as well as of enclaving are often tied to the possibility or fact of commodity exchanges with other, more distant, systems. At every level where a smaller system interacts with a larger one, the interplay of knowledge and ignorance serves as a turnstile, facilitating the flow of some things and hindering the movement of others. In this sense, even the largest commodity ecumenes are the product of complex interactions between local, politically mediated systems of demand.

CONCLUSION: POLITICS AND VALUE

Apart from learning some moderately unusual facts, and regarding them from a mildly unconventional point of view, is there any general benefit in looking at the social life of commodities in the manner proposed in this chapter? What does this perspective tell us about value and exchange in social life that we did not know already, or that we could not have discovered in a less cumbersome way? Is there any point in taking the heuristic position that commodities exist everywhere and that the spirit of commodity exchange is not wholly divorced from the spirit of other forms of exchange?

Politics, in the broad sense of relations, assumptions, and contests pertaining to power, is what links value and exchange in the social life of commodities. In the mundane, day-to-day, small-scale exchanges of things in ordinary life, this fact is not visible, for exchange has the routine and conventionalized look of all customary behavior. But these many ordinary dealings would not be possible were it not for a broad set of agreements concerning what is desirable, what a reasonable "exchange of sacrifices" comprises, and who is permitted to exercise what kind of effective demand in what circumstances. What is political about this process is not just the fact that it signifies and constitutes relations of privilege and social control. What is political about it is the constant tension between the existing frameworks (of price, bargaining, and so forth) and the tendency of commodities to breach these frameworks. This tension itself has its source in the fact that not all parties share the same interests in any specific regime of value, nor are the *interests* of any two parties in a given exchange identical.

At the top of many societies, we have the politics of tournaments of value, and of calculated diversions that might lead to new paths of commodity flow. As expressions of the interests of elites in relation to commoners we have the politics of fashion, of sumptuary law, and of tabu, all of which regulate demand. Yet since commodities constantly spill beyond the boundaries of specific cultures (and thus of specific regimes of value), such political control of demand is always threatened with disturbance. In a surprisingly wide range of societies, it is possible to witness the following common paradox. It is in the interests of those in power to completely freeze the flow of commodities, by creating a closed universe of commodities and a rigid set of regulations affecting how they are to move. Yet the very nature of contests between those in power (or those who aspire to greater power) tends to invite a loosening of these rules and an expansion of the pool of commodities. This aspect of elite politics is generally the Trojan horse of value shifts. So far as commodities are concerned, the source of politics is the tension between these two tendencies.

We have seen that such politics can take many forms: the politics of diversion and of display; the politics of authenticity and of authentication; the politics of knowledge and of ignorance; the politics of expertise and of sumptuary control; the politics of connoisseurship and of deliberately mobilized demand. The ups and downs of the relations within and between these various dimensions of politics account for the vagaries of demand. It is in this sense that politics is the link between regimes of value and specific flows of commodities. Ever since Marx and the early political economists, there has not been much mystery about the relationship between politics and production. We are now in a better position to demystify the demand side of economic life.

CHAPTER TWO

How Histories Make Geographies: Circulation and Context in a Global Perspective

GLOBAL CULTURAL FLOWS

Cultural objects, including images, languages, and hairstyles, now move ever more swiftly across regional and national boundaries. This acceleration is a consequence of the speed and spread of the internet and the simultaneous comparative growth in travel, cross-cultural media, and global advertisement. The power of global corporations to outsource various aspects of their activities, ranging from manufacture and distribution to advertising and commerce, has meant that the force of global capital is now multiplied by the opportunistic combination of cultural idioms, symbols, labor pools, and attitudes to profit and risk. The issue of risk in the current era of financialization is more fully addressed in part 3. Additionally, this volatile and exploding traffic in commodities, styles, and information has been matched by the growth of both flows of cultural politics, visible most powerfully in the discourse of human rights, but also in the new languages of radical Christianity and Islam, and the discourse of civil society activists, who wish to promote their own versions of global equity, entitlement, and citizenship, as the detailed studies of global urban activism in part 2 exemplify. The dynamics of modernization remain an essential feature of global cultural flows. Global corporations now compete for markets, such as bio-technology, digital media, drinking water, energy credits, financial derivatives (as we now know), and other commodity markets which barely existed before 1970.

At the same time, illegal or unofficial markets have emerged everywhere, linking societies and states in different parts of the world. These lateral markets that involve traffic in human organs, armaments, precious metals, and sex work, to name but four examples, make extensive use of the power of the internet, cell phones, and other sophisticated communications technologies. They also take full advantage of the differential policing of national boundaries, the destruction of many rural economies, and the state corruption that characterizes many parts of the world. Such illegal commodity circuits, for example in Africa, also bring apparently desolate economies to major ports and commercial hubs, such as Rotterdam, through the global movement of everyday commodities like refrigerators, air conditioners, cars, and other consumer durables. The diamond market consists of sophisticated networks linking mines and armies, cutting and marketing middlemen in India, as well as major dealers and showrooms in London, Antwerp, and New York; it is now also deeply connected to instances of extreme social violence in such places as Sierra Leone, the Democratic Republic of the Congo, and Angola.[1]

It is important to appreciate that these varied commodity circuits are themselves mutually connected. Thus, the capacity of global financial players to electronically move large sums across national boundaries, and to create and exploit new financial markets across the world, have also produced new inequalities in some of the world's megacities and significantly fueled the recent precipitous global financial meltdown. These inequalities—I think of cities such as Mumbai, Hong Kong or São Paulo—fuel the growth of large urban under classes, which are potential fodder for the work of global crime syndicates engaged in traditional forms of smuggling, cross-border trade, and the relatively new politics of urban terror. The latter kind of politicized crime is perpetrated by criminal networks which grew out of Mumbai and are now located in Karachi, Dubai, Kathmandu, Bangkok, and beyond. They create a new geography relating the Persian Gulf to different parts of South and Southeast Asia; they are directly involved in the politics of violence which exist in Kashmir and elsewhere in South Asia; and, in conjunction with the abovementioned types of commodity links, they underpin the financial infrastructure of networks such as Al-Qaeda, which was originally built through the globalized construction enterprises of the Bin Laden family.

From inspecting these multiple commodity networks and chains, we can conclude that the newer forms of circulation exemplified by global financial markets, instruments, and regulations also affect the overall capitalization of older commodity chains, both illegal and legal, such as those involved in the flows of labor, drugs, arms, and precious metals. Without making too big a case out of this: these new things ride on older things, transform and reinvigorate them. Globalization creates a more volatile and blurred relationship between finance capital and other forms of capital, and a more dangerous relationship between global commodity flows and the politics of warfare, security, and peace in many societies.

The other major factor in all global commodity chains, ranging from the simplest to the most sophisticated, is the explosive growth in highly advanced tools for storing, sharing, and tracking information electronically both by the state and its opponents. For the world, the complexity of global cultural flows has had deep effects on what I once called the "production of locality" and the

1   F. De Boeck, "Garimpeiro Worlds: Digging, Dying and 'Hunting' for Diamonds in Angola," *Review of African Political Economy*, 2001, 28(90), 549–62; C. Nordstrom, *Global Outlaws: Crime, Money, and Power in the Contemporary World*, Berkeley: University of California Press, 2007.

production of local subjectivity.[2] These flows and networks confound older models of acculturation, culture contact, and mixture, since they also brought new materials for the construction of subjectivity. The traffic of images of global suffering, for example, creates new communities of sentiment, which introduce empathy, identification, and anger across large cultural distances. For example, in Europe, wearing a veil, itself highly varied in different parts of the Islamic world, has become a flashpoint for education, fashion, and state authority in countries such as France, which was historically quite comfortable with sumptuous markers of religious identity.

A powerful example of a global discursive flow is the spread of the discourse of human rights into the center of the vocabulary of politics since the birth of the United Nations. In the half century since that time, virtually every known society has generated individuals and groups who have a new consciousness of their political status within the framework of human rights. Minorities of every kind, including women, children, immigrants, refugees, political prisoners, and other weak citizens, now have the capacity to exercise pressure on the state to respect their human rights. This process is of special interest in the history of anthropology, since it brings the social fact of cultural difference squarely into the realm of politics and links cultural diversity to the most essential and universal human rights.

This process is not altogether benign: in many cases the capacity of what I call "small numbers"[3] to press large political claims in the name of cultural difference can produce ethno-national mobilization and contribute to the conditions for genocide. Europe has seen a variety of reactions since the violence in former Yugoslavia in the early 1990s, including the rise of the openly anti-immigrant right in France, Austria, Sweden, Germany, and Italy. Andre Gingrich and Marcus Banks[4] have recently succeeded in assembling something of an answer to this problem from an anthropological view. The global spread of human rights values is also a sign of the complex new forms of law and legality which now affect the relation between order and disorder in many societies undergoing rapid transformation.

In short, global cultural flows have lost the selective and cumbersome qualities that they have had for much of human history, during which most societies found ways to accommodate external systems of meaning within their own cosmological frameworks, hence producing change by dialectical accident and

2   A. Appadurai, *Modernity at Large: Cultural Dimensions of Globalization*, Minneapolis: University of Minnesota Press, 1996.

3   A. Appadurai, *Fear of Small Numbers: An Essay on the Geography of Anger*, Durham: Duke University Press, 2006.

4   A. Gingrich and M. Banks, eds., *Neo-Nationalism in Europe and Beyond: Perspectives from Social Anthropology*, London: Berghahn Books, 2006.

structural combination.[5] Today, global cultural flows, whether religious, political, or market-produced, have entered into the manufacture of local subjectivities, thus changing both the machineries for the manufacture of local meaning and the materials that are processed by these machineries. Consequently, Western citizens, lawmakers, and many liberals debate ideas about refugee rights in terms of multiculturalism, dual patriotism, diasporic dignity, and cultural rights—all of which are as new as the debates they seek to mediate. Likewise, this current period—approximately from the 1970s to the present—is characterized by the flows not just of cultural substances, but also of cultural forms, such as the novel, the ballet, the political constitution, and divorce, to pick just a few examples.

The flow of these forms has affected major world-historical processes such as nationalism.[6] Today, however, the flow of forms also affects the very nature of knowledge, as whole disciplines, techniques, and ways of thinking move and transform in the process. Examples of global flows of such knowledge forms include the spread, say, of internet gaming in China; the growth of day-trading stocks in places like Tokyo, Shanghai, and beyond; the writing of constitutions in post-monarchic societies such as Nepal; and the worldwide popularity of such visual forms as Japanese Manga.

Crucial to an understanding of these cultural flows is *the relationship between the forms of circulation and the circulation of forms*. Forms such as novels, films, and newspapers meet well-established circulatory paths and circuits of religion, migration, and trade. But other cultural forms, such as ballet, animation, fashion photography, and grassroots political activism, create circuits of circulation which did not exist before. Thus, the twenty-first century is witnessing new tensions between the actually circulating cultural forms and the emerging, partially culturally formed circuits or networks that shape and cover the multiple paths of circulation. This dual structure of global cultural forms also generates what we may call the "bumps" or obstacles in regard to many cultural flows. The Chinese state, for example, is very keen to curb the internet, based on its right to regulate information and enforce social morality, just as members of the Falun Gong movement use global techniques of protest and communication to undermine the legitimacy of the Chinese state. Housing activists use the full force of their global allies and circuits to impede the capacity of local and city governments to displace slum populations, a topic addressed in detail in the context of India in part 2. Proponents of women's rights are in a daily race against those who use global cultural circuits to argue and legitimize their own views on gender politics in the name of the value of cultural

5   M. D. Sahlins, *Islands of History*, Chicago: University of Chicago Press, 1987.
6   B. Anderson, *Imagined Communities: Reflections on the Origin and Spread of Nationalism*, London: Verso, 1991 (1983); *The Spectre of Comparisons: Nationalism, Southeast Asia, and the World*, New York: Verso, 1988.

difference. Thus, these global cultural flows have a curious inner contradiction, since they create some of the obstacles to their own freedom of movement and strangely self-regulate the ease with which they cross cultural boundaries. To summarize: knowing that there has always been flow, exchange, and mixture across social boundaries in human history, I take the *longue durée* very seriously. The fact that the same dynamics produce various cultural flows and the very obstacles, bumps, and potholes that impede their free movement constitutes a highly significant, new development in our understanding of cultural flows in the era of globalization; it also ought to comfort those who worry that global flows will result in a simple and homogeneous cultural regime that covers the earth.

SOME DILEMMAS OF METHOD

For some time now, social scientists and area studies scholars, including scholars of built forms, have been wondering about a basic problem: how can we compare social objects in a world where most such objects, whether nations, ideas, technologies, and economies, seem deeply interconnected. The classic idea of comparison in fields as diverse as comparative literature, linguistics, and anthropology relies on the notion that the objects to be compared are distinct and that comparison, therefore, remains unsullied by connectivity. Even in fields like anthropology and evolutionary biology, with their interest in the historical, evolutionary parentage of forms, such as kinship or language, the strategy of comparison treated objects for the purpose of comparison, as if they were formally quite separate. Indeed, comparison was a guide to the study of history and ancestry, rather than vice versa.

I want to suggest that we need to distinguish the problem of circulation from the problem of connectivity, and look at various periods as being characterized by different levels of circulation. For example, there can be periods or contexts marked by a high level of connectivity without a high level of circulation, as in the case of the movement of Buddhism from India to much of Asia in the first millennium of the Christian era. Today, we find ourselves at the other end of the spectrum: we live in a world where both are at very high levels. Many low-tech and geographically isolated societies are limited in regard to both connectivity and circulation. Yet the societies of contemporary Turkey and Germany, with their high level of circulation of Turkish guest workers to and from Germany, do not show a significant increase in connectivity. The politics of value, discussed in chapter 1, primarily addresses the problem of circulation in relation to knowledge in the social life of things. In fact, the politics of value may be regarded as emerging in the friction between circulation and connectivity in the social life of things, which complicates the problem of comparison across regimes of value.

In thinking about area studies, we need to recognize that histories produce geographies and not vice versa. We must get away from the notion that there is some kind of spatial landscape against which time writes its story. Instead, it is historical agents, institutions, actors and powers that make the geography. Of course, there are commercial geographies, geographies of nations, geographies of religion, ecological geographies, any number of geographies, but each of them is historically produced. They did not preexist so that people could act in or with them. To perceive histories as producing geographies promises a better grasp of the knowledge produced in the humanities, the social sciences, and even the natural sciences about the way in which regions, areas, and even civilizations emerge from the work of human beings. This emergence includes what I previously called the "work of the imagination,"[7] which humans do as they strive to extend their chances of survival, improve their horizons of possibility, and increase their wealth and security. Throughout human history, these activities, which are by no means solely the product of modernity, have characterized what I call the "production of locality": while human beings exercise their social, technical, and imaginative capacities, including the capacity for violence, warfare, and ecological selfishness, they literally produce the environments within which they function, including the biological and physical nature of these environments. The idea that histories produce geographies, which of course then in turn shape what happens to historical agents, holds at all scales, including the city scale (see part 2 in this volume). In a variety of fields, the relationship between circulation, comparison, and connectivity features an inner tension between structural approaches stressing comparison and what may be labeled "historical approaches," which stress connectivity. The question, therefore, is whether we can develop a method that does not require a choice between the stress on comparison and the stress on connectivity. For an answer, we have to return to the relationship between "the circulation of forms and the forms of circulation."

THE CIRCULATION OF FORMS

By "forms" I mean to indicate a family of phenomena, including styles, techniques, or genres, which can be inhabited by specific voices, contents, messages, and materials. Unfortunately, the philosophical conundrum of separating form from content cannot be unraveled in this chapter. In using the word "form" I simply wish to temporarily place the issue of global circulation on a slightly more abstract level. The most recent forms to be discussed in this way are the "nation form" and the "novel form," whose relationship was forcefully argued by

---

7   Appadurai, *Modernity at Large*.

Benedict Anderson[8] when he redefined nationalism by linking it to print capitalism, nation and narration, reading and citizenship, imagined and affected communities. There have been some additional inquiries into how the novel form has circulated and how it has been transformed in the process, along with other literary forms and genres. The circulation of the nation form has been the subject of less intense discussion, but Homi Bhabha,[9] Benjamin Lee,[10] and a few others have shown that it, too, moves and inhabits local sites in complex ways. The discussion of the "intimate nation" in chapter 5 illustrates the complex cohabitation of two forms of imagined nation in the same historical and geographical space. Likewise, the analysis of extreme violence in chapter 4 illuminates how political and medical forms can coproduce unexpected forms of political surgery. In a more optimistic vein, Gandhi's way of combining deep genealogies of royal violence with circulating modern ideas of love, tolerance, and civil disobedience illustrates the unexpected ways in which circulation can animate the hybridization of apparently similar forms. The idea of nation also circulates partly due to the production of new reading publics and new forms of writing and publication. The great American constitutional formula "We the People" is not only a performative, as Bonnie Honig[11] and Jay Fliegelman,[12] among others, have shown, but also a circulating performative that produces different local imaginaries about collective identity and democratic projects. The examples of nation and narration are a useful reminder that different forms circulate through different trajectories, generate diverse interpretations, and yield different and uneven geographies. There are novels without nations and nations without novels, so globalization is never a total project capturing all geographies with equal force. Indeed, the circulation of forms produces new and distinct genre experiments, many of which are forced to coexist in uneven and uneasy combinations. One lesson here is that we need to move decisively beyond existing models of creolization, hybridity, fusion, syncretism, and the like, which have largely been about mixture at the level of content. Instead, we need to probe the cohabitation of forms, such as the novel and the nation, because they actually produce new contexts through their peculiar inflection of each other.

A first step to escape the conundrum of the local and the global that many scholars are facing may be to accept that the global is not merely the accidental site of the fusion or confusion of circulating global elements. It is the site of the

8 Anderson, *Imagined Communities*.
9 H. K. Bhabha, *Nation and Narration*, New York: Routledge, 1990.
10 B. Lee, "Peoples and Publics," *Public Culture*, 1998, 10(2), 371–94.
11 B. Honig, "Declarations of Independence: Arendt and Derrida on the Problem of Founding a Republic," *American Political Science Review*, 1991, 85(1), 97–113.
12 J. Fliegelman, *Declaring Independence: Jefferson, Natural Language and the Culture of Performance*, Stanford: Stanford University Press, 1993, ch. 3.

mutual transformation of circulating forms, such as the nation and the novel. Such transformations always occur through what I called earlier the "work of the imagination," which produces locality. In my 1996 work *Modernity at Large*, I stressed that the local was not just an inverted canvas on which the global was written, but that the local itself was a product of incessant effort. Today, that argument is relatively easy to accept, or to agree with, or even to take for granted, but I want to add that this labor and this appropriation are first of all a matter of forms, styles, idioms, and techniques, rather than substantive stories, theories, bodies, or books. Thus, the nation form represents a more vital circulating ingredient than any specific ideology of nationalism. The novel form is more important than any author or variation of the genre. The idea of "the people" is more important than any specific populist ideology. The idea of a foundational legal document for a national polity outweighs this or that particular constitution. Finally, the "work of the imagination" and the circulation of forms produce localities not by the hybridization of contents, art, ideology, or technology, but by the negotiation and mutual tensions between each other. It is this negotiation that creates the complex containers that further shape the actual contents of local practice.

THE FORMS OF CIRCULATION

In closing, let me look at the forms of circulation. These forms are closely tied to the circuits through which they occur, the speed with which they occur, and the scale on which they occur.

Not everything moves through the same circuits: humans move in boats, ships, trains, and cars; pictures, words, and ideas move through a variety of other circuits, which now include cyberpaths of various kinds; blood circulates through certain circuits, money through others, and arms, drugs, and diseases through yet others. Speed is a property that shapes the circulation of different forms; at the same time, it is an element of the forms of circulation. The 2003 invasion of Iraq, for example, clearly shows the uneven speeds of a host of messages, materials, and manpower, as well as media reports.

Spatial scope is another formal key feature of circulatory processes. Linguistically mediated forms tend to have certain genres and produce effects over certain terrains. Therefore, recognizing that circulation itself has some formal properties, mainly in terms of time, space, and scale, I would modify my earlier argument that the uneven relationships between a variety of "scapes"—I used the term "ethnoscapes"—produced these junctures and differences in the global cultural economy. Today, I would make that suggestion more dynamic by arguing that the bumps and blocks, disjunctures and differences are produced by the variety of circuits, scales, and speeds that characterize the circulation of cultural elements. Some examples and questions from Asia will illustrate this point:

Why is there not greater interaction between the film industries of Hong Kong and Mumbai in regard to plots, characters, narratives, finances, production, or distribution? It is true that in the last few decades Mumbai filmmakers include Hong Kong, Singapore, and a few other monumental locations in their films, partly to offset the high costs of exotic locales such as London and New York, but also because some Indian filmmakers, especially from the Madras-based Tamil movie industry, are fascinated by the special consumer cultures of East Asia. However, the reverse is not true: Chinese, Japanese, or other major Asian movie industries do not head south toward India to enrich their own fantasies about the modern. The question is, why not? How many mainland Chinese have seen an Indian soap opera? How many Indians have seen and enjoyed a popular film from the mainland? How many Indian intellectuals can discuss India's relationship with North Korea with any authority? Have India's secular intellectuals wondered why communist China has been remarkably harsh with its own religious minorities? These are all questions about blockages, bumps, and interference in what is otherwise seen as a festival of interaction and celebration between India and China. In general, it is fair to say that any fast and heavy traffic is due to the force of the market of commodities and services, of capital and its flows, and of the energies of entrepreneurship. Where the traffic is weak, it is generally a matter of cultural prejudices and of various state policies. All modernities emerge in the tension between heavy traffic and the opposite, slow traffic. In other words, while it is true that histories produce geographies, the shape, form, and durability of these geographies is also a matter of obstacles, roadblocks, and traffic jams. In order to comprehend how alterity is produced in a globalizing world, we need to consider both the circulation of forms, which I have stressed, and the forms of circulation. In fact, what we need, I believe, is a theory that relates the forms of circulation to the circulation of forms. Such a theory can tell us something useful about the reason why universities move less swiftly than, say, AK-47s, and why, globally, democracy is held in higher esteem than the American presidency.

To really meet the challenge of comparison in a context characterized by high degrees of connectivity and circulation, which I believe defines our era of globalization, we need to understand more about the ways in which the forms of circulation and the circulation of forms create the conditions for the production of locality. I stress locality because, in the end, this is where our vitally important archives reside. Localities—in this world, and in this argument—are temporary negotiations between various globally circulating forms. They are not subordinate instances of the global, but in fact the main evidence of its reality.

CHAPTER THREE

The Morality of Refusal

THE DOUBLE GENEALOGY OF NON-VIOLENCE IN INDIA

This chapter begins and ends with reflection on India, and on the place of Gandhian ideas about non-violence as a form of political action. Gandhi has often been viewed as a great synthesizer of traditional Hindu ideas with modern Western ideas to create his singular vision of non-violence, political protest, and moral mobilization. However, he also is a remarkable example of the interaction of the circulation of political forms with the resemblances between traditional and modern cultural practices. In this regard, he requires us to be especially sensitive to the tension between the forms of circulation and the circulation of forms (see chapter 2). The literature on Gandhi and on his place in the study of non-violence is voluminous. One among the many questions that remain open about Gandhian thought and action is the way in which violence and non-violence are connected in his politics. The argument developed in this chapter is that Gandhian ideas and practices about non-violence have a double genealogy. One genealogy is connected to Indic ideas about asceticism, avoidance, and abstinence, and, in common with other ascetical traditions, relies on the moral virtues and special powers associated with the restraint of bodily appetites. The other genealogy has a different relationship to the world of the senses, of sexuality, and of power, and draws on Indic ideas about kingship, sacrifice, and martial prowess. This latter tradition is not especially anxious about doing harm to sentient life and draws its ethics from the militant logics of sacrifice and warfare in Indic thought. These two genealogies themselves become blurred in the traditions of warrior asceticism in India; hence, this chapter also explores warrior asceticism as a living source for the politics of militant religiosity in India today.

NON-VIOLENCE AS A FORM OF ACTION

Hannah Arendt's reflections[1] on the difference between action and behavior may provide us a good beginning in thinking about the double genealogy of Gandhian non-violence. For human beings, whom Arendt thought of as uniquely capable of action, action meant *starting* something new in the world. Action for Arendt was the distinctive feature of human activity and was

---

1   H. Arendt, *The Human Condition*, Chicago: University of Chicago Press, 1958.

essentially public and political, since it required engagement with other human beings and not just with nature or with machinery.

So let us ask whether non-violence is a way of acting. And if so, what does it inaugurate in the world? This reflection also allows us to consider whether violence and non-violence are in fact activities of the same type, and are thus in some way always related to one another reciprocally or by opposition. Or are they best regarded independently, and related only by their common link to some third activity or situation, such as the production of order or the maintenance of peace? In the conclusion to this chapter, I will suggest that the second alternative offers us a richer way to grasp the relationship between violence and non-violence as historical forms of political action.

NON-VIOLENCE AND ABSTENTION

Non-violence can be viewed as a form of action because it is a form of abstention, and indeed of abstinence. While the Gandhian version of the doctrine of *ahimsa* is frequently tied up with the active project of truthful force, active tolerance, and political love, non-violence is also directly linked with his general interest in avoidance, abstention, and abstinence.[2] It is thus a special form of worldly asceticism. It is worth pausing over abstention as a form of action, because it is action of a unique sort, which is marked by the avoidance of other possible forms of action.

To understand the relation between abstention and action, it is worth pondering again the familiar teachings of the *Bhagavad Gita* about action, renunciation, and attachment. Without conducting a full exegesis of the ideas of the *Gita* about action, renunciation, and attachment, we need to note that Krishna's main advice to Arjuna is to act in the spirit of abstention, and the action in question is violent action. In this instance, it appears that Krishna did not advocate abstention from violent action. But even here, on closer examination, it is abstemious action that Krishna recommends to Arjuna, and the abstention in question is described in the language of detachment from the fruits (*phala*) of action, or, as more commonly translated, from the results or consequences of action. In fact, Krishna's advice to Arjuna is premised on a philosophy of action that distinguishes effects, results, consequences, and rewards. This special ethics of abstention underpins Krishna's advice to Arjuna

---

2 J. Alter, *Gandhi's Body: Sex, Diet, and the Politics of Nationalism*, Philadelphia: University of Pennsylvania Press, 2000; A. Appadurai, "Understanding Gandhi," in P. Homans, ed., *Childhood and Selfhood: Essays on Tradition, Religion, and Modernity in the Psychology of Erik H. Erikson*, Lewisburg, PA: Bucknell University Press, 1978; E. H. Erikson, *Gandhi's Truth: On the Origins of Militant Nonviolence*, New York: W. W. Norton & Company, 1969; I. Rothermund, *The Philosophy of Restraint: Mahatma Gandhi's Strategy and Indian Politics*, Bombay: Popular Prakashan, 1963.

and is worthy of some attention for the light that it casts on Gandhi's understanding of political abstention and detachment.

The common understanding of the doctrine of detachment in *Gita* is based on translations from the original language of the text that tend to conflate effects, results, and rewards into a general concept of consequences. It may be more useful to distinguish these semantic elements and take Krishna's message about violent action to be a doctrine of effects, and in this sense, a pragmatic rather than a moral doctrine. Krishna urges Arjuna to view his duties (as a warrior) as superseding his compunctions as a kinsman, because the salient effect that is desired is victory. Detachment from the effects of his success (the death of his kinsmen) requires commitment to the results, namely victory in war, the dharmic task of the warrior. Gandhi was, from this point of view, committed to the results of his non-violent tactics (to which we shall soon return), and principally, to make it impossible for the British to impose their rule (both as authority and as coercive power) over Indians in India. For this result to be achieved, Gandhi summoned the virtues of bodily detachment and abstention, among whose ascetic virtues was the capacity to withstand the corporeal pain of British armed force. Pain in this ethic is an effect of resistance, but moral victory over the British is the result. Consequences thus divide themselves into two sets, one desired and the other to be ignored or transcended. This division is further facilitated by another feature of the ontology of the *Gita*, which is its doctrine of appearance, *maya*.

This special feature of the philosophy of action is generally important to the Hindu doctrine of *dharma* or of dharmic action, since it represents action as both consequential and compulsory as well as transitory and inconsequential as a result of its being strictly confined to the world of appearance. Here it is important to note that the popular tendency to equate *maya* with "illusion" or "nothingness," in their common English meanings, is misleading. *Maya* may better be understood as "the structure of appearance," which is as an ordering principle with its own rules of shadow and substance, reality and truth, being and representation.[3]

So one genealogical strand, which informs at least some aspects of the Gandhian sense of non-violence as an activity (rather than simply a norm or value), is the idea that abstention from action is itself a form of action, even if both forms of action are equally constrained by being part of the world of appearance. But what exactly makes such abstention best viewed as a form of activity? In Arendt's sense, what does abstention *start* anew in the world?

---

3   I owe this insight to the oral classroom remarks (in the early 1970s) of the late Prof. A. K. Ramanujan of the University of Chicago, who was greatly influenced by the structural linguistics of the 1960s and used the idea of structure to show that the concept of *maya* was not a low-level form of Eastern mysticism, but a rather sophisticated and consistent ontology of appearance.

Here we need to look more closely at abstention in relation to abstinence and avoidance, as a family of actions that together form the moral core of many kinds of ascesis, notably the ascesis of the early Indic world. The standard view of *ahimsa* is that the object of avoidance in *ahimsa* is violent action—specifically action that causes harm to other living creatures—and that is not an incorrect understanding. But it is an inadequate understanding. The Indic understanding of abstention, as the avoidance of harm to other living creatures, is a part of a wider family of disciplines designed to limit attachment, understood as an excessive engagement with sensory results, fruits, and consequences. But abstention is also seen as being a technology with powerful effects.

So now we have the beginnings of an answer to the question of what non-violence as action brings anew into the world. It brings into being the possibility of worldly detachment, or detachment from the world in the world. In this view, non-violence in the Indic tradition takes its meaning not only from a specific philosophy of means and ends, and a particular ontology of appearance, but also from a complex set of practices that surrounds the work of the ascetic and with asceticism as a form of *dharma*, such as the caste *dharma* of the Brahmins. Abstention is the active space for maintaining the tension between being *in* the world and *of* the world, as Max Weber famously characterized the ethos of dharmic Hinduism.[4]

Viewed another way, if we are right in seeing non-violent action as connected in the Indic context with a more general philosophy of abstention, which pertains not just to violence but to a variety of other forms of submersion in the affairs of the world, it opens up another interesting paradox about non-violence, which is its relationship to sacrifice.

NON-VIOLENCE AND SACRIFICE

On the face of it, non-violence stands opposed to sacrifice since sacrifice is usually seen as requiring some form of violence, however derivative or symbolic. In the Indic world, the direct violence that characterized the classical sacrifice gradually gave way, as a consequence of the Hinduistic doctrine of *ahimsa*, to an elaborate doctrine of substitution in Hindu ritual, designed to assure that sentient life was not subtracted or violated in sacrifice.[5] There remains, however, considerable ambivalence about the importance of animal offerings in major Vedic sacrifices in contemporary India.[6]

---

4   M. Weber, *The Religion of India: The Sociology of Hinduism and Buddhism*, Glencoe: Free Press, 1958.

5   F. M. Smith, *The Vedic Sacrifice in Transition: A Translation and Study of the Trikandamandana of Bhaskara Misra*, Poona: Bhandarkar Oriental Research Institute, 1987.

6   T. Lubin, "Veda on Parade: Revivalist Ritual as Civic Spectacle," *Journal of the American Academy of Religion*, 2001, 69(2), 377–408.

Yet this oppositional relationship of non-violence to sacrifice cannot be taken too literally if non-violence is connected to the wider Indic world of abstention and asceticism. Sacrifice, in most theoretical accounts, operates in a space of tension constituted by two poles: one involves the violent cost of the offer; the other is the double communion of the gift, the communion of the givers, and the communion between giver, receiver, and victim.[7] In Indic logic, sacrifice was the exemplary performative act of kingship, as expressed in the elaborate grammar of the *rajasuya*.[8] This is where Indic sacrifice enters a specific constellation of meaning that is not part of the universal logic of sacrifice.

This royal context is worth recalling because it brings back a question we have not discussed much since the 1970s, when Louis Dumont forced a new consideration of the relationship between renunciation and hierarchy, and between the royal and Brahminical order of things.[9] Less remembered about Dumont's argument is the triangular tension that Dumont exposed between Brahmin, ascetic, and king, one that was especially brilliantly elaborated by the late Richard Burghart in the context of Nepal.[10] Dumont's original insight was to suggest that the Indian ascetic was the primordial archetype of the individual in a society otherwise defined by collectivity, community, and what later came to be defined as caste, in Hindu India. Burghart used this insight, which opposed Hindu ascetics both to kings and to Brahmins, by later showing that in Nepal, till recent times, there were multiple social hierarchies organized around kings, Brahmins, and ascetics, with none being reducible to the others. This contribution is a major internal complication for Dumont's ideas about a single hierarchy (founded on a unique principle of purity and pollution) as the very basis of Hindu society. The diversity of these hierarchies is part of what continues to make the moral authority of alternative hierarchical logics available to groups that are marginalized in one hierarchy.

Among the untouchable intellectuals of modern Lucknow, for example, the history of Indian asceticism is consciously deployed against the moral authority of the Brahminic social order.[11] In each of these instances, one marked feature that links ascetics and warriors is their capacity to seek, capture, and deploy force, and to undertake militant actions celebrated in Hindu religious texts and mythological histories. In contrast stands the world of the Brahmin, and of mature Hinduism, in which abstinence becomes tied

---

7   R. Girard, *Violence and the Sacred*, Baltimore: Johns Hopkins University Press, 1977.

8   J. C. Heesterman, *The Ancient Indian Royal Consecration: The Rajasuya Described According to the Yajus Texts*, Gravenhage: Mouton, 1957.

9   L. Dumont, *Homo Hierarchicus: The Caste System and its Implications*, M. Sainsbury, trans., Chicago: University of Chicago Press, 1970.

10   R. Burghart, "Hierarchical Models of the Hindu Social System," *Man*, 1978, 13(4), 519–36.

11   R. S. Khare, *The Untouchable as Himself: Ideology, Identity, and Pragmatism among the Lucknow Chamars*, Cambridge: Cambridge University Press, 1984.

to vegetarianism, regulated social exchange, and a social contract premised on the mutuality of gift exchange rather than the collective public drama of the royal sacrifice.

I refer to these debates in the history of the anthropology of India in order to point out that there is a deep and not fully grasped relationship between royalty, warfare, violence, and asceticism in Indian history. This relationship has its roots in the early Indic paradigm that created an inner bond between ascetics and kings, both masters of the violent sacrifice, in common opposition to the Brahmin, defined mostly by being the apical point in the logic of the gift. We might say, as a simplification, that while *yujna* is the paradigm of the king, *dana* is the paradigm of the Brahmin, though of course these moral orders are deeply reciprocal. The ascetic is the obscure figure here, and there is a rich tradition of thought, especially in the twentieth century, that focuses on the *sadhu*.[12] But the discussion of the inner affinity between kings and ascetics has not been fully explored.

The strong tradition of warrior asceticism has been discussed by several scholars.[13] The most thorough exploration of the relationship between religious orders, ascetic groupings, warfare, and politics has been conducted by William Pinch.[14] This body of work testifies to the deep history of a sub-tradition that remains alive well into the present, forming an important component of the Hindu nationalism of the last two decades. These studies also disclose a distinct sociological paradox about the collective organization of Hindu ascetics, who have also been considered to be exemplars of the logic of individualism in a collectively organized society, by virtue of their freedom from established social categories and locations. This is not the place for any effort to address this well-worn paradox. What is important here is that warrior ascetics are a strong reminder of the inner affinity between ascetic practices and the public conduct of collective violence, in the form of organized warfare. Today the rebirth of the *trisula* (the trident modeled on a fierce icon of Siva), as a public expression of militant street Hinduism, owes itself to the blurring of the roles of king and ascetic in Indic history. While the royal sacrifice is a public performance designed to secure sacred and cosmic order, prosperity and polity, ascetic militancy is more dangerous and disorderly because it lies simultaneously within and without the social order. Peter Van der Veer's groundbreaking study of the

12   Dumont, *Homo Hierarchicus*; G. S. Ghurye, *Indian Sadhus*, Bombay: Popular Prakashan, 1964.

13   C. A. Bayly, *Rulers, Townsmen, and Bazaars: North Indian Society in the Age of British Expansion, 1770–1870*, Cambridge: Cambridge University Press, 1983; D. N. Lorenzen, "Warrior Ascetics in Indian History," *Journal of the American Oriental Society*, 1978, 98(1), 61–75; P. van der Veer, *Gods on Earth: The Management of Religious Experience and Identity in a North Indian Pilgrimage Centre*, London: Athlone Press, 1988.

14   W. R. Pinch, *Peasants and Monks in British India*, Berkeley: University of California Press, 1996; *Warrior Ascetics and Indian Empires*, New York: Cambridge University Press, 2006.

sectarian orders in Ayodhya,[15] especially the Ramanandis, is still the most comprehensive account of the ways in which military organization, commercial aspirations, celibacy, and asceticism come together to inform the ethos of religious life in North India. The fact that these blurrings between warrior and monastic ethics characterize the great pilgrimage centers of North India, in this case of Ayodhya (the mythic birthplace of Rama), throws more than a little light on the proletarian capture of the practices of militant asceticism in India, at least since the rise of the Hindu right since the mid 1980s. We come now to this new form of popular militancy.

From the point of view of public ritual, Indologists agree that the world of the Vedic sacrifice has all but disappeared from India, while the world of the gift not only remains alive but has exploded into numerous forms of sumptuary life, including the wedding, the birthday party, and the bribe, in contemporary India. But while the public ritual of royal sacrifice may have all but disappeared, the inner violence of asceticism is alive and well in Indian public life, in the images of the militant *sadhu*, the *trisula*, and other expressions of masculine abstention as a sign of political power and organized force. The lumpen Hindu militants with their red headbands and tridents, who have captured Indian public space in the *yatras* of the late 1980s and the destruction of the Babri Masjid in 1992, and more recently in the anti-Muslim pogroms in Gujarat, are a reminder of the availability of the paradigm of warrior asceticism for mass democratic politics and ethnocidal mobilization in contemporary India. Here the idioms of sacrifice and violence (as legitimate exercises of male public power) become connected with the idea of the motherland and of distinctly modern ideas of land, territory, ethnicity, and majority. Recent ethnographic work on Gujarat under the leadership of Narendra Modi and his associates shows how Gandhian language can be transformed into a language of sacrifice and cleansing in which the extermination of Muslims can be rewritten as a righteous form of sacrifice for Hindus.[16]

Thus, there is one distinct trajectory that connects abstention—via sacrifice and ascetic militarism—to violence, while Gandhi's trajectory is usually viewed as linking abstention to non-violence. How are we to understand this double trajectory so as to capture the ethical project of non-violence viewed as a form of activity that can "start something new in the world"? Here again, Gandhi's own highly public and publicized strategies of asceticism need to be revisited. What Gandhi did was to make abstention available as a political strategy for the public sphere. This was

15   van der Veer, *Gods on Earth*.
16   P. Ghassem-Fachandi, *Sacrifice, Ahimsa, and Vegetarianism: Pogrom at the Deep End of Non-Violence*, Ithaca: Cornell University Press, 2006.

perhaps most marked in his deployment of fasting as a strategy for mobilizing attention, insisting on his views, and coercing the British and his Indian
opponents to attend to his point of view. Gandhi's idea of the fast unto death
was the most dramatic expression of his idea of *satyagraha*, which is
normally seen as the main way in which non-violence can be an active principle of political action, of civil disobedience, and of refusal. But if we place
the fast unto death in the more general field of Gandhi's strategies and
practices, which included the long marches, the major rituals of civil disobedience, the public sacrifice of British textiles, the active invitation of
physical violence by satyagrahis in relation to the armed force of the Raj,
and the domestic dramas of sexual control and experimentation in Gandhi's
daily life, we are made aware that Gandhian *ahimsa* is indeed closely tied to
the spectacular world of the royal sacrifice and the political power of the
warrior ascetic. Thus, it cannot be seen in isolation from older and newer
forms of Hindu militancy.

This complicated inner affinity may partly account for the irony that Gujarat
today is simultaneously the site of both sides of Gandhi's militant heritage. To
explore this disturbing co-presence of two images of social life that have so
frequently been opposed to one another, we need to take a deeper look at what
I have here called the *morality of refusal*, in light of what has been argued so far
about the double genealogy of Gandhian non-violence.

THE MORALITY OF REFUSAL

Gandhi's story invited us to connect asceticism, abnegation, abstinence, and
refusal as forms of political action. Gandhi was the modern world's first and
greatest refusenik, but his refusal took its meaning from a particular way of
mobilizing the inner link between asceticism, violence, and non-violence in
the Indic world. The best context in which to examine this inner link is to look
once again at the ways in which Gandhi made civil disobedience a major part
of his politics.

Civil disobedience has been argued by some to be the major political innovation that we owe to Gandhi, at least insofar as large-scale resistance to imperial
or colonial rule is concerned. It is certainly that part of the Gandhian heritage
that is most vital to later figures like Martin Luther King and Nelson Mandela.
There is a large technical literature on the history of Gandhian civil disobedience, focused on major events such as the Salt March, the push to refuse the use
of British textiles, and the refusal to accept other British legal impositions. The
story of civil disobedience, as evolved in India by Gandhi, has many dimensions,
including the positive actions entailed by various refusals, actions such as the
collection and processing of salt by Gandhi and his satyagrahis, the active
production of khadi cloth as a form of daily practice and economic resistance,

and the general push to economic self-reliance (*swadeshi*).[17] Nevertheless, refusal is the first principle of civil disobedience (with its roots in Thoreau and the abolitionist movement of the nineteenth century in the United States). In India, and especially for Gandhi, there is a deep connection between refusal, abstinence, and the avoidance of luxury. In other words, Gandhian civil disobedience is shot through with an ascetic ethics, which connects with other forms of abstinence and abnegation (such as fasting, celibacy, and other personal practices). Each of these elements was woven by Gandhi into a larger politics of refusal, which erected personal and bodily abstinence as an answer to the ethics of civil law.[18]

Political refusal, in this Gandhian ethos, was intimately connected with the politics of the body and the morality of avoidance, abnegation, and abstention. The idea of the boycott and the *hartal* capture the political end of this ethos as fasting captures its bodily pole. Both ends are underpinned by an ethics of abstention and an ideology of sacrifice, in the double sense of severance and offering. In the public actions of civil disobedience we see an abstemious, minimalist, and parsimonious echo of the royal sacrifice and of the history of the warrior ascetic in which abstention becomes a weapon of positive action and of militant collective mobilization, in this case against British armed force and the British legal order.

We are now in a better position to answer the question of what sort of action is involved in non-violence. No doubt, non-violence is a particular form of abstinence and of asceticism. But since it is also part of a larger politics of refusal and of sacrifice, it also takes its meaning from the field of violence in two distinct ways. The first—most dramatically captured in the images and reports of the waves of satyagrahis walking toward the British troops in the Salt March, to fall down like ninepins with their skulls bashed in and their bones broken—reminds us that the active work of non-violence is to invite the forces of violence to declare and enact themselves and to manifest themselves practically, rather than as threats or deterrents. The second way in which non-violence takes its meaning from the world of violence is through the more complex genealogy I have tried to describe, which is more Indic in its form, and looks back through the traditions of warrior asceticism to the violence of the royal sacrifice as the supreme form of the political performative. Gandhi's practices of non-violence thus derived their best energies from ideas of militant action that did not simply oppose love to violence, but also opposed an earlier idea of militant asceticism to the imperial forms of organized and legalized police violence. The latter, a completely legalized form of coercive violence, could not have been better designed to fail in the face of the

---

17   R. R. Diwakar, *Satyagraha in Action: A Brief Outline of Gandhiji's Satyagraha Campaigns*, Calcutta: Signet Press, 1949; Rothermund, *The Philosophy of Restraint*.

18   Alter, *Gandhi's Body*.

violence of the militant ascetic, and the harsh discipline of abstention that Gandhi put at the core of his own practices of refusal.

So, non-violence can start something new in the world, and it is certainly not right to view it as the refusal of action, or as quietist in any form. But it is also important to see that the Gandhian version of the ethics of refusal also drew its force from another ethics of violence and power, associated originally with the royal sacrifice in India, and subsequently with militant asceticism. This sort of refusal needs to be handled with care, since it can and indeed has become far too available to the politics of saffron and the vulgarization of the trident in contemporary India.

CONCLUSION: THE PRODUCTION OF ORDER

I began this chapter with the hint that violence and non-violence, as forms of action, may not take their meaning exclusively from their opposed and reciprocal relations to one other but also from some third principle or project. That possibility can now be sketched, as a way to think about some issues that also carry us beyond the concerns of this chapter.

We live in a world characterized by forms of violence that have deep histories, in such forms as rape, torture, warfare, forced ritual mutilation, and so on. These age-old forms have been complicated by new developments such as the census, modern ethno-nationalism, new forms of labor migration, and new flows of technology and information. Especially in the last few decades, ideologies about "suffering at a distance"[19] and recent developments in ideas of humanitarian intervention and universal human rights have produced a renewed concern with looking at the conditions that produce sustainable peace, tolerance, pluralism, and social routine, in the face of massive new forms of exception, emergency, and environmental disaster.

These situations press us to re-open the question of the conditions under which peace can be restored among warring groups, longstanding enmities can be reconciled, and daily practices of tolerance can be actively encouraged to flourish. From the point of view of such categories as "war," "conflict," and "emergency," we are still unable to think of ordinary life, of routine social order, and of ongoing everyday conviviality as anything other than default states, which are the social ground against which the contingencies of violence and conflict produce deviation and distortion.

This default view of the production of the everyday reinforces a foundational tendency in social theory to regard the production of ordinary life as a

---

19   M. Ignatieff, *The Warrior's Honor: Ethnic War and the Modern Conscience*, New York: Owl Books, 1998; L. Boltanski, *Distant Suffering: Morality, Media, and Politics*, New York: Cambridge University Press, 1999.

normal, routine, and functional extension of the existence of society itself. Even though we always have a Hobbesian counter-current in our thinking that reminds us that ordinary life is not a given of human life and nature, the over-riding functionalist view conflates the normal, the routine, the everyday, and the peaceful in social life. We have therefore not paid sufficient attention to the labor or social effort required to produce peace as an everyday fact in human societies. The work of producing the everyday is still seen as the predictable sediment of any organized system of roles, norms, and statuses (to use the jargon of textbook sociology) and imagined as a social version of a perpetual motion machine that functions until some external disturbance throws it into disequilibrium.

There are indeed traditions in social science that have taken a different line. One tradition, best exemplified by the now rather neglected work of Erving Goffman,[20] took the ethnological approach seriously and closely examined the myriad efforts that guarantee the survival of elementary social conventions. Other examples come out of the Freudian tradition, which always remind us of the effort most human beings make to police their impulses, to discipline their drives and fantasies, and to manage their neuro-ses productively. The socio-biologists (mistaken as they are on many basics) are also alert to the thin line between competition and cooperation in human life. Finally, students of the problematic of "everyday life" and the habitus, building on de Certeau[21] and Bourdieu,[22] have attempted to unearth various rituals and strategies whose main purpose is the perpetuation of routine social life.

But none of these traditions has given us an adequate basis for under-standing the quality, frequency, and intentionality that must go into the maintenance of routine understandings, elements that go into what I have elsewhere called "the production of locality."[23] Similarly, the production of routine social life is a complex project in which ordinary persons strive to find the right balance between attention and distraction, compromise and confron-tation, visibility and recessiveness in their bodily presence, and between greater or lesser knowledge of the circumstances of their daily lives.[24] We need to look more closely at the social and the cultural resources that ordinary

---

20   See, for example, E. Goffman, *The Presentation of Self in Everyday Life*, London: Allen Lane, 1969.

21   M. de Certeau, *The Practice of Everyday Life*, Berkeley: University of California Press, 1984.

22   P. Bourdieu, *Outline of a Theory of Practice*, R. Nice, trans., Cambridge: Cambridge University Press, 1977.

23   A. Appadurai, *Modernity at Large: Cultural Dimensions of Globalization*, Minneapolis: University of Minnesota Press, 1996.

24   V. Das, *Life and Words: Violence and the Descent into the Ordinary*, Berkeley: University of California Press, 2006.

people must deploy in order to increase predictability in lives that are regularly challenged by exception, emergency, and disaster. In a world of rapid motion, fast-moving social messages, multiple channels of seductive propaganda, intense overcrowding and heavy pressure to contest or exit, rather than to conform, daily routine requires a miracle of cooperation. So, especially for the poorer sections of society—and even more, for the women, children, and older members of these societies—life is increasingly lived under the sign of the exception. Examples of this predicament include: the massively crowded commuter trains of Mumbai or Tokyo; the criminalized civil societies of the great favelas and slums of our megacities; the refugee camps in Darfur, Thailand, Somalia, Palestine, and numerous other places; the emergency communities produced by major environmental disasters in Pakistan, Indonesia, Sri Lanka, and New Orleans.

If we are willing to concede that the maintenance of routine social and cultural expectations requires increased investments among individuals and communities of many kinds, and is increasingly a product of improvisation rather than of habit, it is incumbent upon us to rethink the elementary logics of sociality once again. That larger project can only be hinted at here, and it is connected to what I have earlier identified as "the work of the imagination."[25]

The analysis of the inner relationship of violence to non-violence, as in the Indic example, has something to offer to this deeper question about social order as a generally vulnerable outcome of uncertain social processes. The preceding analysis of Gandhian non-violence suggests that it has two genealogies: one is the doctrine of *ahimsa*, with its positive injunction to avoid harm to other sentient beings, turned in Gandhi's hands into a broader morality of refusal, with consequences for the politics of non-cooperation, civil disobedience, passive resistance, and other forms of peaceful opposition to established legal orders. The other genealogy explains the active part of non-violence, of non-violence as a principle of activity, by referring to the violence of the sacrifice, to the logic of martial asceticism in India, and to the more general possibility that non-violence also requires its special forms of militancy, associated with abnegation, abstinence, and refusal.

This double genealogy for Gandhian non-violence may offer us a new way to characterize the special disciplines and aggregate efforts now required for ordinary people to produce some degree of routine and predictability in circumstances that offer many incitements to violence against life in all its forms. In other words, we may need to see violence and non-violence as principles of action that actually have independent genealogies and offer different resources for managing social life, and are not just reciprocal and symmetrical forms,

---

25   Appadurai, *Modernity at Large*.

occupying essentially the same social terrain by inversion or by serial exhaustion. Non-violence as a militant morality of refusal may offer us a new angle on the ways in which many ordinary communities snatch predictability from the jaws of exception.

CHAPTER FOUR

The Offending Part:
Sacrifice and Ethnocide in the Era of Globalization

PARTS AND WHOLES

The problem of the whole and the part has been one of the central problems of Western social thought since its formal beginnings. Classical Greek thought introduced formal ontological and metaphysical considerations into the discussion of the part and the whole, whereas the prior discussion of the part and the whole had been primarily ritual and ethical.

In the modern social world, the most sacralized example of the social whole is the nation, which has exceeded other ideals of social sacrality such as the brotherhood of mankind and the community of believers. Various religious traditions, such as Buddhism, Islam, and Christianity, still seek to maintain the primary value of the *sangha*, the *'umma*, and the church over that of the nation-state. But as many scholars have shown, sometime in the course of the seventeenth century the nation emerged as the most general form of the sacred social collectivity. Conceived as a sacred whole, the modern nation-state, in common with earlier ideas of the nation, imbued itself with a series of somatic attributes, the most notable of which was the soil, the others being language, blood, race, and religion. The somatic undergirding of this unique social ideology was the primary force to cause pre-Westphalian ideas of authority and jurisdiction to become de-sacralized and replaced by the blood of the nation, the soul of the folk. Foucault, among others, has allowed us to see that the focus of the modern state on borders and territories was essential to the emergence of the idea of a people in the modern sense, a people who were defined by their territorial co-presence, their countability, and their accountability to the apparatus of the territorial state. In this modern formation, the idea of ethnic genius and substance was connected to the emergence of borders, of territory, the census, and a new articulation with the power of the bureaucratic state. Thus, the seventeenth and eighteenth centuries mark the true beginnings of national geography, subsequently elaborated in ideas of national sovereignty, national economy, national security, and various other refinements. I have written elsewhere of the ways in which land, soil, and territory became both distinct and connected in this new moment, so that ideas of dominion, ideas of identity, and ideas of property and tenure could be re-articulated under a new social covenant, although each of these elements had a venerable prior history.[1]

This new social whole, the nation-state, now a little more than three centuries old, has spread through the growth of capitalism and empire to much of the world, and is still the regnant principle of political affiliation, complicated as it might be by new forms of loyalty and mobility produced through the forces of globalization. Some idea or other about ethnic singularity and purity is always present when national peoplehood is discussed and defined, thus producing an enduring tension between the idea of citizenship as a formal political fact and peoplehood as a substantive somatic fact, the latter always being rooted in some pre-contractual sense of affinity. Blood and race are invariably involved in this underlying ideology, and preoccupations with national identity and authenticity are invariably tied up with ideas of national purity. The sacredness of the nation, the purity of its people, and its meaningfulness as a social whole are always present in the relations within and between nations.

In this context, the problem of the part is at once technical and procedural: subgroups, sub-territories, local authorities, electorates, and even individual voter citizens are managed by different nation-states through different techniques of representation, proportion, voice, and balance, depending on the extent and form of commitment to democratic principles in any given nation-state. But this aspect of the problem of parts within the national whole is not my central question today, since it is primarily about governance, administration, and procedural rationality. I am concerned with the problem of the part insofar as it affects the logic of national purity. This requires us to consider the issue of sacrifice. In chapter 3, I argued that Gandhi's unique brand of non-violent resistance to the British was in fact a complex hybrid of classical ideas of violent religious action and ascetical forms of abstention and moral purification. In this chapter, sacrifice can be seen to have a much darker hybrid potential in which ideas of reduction and subtraction animate terrifying forms of bodily violence.

BLOOD, SACRIFICE, WAR

In order to arrive at a fuller understanding of the role of sacrifice in the practices of the modern nation-state, we need to return to some basic arguments from comparative religion and anthropology. As far as sacrifice is concerned, the most sustained effort to confront the close relationship between violence

---

1 A. Appadurai, *Modernity at Large: Cultural Dimensions of Globalization*, Minneapolis: University of Minnesota Press, 1996.

and the sacred is René Girard's brilliant study of the subject.[2] Though this work is idiosyncratic in many regards, it makes an effort to understand sacrifice in the Greek ritual world, and takes what is most interesting from the structuralist and psychoanalytic traditions to remind us that violence is not just the thematic of sacrifice, but also its problematic. Girard argues that the unresolved and still active question of violence in human life is addressed in sacrifice by what he calls the role of the surrogate victim. There are many difficulties with a direct application of Girard's argument, drawn largely from the corpus of Greek texts and ethnographic reports from the archive of social anthropology. Yet there are several striking features of Girard's analysis that can be of help to us. The first is to remind us that violence in ritual contexts is not merely or thinly metaphorical. It is rather a serious effort to address the generative violence of human societies, and to manage it by directing it onto the person of a surrogate victim. This surrogacy is calculated to manage violence through violence, and for Girard "sacrifice is primarily an act of violence without the risk of vengeance."[3] This view of sacrifice (based on a view of social life as fundamentally and perennially prone to violence and vengeance) sees it as preventive, practical, and prudential. In Girard's analysis, the sacrificial victim must be both inside and outside the community, in some way recognizably similar to and yet different from the members of the community. I quote Girard here:

> If we look at the extremely wide spectrum of human victims sacrificed by various societies, the list seems heterogeneous, to say the least. It includes prisoners of war, small children, unmarried adolescents, and the handicapped, it ranges from the very dregs of society, such as the Greek *pharmakos*, to the king himself.[4]

This core idea about the surrogate victim, the loss of whose blood prevents the uncontrolled loss of communal blood through the spiral of vengeance, leads Girard to a series of valuable ideas about ritual substitution in the practices of sacrifice, about the connection between cure and poison at the heart of the Greek idea of the *pharmakon*, and, most important for our purposes, a fascinating discussion of the role of the term *katharma*, which was not unconnected to the term *pharmakos* in Greek texts. Girard's brilliant reading of the terms *katharma* (etymologically and conceptually linked to Aristotle's doctrine of catharsis) and *pharmakos*, whatever his interpretive excesses, and however far his arguments may be from the world we seek to address today, offer us a philological foundation for understanding the links between purification,

---

2   R. Girard, *Violence and the Sacred*, Baltimore: Johns Hopkins University Press, 1977.
3   Ibid., 13.
4   Ibid., 12.

substitution, catharsis, and purgation. Again, I offer a quotation from Girard, which links up to our concern with excision and extrusion from the social body:

> Whenever we describe the generative process or its products in terms of expulsion, purgation, or purification, we are attributing natural causes to phenomena that are not in the least natural, because they derive from violence. Expulsions, evacuations, and purgations are found in nature; the natural model does indeed exist. But its reality should not distract us from the extraordinary role that this model has played in the history of the human imagination, from primitive religious rituals and shamanistic medicine to the present day . . .
>
> The obsessive concern during the seventeenth century with clysters and bleedings, with assuring the efficient evacuation of peccant humors, shows plainly that the medical practices of that age were based on the principle of expulsion and purification. These practices constituted, in fact, a slightly refined variant of the shaman's approach with its emphasis on the extraction of the physical *katharma*.[5]

As it happens, Girard's line of reasoning leads him to make some interesting observations about purging, inoculation, and immunization in the subsequent history of medicine, but it can also be directed toward the history of surgery, as I will suggest when I turn to the question of amputation and excision.

Girard's line of thinking has an interesting counterpart in the important work of Mary Douglas on *Purity and Danger*, which has influenced many anthropologists who tackle the paradoxes of nationalism, including Michael Herzfeld,[5] Lisa Malkki,[6] and myself, among others. This body of work, in various ways, has convincingly shown that the problem of dirt, of impurity, and of matter out of place is not just a quaint problem of structuralist analysis or a theory for the never-never lands of small and faraway societies, but can also illuminate the logic of modern ethnocidal processes and mass refugee movements in Europe, Africa, India, and beyond. Though this ongoing work in social anthropology takes "blood" seriously and places it firmly in the practical mission of metaphor,[7] it does not yet connect fully with a distinct tradition of interest in sacrifice, memory, and the shedding of blood, which characterizes the work of Anderson, Balibar, and Claudio

---

5   M. Herzfeld, *Cultural Intimacy: Social Poetics in the Nation-State*, New York: Routledge, 1997.

6   L. H. Malkki, *Purity and Exile: Violence, Memory, and National Cosmology among Hutu Refugees in Tanzania*, Chicago: University of Chicago Press, 1995.

7   J. Fernandez, "The Mission of Metaphor in Expressive Culture, with Comments and Rejoinder," *Current Anthropology*, 1974, 15(2), 119–45.

Lomnitz,[8] all of whom are preoccupied with the mobilization of death in the birth and eschatology of nations. These scholars are concerned less with the semiotic and structural understanding of blood, sacrifice, impurity, and intimacy. They are more concerned, though they are not necessarily of one mind, with the larger implications of death, sacrifice, and war in colonial, postcolonial, and global settings. I turn now to Benedict Anderson's reflections on the topic in the expanded edition of his classic work on nationalism,[9] and to Etienne Balibar's ideas about war in the "production of the people."[10]

Their efforts to tackle the question of sacrifice in modern settings offer some lessons about the relationship between what we may call "shed" blood and "shared" blood in the contemporary world. Anderson puts the central question this way, when he states that the nation

> is imagined as a *community*, because, regardless of the actual inequality and exploitation that may prevail in each, the nation is always conceived as a deep, horizontal comradeship. Ultimately it is this fraternity that makes it possible, over the past two centuries, for so many millions of people, not so much to kill, as willingly to die for such limited imaginings. These deaths bring us abruptly face to face with the central problem posed by nationalism: what makes the shrunken imaginings of recent history (scarcely more than two centuries) generate such colossal sacrifices?[11]

It seems ungenerous to say that Anderson did not quite manage to reconcile his deep admiration for the power of the social imaginary of the nation with his sense that it was somehow "shrunken," and thus could not really provide a convincing answer to the question of why some were willing to kill for the nation and others to die for it. Perhaps he should have pondered Girard's struggles with the question of violence and the sacred more fully. In Etienne Balibar, we have a more convincing answer to this question, first sharply posed by Ernest Renan in the late nineteenth century. Balibar's answer to why nationalism succeeds in convincing so many of the virtues of its demands for loyalty, sacrifice, and death invokes a series of pedagogical practices instituted by modern nation-states, among them the mobilization of many members of their population into armies whose sole purpose was war in the name of the nation. By becoming surrogate victims, the young men who were mobilized into the mass

---

8   C. Lomnitz, *Death and the Idea of Mexico*, Cambridge, MA: Zone, 2005.

9   B. Anderson, *Imagined Communities: Reflections on the Origin and Spread of Nationalism*, London: Verso, 1991 (1983).

10   E. Balibar, "The Nation Form: History and Ideology," in E. Balibar and I. M. Wallerstein, eds., *Race, Nation, Class: Ambiguous Identities*, New York: Verso, 1991.

11   Anderson, *Imagined Communities*.

armies of the modern nation-state, in Balibar's argument, become both the perpetrators and the surrogate victims of modern national communities, if we look at them as Girard might have us do. The work of modern war thus is not so much a product of the sentiment of the imagined community as it is a major pedagogical source of this sentiment. Put more starkly, self-sacrifice and killing in the process of war is what produces the sense of horizontal comradeship that Anderson describes, since it is what produces the very mix of national memory and amnesia that Renan, Anderson, and many others seek to explain.

Even this interpretative move, putting Balibar's ideas about military mobilization and Girard's ideas about surrogacy, substitution, and sacrifice into a single framework, does not quite get us to where we want to go, for it only explains the productive force of the violent taking and giving of human life in reference to official nationalism, the modern state, and state-sponsored warfare. It does not get into the central features of the late twentieth century, which typically involve intra-state wars, ethnicized minorities, genocidal mobilizations, and planned atrocities as instruments of warfare. For this, we need a different way to think about sacrifice, mutilation, and the problem of minorities.

FEAR OF SMALL NUMBERS

This section draws substantially on chapter 1 of my recent book on global violence in the 1990s.[12] The inherent ethnicist tendency in all ideologies of nationalism does not explain why only some national polities become the scenes of large-scale violence, civil war, or ethnic cleansing. Here we need recourse to the place of social uncertainty in social life. I have elsewhere developed an argument about the ways in which social uncertainty can drive projects of ethnic cleansing that are both vivificationist and verificationist in their procedures.[13] That is, they seek uncertainty by dismembering the suspect body, the body under suspicion. I argue further that this species of uncertainty is intimately connected to the reality that today's ethnic groups number in the hundreds of thousands, and that their movements, mixtures, cultural styles, and media representations create profound doubts about who exactly may be among the "us" and who among the "them."

In this context, in myriad ways, some essential principles and procedures of the modern nation-state—the idea of a sovereign and stable territory, the idea of a containable and countable population, the idea of a reliable census, and the idea of stable and transparent categories—have come largely unglued in the era of globalization. Above all, the certainty that distinctive and singular peoples

12   A. Appadurai, *Fear of Small Numbers: An Essay on the Geography of Anger*, Durham: Duke University Press, 2006.

13   A. Appadurai, "Dead Certainty: Ethnic Violence in the Era of Globalization," *Public Culture*, 1998, 10(2), 225–47.

grow out of and control well-defined national soil has been decisively unsettled by the global fluidity of wealth, arms, peoples, and images that I described in *Modernity at Large*.[14]

In simpler words, though the lines between "us" and "them" may have always, in human history, been blurred at the boundaries, unclear across broad spaces and large numbers, globalization exacerbates these uncertainties and produces new incentives for cultural purification, as more nations lose the illusion of national economic sovereignty or well-being. This reminds us that large-scale violence is not simply the product of antagonistic identities, but that violence itself is one of the ways in which the illusion of fixed and charged identities is produced, partly to allay the uncertainties about identity that global flows invariably produce. In this regard, Islamic fundamentalism, Christian fundamentalism, and many other local and regional forms of cultural fundamentalism may be seen as a part of an emerging repertoire of efforts to produce previously unrequired levels of certainty about social identity, values, survival, and dignity. Violence, especially extreme and spectacular violence, is a mode of producing what I have elsewhere called "full attachment,"[15] especially when the forces of social uncertainty are allied to other fears about growing inequality, loss of national sovereignty, or threats to local security and livelihood. In this sense, to use Philip Gourevitch's brutal aphorism about Rwanda, "genocide, after all, is an exercise in community-building,"[16] an aphorism to which I return in the concluding portion of this chapter.

The social productivity of violence does not in itself account for the special ways in which violence against groups defined as minorities seems to have taken on a new life in the 1990s, from the United States to Indonesia, and from Norway to Nigeria. One could argue that the emerging European Union is in many ways the most enlightened political formation in the post-national world. Yet there are at least two Europes in evidence today: the world of inclusion and multiculturalism in one set of European societies, and the violent xenophobia of what we may call Anders Breivik's or Pim Fortuyn's Europe in the other. The growing legitimacy of right-wing ideologies throughout Europe in the past decade puts it firmly on the map of global racial xenophobia.

The tip over into ethno-nationalism and even ethnocide in democratic polities has much to do with the strange inner reciprocity of the categories of "majority" and "minority" in liberal social thought, which produces what I call *the anxiety of incompleteness*. Numerical majorities can become "predatory" and ethnocidal with regard to "small numbers" precisely when some minorities (and their small numbers) remind these majorities of the small gap that lies

---

14   Appadurai, *Modernity at Large*.
15   A. Appadurai, "Full Attachment," *Public Culture*, 1998, 10(2), 443–9.
16   P. Gourevitch, *We Wish to Inform You That Tomorrow We Will Be Killed With Our Families: Stories From Rwanda*, New York: Farrar, Straus and Giroux, 1998.

between their condition as majorities and the horizon of an unsullied national whole, a pure and untainted national ethnos. This sense of incompleteness can drive majorities into paroxysms of violence against minorities. Globalization, as a specific way in which states, markets, and ideas about trade and governance have come to be organized, exacerbates the conditions of large-scale violence because it produces a potential collision course between the logics of uncertainty and of incompleteness, each of which has its own form and force. As a broad fact about the world of the 1990s, the forces of globalization produce conditions for an increase in large-scale social uncertainty and also in the friction of incompleteness, produced in the traffic between the categories of "majority" and "minority." The sense of incompleteness (in the project of complete national purity) and the sense of social uncertainty about large-scale ethno-racial categories can produce a downward spiral, which is the road to genocide.

This approach to the growth in large-scale cultural violence in the 1990s gives us a way to recognize when the anxiety of incompleteness and unacceptable levels of uncertainty combine in ways that spark large-scale ethnocidal mobilization. One might argue that the co-presence of high levels of both sentiments is a necessary condition of large-scale violence. But sufficiency, as is so often the case in the social sciences, is another matter. In some cases, sufficiency might be provided by a rogue state (Iraq and the Kurds); in other cases by a racist colonial structure (Rwanda); in yet other cases by a tragically ethnicized constitution-building process (Yugoslavia after Tito); or again, by criminal leaders driven by personal greed and illicit commodity networks (Liberia, Sudan). In the case of India, the condition of sufficiency appears to have to do with a special contingency that links a major political partition to a series of internal legal and cultural fault lines.

One more point needs to be made in this brief overview of the argument of my book *Fear of Small Numbers*. The large-scale violence of the 1990s appears to be typically accompanied by a surplus of rage, an excess of hatred, which produces untold forms of degradation and violation, both to the body and the being of the victim: maimed and tortured bodies, burnt and raped persons, disemboweled women, hacked and amputated children, sexualized humiliation of every type. What are we to do with this surplus, which has occurred most often in public actions, often among friends and neighbors, no longer conducted in the covert ways in which the degradation of group warfare used to occur in the past? I suggest that the surplus of rage, the urge to degradation, which drives the narcissism of "minor differences" is now vastly more dangerous than in the past because of the new economy of slippage and morphing that characterizes the relationship between "majority" and "minority" identities and powers. Since the two categories, owing to the pliability of censuses, constitutions, and changing ideologies of inclusion and equity, can plausibly change places, "minor" differences are no longer just critical tokens of an uncertain self, and thus especially to be guarded, as the original Freudian insight might suggest. In fact, minor differences can become the least acceptable, since they further lubricate the slippery two-way traffic between the two categories. The brutality, degradation, and dehumanization that frequently accompany the ethnicized violence of the last fifteen years are a sign of conditions in which the very line between minor and major differences has been made uncertain. In these circumstances, the rage and fear that incompleteness and uncertainty together produce can no longer be addressed by the mechanical extinction or extrusion of unwanted minorities. In these conditions, minority is the symptom but difference itself is the underlying problem. Thus, the elimination of difference itself (not just the hyper-attachment to "minor" differences) is the new hallmark of today's large-scale, predatory narcissisms. Since this project is fundamentally impossible in a world of blurred boundaries, mixed marriages, shared languages, and other deep connectivities, it is bound to produce an order of frustration that can begin to account for the systematic excess that we see in today's headlines. It is this excess that I address in the following, final section of this chapter.

POLITICAL SURGERY AND THE OFFENDING PART

I use the term "political surgery" to describe the performance of violent operations on body parts and constituents to create a variety of political effects. It is a new phase in the history of human violence, and it requires us to tolerate the tremendous strain of understanding, yet again, the monstrous extensions of otherwise responsible technologies of therapy and disease management.

We live in a post-structuralist world, both in theory and in practice. Parts and wholes do not anymore obey any obvious Saussurean logic. Nor do they conform to the sort of relationship that allowed Louis Dumont, building on the work of Raymond Apthorpe and the general tradition of Durkheim, to posit that parts and wholes were related not just formally but ethically, through hierarchical subordination to some sort of fundamental principal of hierarchy. Nations, conceived as sacred wholes, increasingly fear their minor parts, since those parts have increasingly become both more substantive and more political. Bodies have come apart in myriad ways that social scientists have begun to document closely. Organs have become part of a global commodification, thus leading lives that require severance from their earlier bodily homes. Techniques of sexual surgery make it possible to add and subtract bodily parts across previously unbridgeable gaps of age and gender. Plastic surgery promiscuously adds, subtracts, and redistributes fat to reorganize the aesthetics of the bodily whole. Cloning of every kind makes it hard to use the idea of the original to discriminate new from old forms. Outsourcing, in such forms as call centers, has almost completely divorced names, accents, voices, and identities from their actual bodily bearers. Life on the internet has encouraged numerous forms of multiplication and division of names, identities, images, voices, and lives, so that a parallel cyber-world of parts and wholes has come to exist whose logic is different from first-order social life. In all these ways, bodies have become the material for recombinations of larger social forms and visions. The world of medicine is certainly a major site for this recalibration of the relationship of parts to wholes, and surgery is an important technique for this recalibration.

I come to surgery because some of the most monstrous acts that accompany large-scale violence in the last two decades involve para-surgical techniques: amputation, excision, sub-incision, and other forms of separation of parts from the bodily whole are now standard parts of large-scale violence. These practices join other forms of ethno-surgery, such as scarification, clitero-dectomy, and other routinized practices of surgical violence that are still rampant in many parts of the world.

Recalling Mary Douglas and René Girard, it is worth noting that there is a longstanding link between violence, bodily sacrifice, purification, and social reproduction in the course of human history. And Girard's reference to expurgation and catharsis as critical medical techniques reminds us that violent political surgery has a complicated history in which the seventeenth century may well mark a turning point or pivot in the history of political surgery in the West. Somewhere during the eighteenth and nineteenth centuries, the idea of the "offending part" completes its journey from the Bible to the medical world and becomes part of the language of medical practices. The biblical genealogy of the idea of the "offending part" is important, because the current fear of minorities is intensely and intimately tied up with the discourse of dirt, of disease, of deformity, and of malignancy. Nazi discourse[17] is a spectacular instance of this conjuncture. And examples of this discourse, and of related calls to excision, amputation, and extrusion appear repeatedly in the context of ethnocidal mobilization and planned episodes of mass violence.

Before pondering a few examples of this most difficult of ethical terrains, it is worth asking why one needs to make this journey when we can learn so much by looking at massive social violence in light of contextual causes such as poverty, failed states, struggles over scarce resources, forced displacements, runaway economic stress, and the like. The answer is simple and important. Much extreme bodily violence since the late 1980s, in many different parts of the world, shows little kinship with ordinary logics of

---

17   As shown, for example, by R. Proctor, "The Destruction of 'Lives Not Worth Living,'" in J. Terry and J. Urla, eds., *Deviant Bodies: Critical Perspectives on Difference in Science and Popular Culture, Race, Gender, and Science*, Bloomington: Indiana University Press, 1995.

exclusion, minoritization, competition, and political calculation. It is often both extreme and excessive in ways that appear regularly to confound the means-ends rationalities for political violence. Torture, bodily mutilation, rape, and sexual abuse of almost every imaginable sort appear to exceed the wildest hopes of their planners and the worst fears of the victims. In scale, scope, and intensity, we witness forms of rampant and large-scale bodily cruelty, linked to some sort of political project, that do not yield to any instrumental or functional calculus. This is why we have no choice but to explore such thinkers as Mary Douglas and René Girard (and perhaps even Arnold van Gennep) in asking what the social ambitions of this sort of extreme bodily violence might be. What is their social point, what do they seek to accomplish, what is their project, however dystopic and repellent?

Let us work from a few examples. Let us ask whether the practices associated with the bodily mutilation of young women, in many societies, particularly in the northern parts of Africa, can anymore be seen as narrowly traditional practices? Clearly they are part of an angry assertion that women's bodies cannot be placed in the public realms either of human rights, or of modern medical ethics, or of simple medical security. In other words, the insistence by men (and a few women) of the rights of various communities to practice genital mutilation (often referred to as sub-incision) must be seen as belonging to the family of what I have here called political surgery, that is, surgery with the intention of accomplishing a political purpose. In this instance, the purpose is to forcibly assert the availability of the female body to serve as a theater for patriarchal traditions and anti-state rage. Honor killings in Pakistan, public stonings in the Middle East, and other forms of death or damage inflicted on women (and men) clearly belong to this general category. In this light, we can also recategorize the forced and arms-backed rapes of civil wars as far from each other as those of Aceh, Sierra Leone, and Bosnia in the same general framework as being acts of political surgery designed to make political interventions and inflict bodily harm in the name of some larger project of cleansing or minoritization.

The case of Sierra Leone especially demands our attention because it appears remarkably free of ethnic, religious, or racial subtexts. Thus, it is sometimes discussed as the most horrifying of the recent archives of large-scale bodily violence because it seems to be outside the known parameters of cleansing or other culturally motivated violence. The rapes, amputations, and murders of the last decade in Sierra Leone, especially those engineered during the rule of Charles Taylor in neighboring Liberia, appear to be narrowly, even inscrutably, political in nature. Since Sierra Leone seems to be especially the site of amputations as forms of political violence, and since these amputations were also substantially directed at children, we must pause over this particular site of political surgery.

I do not write as an expert on Sierra Leone or on West Africa. Yet a few possibilities emerge during the trial of Charles Taylor and his period of rule over neighboring Liberia (1997–2003). The first is the immense involvement of children, both as perpetrators and as victims of mass violence in Sierra Leone. This factor has rightly been connected to the interest of Taylor and others who orchestrated the context for this violence, in the creation of a profound gap between the generations in Sierra Leone and their success in producing the message that parents, elders, and traditional adults in Sierra Leone were somehow evil. The second striking fact is that this sense of the older generation as evil did not save many children from severe political surgery, sometimes at the hands of other children. The third theme is that the amputations were not a result of failures to kill, but were deliberate efforts to subtract body parts and end their productive use. The fourth is that the systematic use of amputations was also tied up with large scale and intentional sexual brutality directed against women. The fifth and most important is that they were in some sense communicative efforts intended to produce fear, and that they were at least in some instances deliberate statements intended to be parts of a bizarre dialogue with internal opponents or with external peacekeepers. I have no deeper understanding to offer of the special case of Sierra Leone except to observe that it is a case of the super-pathology of a preoccupation with the parts and of the direct use of para-surgical means. In one instance, a representative of one of the major rebel groups, the RUF, based his denial of their involvement in many amputations on the grounds that there were clear differences in the techniques of amputation (across the palm in one case and at the elbow in the RUF technique).

This deliberate communicative use of political surgery is a different road to this sort of activity in its capacity to serve what I have already referred to as a vivisectionist or discovery function.[18] It may well be that this vivisectionist or discovery function is more salient to those situations in which large numbers and a plausible set of ethno-religious or ethnic differences are involved. Where deeply interlinked histories, large numbers of mixed marriages, and close linguistic relations, as well as long histories of migration and co-residence are involved (as with Serbs and Croats in Eastern Europe, Hindus and Muslims in India), there seems to arise a major concern with establishing "unmixed" identities (to borrow Robert Hayden's striking usage) and to use violence and physical damage to "establish" certainty about the identity of the victim. The links of this vivisectionist mode of bodily damage to political surgery can also be seen in India in the riots against Muslims in the early 1990s and the efforts of Hindu mobs to check male penises for circumcision to assure that a victim was Muslim (or not). Indeed, vivisection and verification may join with excision and

---

18   Appadurai, "Full Attachment."

expurgation since both have to do with heightened rage and doubt about "the offending part."

In general, while instances of political surgery can be multiplied in the period after 1990, especially but not only in Africa, it may be generally linked to a sort of monstrous allegorical practice in which the relationship of part and whole in the body serves as a narrative of the part and the whole in the polity. On each register, the amputation of the offending part might at first glance appear to be an act of revenge (in the mode of an eye for an eye). This interpretation might even make some limited sense in situations characterized by rage and vengefulness. However, the allegory appears more deeply connected to the problematic of the offending part, the part that produces, however suddenly or absurdly, the anxiety of incompleteness. The irony of amputation in particular, and of political surgery in general, is that it addresses the anxiety of incompleteness by inscribing incompleteness on the minor body instead of simply killing or extruding it.

This is very tricky terrain indeed, for in this regard much of the worst violence of the 1990s and since does not have the machine-like coldness of the German holocaust machinery, which seemed mostly intent on the finality of the Final Solution. It is true that the Nazi murder squads, both within and outside the death camps, were also anxious to degrade the Jews and other "imperfect" Germans in every way imaginable before killing them, but they did not seem to be interested in partial damage and partial recovery. In at least some of the most horrific social violence of the last fifteen years, the problem of civil struggle, especially when it has an ethnic plot, seems to lead to deliberately partial damage, damage from which recovery is possible but forgetting is impossible. Hindu violence against Muslims, up to and including the pogroms in Gujarat, seems to have this oddly unfinished quality to it, the quality that pushes toward surgery, arson, and incomplete damage to property and to person, which is not the true hallmark of a genocidal project.

We are here pushed to recall why we are making this inquiry and to remind ourselves why we began with René Girard and the inner violence of sacrifice. It is not hard to see, in an era of growing economic disparities, failed and corrupt states, cynical multilateral economic policies, massive disease and dislocation, private militias and semi-legitimate warlords, illegal traffic in diamonds, arms, bodies, and body parts, why intrastate violence might be on the rise or why scapegoating and stereotyping might produce conflict, resentment, or even large-scale rioting.

What is much harder to grasp is why the last two decades have seen an enormous increase in social violence that stretches the boundaries of the imaginable, that appears to be driven by a rage that exceeds all political calculation or management, and that uses strategies of violation that put the humanity of both perpetrator and victim in common question. It is this stunning surplus of rage and excess of violation that forces us to open interpretive horizons that might otherwise seem tasteless in their abstraction or their arbitrariness.

By going back to Girard's thoughts on the affinities between the surrogate victim, the ritual substitution, the logic of purification, and the peculiar logic of the *pharmakos* and the *katharma*, what do we gain? What we gain is a way to explore how the logics of expulsion, expurgation, and elimination, in these monstrous situations, bring together some dangerous affinities between our technologies of therapy, of sacrifice, and of social redemption.

Let us revisit Philip Gourevitch's brutal aphorism about the mass violence in Rwanda in the early 1990s.[19] Examining the ways in which the Hutu murder squads were mobilized by the radio messages of their political handlers, Gourevitch was moved to state that "genocide, after all, is an exercise in community-building." Taking a cue from Gourevitch, we must concede that humans, unfailingly social in their being, are never lacking in social ambitions, even in their most horrifying collective projects. Put another way, when extreme violence is part of repetitive, collective action, we do not have the option to make the motivation of its perpetrators a black box and to move directly to reconciliation, to therapy, or to punishment. We are obliged to provide some sort of interpretation. In building such an interpretation, we must begin with the concession that collective violence, like all forms of collective action, always has ambitions. We may call these ambitions dystopic, and we may condemn these social projects, but to avoid grasping them as projects is to give up too easily.

In suggesting some ways in which the languages, the practices, and the diverse logics of surgery, purity, and the elimination of undesirable social parts may become intertwined in the practices of cleansing, burning, cutting, and chopping (the slash and burn of ethnocide, we might say), we may be forced to look again, as René Girard did, into the desire for purgation and purification at the dark heart of rituals of violence.

In so doing we may have to reopen the long tradition, at least as old as Durkheim, of placing anomie at the heart of social dysfunction, an approach that is fundamentally circular. We may need to reexamine what happens to classical rites of passage when soil, territory, and identity become ruthlessly delinked. We may need to rethink our strong inclination to see extended conflict as, in the final instance, a redress of harm or restoration of default equilibria, a view as old as Simmel in social theory. And we may have to look again at the Freudian tradition to understand how self and other can become incitements to reciprocal political surgery. All of this requires a fresh resolve to stare at the heart of darkness. If we are willing to do so without playing favorites among our classical theoretical sources, this journey may also let us return afresh to

---

19   Gourevitch, *We Wish to Inform You That Tomorrow We Will Be Killed With Our Families.*

theorizing the sources of order in social life, apart from the settling of conflicts, the healing of imagined and symbolic wounds, the therapies of forgiveness and reconciliation, or the politics of reparation. Each of these projects has its virtues and rewards, but none of them guarantees a sufficiently deep understanding of the ambitions of social violence.

CHAPTER FIVE

In My Father's Nation:
Reflections on Biography, Memory, Family

THE INTIMATE NATION

It has frequently been remarked that nations inspire deep sentiments. People, at least some people, live and die for them. Nations are sometimes referred to as father and mother lands. Even moderate nationalists understand less moderate ones.

Even though some of the best work in the social sciences and in the humanities in the last few decades has been devoted to nations and nationalism,[1] there is still something uncanny about a form of social organization that has a relatively brief history, even in the West, and has not only come to seem natural and necessary, but is also deeply felt and valued.

There is no doubt that we now have a vigorous debate about the future of the nation-state, especially in the context of globalization, but the tone of these debates is rarely quiet or dispassionate. Those who argue that the nation-state may be undesirable or waning are seen as not just wrong, but wrongheaded, or worse. So we have a simple but difficult question: why is a large, abstract, and recent form of social organization the project of such intense affect, usually positive?

Of course, there have been several efforts to engage this question, and some of them are closer to the mark than others. Before I indicate my own sympathies on this issue, let me note that there is a family of approaches to this question that I now take to be fully discredited, and it is the family we call "primordialist," which tends to account for newer and larger attachments by reference to older, smaller, more intimate ones, usually conceived in terms of blood and kinship. The primordialist approach is problematic in several ways, but it often appears even in the work of those who want to resist it, partly because it has become so deeply embedded in our common sense and partly because we have no good alternatives to it. I will not rehearse my own list of objections to this position in this context. But I will note that in one important sense the problem with

---

1   B. Anderson, *Imagined Communities: Reflections on the Origin and Spread of Nationalism*, London: Verso, 1991 (1983); E. J. Hobsbawm, *Nations and Nationalism since 1780: Programme, Myth, Reality*, Cambridge: Cambridge University Press, 1990; and P. Chatterjee, *Nationalist Thought and the Colonial World: A Derivative Discourse*, Minneapolis: University of Minnesota Press, 1986, are just a few examples.

primordialism is that it fails to explain the most important matter in any extensionist argument, which is the question of why certain primary loyalties seem expandable in scale and why, furthermore, some large-scale forms, notably the nation, seem to inspire the extension of primary attachments and others do not. No one seems to want to kill or die because they share an attachment to the global collectivity of mathematicians, for example. Indeed, one might methodologically invert the question and ask why, once the nation is a going concern, smaller-scale arenas and relations become quickly suffused with the discourses and tropes of the nation, and little collectivities begin to operate under the sign of the nation.

If the primordialist approach, broadly conceived, is misleading, where else can we turn? Here the primordialist approach itself provides the beginnings of a clue, in its preoccupation with blood and family. Blood is a critical part of much nationalist discourse, and that in two ways. On the one hand, by linking ideas of family, ethnos, and race, the culturally varied languages of sanguinity are critical elements of the structure of national affect. This fact led primordialists into the impression that blood, misread as a universal biological fact, was the natural basis for more extensive relations, such as those of the tribe, the caste, the region, and the nation. In fact, blood is one of these great human universals whose universality lies not in its biological truth but in its universal availability for a large variety of metaphorical missions. Blood is indeed always present in the great human moments of birth, marriage, and death, but the difficult question is how nations—large, artificial, abstract, and distant—have captured parts of the energy of the discourse of blood. This question directs us to another set of contexts in which blood arises, and this is the context of blood in warfare, sacrifice, and the killing of living beings, whether in the name of religion or in other forms of homicide. This set of contexts, amply discussed in its own right, has not been carefully connected to the life-cycle contexts in which blood universally appears as the linking element. Co-examining these two sets of contexts allows us to make a different sort of link between intimacy, sacrifice, and violence, which were discussed in chapters 3 and 4 from a somewhat different angle. I suggest here that the nation accomplishes the mobilization of affect by linking violence to intimacy through the shedding of blood, itself metaphorically constructed in the idioms of sacrifice, valor, and heroism. This mobilization is accomplished through narratives, both public and intimate, which are especially powerful when they saturate the private sphere and the world of the family.

Making the link between blood and belonging in this way allows us to cast a slightly different light on the well-known affinities between religion and nationalism, whose relations have been remarked on by many scholars.[2]

---

2   Anderson, *Imagined Communities*; P. van der Veer, *Religious Nationalism: Hindus and Muslims in India*, Berkeley: University of California Press, 1994.

Thinking about this link through the mediation of the practices of violence has been given plausibility in another line of work, such as that of Etienne Balibar,[3] who identified the important place of military mobilization in generating attachment to the nation-form, and more recently in a series of essays by the African social critic Achille Mbembe.[4] The common thread in these accounts forces us to confront the strange institutional productivity of large-scale violence. This kind of productivity allows us to see how blood and belonging are made to collaborate in the creation of national affect.

THE PRODUCTIVITY OF VIOLENCE

There are many ways in which violence can seem to be, albeit in a malignant way, productive. It yields powerful scenes of identification, new stimuli to social participation, and new senses of social collectivity; it renews social ties. We can see these aspects of violence in the bored anger of soccer thugs as described by Bill Buford;[5] in the manic energy of the genocidaires in Rwanda; in the banding and bonding of soldiers; in a Hollywood theme from Audie Murphy to Tom Hanks; in the camaraderie of the SS in the Nazi Holocaust; in the converted soccer stadiums of many cities in the world, where executions and floggings are used to entertain citizens; and in many other scenes of sociality produced by the physics of violence.

This kind of sociality produced in the mobilizing carnage of group violence should hardly come as a surprise if we remind ourselves of two familiar themes from the *longue durée* of many human societies. The first—warfare—has always produced its own solidarities, first among trainees for military service, then among combatants, then among their families and friends who have always found in the death of the soldier a reason for love of society, rather than alienation from it. The deliberate mobilization of aggressive solidarity among soldiers is indissolubly linked to wartime xenophobia throughout human history. The second theme, not quite as universal, and somewhat more varied in its expression, is the practice of sacrifice, in which the loss of precious bodies and body parts is tied to ideas of cosmic justice, the appeasement of the gods and the maintenance of various ideas of compensation, exchange, and long-term social security. In the work of Marcel Mauss, famously, we are reminded of the inner affinity between gift and sacrifice, both involving exchange and divestment in the service of social solidarity and reproduction.

3   E. Balibar, "The Nation Form: History and Ideology," in E. Balibar and I. M. Wallerstein, eds., *Race, Nation, Class: Ambiguous Identities*, New York: Verso, 1991.

4   A. Mbembe, *On the Postcolony: Studies on the History of Society and Culture*, Berkeley: University of California Press, 2001.

5   B. Buford, *Among the Thugs*, New York: W. W. Norton & Co., 1993.

Thus, we need not look at the social productivity of group violence in modern times with any surprise. The question about this sort of productivity is its special relationship to the investment of the nation with special effects and affects. Modern nations are organized around ideas of ethnos, territory, and sovereignty, as we all know, and states make these ideas real through the ideologies of borders, armies, and the defense of national sovereignty. This ideology is the basis of the formation of modern armies, which not only assume the state's monopoly over legitimate violence but also tie this monopoly to the idea of a "people," conceived fundamentally as some sort of ethnos. Hannah Arendt[6] was perhaps the first to notice this fatal feature of the nation form, and its deep tension with ideas of universal democracy and citizenship. Nations cannot exist without some sense of peoplehood, and peoplehood, whatever the mix of *volkisch* elements involved in any particular case, depends on some sense of kind that is bounded and distinct. Since this sense of distinction has to cover large and complex spaces, it cannot avoid some racialized elements, and these racialized elements can and do become, under various conditions, mobilized as racism. War is a classic occasion for the mobilization of this kind of racism, but we know now that many other forms of social stress can also awaken the inner affinity between nation, ethnos, and race.

This inner affinity returns us to the question of blood, sacrifice, and war. By invoking the idiom of the shedding of blood, modeled as sacrifice, in just wars, usually in preparation for real or imagined defense of the national body and national soil, modern states are able to rewrite the family as a site of consanguinity. Blood relations and bloodshed become connected, and the nation imagined as a space of endangered consanguinity and blood becomes the site both of purity and of connectivity. The strength of the metaphorical power of blood, so far as the nation is concerned, is that it connects the idea of the ethnos to the idea of the people and the soil, through the many languages of purity. It is thus no accident that in the era of globalization, we have witnessed a new concern with ethnic cleansing or purification, since the idea of blood allows an endlessly varied repertoire of ways to connect family and sacrifice with the fear of a contaminated national ethnos. The argument so far seems logical but somehow abstract, far from the processes by which the narratives of purity, of kinship, and of nation actually come to infuse each other in the empire of affect. And this brings me to how I came to live in my father's nation.

---

6   H. Arendt, *The Human Condition*, Chicago: University of Chicago Press, 1958.

My father, S. A. Ayer, died in 1980, at the age of eighty-two. He was a journalist for most of his working life, except for one remarkable interlude that is the basis for this chapter. In 1941, he met Subhas Chandra Bose, subsequently known to him and our family, and to most people in India, as Netaji (Leader), while he was a Special Correspondent for Reuters, based in Bangkok. In and through a remarkable adventure, Bose, a charismatic Indian nationalist born and raised in Calcutta, had come to split with Gandhi and Nehru on many things about the struggle for India's independence, notably on the question of armed resistance to the British. He escaped from house arrest under the British in India and, after a risky and romantic set of global journeys, aided by the Germans and the Italians, ended up in Southeast Asia. He formed an army, the Indian National Army (INA); created an exile state, the Provisional Government of Azad Hind (Free India); and worked closely with the Japanese to set up an army made up of Indian troops taken prisoner by the Japanese in various battles against the British in Southeast Asia. His aim was to fight side by side with the Japanese and to enter India with an independent armed force representing an Indian government in exile.[7]

This extraordinary vision, running expressly against the official and sacred nationalist agenda set by Gandhi and Nehru, failed, as did the Japanese in the larger drama of World War II in the northeastern regions of British India (today's Myanmar and Assam). The INA was savagely defeated, but, as my father never tired of saying to us in the decades after the war, the INA did manage to set foot on what he called "Indian soil" in some desperate thrusts into the present day state of Assam.

In the aftermath of the defeat of the Japanese and the INA, Bose died in the crash of a Japanese plane, which was on a flight from Formosa to Manchuria, after the official surrender of the Japanese. A major trial was held in Delhi shortly after the end of the war. This trial, known ever after as the Red Fort Trial, put in the dock three senior Indian officers from the INA, on grounds of treason for having deserted the British Indian army and gone over to the enemy, that is, to the Japanese. This extraordinary trial galvanized an already powerful nationalist mood in India and made heroes of the men on trial, brought Bose and the INA into the center stage of the struggle for independence, and, in my father's opinion, hastened the exit of the British from India by at least a decade.

My father met Gandhi, Nehru, Patel, and the rest of the Indian Congress leadership after he made a hazardous return to India at the end of the war,

---

7 S. Bose, *His Majesty's Opponent: Subhas Chandra Bose and India's Struggle against Empire*, Cambridge, MA: Belknap Press of Harvard University Press, 2011, ch. 6.

jobless and penniless. Thus began another drama in which the INA was momentarily a glorious force in the national narrative, though it was soon to be relegated to the sidelines by the ruling Congress, whose leadership never forgave Bose for breaking with Gandhi, taking aid from the Axis, and challenging the destiny of the Congress to lead independent India. INA soldiers were rarely given the rewards of other "freedom fighters" in the new India, and Netaji did not get even a postage stamp in his name until the mid 1960s, long after a pantheon of minor notables had made the list. The story of the INA was largely suppressed, though some of its leaders became important figures in the new Indian state. Bose was remembered most vividly in Bengal and to some extent by various subaltern nationalists elsewhere in the country, but, for many years after Indian independence, he was anathema to official nationalism. For Nehru and his close associates, Bose was a dubious nationalist, too cozy with the Japanese and the other members of the Axis, vaguely fascist in his own militarized personal style and the cult of personality that surrounded him.

At the same time, many people in India, notably an important segment of the large Bose family in Calcutta, refused to believe that Bose had really died in a plane crash in 1945. Ever since there have been several commissions of inquiry into Bose's death (my father was pressed to testify under cross-examination at most of them that occurred before his death). There are still reports of sightings of Bose, frequently in the form of a "holy man" in some remote forest or sacred sanctuary. The rumors rise and fall, the calls for inquiries come and go. Bose would have been a hundred and fourteen years old were he alive in 2011, but that does not seem to still the mixture of family politics and national yearning that produces these sightings of a figure that has certainly captured a critical part of the Indian nationalist imagination.

My father was, in all this, twice estranged. Although a staunch bourgeois liberal in many ways, his three-year experience with Bose (two of which he was with Bose almost on a daily basis and served as Minister for Publicity and Propaganda in Bose's exile cabinet) convinced him of the virtues of charismatic leadership, total commitment, and a military approach to India's independence. He hated the idea that the INA was a puppet of the Japanese, and remained absolutely certain that had the Japanese won the war and ousted the British from India and tried to become its new hegemons, Bose would have risen against them as surely as he did against the British. My father, as a journalist and nationalist, was also given some grudging recognition by the rulers of the new India, after 1947. Reuters offered him his old job (in a wild display of British benevolence toward a man who had ditched them in the thick of the war and organized radio propaganda by jamming BBC airwaves in India, whenever possible, on behalf of Netaji). But my father refused, on grounds of principle.

Meanwhile, my mother had five grown sons, ranging in age from five to fifteen, one of whom had never really seen my father. She lived through the war years under the vague protection of her father in the small southern temple town of Madurai, a virtual widow, while her husband was in the service of a rogue nationalist in the towns and jungles of Southeast Asia. She supported her sons and herself on a salary that Reuters (again remarkably) paid her as a quasi-widow for the duration of the war, thus avoiding abject dependence on her father's domestic resources. She and my father set up house again in Bombay, where they had lived off and on for several decades before the war. My father took several jobs, in some sort of media and publicity capacity, for about eight years before returning to active journalism, sometime in the mid 1950s, and finally retired in the mid 1960s, when his health began to fail. Another child, my sister, was born to my parents in 1946, and I was born in 1949, into a household already devoted to the memory and significance of Bose.

Although my father did various things for a living after the war, he lived only to tell Bose's story, which he did in many books, speeches, and articles, and in a variety of public contexts. Nothing engaged him like the memory of Bose, nothing pained him as much as a harsh word said about Bose, and nothing gave him more pleasure than to talk to his children, including me, about Bose, frequently in the form of vivid anecdotes about his daily life with the great leader. Books about Bose and the INA, photographs, flags, medals, old uniforms were woven into the material life of our flat in Bombay.

And there were the visitors. There was a constant stream of friends, colleagues, and fellow workers from the INA days in our house. These included men who had become important leaders in the new state; businessmen who had lent financial support to Bose in Southeast Asia and who were now prospering in Bombay; young men who had fought for the INA and who were now in need of jobs or loans; and women and children who were, like my family, steeped in the lore of Bose. These men and their families came from many castes and communities, but when they met, though they were all fluent English speakers, they always greeted each other with the INA slogan "Jai Hind" ("Victory to India"), and frequently spoke in the chaste Hindustani that Netaji had made the lingua franca of his followers and army. This was the nation that official nationalism forgot, and it was woven coarsely into the upbeat world of India in the 1940s and 1950s. It remained a counterculture, with mostly its own memories and its own stories, texts, meetings, celebrations, and commemorations. It was not an illegal world, but it was a shadow world, marginalized by Congress nationalism, wounded by the absence of its leaders, divided on the question of Bose's death in a plane crash, divided too by differences among its members in their views of politics in independent India.

But it was above all a nation in memory, a nation of remembrance, a nation of and by narration, and at the center of all the narratives was Netaji himself. My father would find himself in tears when close male members of the Bose family visited us in Bombay, because some of them looked and sounded so much like

Netaji himself. On one such occasion, when I asked my father why his eyes were wet, my father told me about this sensory rush. This was my father's nation, and it was a nation that was almost completely deleted from the Indian public sphere. It did have its own, limited public sphere of meetings, rallies, social occasions, and gatherings. But these occasions were few and the books written about Bose were consumed only by a limited number of readers. On the whole, this nation lived in the space of the family, the social visit, and in private encounters in the security of the home. Homes were the most important "places of memory" for this nation, and so children like me grew up, in effect, in two nations.

One nation, Nehru's India—scientific, secular, socialist, confident of the great project of beating poverty, industrializing the village, and making India a big player in Asia and the world—was the one of our textbooks and public holidays, our major politicians and scandals, our livelihoods and crises of public life. The other nation, the nation of narration, was homebound, subcutaneous in its style, capillary in its modalities. It was a nation by anecdote. It was a nation of romance, adventure, thrill: Netaji's escape from house arrest, his dangerous submarine journey to Asia from Europe, the valor of the women's regiment of the INA (the Rani of Jhansi Regiment), the tragic defeat in the jungles of Burma and Assam. It was a vaguely seditious nation, still suspicious of Nehru, bitter about its marginalization by the Congress, ambivalent even about Gandhi. My father remained close to key friends and colleagues from Japan, who had worked with him when he was in the INA, and in 1951 he even made a journey to Formosa to confirm firsthand what had happened when Netaji's plane crashed. He then took what he firmly believed to be Netaji's ashes to a Shinto shrine in Tokyo where they are to this day, since Netaji's family refused to accept that the great leader was dead, and thus was opposed to bringing his ashes back to India. The Japan connection, though slender, stayed with our family for decades, and even as late as the mid 1980s a senior delegation of men who had known Netaji from their days in the Japanese Armed Forces paid a ceremonial visit to the home of my eldest brother, in Bombay, in memory of Bose and my father. It was perhaps this Japanese subtext that was the most graphic reminder of the seditious nature of this nation of narration, since even those with only a vague sense of the players in World War II recalled that the Japanese were somehow not the best side to be allied with in that great struggle.

Still, my father, who often reflected on his guilt for abandoning my mother to many years on her own, with five children, usually ended these reflections with the admission that he would, and could, have done nothing else once he met Netaji. So we always lived with the story, and it appeared in many pieces, versions, fragments. It was a counter-narrative whose sacred places were to the East of India, in places already strange to those of us who were growing up in another geography, in places like Taihoku and Singapore, Rangoon and Kuala

Lumpur, Tokyo and Mandalay. This nation was somewhere east of India. But it lived in and through the practices of memory, like the public, official Indian nation, but as its anecdotal other. It lived behind the veil so that the India of Gandhi, Nehru, and the Congress could occupy the largest share of the places of official memory. It was not just a remembered nation, as all nations necessarily are; it was a nation of remembrance, thus a nation of narration. It was a nation that lived, for those who grew up in families that were somehow linked to Bose, if only sentimentally.

BLOOD, MEMORY, FAMILY

I have left out much in the story of Netaji, the INA, and my father's relation to them, and I have left out even more of the myriad ways in which the nation of narration entered my own family drama. But perhaps enough has been said to pull together some of the threads, and to ask how and why this strange, personal story might have something to offer to the question of how nations succeed in making themselves objects of intimacy and affect, and thus acquire the practical aura of consanguinity.

I began by suggesting that we should not ask how sentiments of the small worlds of family, marriage, and kinship can be extended upwards to the scale of the nation, but rather the reverse question: how does the nation succeed in suffusing the world of one's near and dear, in spite of its large and remote characteristics? I also suggested that ideas of blood, as mediated by tropes of sacrifice and peoplehood, were the symbolic source of this implosion, which appears, in ordinary experience, as its reverse. Most important, I argued that it was the practices of violence that laid the grounds for the felt sacrality of the nation and that the reverse dialectic was the derivative one. How do these ideas gain strength from the story I have told of my own family romance, and the way in which it was the space of Netaji and the INA, my father's nation of narration?

It would seem at first sight that this exceptional, even ersatz nationalism is precisely opposed to the official mass nationalism of Gandhi, Nehru, and the Congress, and thus can tell us little about such official, large-scale nationalisms. Thriving as it did largely behind the purdah of the family world, it was a public secret, a hidden counterpoint to the ways in which official India took on its force—the force that today inspires the Hindu right, underwrites the Indian Bomb, and threatens secularism deeply in India. What can the INA story, the story of my father's nation, tell us about the very process by which it was driven into a quasi-private sphere?

To answer this requires one more move in the story of the INA and into the nature of memory and narrative as they infuse personal biography and family history. The fact is that the narration of my father's nation—which was no more than a nation of narration—occurred through stories in which official nationalism was always present. The stories of the INA always involved the great dramas of the middle of the twentieth century, the struggle between the Allies and the Axis, the dramatic break between Gandhi and Nehru, the old jealousies between Nehru and Netaji, the complex relations between those who were ostracized by the new powers of independent India and those who managed to find high places in it. The stories I heard were never unrelated to the dramas and personalities of official nationalism, both as it was recalled and as it was lived in the 1950s and 1960s. In other words, the story of the INA—the nation of narration—was never told in anything but a complex tension with the official narrative of the public nation. In the process, these stories, embedded of course in the post-independence hopes and dramas of the main protagonists, were not in fact as privatized as they might first seem. They were always the resource from which my father and his friends drew their sense of self and society as they negotiated with the world of the victors, the world of the Congress and its allies. This was a complex matter, not driven solely by the fact that these men and their families had to live and survive and find jobs and incomes after the war. But they themselves were not prepared to live wholly in a nation of narration. They were nationalists still, and thus it was vital for them to seek, each in his own manner, a way to tie their memories to their aspirations. They did this in many ways, among them by telling the stories of their lives in the years between 1940 and 1945 so that there was always a moral that said something to the present, often presented as Netaji's truth speaking to Nehru's power. The highly personal, collective biographical fabric that was woven when these men met and talked (with women and children usually present, listening, questioning, commenting) about past and present was always by its narrative nature intimate, personal, and circumstantial. As such, this fabric also drew official nationalism into its emotional orbit, and made its heroes and sacred events part of the intimate space created in the nation of narration centered on Netaji and his life and death. Thus was the story of his struggles, his heroism, his sacrifice, and his death drawn into the felt sense that everyone in this nation of narration had also made a mimetic sacrifice, giving up money, or families, or years, or hopes to their leader, often at great cost to their lived present in Nehru's India. Thus, the INA's blood, Netaji's death, their own sacrifices, all became elements of a felt nation that refused to die with the end of the war. And in the dialogue between the stories of this nation and the public narratives that surrounded us all, official India also took on the magic of blood and the mystique of sacrifice. These INA families thus became suffused with a complex and multiplex sense of India, one to which they did not extend a priori the love they had of their near and dear ones. Rather, their sense of Netaji's India, with its specific histories and geographies, lent to their family lives and worlds some of the drama of the nation of narration. But—and here the dialectic certainly goes both ways—this transformed family sphere, seen as the theater of sacrifice, loss, and self-respect, also fed back into that sense of national affect whose grounds we have been trying to explore.

This suggestion can at least potentially be generalized beyond the odd case of my father's nation and the world of Netaji and the INA nation. Many families and groups in places like India indeed occupy oblique and unofficial places in relation to what later becomes a single nation, with a single major narrative. Everyone lives in, or near, some sort of nation of narration—the Communists, the Dalits, women, people nearer or further from Partition, peasants, techno-crats. No one is immaculately conceived within the narratives of the official nation. Everyone, at least in places like India, lives also by anecdote, in smaller privatized spaces of recollection and loss, heroism and suffering, which speak, even if sometimes in a whisper, to the grand narrative of India after 1947. In adding this biographical twist to a larger collective saga, I hope to have contrib-uted a further piece to the puzzle surrounding the intensities of affect that surround the nation-form and the sense of national intimacy that defies the vastness of its spaces and the empire of its numbers.

Part II

THE VIEW FROM MUMBAI

CHAPTER SIX

Housing and Hope

Today, housing for the poor, and especially housing for the urban poor, is intimately connected to a whole set of processes that characterize the modern world: overcrowded megacities; complicated forms of taxation, credit, and debt that tend to exclude the poor and advantage the rich; legal formats and fora that have evolved over the last three hundred years to turn housing into a form of property, which can be bought, sold, and exchanged without any regard to equity; forms of politics and governance that have made housing a pawn in high-order corruption, criminalization, and political warfare, so that housing in many cities is a literal battlefield—from Gaza to Baghdad, from Harare to Beijing. So to create solutions to the housing problems of the urban poor requires us to tackle an intricate web of social arrangements that connect politics, finance, crime, architecture, engineering, and real estate.

But this was not always so. In the long story of the search of humans for secure habitations, and as societies juggled their strategies between hunting and gathering, animal husbandry, farming, trade, conquest, and other modalities for socio-economic organization, housing was not generally a matter of law, private property, or speculative commoditization. Rather, housing was part of a more informal way in which human communities allocated their collective spatial resources. In some cases, hunters and gatherers simply cleared land, built settlements with various forms of quasi-private shelter for families or other small kinship units. In other cases, such as those of nomadic communities, houses were temporary and were set up along pastoral and seasonal routes. In the case of different forms of peasant communities, housing tended to be both more elaborate and more durable, but was nevertheless hardly ever associated with cash, taxation, or legal documentation, except at the level of whole communities or groups (such as castes or clans in India).

These observations are not just of interest for historians and students of human evolution and cultural development. Many of these forms of housing and community are with us still, in many parts of the developing world. In India, my own country, hill- and forest-dwelling groups still struggle to maintain their life ways and material environments in the face of agriculture, big dams, commercial forestry, and police repression. This is also the case in many parts of Southeast Asia, Latin America, and Africa, leading to the phenomena of activist movements and networks which link indigenous groups across the world. For many of these communities, they are facing not only the destruction of their habitats and livelihoods, but also their communities and forms of habitation.

Even today, in these diverse communities, which include peasant communities from Brazil to Ireland and Italy to Malaysia, social groups are striving to maintain the integrity of their communities, which is often embodied and embedded in their housing forms. Anthropologists have made many careful studies of the ways in which housing forms and structures around the world reflect and enact core community values about life and death, gender and reproduction, man and the cosmos, animals and humans, and other fundamental features that give meaning and cultural life to human communities.

These studies are not invitations to nostalgia and are better seen as a living testament to the ways in which housing, habitation, and home are deeply related ideas. Whenever and wherever human beings find forms in which to build shelters for primary groups, they are not only or primarily seeking protection from the elements, safety from predators, and privacy from the gaze of strangers. They are also marking the very meanings of their humanity in the materials of grass and thatch, bamboo and stone, mud and brick, wood and clay. The range of housing forms in human history, and around the world today, are a testament to the intimate connections between family life, design, cosmology, and the social imagination. Nor do these links require wealth, stability, or security to achieve their force. Even homes created in the midst of chaos, in the face of ecological disaster or political holocaust, never cease to carry a trace of the human need to expand the meaning of human life by association with elementary forms of shelter. Philosophers like Martin Heidegger and Emmanuel Levinas have recognized the importance of ideas such as "dwelling" and "habitation" in the struggle of human beings to craft their humanity, but they have not always been sufficiently literal in their theories. In my own earlier work,[1] I have argued that the local is not merely an inert canvas upon which the moving space of globalization is painted, but the local is itself is a constant and laborious work in progress, so that the production of locality is a fundamental and never-completed site of human action.

In fact, it is not only in the housing forms of the Shona or the Kwazulu, or the Inuit, or the Maori or the Navajo peoples today that we can see humans reaching toward material ways of arranging their most intimate possessions, relations, and resources in the constant work of producing locality. We can see this also in the humblest of slum dwellings throughout the world today. In the favelas of Brazil, James Holston[2] has shown that slum dwellers choose and

---

1   A. Appadurai, *Modernity at Large: Cultural Dimensions of Globalization*, Minneapolis: University of Minnesota Press, 1996.

2   J. Holston, "Autoconstruction in Working-Class Brazil," *Cultural Anthropology*, 1991, 6(4), 447–65.

arrange the materials of their housing with a highly specific aesthetics, which reflects more than a mechanical use of the materials at hand. Pavement dwellers in India always take some care to arrange their meager possessions in a manner that amplifies their claims to family life, social respectability, and personal dignity. We know that residents of the townships of South Africa have not given up on the effort to make homes places of order, both real and aspirational, where small businesses, domestic life, and the entertainment of guests and friends can carry on with some semblance of regularity and respectability.

Thus, the deep human significance of housing lies in its intimate connection to dwelling, dignity, and the cultural design of physical intimacy. Housing provides the link between kinship, reproduction, dignity, and shelter. It is the place where even the poorest of humans can connect shelter with their humanity. It is on this foundation that the struggle for secure housing today must be placed.

INSECURITY AND BARE CITIZENSHIP

The predicament of the urban poor in today's world requires us to step back from the normal language of public policy and urban studies and consider urban poverty from a more fundamental point of view. In many premodern traditions and societies, poverty was not seen as a statistical or political fact. Today's understandings of poverty and the poor are closely tied up with the emergence of demography, development studies, and twentieth-century applications of census techniques and approaches. One result of this is that poverty has come to be seen as largely an effect of failed policies, and the poor, especially the urban poor, have been turned into an impersonal mass, a statistical aberration, a disease of numbers. This is a far cry from the complex ways in which "poverty" was viewed as a human predicament before it was turned into a "demographic" and developmental category. The result of this change, which is largely a product of the late nineteenth and early twentieth centuries, is that the condition of poverty has gradually been moved from the space of ethics and resituated in the space of technology and public policy.

Before this great transformation, the fact of poverty was not in itself a disqualification that made an individual (or a group) lose the claim to contest those in authority, and claim charity and generosity from those better off than themselves. Indeed in various great religious traditions, poverty was often tied to purity, to asceticism, to various forms of virtue, and to some forms of power. So we have here a strange paradox. Before the full acceptance of the liberal presumption of the equality of all human beings before the law, the state, and their fellow citizens, the poor may have lacked in political voice and suffered all manner of political exploitation. But their humanity was not usually in question. With the worldwide spread of the ideals of liberal democracy in the West, and the concomitant spread of the idea of the "people" as a global fact that united liberal, socialist, and fascist polities in the twentieth century, poverty became increasingly an effect of measurement and the poor were steadily turned into what, following Giorgio Agamben, we may call "bare citizens."

I am recalling here the distinction that Agamben[3] makes between "bare life" (*zoe*) and political life (*bios*), a distinction in which he builds upon Hannah Arendt's powerful idea of "naked life" in her classic work on *The Origins of Totalitarianism*, published in 1951. Arendt was reflecting on the prisoners in the death camps of Nazi Germany and on the status of refugees in the middle of the twentieth century, both of whom had essentially lost all rights in the eyes of the sovereign power. Agamben has drawn on this same idea of "bareness" or "nakedness" to discuss the plight of the prisoners in Guantanamo, who were placed in a state of exception and reduced to the conditions of "bare life."

I suggest that the large masses of the urban poor have been, in this same sense, pushed into a state of bare citizenship in the societies in which they live. They have become, to some extent, invisible in the eyes of the law, stripped of many normal rights and privileges, and placed in much the same status as refugees, prisoners of war, aliens, and other "bare citizens." If this seems like an extreme characterization, I draw your attention to the current frequency and scale of slum demolitions and evictions throughout the world.

In looking more closely at the global picture on evictions and demolitions as a connected set of actions and tragedies, I wish to bring to broader attention a set of gross violations of human rights that have largely escaped the attention of activists, politicians, and human rights experts, except those who have specialized interests in the problems of the urban poor.

Let me begin with the case of India, which continues to advertise itself as the world's largest democracy, which has proudly advertised its massive growth rates in the last decade or so, which proudly competes with China for leadership in Asia, and which now is considered to be both a massive market for global middle-class goods and a formidable player in international high-tech and software industries. Even more to the point, India is now one of the favored targets of international real estate developers, speculators, and architects, who are engaged in the building of offices, malls, and apartment buildings for the growing upper and middle classes. Because of India's reputation for bureaucratic corruption and infrastructural deficiencies, global manufacturing interests have been ambivalent about India, but the real obstacle to opening India's markets to every form of global investment is the problem of India's urban poor, who are viewed as a blight on its urban landscapes, a drain on its public resources, a clog in its infrastructure, and a drag on its productive efficiency.

---

3   G. Agamben, *Homo Sacer: Sovereign Power and Bare Life*, Stanford: Stanford University Press, 1998.

Each of these facts is highly contestable, and taken together they form an ideology of anti-poor sentiment that amounts to a quasi-racist ideology.

This prejudice is hidden from explicit articulation because of India's constitutional commitment to the need for alleviating poverty, for correcting historical damage to the weaker groups in society, and for moving the poor not only into the democratic electorate but also into active and equitable forms of wealth-sharing and political participation. The Indian state has substantially failed in these quasi-socialist aspirations, and the successes of the current government to encourage massive liberalization and wealth creation have far outweighed their successes in poverty alleviation. The poor cannot be totally ignored, because their votes do count in India's regular elections at all levels, from wards and municipalities to regional legislatures and the national parliament. Thus, a great deal of populist lip service is paid to the poor, especially at election time, but their real power and voice in matters of daily life, security, and access to economic resources and opportunities is negligible. On the other hand, as I will now show, the hostile record of the Indian state in regard to its slum dwellers is unmatched.

There is a deeper and broader issue that we must consider when we look at the worldwide data on violence against the urban poor as expressed in demolitions and evictions as a regularized tactic of state terror. These statistics are in fact less revealing than they seem. For they disguise the structurally even more widespread conditions of insecure housing that are involved when we count—worldwide—the populations of illegal migrants within and across societies, who are officially bare citizens, including the numerous populations of internally displaced persons (IDP), refugees, and forcibly relocated citizens such as those affected by the Three Gorges project in China.

In regard to IDP populations, who are typically contrasted with refugees on the basis that their displacement does not involve the crossing of state borders, the numbers are based on estimates, because IDP populations are constantly fluctuating: some IDPs may be returning home while others are fleeing, others may periodically return to IDP camps to take advantage of humanitarian aid. While the cases of IDPs in large camps such as those in Darfur, western Sudan, are relatively well reported, it is difficult to assess the numbers of those IDPs who flee to larger towns and cities. It is necessary in many instances to supplement official figures with additional information obtained from operational humanitarian organizations on the ground. Additionally, most official figures only include those displaced by conflict or natural disasters. Development-induced IDPs often are not included in assessments. Still, based on a variety of sources, the number of IDPs today approaches 25 million.

The complexity of overlapping categories and counts make it hard to establish clear statistical distinctions between urban populations locally devastated by campaigns of slum demolition and eviction, internally displaced populations produced by ecological projects, civil war, or other national problems, and the worldwide categories of refugees and illegal immigrants. In addition, a genuine count of these bare citizens must also include victims of sex trafficking, human trafficking, and new forms of economic slavery, which often thrive because the victims are first forcibly separated from their original families and homes. Together, all these categories may well be anywhere between 75 million and 100 million of the world's population, i.e. around 1 percent of the world's population. This may seem like a small number, but it is probably an underestimate and it should be treated less as an absolute number than as a window into the potential vulnerability of the larger urban poor of the world who are a growing proportion of the total population.

It is worth thinking about this global population of the world's "bare citizens" for a variety of reasons. First of all, thinking about them in this broad and holistic way draws attention to the fact that the state of inadequate, insecure, temporary, dangerous, or unhealthy housing (or no housing at all) is a problem that goes far beyond the scope of urban planning, architecture, or municipal authority. It is a product of today's unholy mix of warfare, real estate markets, poorly enforced housing laws, runaway technological disruptions, and, above all, a wholesale failure in the implementation of human rights laws and norms when it comes to the insecurity of housing for millions of human beings.

In other words, insecure housing is a lens into a variety of fundamental crises of the current world system which make it impossible to reliably guarantee the simplest protections to the most vulnerable populations in locations as different as Sudan, Brazil, South Africa, India, and Cambodia. In some sense, longstanding "squatter settlements,"[4] in spite of their tremendous vulnerabilities in megacities such as Mumbai, Delhi, Mexico City, Harare, Lagos, and Bangkok, to name just a few, point to an even larger failure in the zone where development and global economic transfers meet human rights law and democratic constitutions. This can be considered a crime against humanity of colossal proportions, whose perpetrators cannot be easily identified and prosecuted because they are so varied, so protean, and so interconnected with routine procedures of law and market in the current world. Crimes against humanity, which strip persons to "bare citizens" by depriving them of secure housing, have a deep and multiplex relationship to broader issues of citizenship and dignity, as we shall now see.

UNHOUSED CITIZENSHIP

In the context of the extraordinary range and scope of the forces that produce insecure housing, or no housing at all, for such a large number of human beings, we need to reexamine the basic links between housing, citizenship, and dignity.

---

4   R. Neuwirth, *Shadow Cities: A Billion Squatters, a New Urban World*, New York: Routledge, 2004.

It is easy enough to see that the state of "bare citizenship" that I have described makes a mockery of most current constitutional documents and official governmental claims to honor the norm of housing as a basic human right.

If citizenship is seen as an active and dynamic condition and not merely as a passive belonging to a territory, an ethnos, or a polity, then the bare citizenship that characterizes those whose houses are dramatically insecure is not merely a deficit. It is a deficit that offers us a different lens on citizenship. The sort of bare citizenship that insecure housing brings is inherently unstable, volatile, and ephemeral. In short, if you cannot be sure about the walls (however thin) that mark off your intimate sphere from the wider world and the roof above your head as a shelter from the elements, then the physical basis for citizenship as a series of spatial activities is highly circumscribed.

The relationship between space and urban citizenship is intricate and multilayered.[5] Many cities allocate access to rationed foods, energy, and sanitary facilities on the basis of one sort of identity card that requires a governmentally recognized address. Lacking such an address, urban slum dwellers and other bare citizens become immediate parts of what in Francophone Africa is sometimes called a *population flottante* (floating population). Employers of such poor citizens, even in the formal economy, like to know where their employees live, for similar reasons having to do with monitoring and reliability. The many urban poor who belong to the "toilers"[6] of megacities and work in casual and seasonal jobs such as scavenging, physical lifting, and moving of goods, emergency infrastructure projects, time-bound construction projects, and so on depend on learning about work opportunities, which in turn depends on knowing where others can find you reliably. For the middle classes, this is your home. For the urban poor, this location is unstable and dispersed, thus endangering access to jobs even in the bowels of the urban economy. The services of the police for dealing with local crime and of the municipality for dealing with problems of flooding, sewage, or other physical hazards are likewise unavailable for those without housing expressed as an address. Further, political parties deliver their patronage services in exchange for electoral promises from colonies and settlements of squatters, but even these quasi-corrupt forms of participation in political life are threatened by every act of displacement, eviction, or demolition. When these disasters reduce citizens to bare citizens, their claims on even the weakest forms of political patronage also disappear.

For those who have no housing, live in virtual hovels, or lose their housing through the many dynamics that produce insecurity in housing, there are a

---

5   A. Appadurai and J. Holston, "Introduction: Cities and Citizenship," in J. Holston, ed., *Cities and Citizenship*, Durham: Duke University Press, 1999.

6   S. Pendse, "Toil, Sweat and the City," in S. Patel and A. Thorner, eds., *Bombay: Metaphor for Modern India*, Bombay: Oxford University Press, 1995.

series of further losses in social capital and cultural credibility. They lose their capacity to host friends and kinsmen visiting from the country, and, in losing this capacity for domestic hospitality, they further erode their already thin social ties, with possibly negative effects in all forms of social networking, including job possibilities, help from their relatives in other towns or villages, and marriage possibilities for their daughters. This is one of the ways that life in rural areas (so long as they are not subject to massive ecological or development dislocation) retains some social advantages for even poor peasants, because they and their habitations are part of a reasonably secure and legible social map. In the crowded slum areas of large cities, where demolition, eviction, criminalization, and urban upgrading projects entail de-housing the very poor, the social dimensions of citizenship are thinned out, since among the poorest of the poor in many societies, there is an even greater dependence on issues of status, trust, rank, and social connectivity than among the middle and upper classes. For those who doubt that even the poorest of groups in the most hierarchical of societies operate through conventions of dignity, rank, and prestige, they need only to consult studies of hierarchy *within* rural untouchable communities in India,[7] as one forceful example.

In short, secure housing is the critical mediating device that stands between the poor and the bare citizenship produced by demolition, eviction, migration, trafficking, war, and other social catastrophes. Housing is the bridge between political citizenship (which allows for claims on parties, municipalities, war bosses, city bureaucracies, banking institutions, and the police) and social citizenship (which involves the transactions of debt, consumption, marriage, work-related information, and social standing in a community or neighborhood).

Secure housing certainly needs to be viewed as a primary and unquestionable human right whose destruction and deconstruction could be seen as a crime against humanity. But I have tried to argue that this is not only because housing is a primary bio-evolutionary need, alongside food, but because it is the pivot, platform, and prerequisite of political and social citizenship, especially for the urban poor. In this sense, we should see housing, habitation, and dwelling not only as the centrifugally organized focus of privacy, intimacy, and sociality within domestic life, but also as the centripetal focus of energies that guarantee fuller access to wider social networks, a more dignified social role for individuals and families, and a more deep bank for accumulating information, credibility, and dignity for the urban poor in public life as well.

Secure housing, in other words, is the critical source of stability and anchorage that allows citizens the ability to engage in the dynamic actions and transactions that constitute citizenship as an activity rather than as a mere

---

7   M. Moffatt, *An Untouchable Community in South India: Structure and Consensus*, Princeton: Princeton University Press, 1979.

statistical or civic fact. In big cities, the flow of information, the evolution of social relationships, the change of places of work and worship, the shifting dynamics of informal markets, the vagaries of weather and seasonality, are all built-in sources of volatility. For those whose housing is under constant threat, these external volatilities are turned into a double nightmare when the ground under their feet and the roof above their heads is also always threatening to dissolve or collapse.

HUMAN WASTE AND WASTE HUMANS

Fortunately, we are facing this situation armed with some serious ideas and already existing strategies based on hope. Before turning to some of these specific strategies, I wish to refer, briefly, to the ideas and possibilities that have occurred to me in the course of my multiyear, collaborative, advocacy-based research with the Shack/Slum Dwellers International (SDI) and especially with its Indian partners, located in three Indian organizations, one an NGO called the Society for the Protection of Area Resource Centres (SPARC), the other a national community-based organization (CBO) called the National Slum Dwellers Foundation, and the third a national CBO called Mahila Milan, built on women's voices, aspirations, and strengths across the slum communities of India. This network has been the subject of previous work and in the following chapters I highlight their distinctive character, strategy, and politics.

This network of community-based activists has managed to seize and capture the attention of city, regional, and federal governments across the world, and also finds means of collaborating creatively with major multinational funding agencies, private local donors, and other like-minded activists from civil society at every level. This alliance has catalyzed fragmented and disempowered slum communities to exchange local experiences and create cross-national learning strategies; it has balanced resistance to slum demolitions and evictions with reasoned collaborations with the state at every level; it has insisted on increasing the capacity of local communities to build their own finances and expand their own skills in engineering construction and housing design; and it has extended their clout with local politicians and administrators without falling prey to becoming vote banks or slum armies for corrupt politicians. At the same time, they have resisted the major efforts by various local governments to push slum dwellers out of increasingly valuable urban real estate, which is coveted by global developers, speculators, and their hired architects and planners and they have developed local strategies for securing housing rights for the urban poor in such highly volatile cities as Mumbai, Nairobi, and Phnom Penh.

The recent struggles over urban development and real estate exploitation in the famous megaslum of Dharavi in Mumbai have highlighted the many complexities of resisting the forces of global capital and urban housing speculation in a major Indian megacity. The unfolding story of the struggles for Dharavi can be understood more fully in the growing base of documentation of the facts on the ground in this extraordinary squatter city.[8] Here, the Indian organizations that are part of SDI have joined hands with a variety of other CBOs in a remarkable effort to resist wholesale displacement and relocation of up to a million residents of this massive mini-city of informal settlements, and have succeeded in slowing down an extraordinarily powerful combination of forces from the state and city governments, as well as from local and global housing moguls and developers who want to grab this valuable piece of land, valued by some at up to $1500 per square foot, for prices as absurdly low as $150 per square foot, and this without anything but the most shoddy planning for where these poor people might be resettled, reemployed, or rehabilitated. In a city like New York, London, or Paris, such a process would have led to a veritable social revolution, involving as it does the potential devastation of several hundred thousand people, hundreds of businesses (many of them home based), and more than a hundred distinct mini-communities (occupational, linguistic, and religious), some of whom lived in this part of Mumbai before the rest of the city even existed! The struggle over Dharavi is important not only because of its inherent importance as a major and historically deep slum community, but because Mumbai, a city of about 15 million people, is at least 50 percent composed of slum, squatter, or informal shanty communities, in the shadow of the office buildings, malls, skyscrapers, and flyovers of a city that aspires to be India's equivalent of Shanghai. My earlier discussions of slum demolitions in Mumbai argued that they are completely extraordinary for a country that prides itself on its sixty-year-old democracy, its traditions of non-violence and social cooperation, its international prestige and growing global economic power. It combines the brutality of Harare in an economy that is more like Brazil or Italy.

The ongoing Dharavi struggle holds many lessons, but in terms of the politics of hope it has special significance. The first has to do with a highly material way in which Heidegger's and Levinas's ideas about building and dwelling actually inform the history of squatter families. In the case of the settlement of Dharavi, this area was carved out of marshy lowland that nearby settlers from many different parts of India made habitable by their own processes of infill with garbage and different forms of non-perishable waste. Dharavi today has a vast array of housing forms, alleys and paths, spaces of leisure and worship, work and play, all in the absence of full municipal recognition, legal security, or good infrastructure for sanitation, water, or power. Yet, over almost a century,

8   K. Sharma, *Rediscovering Dharavi: Stories from Asia's Largest Slum*, New York: Penguin Books, 2000; J. Engquist and M. Lantz, eds., *Dharavi: Documenting Informalities*, New Delhi: Academic Foundation, 2009; A. Jockin, S. Patel, and S. Burra, "Dharavi: A View from Below," *Good Governance India Magazine*, 2005, 2(1).

the urban poor have gradually constructed a complex network of dwellings that has been directly produced by their actions of building. Thus, the value which Heidegger and Levinas have argued for, in terms of the metaphysics of human life, of being at home in the world, and of resisting the "enframing" of all human life by exploitative technologies, is in such informal settlements enacted in dwelling-through-building and building-through-dwelling.

In many major cities of the world, we have large communities that literally live on mountains of compacted trash, which constitutes the earth beneath their feet and the sky that defines their horizons. This is a far cry from the detailed pictures of German peasant homes that Heidegger used to exemplify the metaphysics of dwelling. In these communities of garbage, living in trash has been made the basis of economies of scavenging and recycling, imaginative use of the waste materials of middle-class consumption and industrial byproducts from small-scale enterprises in a large variety of industries from leather and glass to paper and clay. Dharavi here fits into a global array of *cities of disposal*, such as Payatas in Manila, Victoria Island in Lagos, and many other places, where trash, waste, and garbage are part of the material through which building produces a dwelling for slum communities. Though these communities face many kinds of daily hazard, which endanger their health, their physical security, and the security of their possessions, their hardest burden is that they are themselves regarded as somehow disposable, degradable, and recyclable. In the largest Nazi death camps, such as Auschwitz, we are familiar with the mountains of personal property, such as clothing, jewelry, false teeth, tools, and hair that the inmates were forced to sort through, sift, and inhabit in order to extract their own material wealth for their inhuman captors. The disposable cities where informal communities build their lives, in part, out of disposable materials are not quite as degrading. But they certainly always carry with them the stigma of waste, the sign of social invisibility, and the potential for "creative destruction" in the name of health, wealth, or civic beauty.

PATIENCE, RISK, AND HOPE

The recent movements to save Dharavi for those who have made it habitable, for those who have made a landscape of waste into a landscape of dwellings, have brought to light the remarkable internal diversity, the rich variety of cultural histories, the complex and massive contributions to the urban economy, and the remarkable capacity for internal governance and self-representation that have been contained within these invisible cities of disposal. In the last few years, a genuine social movement has emerged in Dharavi, which brings together community-organized censuses, successful though peaceful public marches, strong collaborations between local nongovernmental organizations and local communities, and most remarkably, a considerable degree of cooperation among political parties who have frequently been at each other's throats. I was myself witness to a remarkable informal meeting between local representatives of the Bharatiya Janata Party, the Communist Party, and the ruling Congress Party, who were also embedded in specific sub-communities within Dharavi, in the office of the National Slum Dweller's Federation, discussing and negotiating resistance strategies with Jockin Arputham, a leader within the SDI.

Here a practical history of communities built on linking building with dwelling, in the harsh conditions of bare citizenship and in the material context of cities of disposal, tells us that human waste need not imply wasted humans. Indeed, as the residents of Dharavi mobilize to resist the argument of their superfluity and the sustained campaign to separate their painstakingly achieved settlements and to convert them into commoditized real estate, they also make it impossible for the state and its market allies to treat them as human waste, as disposable humans. This sort of resistance to eviction, commodification, and demolition is not always successful or even registered for a wider global public.

All campaigns to claim full citizenship, to claim permanence in the face of the temporary, to claim dignity against the argument of disposability, are exercises in building what I call "the capacity to aspire" (see chapter 9), a navigational capacity through which the poor can redefine the terms of trade between recognition and redistribution, and through their confrontations and negotiations with state and market power, demonstrate and perform their ability to construct collective hope and to draw others around them into public dialogues and contracts to respect their claims to durability and permanence.

Such efforts themselves rest on other strategies that have been nurtured by community-based housing activists for several decades, both local and globally networked. One strategy, especially relevant to the politics of hope, is to be found in the ways that these communities oppose the politics of catastrophe, exception, and emergency with their own politics, which is frequently the politics of patience, which can even more accurately be called the politics of waiting. I will point more fully to the importance of the politics of patience in Mumbai's housing movement in chapter 8. Here I want to highlight this discipline from a different perspective.

The unhoused or underhoused millions in a city like Mumbai or Delhi or Calcutta, or in Cape Town or Johannesburg or Durban, mobilize themselves to demand better housing under more favorable and secure conditions. They know that they are always entering an unknown period of waiting: waiting for policymakers to agree on the plan, waiting for funders to shake up the complacency of local and national governments, waiting for builders and contractors to fulfill their promises to build new housing, and waiting for their own turn at the head of the queue. In most cases, the numbers are such that individual families and communities must prepare to wait years, even decades, for even a reasonable chance to see that their time has come. This requires them to learn to regard their own temporary dwellings as themselves parts of a temporary condition which is sure to change. Such patience, such waiting is always heroic, but it is even more so when it has to be mobilized in an atmosphere where rapacious real estate development projects as well as state-sponsored exercises in demolition, relocation, or eviction create a constant atmosphere of plausible emergency. Here is the difference between hoping and dreaming, for hoping for change in this context requires a disciplined dialogue between the pressures of catastrophe and the disciplines of patience. Politically organized hope mediates between emergency and patience and produces in bare citizens the internal resources to see themselves as active participants in the very process of waiting. Hope in this context is the force that converts the passive condition of "waiting for" to the active condition of "waiting to": waiting to move, waiting to claim full rights, waiting to make the next move in the process that will assure that the queue keeps moving and that the end of the rainbow is not a broken promise.

For the politics of hope to succeed in negotiating the risky terrain where emergency confronts the need for patience, one other tactic is important to mention, and it has been written about elsewhere both by academics and by activists: this is the role of precedent (see also chapter 8 in this volume). Precedent-setting has been a long-term and carefully refined strategy of the SDI and its Indian network partners. Precedent can affect a variety of domains, including politics, policing, finance, construction, and, not least, housing construction and rehabilitation. In their negotiations with local governments, with funders, with local and global housing agencies, with bankers, and with architects, precedent-setting involves a persistent effort to persuade the agencies that have power over slum residents to engage with them in collaborative exercises of one or another type. A precedent could involve asking a poor slum woman to give a speech at a major political rally; it could involve giving a contract for building a community toilet to a local slum organization rather than to outside contractors; it could involve the agreement of a mayor, housing bureaucrat, or police official to participate in some public event or process designed by slum dwellers; it could involve the design of an unconventional loan to a savings group within a slum community. In each of these cases—and there are myriad others— the setting of a precedent does not involve a legal or administrative machinery or process. Rather, it involves the creation of an ethos of trust and joint risk-taking, in which slum dwellers and various other powerful individuals and agencies learn how to share and distribute risk in important ventures where shared interests are involved. Since slum dwellers are by definition bare citizens, these precedent-setting actions are critical resources in their effort to enter the space and master the culture of legal/bureaucratic processes, and it helps to create a potential value-multiplying chain of examples (precedents) which provide a sort of social infrastructure to fortify the otherwise intolerable burdens of "waiting" and the constant threat of "disposal" and de-recognition. Thus, precedent-setting is a crucial weapon in the politics of hope, for it provides living instances of the possibilities of collaboration between the slum dwellers and those who generally appear as their enemies or tyrants. It is a tool for the building of social capital, capital which takes the form of trust in joint risk-taking.

The subject of risk brings us to the last important feature of the politics of hope insofar as housing and bare citizenship are concerned. The vulnerability of the urban poor, those whom I have described as bare citizens in this chapter, is above all a result of the uncertainty built into their incapacity to build their citizenship on the basis of secure housing. As I argued here earlier, secure housing is not only a part of full citizenship; it is also a vital means for full citizenship as a dynamic practice rather than a passive identity. In the absence of secure housing, not only is the journey from bare citizenship (*zoe*) to political citizenship (*bios*) always precarious, but its insecurity produces a toxic and permanent state of uncertainty about the journey from *zoe* to *bios*, from bare citizenship to active citizenship. Following the classic economic distinction articulated by Frank Knight,[9] the general and immeasurable uncertainty of insecure housing is not convertible to the calculable terrain of risk, which has the advantage that it permits measurement, assessment, and some measure of informed *experimentation*.

I use the word "experimentation" deliberately because I am convinced that there are no easy and preexisting solutions to addressing the massive problems of housing for the urban poor in today's world. Everywhere there are deep and irreconcilable debates among planners, funders, slum communities, and architects about the best fiscal and physical designs that might resolve the absence of secure housing in a humane and democratic manner. There are battles about community participation, about transparency and accountability, about low-versus high-density solutions, about moving manufacture versus moving services, about the challenges of whether jobs or housing should be the primary goal, about the tradeoffs between environment and equity, and a host of other debates. In this context, which characterizes the dilemma of large cities worldwide, it is clear that the only way forward is by *collaborative risk-taking*, in which poor communities themselves are encouraged to participate in the experiments to partner in the possible designs of and to share in the risks of specific investments in space, infrastructure, and urban services.

Such collaborative risk-taking, which I have observed firsthand especially in the federated communities which belong to the Alliance of SPARC, NSDF, and Mahila Milan in India, has multiple advantages. It allows politicians and bureaucrats the chance to receive credit for joining hands with the urban poor,

---

9   F. H. Knight, *Risk, Uncertainty and Profit*, Boston: Houghton Mifflin Co., 2009 (1921).

a form of credit that certainly has positive value in Indian politics and government. It allows poor communities the chance to gain ownership and comfort with technical skills and resources (in finance, construction, and design, for example), which multiply their future capacity for negotiation and collaboration. It allows the wider public, through the media, to witness such collaborations and to grow comfortable with the idea that the poorest communities can have articulate voices and credible technical competences. And finally, and certainly not least, these collaborations help to make the politics of hope, and the potentially negative politics of waiting, less of a vacuum, since these experimental and collaborative risks provide tangible signs, maps, and guides to what a sustainable future could look like. Thus, converting the free-floating uncertainty that goes with insecure housing into the calculated risks that accompany the politics of hope is one way in which bare citizens can practice the arts of full, political citizenship, even before they have acquired the formal requirements for that status. In short, any act of participation in the design of their own future habitations becomes for unhoused or insecurely housed citizens an act of building, and a step toward dwelling—not only as bare citizens—in the cities of the future. In this sense, the politics of hope depends on increasing the opportunities for the poor to convert uncertainty into risk, by seizing every opportunity to collaborate, experiment, and aspire in the public domain, not just with their allies but also with their many opponents.

CHAPTER SEVEN

Spectral Housing and Urban Cleansing: Notes on Millennial Mumbai

A BRIEF HISTORY OF DECOSMOPOLITANIZATION

Cities like Bombay—now Mumbai—have no clear place in the stories told so far that link late capitalism, globalization, post-Fordism, and the growing dematerialization of capital. Their history is uneven—in the sense made commonsensical by a certain critical tradition in Marxism. It is also character-ized by disjunct, yet adjacent, histories and temporalities. In such cities, Fordist manufacture, craft, and artisanal production, service economies involving law, leisure, finance, and banking, and virtual economies involving global finance capital and local stock markets live in an uneasy mix. Certainly, these cities are the loci of the practices of predatory global capital—here Mumbai belongs with Bangkok, Hong Kong, Sao Paulo, Los Angeles, Mexico City, London, and Singa-pore. But these cities also produce the social black holes of the effort to embrace and seduce global capital in their own particular ways, which are tied to varied histories (colonial and otherwise), varied political cultures of citizenship and rule, and varied ecologies of production and finance. Such particularities appear as images of globalization that are cracked and refracted. They are also instances of the elusiveness of global flows at the beginning of the new millennium.

Typically, these cities are large (10–15 million people) and are currently shifting from economies of manufacture and industry to economies of trade, tourism, and finance. They usually attract more poor people than they can handle and more capital than they can absorb. They offer the magic of wealth, celebrity, glamour, and power through their mass media. But they often contain shadow economies that are difficult to measure in traditional terms.

Such cities, too, are the site of various uncertainties about citizenship. People come to them in large numbers from impoverished rural areas. Work is often difficult to obtain and retain. The rich in these cities seek to gate as much of their lives as possible, travelling from guarded homes to darkened cars to air-conditioned offices, moving always in an envelope of privilege through the heat of public poverty and the dust of dispossession. Frequently, these are cities where crime is an integral part of municipal order and where fear of the poor is steadily increasing. And these are cities where the circulation of wealth in the form of cash is ostentatious and immense, but the sources of cash are always restricted, mysterious, or unpredictable. Put another way, even for those who have secure salaries or wages, the search for cash in order to make ends meet is endless. Thus everyday life is shot through with socially mediated chains of debt—between friends, neighbors, and coworkers—stretched across the continuum between multinational banks and other organized lenders, on the one hand, and loan sharks and thugs, on the other.

Bombay is one such city. It has an interesting history as a set of fishing villages, many named after local goddesses, linked by bridges and causeways and turned into a seat of colonial government in western India. Later, in the second half of the nineteenth century, it blossomed as a site of commercially oriented bourgeois nationalism, and, until the 1950s, it retained the ethos of a well-managed Fordist city, dominated by commerce, trade, and manufacture, especially in the realm of textiles. Well into the 1970s, in spite of phenomenal growth in its population and increasing strain on its infrastructure, Bombay remained a civic model for India. Most people with jobs had housing; most basic services (such as gas, electricity, water, and milk) reliably reached the salaried middle classes. The laboring classes had reasonably secure occupational niches. The truly destitute were always there, but even they fit into a complex sub-economy of pavement dwelling, rag picking, petty crime, and charity.

Until about 1960, the trains bringing in white- and blue-collar workers from the outer suburbs to the commercial and political core of the city (the Fort area in South Bombay) seemed to be able to move people around with some dignity and reliability and at relatively low cost. The same was true of the city's buses, bicycles, and trams. A three-mile bus ride in 1965 Bombay cost about 15 paise (roughly the equivalent of two US cents at then-current rates). People actually observed the etiquette of queuing in most public contexts, and buses always stopped at bus stops rather than fifty feet before or after them (as in most of India today).

Sometime in the 1970s all this began to change and a malignant city began to emerge from beneath the surface of the cosmopolitan ethos of the prior period. The change was not sudden, and it was not equally visible in all spheres. But it was unmistakable. Jobs became harder to get. More rural arrivals in the city found themselves economic refugees. Slums and shacks began to proliferate. The wealthy began to get nervous. The middle classes had to wrestle with overcrowded streets and buses, skyrocketing prices, and maddening traffic. The places of leisure and pleasure—the great promenades along the shore of the Arabian Sea, the wonderful parks and *maidans* (open grass fields designed for sport and pastime in the colonial era), the cinema halls and tea stalls—began to show the wear and tear of hypermodernization.

As this process began to take its toll on all but the wealthiest of the city's population, the groundwork was laid for the birth of the most markedly xenophobic regional party in India—the Shiva Sena—which formed in 1966 as a pro-native, Marathi-centered movement for ethnic control of Bombay. The Shiva Sena still has a significant national profile as one of the many parties that form the Sangh

Parivar (or coalition of Hindu chauvinist parties). Its platform combines language chauvinism (Marathi), regional primordialism (a cult of the regional state of Maharashtra), and a commitment to a Hinduized India (Hindutva, the ideology of Hinduness). The Shiva Sena's appeal goes back at least to 1956, shortly before Bombay was made the capital of the new linguistic state of Maharashtra and after intense rioting in Bombay over the competing claims of Gujaratis for Bombay to be in their own new linguistic state. In retrospect, 1956 marks a moment when Bombay became Mumbai, the name now insisted on by the official machineries of the city, all of which have been influenced by the Shiva Sena. Since this period, mostly through the active and coercive tactics of the Shiva Sena and its cadres, Bombay's Marathi speakers have been urged to see the city as theirs, and every few years a new enemy is found among the city's minorities: Tamil clerks, Hindi-speaking cabdrivers, Sikh businessmen, Malayali coconut vendors—each has provided the "allogenic" flavor of the month (or year).

A high point of this ethnicization of the city was reached in late 1992 and early 1993, when riots broke out throughout India after the destruction of the Babri Masjid in Ayodhya (in the state of Uttar Pradesh in north India) by Hindu vandals on December 6, 1992. Bombay's Hindu right managed in this period to join the national frenzy of anti-Muslim violence, but this violence, too, had a Bombay flavor. In keeping with more than two decades of the Shiva Sena's peculiar mix of regional chauvinism and nationalist hysterics, Bombay's Hindus managed to violently rewrite urban space as sacred, national, and Hindu space. The decades of this gradual ethnicizing of India's most cosmopolitan city (roughly the 1970s, 1980s, and into the 1990s) were also the decades when Bombay became a site of crucial changes in trade, finance, and industrial manufacture. This chapter is in part an effort to capture this more than circumstantial link. I turn now to a series of ethnographic interventions whose purpose is to think through the complex causalities that mediate between the steady dematerialization of Bombay's economy and the relentless hypermaterialization of its citizens through ethnic mobilization and public violence.

I have suggested so far that Bombay belongs to a group of cities in which global wealth and local poverty articulate a growing contradiction. But this chapter is not an effort to illuminate a general class of city or a global urban dilemma. It is an effort to recognize two specificities about Bombay that mark and produce its singularity. The first is to note the peculiar ambiguities that divide and connect cash and capital (two quite distinct forms of wealth) from one another. The second is to show that this disjuncture is part of what might let us understand the peculiar ways in which cosmopolitanism in Bombay has been violently compromised in its recent history. I do this by sketching a set of circumstances to make an argument about wealth, housing, and ethnic violence, that is, at this stage, circumstantial. Future work on Mumbai may allow me to be more precise about causalities and more definite about comparisons.

CITY OF CASH

In some ways, Bombay is as familiar with the history of capital as the most important cities of Europe and the United States. Long a site of seafaring commerce, imperial trade, and colonial power, Bombay's colonial elite— Parsis, Muslims, and Hindus (as well as Baghdadi Jews, Syrian Christians, Armenians, and other exotics)—helped shape industrial capitalism in the twilight of an earlier world economy built around the Indian Ocean. That earlier world economy (made vivid in Amitav Ghosh's *In An Antique Land*) can still be glimpsed in the traffic of dhows between the west coast of India and the states of the Persian Gulf, in the escalating illegal traffic in gold along this circuit, in the movement of thousands of migrants to the Gulf states from Kerala and elsewhere on the west coast, in the post-OPEC invasion of Arab tourists into Bombay seeking the pleasures of the monsoon, cheap medical care, the flesh trade, and the cheaper-than-Harrod's prices for many delicious goods. Bombay's citizens began to complain that they could no longer afford their favorite summer fruit—the Alphonso mango—because exports to the Middle East had shrunk local supplies and pushed mango prices beyond their reach.

Partly because of its huge film industry (still among the world's largest); partly because of its powerful role in trade, banking, and commerce; and partly because of its manufacturing sector, centered on textiles but extending to metal-works, automobile factories, chemical industries, and more—for all these reasons, Bombay after World War II was quintessentially a cosmopolis of commerce. People met in and through "business" (a word taken over from English and used to indicate professions, transactions, deals, and a whole ethos of commerce), and through "business" they forged and reproduced links across neighborhoods, ethnicities, and regional origins. No ethnicity in Bombay escaped stereotyping, and all stereotyping had its portfolio of jokes. What counted was the color of money.

And money leads a complex life in today's Mumbai. It is locked, hoarded, stored, and secreted in every possible way: in jewelry, in bank accounts, in household safes and mattresses, in land and housing and dowries, in boxes and purses and coffee tins, and behind shirts and blouses. It is frequently hidden money, made visible only in the fantastic forms of cars and mansions, sharp suits and expensive restaurants, huge flats and large numbers of servants. But even more, Mumbai is a city of visible money—of CASH—where wads, stacks, piles of rupees are openly and joyously transacted.

I remember a local street hood in my 1950s Bombay neighborhood who managed to become the local controller of the numbers racket. He wore a teryl-ene shirt with semitransparent pockets in which there was always the glimmer and clink of a huge number of little coins, the currency of his trade. The numbers racket then was tied to the daily close of the New York Cotton Exchange (or so I was told), and this flashy fellow never tired of strolling around with a little jingle sounding from his chest. He would laugh as he bought *pan* (betel nut rolled in betel leaf) from the local *panwalla* "on credit"; and when the *panwalla* would grab for his transparent pocket, he would flit away, laughing, gently guarding the coins near his heart. Coins were still tokens of wealth then. Today, he would need paper money in order not to look silly.

And it was also widely felt that cash, chance, and wealth were linked. This same numbers racketeer, who happened to come from the Tamil south of India and thus could speak to me in my native Tamil, always grabbed me on the street to ask, with a half smile, for me to give him two numbers so that he could use them to place his own bets. At issue was some notion of small children as bearers of good luck, idiot savants of probability, and I, a Brahmin child from a respectable Tamil family, probably embodied bourgeois prudence as well. This flashy hood somehow fell out with his bosses, turned into a humiliated beggar over a period of a few years, and, spurned by those very street people he had used and perhaps cheated, died broke. He surely never moved out of the magic circle of cash into the hazy world of bank accounts, insurance policies, savings, or other prudential strategies. He represented the raw end of the cash economy. Today, the numbers trade, still a major part of Bombay's street economy, has shifted away from the proto-global link to US commodity markets to—so the popular narrative goes—the play of pure chance: the pulling of cards out of a pot in a rumored-to-be real location in suburban Bombay every evening, with runners fanning out in minutes to report the results. This system is simply called *matka* (pot).

Yet there is a lot of interest in today's Bombay in such things as bank accounts, shares, and insurance policies—instruments all concerned with protecting money, providing against hazard, hedging risk, and enabling enterprise. Bombay's commercial economy includes a large part of its citizenry. Even poor wage-earners strive to have small savings accounts (with passbooks), and, more fascinating, no one is immune from the seduction of "whole-life" insurance. I have sometimes suspected that all of India is divided into two groups: those who sell insurance (an extremely popular trade for the less credentialed among the literate classes) and those who buy these policies. In Bombay, the Life Insurance Corporation of India is mainly housed in a building the size of a city block—a monumental vault that contains hundreds of thousands of small policies bought and sold most often from one individual to another. Starting as early as the 1960s, ordinary middle-class housewives began to see the benefits of various forms of corporate paper, including stocks, shares, and related instruments. These were bought mostly to be held—not sold—and their circulation through various financial markets was restricted and sluggish, until the last few years, when money markets have begun to get fast, volatile, high-volume, and speculative.

But back to cash. Much of Bombay's film industry runs on cash—so-called black money. This is a huge industry that produces more than three hundred Hindi films a year for a worldwide market and reaps huge revenues at the box office. As a shrewd local analyst said to me, there is no real film *industry* in Bombay, since there is no money that is both made and invested within the world of film. Rather, film financing is a notoriously gray area of speculation, solicitation, risk, and violence, in which the key players are men who have made killings in other markets (such as the grain trade, textiles, or other commodities). Some of them seek to keep their money out of the hands of the government, to speculate on the chance of financing a hit film and to get the bonus of hanging out with the stars as well. This sounds similar to the Hollywood pattern, but it is an entirely arbitrary cast of characters who might finance a film, so much time is spent by "producers" in trolling for businessmen with serious cash on their hands. And since these bankrolls are very large, the industry pays blockbuster prices for stars, and the entire cultural economy of the film world revolves around large cash transactions in black money. Periodically, big stars or producers are raided by income tax officials and a media bloodletting about seized assets is offered to the public, before business as usual resumes.

This sort of cash is everywhere in Bombay's "business" world, in huge rumored payments to government officials or businessmen to get things done, and equally in the daily small-scale traffic in black-market film tickets, smuggled foreign goods, numbers racket payments, police protection payments, wage payments to manual labor, and so on. It has been said that the "parallel" or "black" economy in India might be half again as large as the tax-generating, official economy. In Bombay, the ratio is probably higher.

Money is still considered real—in most circles—insofar as it is readily convertible to cash. Liquidity is the dominant criterion of prosperity, for both corporations and individuals, and new understandings of monetary phenomena such as credit, mortgages, and other technical or temporal "derivatives" are only now entering Bombay—and that, too, for its upper middle classes. Even the most sophisticated international and national financial strategists and czars, who are now responsible for putting Bombay permanently on the map of global investment, find it difficult to escape the sensuous appeals of cash. Wealth is understood to be an abstraction, but it is never seen as fully real in forms of paper that are not currency.

Bills and coins are not primarily what moves global wealth through Bombay's industrial houses, government offices, and corporate headquarters, but they are still the hallmarks of wealth and sociability, anchors of materiality in a world of invisible wealth. This is a shadow economy whose very shadows take on their density from the steady flow of real bills and coins through the lives of many kinds of transactors. Nor is this just money fleeing the tax collector. It is also money seeking immediate expenditure, racing from pocket to pocket without the logistical drag of conversion, storage, restriction, accounting, and dematerialization to slow the fuel of consumption. And this is true for the poor and for the rich. Whether you want 10 rupees to send to your mother in a postal money order or 4,000 rupees to have a bottle of Chivas Regal delivered to your door, cash is king. The rest is rumor.

Note that none of this has much to do with galloping inflation, any simple kind of fetishization, or the absence of immense local skills in money handling, credit, trade, and trust-based transactions that are truly global. It is entirely wrong to imagine that cash transactions imply limited trust. On the contrary, since parting with cash is decisively terminal, giving and taking cash requires larger amounts of trust than dealings in other sorts of monetary instruments. Cash handed over—even more than in other cases in the world—vanishes without a trace. The diamond industry, for example, which links cutters and polishers in coastal Surat (Gujarat) with caste-linked traders in Bombay, London, Antwerp, and beyond, is an exquisite case of global transfers that use every available form of credit (based on trust) but run on the fuel of hard cash at every critical switch point.

Nor is this corruption-at-large, where cash is best for extortion and fraud, though both exist in substantial measures. Rather, cash rules in Bombay as the mobile and material instantiation of forms of wealth that are known to be so large as to be immaterial. This is more nearly a commoditization of the fetish than a fetishization of the commodity, since currency here is itself treated as powerful in the extreme. What is invisible is not the currency behind the currency at hand but the wealth embedded in it. So moving currency around takes materialities that are themselves deeply powerful—fetishes, if you will— and puts them into generalized circulation. Cash here, to borrow Fredric Jameson's phrase from a very different context, is a central "signature of the visible."

What we know about Bombay in the nineteenth century and—more hazily—before that time certainly suggests that cash and its circulation through various kinds of commerce was a vital ingredient of sociality. It was the guarantee of cosmopolitanism because its sources were distant and varied, its local traffic crossed ethnic and regional lines, and its presence was both entrepreneurial and civic. The vital importance of Parsi philanthropists in the civic and public life of nineteenth- and twentieth-century Bombay is one of many examples of the cosmopolitanism of its public sphere.

What then is new today about cash in the city of cash? One answer is that cash and capital have come to relate in a new and contradictory manner in Bombay since the 1970s. While cash still does its circulatory work, guaranteeing a complex web of social and economic relations and indexing the fact that the business of Bombay is "business," capital in Bombay has become more anxious. This can be seen in two areas. The first is the flight of industrial capital away from the city, which is addressed later in this chapter. The second is that financial capital in Bombay operates in several disjunct registers: as the basis for multinational corporations tempted by new market seductions in India, as speculative capital operating in illegal or black markets, and as entrepreneurial energy operating in a city where it is increasingly difficult to coordinate the factors of capitalist production. Yet a large cash economy still governs Bombay. This uneasy relationship between cash and capital can be seen in a variety of arenas, but housing is perhaps the best place to follow how this disjunct relationship helps create the conditions of possibility for ethnic violence.

SPECTRAL HOUSING

It is a banality to say that housing is scarce in Bombay. This is so widely known to be true that it is scarcely ever discussed abstractly. But it haunts many conversations about resources, plans, hopes, and desires among all of its citizens, ranging from those who live in multimillion-dollar penthouses to those who pay protection money for rights to six feet of sleeping space in an aqueduct. It is always at issue when jobs are mentioned (But where will you live?), when marriages are negotiated (Will you give my son part of your flat as part of his dowry?), when relatives are visited (Is cousin Ashok staying with you now?), or when neighbors speculate on the identities of people going in and out of each other's flats (Is X a subtenant or a relative, or both?).

To speak of spectrality in Bombay's housing scene moves us beyond the empirics of inequality into the experience of shortage, speculation, crowding, and public improvisation. It marks the space of speculation and specularities, empty scenes of dissolved industry, fantasies of urban planning, rumors of real estate transfers, consumption patterns that violate their spatial preconditions, and bodies that are their own housing. The absent, the ghostly, the speculative, the fantastic all have their part to play in the simultaneous excesses and lacks of Bombay's housing scene. It is these experienced absurdities that warrant my use of the term *spectral* in a setting where housing and its lack are grossly real. What are these swollen realities?

The social traffic on Bombay's extraordinary vital metropolitan train service is entirely premised on the fact that millions of people travel increasingly huge distances (two hours and fifty miles is not uncommon) to get from home to work and back. And many of them undergo complex transformations in transit, turning from oppressed dwellers in shantytowns, slums, and disposable housing into well-dressed clerks, nurses, postmen, bank tellers, and secretaries. Their "homes" are often unstable products—a bricolage of shoddy materials, insecure social relations, poor sanitation, and near-total lack of privacy. As they move into their places of work, this vast army of the middle and working classes usually moves into more secure spaces of recognition, comfort, and predictability than the "homes" they return to at night, even when their jobs are harsh, poorly paid, or dangerous.

And this does not speak of the truly destitute: beggars; homeless children; the maimed and the disfigured; the abandoned women with small children; and the aged who wander deaf, dumb, or blind through Bombay's streets. These are the truly "homeless," who wander like their counterparts in other world cities from Chicago and Johannesburg to Frankfurt and Bangkok. These are in some cases "street people," although this category must not be taken to be wholly generic across different cities and societies. And that is because the streets themselves constitute specific forms of public space and traffic.

Much could be said about Indian street life and the life of Bombay's streets in respect to housing. But a few observations must suffice. Bombay's "pavement dwellers" (like Calcutta's) have been made famous in both sociology and popular media. It is true that there is a vast and semi-organized part of Bombay's population that lives on pavements—or, more exactly, on particular spots, stretches, and areas that are neither building nor street. These pavement dwellers are often able to keep their personal belongings with others in shops or kiosks or even inside buildings (for some sort of price, of course). Some actually live on pavements, and others sleep in the gray spaces between buildings and streets. Yet others live on roofs and on parapets, above garages, and in a variety of interstitial spaces that are not fully controlled by either landlords or the state. As we shall see in the concluding section, "pavement dwellers" and "slum dwellers" are no longer external labels but have become self-organizing, empowering labels for large parts of the urban poor in Bombay.

The important point here is that there is a vast range of insecure housing, from a six-foot stretch of sleeping space to a poorly defined tenancy situation shared by three families "renting" one room. Pavements shade into *jopad-pattis* (complexes of shacks with few amenities), which shade into semi-permanent illegal structures. Another continuum links these structures to *chawls* (tenement housing originally built for mill workers in Central Bombay) and to other forms of substandard housing. Above this tier are the owned or rented flats of the large middle class and finally the fancy flats and (in a tiny number of cases) houses owned by the rich and the super rich. These kinds of housing are not neatly segregated by neighborhood, for one simple reason: the insecurely housed poor are everywhere and are only partly concentrated in *bastis* (slums), *jopad-pattis*, and *chawls*. Almost every one of these kinds of housing for the poor, including roofs, parapets, compound walls, and overhangs, is subject to socially negotiated arrangements. Very often, control over these insecure spaces is in the hands of semi-organized crime, where rent and extortion shade into one another.

Even in the apartment buildings of the rich and upper middle class, especially in the commercial core of South Bombay and in the posh areas of Malabar Hill, Cuffe Parade, Worli, and Bandra, there is a constant pressure from the house poor. The poor set up house anywhere they can light a fire and stretch out a thin sheet to sleep on. As domestic servants, they often have small rooms in the large apartment buildings of the rich, and these servants (for whom such housing is a huge privilege) often bring friends and dependents, who spill out into the stairwells, the enclosed compounds, and the foyers. The official tenants, owners, and landlords wage a constant war against this colonization from below, but it is frequently lost because—as in all societies based on financial apartheid—one wants the poor near at hand as servants but far away as humans.

At the same time, small commercial enterprises sprout on every possible spot in every possible street, attached to buildings, to telephone poles, to electricity switching houses, or to anything else that does not move. These petty enterprises are by nature shelters, so many commercial stalls are, de facto, homes on the street for one or more people. The same is true of the kitchens of restaurants, parts of office buildings—indeed, any structure where a poor person has the smallest legitimate right to stay in or near a habitable structure, especially one that has water or a roof. Electricity and heat are rare luxuries, of course.

In this setting, for the very poor, home is anywhere you can sleep. And sleep is in fact the sole form of secure being. It is one of the few states in which—though usually entirely in public—there is respite from work, from harassment, and from eviction. Sleeping bodies are to be found everywhere in Bombay and indeed at all times. People walk over sleeping bodies as they cross streets and as they go into apartments, movie theaters, restaurants, and offices. Some of these people are sleeping in spaces to which they are legitimately connected through work or kinship. Others, as on park benches and street corners, are simply taking their housing on the hoof, renting sleep, in a manner of speaking. Public sleeping is the bottom of the hierarchy of spectral housing, housing that exists only by implication and by imputation. The sleeping body (which is almost always the laboring body or the indigent body) in its public, vulnerable, and inactive form is the most contained form of the spectral house. Public sleeping is a technique of necessity for those who can be at home only in their bodies.

Here we must resituate the sleeping, indigent, and exhausted body back in the specificities of Bombay's terrain of habitation, lest we slip into the generic sense of the urban poor as a global type. For the huge presence of the not-properly-housed is part of a bigger network of fears, pressures, and powers that surround housing for everyone in Bombay. Bombay has a shrinking but still large body of tenants, governed by an obsolete rent control act that has been the subject of enormous contention since the beginnings of economic liberalization in the early 1990s. Landlords, especially in South and Central Bombay, are at war with their "old" tenants, who pay tiny rents for real estate worth fortunes in these desirable parts of Bombay. In the mid 1990s, in spite of a dramatic drop in real estate prices across the country, prices per square foot for flats in the most desirable parts of Bombay were between 8,000 and 12,000 rupees. Thus, in US dollars, a fifteen-hundred-square-foot apartment would be valued at between $300,000 and $350,000. Prices in less desirable areas were predictably lower, but consider such prices in a country where more than 40 percent of the population live below the poverty line.

Since about 1992 there have been wild swings in the real estate market, partly fueled by financial speculators, both local and global. Since 1994 or so, when real estate prices hit their all-time high, there have been drops. There is a complex legal battle, involving the city of Bombay, the state of Maharashtra, and the union government (in Delhi) to reform the tenancy acts pertaining to urban real estate to give some semblance of market rationality to real estate prices. But the tenants are powerfully organized (though relatively small in number), and the landlords like the inflated prices when they sell but not when they have tenants who pay old rent. Homeowners, in cooperatives and condominium-style arrangements, also help the upward spiral since they have to think of housing as their most precious possession, potentially convertible into all sorts of other privileges.

In this context, mythologies of housing run rife, and no one is immune from dreams and fantasies. Tenants dream of a day when they will be allowed— by state fiat—to buy their houses for, say, fifteen years' worth of the "old" rent, which, from the point of view of the market, is a pittance. Landlords dream of a free market where they can kick out their poor tenants and bring in wealthy multinationals (believed to be honest and evictable). In the meantime, they allow their buildings to decay, and the municipality has now imposed a forced program of repair and restoration since the façades of these buildings and their internal structures are falling apart, creating a few major collapses and lots of accidents. So South and Central Bombay are strewn with repair projects based on a forced levy on tenants and landlords. Meanwhile, many of these old rent buildings feel like mausoleums, as tenants die or move but hold onto their places by locking them up or having servants take care of them. The vista look-ing from one of these buildings to another is of ghostly spaces, shut windows, silent verandas—spaces of houses without occupants, often gazing at bodies without houses on the streets and pavements below.

The market in "rental" houses is brisk and illegal, involving vast sums of cash, transacted as so-called *pagri* (key money), which often amounts to more than the market value of the house. The *pagri* is paid by the new "tenant," who comes in on a much higher rent, and is shared by the landlord and the "selling" tenant who, in fact, is selling his right to stay on distorted rental terms. The landlord seeks the best black money deal, and the buyer pays whatever the market demands.

This black market in "rentals" is even more distorted because its up-market end is occupied by the multinationals who (through their middlemen) are willing to pay huge down-payments (equivalent sometimes to rent for twenty years), along with a high monthly rental. In addition, dealings with multinationals allow such transactions to be legally binding and relatively transparent, as well as, in some ways, prestigious. The growing presence of multinationals with needs for office and residential space has done much to keep real estate values very high in the best parts of Mumbai, in spite of the emergent drift to find headquarters outside the city. This upper end of the market is also the zone of indigenous speculators with large amounts of black money who wish to make big returns. Below this level is the universe of middle-class owners and renters who typically entertain dreams of the big kill when they are in a position to sell their property or their rental rights. And still further down the hierarchy are the varieties of rights in tenements, slums, pavements, and shantytowns, where the buying and selling of rights is decisively connected to local thugs, ward-level politicians, and other small-time peddlers of influence.

Knitting together this complex edifice of housing-related hysteria is a huge disorganized army of brokers and dealers, whose subculture of solidarity, networking, and jealousy is notorious and resembles that of pimp sociologies in many big cities. These are the individuals who turn up like vultures in every context of viewing or potential sale or change of tenant, ever fearful that buyer and seller will cut them out or that they will lose their share of the deal to others in their own business. These are the individuals who constitute the fiber optics of rumor, price information, news about potential legal changes, and solutions to tricky problems of money transfer, security, and value. They are the foot soldiers of the spectral housing scene, themselves fueled not by the volume of transactions but by the ideology of the big hit, when a single big transaction will make their fortunes. They are also critical parts of the "nervous system" of spectral housing in Mumbai, in which rumors of big sales, big fees, and "good" and "bad" landlords circulate. It is also these brokers who ruthlessly boycott tenants who "show" their flats just to check the market but always back out at the last moment, just as certain buyers always back out after everything has been settled. Given the huge cash sums, the secrecy and fear, the greed and transient trust that is required for these deals to be consummated, a reputation for being a "tease" in this market can be fatal.

Beyond all this nervous greed and fluid dealing, in which few explorations actually lead to real changes of owner or occupant, and against the steady buzz of rumors about changes in the law that governs tenancy, ownership, sales, and rights, there is a larger picture of globalization, deindustrialization, and urban planning in which the nervous system of real estate deals meets the muscularity of long-term structural developments in Mumbai's economy. This story has several interactive parts.

Over the last thirty years or so, Bombay has been steadily deindustrialized, especially in its historically most important industrial sector, the production of textiles. An industry that represented the clearest case of a workable compact between state support, entrepreneurial skill, civic amenities, and productive union organization, the mill sector of Central Bombay was for decades the heart of the modernist geography of manufacture in Bombay, with the mills and their associated tenement houses occupying an area of several square miles in Central Bombay (and smaller areas elsewhere). These were solidly working-class neighborhoods, much as in the industrial cities of Europe and the United States at the height of the industrial revolution, and, like them, tied to the imperial-global economies of the nineteenth century. Over the last two decades, several forces have played havoc with this manufacturing core of Bombay. These include the growing obsolescence of equipment, as textile industries worldwide become high tech, and the reluctance of Bombay's indigenous capitalists to negotiate with the unions, stemming from their recognition that cheaper and less militant labor was available in the smaller towns of Maharashtra state (Nasik, Pune, Aurangabad, Nagpur, and many others). This process (as in many parts of the world) has been both a cause and an effect of the move toward flexible, part-time, and insecure forms of labor, the growth in which has steadily taken the fangs out of the union movement in Bombay. In recent years, a more disturbing global pull has reinforced this local process, as major multinationals also start to flee Bombay seeking lower rents, cleaner environments, more pliant labor, and simpler logistical systems.

This trend, in which national and transnational manufacturing is steadily leaving Bombay, is counterbalanced by the continued importance of Bombay's legal, political, and fiscal infrastructure, which cannot be fully outsourced to smaller towns and industrial centers. So the new geography of post-Fordism in Bombay has a set of abandoned factories (or unprofitable ones) at its heart, a growing service economy that has locational advantages not yet matched by smaller towns, a working class that is little more than a host of fragmented unions, and a workforce that has massively shifted to the service sector—with jobs in restaurants, small offices, the film industry, domestic service, computer cafes, "consulting" outfits, street vending, and the university system. In this regard, Bombay fits the broad global profile of swollen megacities that localize national/global speculative and service-oriented interests. In a sense, these are "octroi" economies that subsist by charging fees for intermediary services in transport, licenses, and the like, as industrial work fails to sustain a substantial proletariat.

Among the families that control large parts of these manufacturing enterprises that are being moved out to smaller towns, there is an effort to repackage their motives in the idiom of real estate, arguing that, as they vacate their erstwhile mills, large spaces will be opened up for the "homeless" with appropriate compensation for themselves through the state. Here is another major spectral narrative that dominates the upper ends of the nervous system of Mumbai's housing. A new imaginary is afloat, where thousands of acres of factory space are rumored to be lying idle behind the high walls that conceal the dying factories. Workers still live in the tenements of Parel, Worli, and Nagpada, and many of them listen to the sirens of the factories as they trudge toward this dying field of industrial dreams. But many of the buildings behind these high walls are silent, and, it is rumored, deals are being brokered between these industrialists, big developers, large corporations, and criminal syndicates to harvest these imagined thousands of acres in the very industrial heart of Mumbai. Rumors abound of major presentations by big developers in corporate boardrooms, displaying these lands with aerial shots and projecting the feast of hidden real estate just beyond the famine of the streets and buildings of visible Mumbai.

Here is the great imaginary of vast lands for Mumbai's poor and homeless, which might magically yield housing for those who, for a few decades, have had to go farther and farther out in order to find a space to live. This is the master specter of housing in Mumbai, a fantasy of huge tracts, some with very few structures on them, ready to be transformed, at the stroke of someone's pen, into Mumbai's paradise of habitation. Thus is the logic of deindustrialization and capital flight rewritten as the story of a chimerical landscape of trees, lakes, and open air waiting to be uncovered just behind the noise of the madding crowd of Central Mumbai. Yet global finance and its indigenous counterparts—as well as a host of other enterprises that rely on trade, speculation, and investment—still find Mumbai seductive, so that the pyramid of high prices and rampant inflation is kept alive and every square foot of housing is defended as personal patrimony.

From the point of view of street life, consumption is fueled by the explosive growth in small-scale hucksters, vendors, and retailers that have flooded Mumbai's pavements, rendering them almost impassable. Many of these vendor-dominated streets peddle items having to do with the fantasy of a global, middle-class consumer, with the truly smuggled, the imitated pirates, and the homegrown simulacrum all joyously mixed with each other: bras and juicers, lamps and window shades, underwear and cutting knives, sandwich makers and clothespins, decorative kitsch and T-shirts, women's dressing gowns and men's Levis. There seems to be no real annoyance with these vendors, despite the fact that they put pedestrians in the awkward position of either walking on the road (nudged by cars that could kill them), falling into the sewage grates just next to the curb (which are sometimes open), or picking their way through

carpets of T-shirts, sneakers, and drinking glasses. In this extraordinary efflorescence of street vending, we see again that cash is king, that money moves,
and that some entrepreneurial energy in the greater Mumbai area has moved
massively into this retail sector, its provisioning, and its marketing. This market
in petty goods, itself fueled by Mumbai's relatively high wages, has taken the
place of other forms of income (for the sellers) and of expenditure (for the
buyers).

This immense landscape of street-level traffic in the petty commodities of
everyday life is often physically contiguous to permanent shops and glitzy stores
where the A-list versions of the street commodities are also on display. These
street markets (a late industrial repetition of the sort of medieval European
markets described by Fernand Braudel) allow Mumbai's poorer working people,
whose money is scarce but who have bought into the object assemblages of
Mumbai's cashocracy, to enter the world of consumption—a world deeply influenced by real or imagined foreign objects, their local incarnations and
applications.

But there is more to this than a surfeit of cash among Bombay's middle and
working classes (for the indigent can only gaze at these piles of cargo). The key
elements of these street bazaars (though the full taxonomy of vendor's goods is
as complex as anything Jorge Luis Borges might have imagined) are the materialities of modern domesticity: children's underwear, women's dresses, men's
T-shirts, cheap lipstick, talcum powder, decorative kitsch, sheets and pillows,
mats and posters. The people who throng these places and succeed in negotiating their deals walk away with virtual households, or elements of the collection
of goods that might constitute the bourgeois household in some abstract
modernist dream. Among other things, there are hundreds of vendors in
Mumbai who sell old magazines from the West, including such oddities as
Architectural Digest and *House and Garden*, ostensibly meant for the creative
designer in Mumbai but actually looked at by humbler consumers living in one-
or two-room shacks.

These public dramas of consumption revolving around the accoutrements
of domesticity constitute an investment in the equipping of houses that may be
small and overcrowded, where individual space and rights may be highly
restricted, and where much in the way of modern amenities may be limited or
absent. These humble objects of domestic life are thus proleptic tools of a
domesticity without houses: houseless domesticity. In the purchase and assemblage of these objects, which imply a domestic plenitude that is surely
exaggerated, Bombay's working poor and nonprofessional service classes
produce their own spectral domesticity, which in its sensuous, cash-based,
pleasurable social reality recognizes the shrinking horizon of the actual houses
in which these objects might have a predictable life. Of course, all modern
shopping (in Mumbai and beyond) has the anticipatory, the imagined, the

auratic, and the possessive about its ethos. But street shopping in Mumbai, like public sleeping, is a form of claim to housing that no one can contest or subvert in the city of cash. This is where the specters of eviction meet the agencies of consumption.

We now turn to an explicit effort to engage the slippage between Bombay and Mumbai, in this chapter and in the social usages of the city. If Bombay was a historical space of commerce and cosmopolitanism, through what project did Bombay become Mumbai, so that, today, all official dealings—from control-tower traffic at Sahar airport to addresses on letters mailed to the city—must refer to Mumbai? What killed Bombay?

In the section that follows, I try to answer this question by linking the problems of scarcity and spectrality in the housing market to another kind of shrinkage, which is produced by the repositioning of Bombay's streets, shops, and homes as a sacred national space, as an urban rendition of a Hindu national geography. As struggles over the space of housing, vending, and sleeping gradually intensified, so did the sense of Bombay as a site for traffic across ethnic boundaries become reduced. The explosive violence of 1992–1993 translated the problem of scarce space into the imaginary of cleansed space, a space without Muslim bodies. In and through the violence of these riots, an urban nightmare was rescripted as a national dream.

URBAN CLEANSING

In 1996 the Shiva Sena proclaimed that Bombay would henceforth be only known as Mumbai. Even prior to this date, Mumbai had been the name for the city preferred by many of the Marathi-speaking majority, and especially by those who identify with the Shiva Sena. In one sense, the decision to officialize the name "Mumbai" is part of a widespread Indian pattern of replacing names associated with colonial rule with names associated with local, national, and regional heroes. It is an indigenizing toponymic strategy worldwide in scope.

In the case of Bombay, the move looks backward and forward simultaneously. Looking backward, it imagines the deity Mumba Devi (a goddess of one of the shrines that was vital to the fishing islands that later became Bombay). It evokes the fishing folk of these islands, and, because it is the name that was always used by Marathi speakers, it privileges their everyday usage over those of many other vernacular renditions of the name (such as the "Bambai" favored by Hindi speakers and the "Bambaai" of Tamil speakers). Of course, it gains respectability as an erasure of the Anglophone name, Bombay, and thus carries the surface respectability of popular nationalism after 1947. But its subtext looks to the future, to a counter-Bombay or anti-Bombay, as imagined by the Shiva Sena, whose political fortunes in the city wax and wane but whose hold on urban life no one has dared to write off.

This is a future in which Marathi and Maharashtrian heroes and practices dominate urban culture, and this purified regional city joins a renascent "Hindu" India; it is a future that envisions Mumbai as a point of translation and mediation between a renascent Maharashtra and a re-Hinduized India. This Mumbai of the future is sacred national space, ethnically pure but globally competitive. Balasaheb Thackeray, the vitriolic head of the Shiva Sena, was happy to welcome Michael Jackson to his home and had no trouble facilitating a major deal for Enron, the Texas-based multinational that wanted a major set of concessions for a new energy enterprise in Maharashtra, now no longer in business. So the transformation of Bombay into Mumbai is part of a contradictory utopia in which an ethnically cleansed city is still the gateway to the world.

When the mosque of Babri Masjid in Ayodhya was destroyed by Hindu vandals on December 6, 1992, a watershed was marked in the history of secularism in India, in the context of a big effort to Hinduize India and to link local ethnopolitics and national xenophobia. The events of December 1992 were themselves the product of an immensely complex process by which the major political parties of the Hindu right, most notably the BJP (Bharatiya Janata Party), managed to turn a series of recent political changes in the Hindi-speaking northern part of India to their advantage. These changes—most important among them the new political power of lower castes—were often results of violent confrontations between lower and upper castes over land tenure, government job quotas, and legal rights. In the late 1980s, building on a century of localized movements toward Hindu nationalism and nationalized Hinduism, the BJP and its allies had mobilized hitherto fragmented parties and movements under the single banner of Hindutva (Hinduness). Seizing on the failures of other national parties, they managed to launch a full-scale frontal attack on the ideals of secularism and interreligious harmony enshrined in the constitution and to convince Hindus of all classes that their salvation lay in Hinduizing the state.

In the process, they focused particularly on a series of neoreligious strategies and practices, drawing on existing cultural repertoires, to construct the imaginary of a Hindu soil, a Hindu history, and Hindu sacred places that had been corrupted and obscured by many outside forces, none worse than the forces of Islam. Anti-Muslim sentiments, available in various earlier discourses and movements, were transformed into what Romila Thapar called "syndicated" Hinduism, and one form of this politicized Hinduism took as its major program the liberation of Hindu temples from what were argued to be their illegitimate Muslim superstructures. The Babri Masjid became the symbolic epicenter of this more general campaign to cleanse Hindu space and nationalize the polity through a politics of archaeology, historical revisionism, and vandalism. The story of the events surrounding the destruction of the Babri Masjid has been well told elsewhere, and many scholars have placed these events in the deep history of Hindu-Muslim relations on the subcontinent.

There were riots throughout India after December 6, 1992, substantially amounting to a national pogrom against Muslims (though there was some Muslim violence against agents and sites of state power). But this was the first time there was a massive, nationwide campaign of violence against Muslims in which soil, space, and site came together in a politics of national sovereignty and integrity. Not only were Muslims seen as traitors (Pakistanis in disguise), but also their sacred sites were portrayed as a treacherous geography of vandalism and desecration, calculated to bury Hindu national geography at both its centers and its margins. In a sense, the political geography of sovereignty, focused on border wars with Pakistan, was brought into the same emotional space as the political geography of cultural purity, focused on the deep archaeology of religious monuments.

As it was the home of the Shiva Sena, Mumbai was drawn into this argument about national geography as Hindu geography in December 1992 in a special way. The story of the growth of the Shiva Sena from the 1960s to the present has been well told and analyzed elsewhere, so just a few points need be made here. The party has succeeded in identifying with the interests of Mumbai's growing Marathi-speaking lumpen proletariat while also actively destroying its left (communist) union culture. After starting mainly as a group of urban thugs, the Shiva Sena has managed to become a regional and national political force. It has hitched its regional nationalism (with deep roots in Maharashtra's ethnohistory and vernacular self-consciousness) to a broader national politics of Hindutva. It has created a relatively seamless link between its nativist, pro-Maharashtrian message and a national politics of confrontation with Pakistan. It has sutured a specific form of regional chauvinism with a national message about Hindu power through the deployment of the figure of the Muslim as the archetype of the invader, the stranger, and the traitor. The Shiva Sena has achieved this suture by a remarkably patient and powerful media campaign of hate, rumor, and mobilization, notably in the party newspaper *Saamna*, which has been the favorite reading of Mumbai's policemen for at least two decades. The Shiva Sena has done all this by systematically gutting the apparatus of city government, by criminalizing city politics at every level, and by working hand-in-glove with organized crime in many areas, notably in real estate, which brings us back to space and its politics in Mumbai.

Here we need to note certain important facts. According to several analysts, about 50 percent of Mumbai's 12 million citizens live in slums or other degraded forms of housing. Another 10 percent are estimated to be pavement dwellers. This amounts to more than 5 million people living in degraded (and degrading) forms of housing. Yet, according to one recent estimate, slum dwellers occupy only about 8 percent of the city's land, which totals about 43,000 hectares. The

rest of the city's land is either industrial land, middle- and high-income housing, or vacant land in the control of the city, the state, or private commercial
interests. Bottom line: 5 million poor people live in 8 percent of the land area of
a city no bigger than Manhattan and its near boroughs. As some have observed,
it is amazing that in these conditions of unbelievable crowding, lack of amenities, and outright struggle for daily survival, Mumbai's poor have not exploded
more often.

But they did explode in the riots of 1992–1993. During the several weeks of
intense rioting after December 6, there is no doubt that the worst damage was
done among those who lived in the most crowded, unredeemable slums. The
worst zones of violence were among the very poorest, in areas such as Behram-
pada, where Hindu and Muslim "toilers," in Sandeep Pendse's powerful usage,
were pitted against each other by neighborhood thugs, Shiva Sena bosses, and
indifferent police. Though the Indian Army was called in to impose order, the
fabric of social relations among Mumbai's poor was deeply damaged by repeated
episodes of arson, rape, murder, property damage, and eviction.

In these few weeks of December 1992 and January 1993, there was also a
frenzied mobilization by the Shiva Sena of its sympathizers to create public
terror and to confront Muslims with the message that there was no public space
for them and that they would be hunted down and killed or evicted from their
homes wherever possible. There was a marked increase in ethnocidal uses of a
new ritual form—the *maha arati*[10]—which was a kind of guerrilla form of public
worship organized by Hindu groups to push Muslims out of streets and public
spaces in areas where the two groups lived cheek by jowl. These ritual acts of
ethnic warfare were mostly conducted in the middle-class rental zones of
Central Mumbai; but in the slums and *jopad-pattis* of the north and west there
were firebombings and arson, street murders and beatings, and the main victims
were the poorest of the Muslim poor—rag pickers, abattoir workers, manual
laborers, indigents. Across the city, the Shiva Sena mobilized a national geography, spreading the rumor that the Pakistani navy was about to attack Mumbai
from its shoreline on the Arabian Sea, and anxious Hindu residents turned
searchlights onto the ocean to spot Pakistani warships.

---

10   The *maha arati* is widely conceded to be a ritual innovation by the Shiva Sena, first
developed in December 1992, in which a domestic Hindu ritual, traditionally conducted indoors,
was converted into a large-scale, public devotional offering to various Hindu gods and goddesses.
It is marked by the centrality of sacred fires (as in most domestic worship among Hindus) and,
in this new format, was also accompanied by elaborate and incendiary anti-Muslim speeches and
exhortations by pro-Hindu politicians and public figures. By various reliable estimates, it appears
that several hundred of these inciting rituals were staged in the period between December 6, 1992,
and January 15, 1993, in major streets, intersections, parks, and neighborhoods in Bombay. The
Report of the Srikrishna Commission notes the high correlation between these public rituals and
the frenzied destruction of Muslim lives and property when the crowds dispersed after these high-
intensity politico-ritual spectacles.

Meanwhile, inside the city, Muslims were cornered in slums and middle-class areas, in their own crowded spaces, hunted down with lists of names in the hands of organized mobs, and Muslim businesses and properties were relentlessly put to the torch. There was a strange point of conjuncture between these violent efforts to create Hindu public spheres and spaces, to depopulate Muslim flats and neighborhoods, and to destroy Muslim bodies and properties, and an ongoing form of civic violence directed against Mumbai's street dwellers, which I discuss below.

In the weeks preceding December 6, 1992, there had been a renewed effort by the Municipal Corporation to destroy the structures built by unlicensed street vendors and to destroy unauthorized residential dwellings that had sprouted throughout Mumbai. Here, municipal zeal (personified by G. Khairnar, an overzealous city official who was strangely not a Shiva Sena client) joined with political propaganda to create a tinderbox in the heavily Muslim areas of Central Bombay from Bhendi Bazaar to Byculla, especially along Mohammed Ali Road, the great Muslim thoroughfare of contemporary Mumbai. In this neighborhood, Muslim gangsters had worked with the connivance of shady financiers and corrupt city officials to build many unauthorized residential structures (through intimidation, forgery, and other subversions of the law) while terrorizing any potential resistors with armed force.

The Bombay municipality has had a tradition of chasing after street vendors for at least three decades in a constant public battle of cat-and-mouse that the vendors usually won. There was also a long and dark history of efforts to tear down slum dwellings, as in other cities in India. But in the late 1980s, this battle was intensified, as the nexus between real estate speculators, organized crime, and corrupt officialdom reached new heights. Although this nexus involved illegal housing and unlicensed vending throughout Mumbai, Khairnar's municipal gendarmerie just happened to focus their civic violence on an area dominated by the Muslim underworld. Thus, tragically, just before the Babri Masjid was destroyed in Ayodhya, Bombay's Muslim underworld was in a rage, and Mumbai's Muslim residents were convinced that there was, indeed, a civic effort to dismantle their dwellings and vending stalls. This is where the battle for space—a heated triangle involving organized mafias, corrupt local officials and politicians, and a completely predatory class of real estate speculators—met the radical politics of Hindutva in December 1992.

The geography of violence in Mumbai during December 1992 and January 1993 is overwhelmingly coincident with the geography of urban crowding, street commerce, and housing nightmares in Mumbai. In this violence, two grisly specters came to haunt and animate one another in the world of Mumbai's poorest citizens, as well as its working classes: the specter of a zero-sum battle for residential space and street commerce, figured as a struggle between civic discipline and organized crime; and the specter of

Mumbai's Muslims as a fifth column from Pakistan, ready to subvert Mumbai's sacred geography.

In this macabre conjuncture, the most horrendously poor, crowded, and degraded areas of the city were turned into battlegrounds of the poor against the poor, with the figure of the Muslim providing the link between scarce housing, illegal commerce, and national geography writ urban. In 1992–1993, in short, spectral housing met ethnic fear, and the Muslim body was the site of this terrifying negotiation. Of course, the middle and upper classes suffered as well, largely through the stoppage of commerce, movement, and production. But the overwhelming burden of violence—both its perpetration and its suffering—was borne by the bodies of Mumbai's toilers, and the massive sense of having no place in Mumbai (reinscribed as India) was overwhelmingly borne by its Muslims.

Here we must return to consider the links between spectral housing, the decosmopolitanizing of Bombay, and the ethnic violence of 1992 and 1993. The deliberate effort to terrorize Bombay's Muslims, to attack their vending stalls, to burn their shops and homes, to Hinduize their public spaces through violent ritual innovations, and to burn and maim their bodies can hardly be seen as a public policy solution to Bombay's housing problems. Neither can it be laid at the door of a single agency or power, even one so powerful and central to these events as the Shiva Sena. But it does seem plausible to suggest that in a city where daily sociality involves the negotiations of immense spatial stress, the many spectralities that surround housing (from indigent bodies to fantasy housing schemes and empty flats) can create the conditions for a violent reinscription of public space as Hindu space. In a city of 12 million persons, many occupying no more space than their bodies, it is not hard to see that imagining a city without Muslims, a sacred and Hindu city, free of the traffic of cash and the promiscuity of "business" (think of all the burnt Muslim shops of 1992 and 1993), could appear—briefly—to be a bizarre utopia of urban renewal. This monstrous utopia cannot be imagined without the spectral economies of Bombay's housing. But it also needed a political vision—the Shiva Sena's vision of a Hindu Mumbai—to move it toward fire and death.

The rest was contingency—or conjuncture.

ARGUMENTS FOR THE REAL

This is a grim story about one of the world's most dramatic scenes of urban inequality and spectral citizenship. But specters and utopias—as practices of the imagination—occupy the same moral terrain. And Bombay does not lack for a complex politics of the real. Throughout the twentieth century, and even in the nineteenth century, Bombay had powerful civic traditions of philanthropy, social work, political activism, and social justice. These traditions have stayed powerful in the last three decades of the twentieth century and at the beginning of the twenty-first century, where globalization, deindustrialization, and ethnourbanism have become linked forces. Both before and after the 1992–1993 riots, there have been extraordinary displays of courage and critical imagination in Mumbai. These have come from neighborhood groups (*mohulla* committees) committed to squelching rumors and defusing Hindu-Muslim tensions; from housing activists; from lawyers and social workers; and from journalists, architects, and trade union activists. All of these individuals and groups have held up powerful images of a cosmopolitan, secular, multicultural Bombay, and a Mumbai whose 43,000 hectares could be reorganized to accommodate its 5 million poorly housed citizens.

These activist organizations—among them some of the most creative and brilliant pro-poor and housing-related nongovernmental organizations (NGOs)—are making their own arguments about the political real in Mumbai. Their story, which, among other things, has forced the publication of an extraordinary judicial report on the 1992–1993 riots (which the Shiva Sena government tried mightily to bury), has been told elsewhere. This story is also linked to the extraordinary courage of ordinary people in Mumbai, and often among the poorest of the poor, to shelter their friends and neighbors from ethnocidal mob violence. These utopian visions and critical practices are resolutely modernist in their visions of equity, justice, and cultural cosmopolitanism. In the spectral world that I have described, they are not naïve or nostalgic. They are part of the ongoing struggle for that space where Mumbai's Real meets the real Bombay.

CHAPTER EIGHT

Deep Democracy: Urban Governmentality and the Horizon of Politics

GLOBALIZATION FROM BELOW

Post-1989, the world seems marked by the global victory of some version of neoliberalism, backed by the ubiquitous presence of the United States and sustained by the common openness to market processes of regimes otherwise varied in their political, religious, and historical traditions. At the same time, long after the fall of the Soviet order, it is clearer than ever that global inequality has widened, intranational warfare has vastly outpaced international warfare (thus leading some observers to suggest the image of a Cold Peace), and various forms of violent ethnicization seem to erode the possibilities of sustainable pluralism. All this in a period that has also witnessed increased flows of financial capital across national boundaries and innovations in electronic communications and information storage technologies—the paradoxes abound, and have led to the proliferation of new theories of civilizational clash and of global gaps between safe and unsafe physical zones and geographical spheres. Fears of cyber-apartheid mix with hopes for new opportunities for inclusion and participation.

In this confusion, now exacerbated by the knowledge that neither the most recent innovations in communications nor the defeat of the Soviet Union has created the conditions for global peace or equity, two great paradigms for enlightenment and equity seem to have become exhausted. One is the Marxist vision, in all its global variants, which promised some sort of politics of class-based internationalism premised on class struggle and the transformation of bourgeois politics by proletarian will. This is an internationalist vision that nevertheless requires the architecture of the nation-state as the site of effective struggle against capital and its agents. In this sense Marxism was, politically speaking, realist. The other grand vision, salient after 1945, was that of modernization and development, with its associated machinery of Western lending, technical expertise, and universalist discourses of education and technology transfer, and its target polity of the nationally based electoral democracy. This vision, born in such experiments as the Marshall Plan, has been subjected to intense criticism on numerous scores, but the starkest challenge to it is presented by the fact that today, over half a century after the Bretton Woods accords, more than half of the world's population lives in severe poverty.

In this context, a variety of other visions of emancipation and equity now circulate globally, often at odds with the nationalist imagination. Some are culturalist and religious, some diasporic and nonterritorial, some bureaucratic and managerial. Almost all of these recognize that nongovernmental actors are here to stay and somehow need to be made part of new models of global governance and local democracy.

The alliances and divisions in this new global political economy are not always easy to predict or understand. But among the many varieties of grassroots political movements, at least one broad distinction can be made. On the one hand are groups that have opted for armed, militarized solutions to their problems of inclusion, recognition, and participation. On the other are those that have opted for a politics of partnership—partnership, that is, between traditionally opposed groups, such as states, corporations, and workers. The alliance of housing activists whose story occupies the bulk of this essay belongs to the latter group and is part of the emergent process through which the physics of globalization is being creatively redeployed.

THE STORY

What follows is an analysis of an urban activist movement with global links. The setting is the city of Mumbai, in the state of Maharashtra, in western India. The movement consists of three partners, and its history as an alliance goes back to 1987. The three partners have different histories. The Society for the Promotion of Area Resource Centers, or SPARC, is an NGO formed by social work professionals in 1984 to work with problems of urban poverty in Mumbai. NSDF, the National Slum Dwellers Federation, is a powerful grassroots organization established in 1974 and is a CBO, or community-based organization, that also has its historical base in Mumbai. Finally, Mahila Milan is an organization of poor women, set up in 1986, with its base in Mumbai and a network throughout India, which is focused on women's issues in relation to urban poverty and concerned especially with local and self-organized savings schemes among the very poor. All three organizations, which refer to themselves collectively as the Alliance, are united in their concern with gaining secure tenure of land, adequate and durable housing, and access to elements of urban infrastructure, notably to electricity, transport, sanitation, and allied services. The Alliance also has strong links to Mumbai's pavement dwellers and to its street children, whom it has organized into an organization called Sadak Chaap (Street Imprint), which has its own social and political agenda. Of the six or seven nonstate organizations working directly with the urban poor in Mumbai, the Alliance has by far the largest constituency, the highest visibility in the eyes of the state, and the most extensive networks in India and elsewhere in the world.

This chapter represents an effort to understand how this came to be by looking at the horizon of politics created by the Alliance and by seeing how it has articulated new relations to urban governmentality. It is part of a larger ongoing study of how grassroots movements are finding new ways to combine local activism with horizontal, global networking. It is also, methodologically speaking, a partial effort to show how the anthropological study of globalization can move from an ethnography of locations to one of circulations. In my conclusion, I use the story of this particular network to discuss why it is useful to speak of "deep democracy" as a concept of wider potential use in the study of globalization.

THEORETICAL POINTS OF ENTRY

Three theoretical propositions underlie this chapter's presentation of the story of the Alliance in Mumbai.

First I assume, on the basis of my own previous work[1] and that of several others from a variety of disciplinary perspectives,[2] that globalization is producing new geographies of governmentality. Specifically, we are witnessing new forms of globally organized power and expertise within the "skin" or "casing" of existing nation-states.[3] One expression of these new geographies can be seen in the relationship of "cities and citizenship,"[4] in which wealthier "world-cities" increasingly operate like city-states in a networked global economy, increasingly independent of regional and national mediation, and where poorer cities—and the poorer populations within them—seek new ways to claim space and voice. Many large cities like Mumbai display the contradictions between these ideal types and combine high concentrations of wealth (tied to the growth of producer services) and even higher concentrations of poverty and disenfranchisement. Movements among the urban poor, such as the one I document here, mobilize and mediate these contradictions. They represent efforts to

---

1   A. Appadurai, *Modernity at Large: Cultural Dimensions of Globalization*, Minneapolis: University of Minnesota Press, 1996.

2   M. Castells, *The Rise of the Network Society*, Cambridge, MA: Blackwell, 1996; A. Giddens, *Runaway World: How Globalization Is Reshaping Our Lives*, New York: Routledge, 2000; D. Held, *Democracy and the Global Order: From the Modern State to Cosmopolitan Governance*, Stanford: Stanford University Press, 1995; J. Rosenau, *Along the Domestic-Foreign Frontier: Exploring Governance in a Turbulent World*, Cambridge: Cambridge University Press, 1997.

3   S. Sassen, "Spatialities and Temporalities of the Global: Elements for a Theorization," *Public Culture*, 2000, 12(1), 215–32.

4   A. Appadurai and J. Holston, "Introduction: Cities and Citizenship," in J. Holston, ed., *Cities and Citizenship*, Durham: Duke University Press, 1999.

reconstitute citizenship in cities. Such efforts take the form, in part, of what I refer to as *deep democracy*.

Second, I assume that the nation-state system is undergoing a profound and transformative crisis. Avoiding here the sterile terms of the debate about whether or not the nation-state is ending (a debate to which I myself earlier contributed), I nevertheless wish to affirm resolutely that the changes in the system are deep, if not graspable, as yet, in a simple theory. I suggest that we see the current crisis as a crisis of redundancy rather than, for example, as one of legitimation.[5] By using the term *redundancy*, I mean to connect several processes that others have identified with different states and regions and in different dimensions of governance. Thus, in many parts of the world, there has been undoubted growth in a "privatization" of the state in various forms, sometimes produced by the appropriation of the means of violence by nonstate groups. In other cases, we can see the growing power in some national economies of multilateral agencies such as the World Bank and International Monetary Fund, sometimes indexed by the voluntary outsourcing of state functions as part of the neoliberal strategies that have become popular worldwide since 1989. In yet other cases, activist NGOs and citizens' movements have appropriated significant parts of the means of governance.

Third, I assume that we are witnessing a notable transformation in the nature of global governance in the explosive growth of nongovernment organizations of all scales and varieties in the period since 1945, a growth fueled by the linked development of the United Nations system, the Bretton Woods institutional order, and especially the global circulation and legitimation of the discourses and politics of "human rights." Together, these developments have provided a powerful impetus to democratic claims by nonstate actors throughout the world. There is some reason to worry about whether the current framework of human rights is serving mainly as the legal and normative conscience—or the legal-bureaucratic lubricant—of a neoliberal, marketized political order. But there is no doubt that the global spread of the discourse of human rights has provided a huge boost to local democratic formations. In addition, the combination of this global efflorescence of nongovernmental politics with the multiple technological revolutions of the last fifty years has provided much energy to what has been called "crossborder activism" through "transnational advocacy networks."[6] These networks provide new horizontal modes for articulating the deep democratic politics of the locality, creating hitherto unpredicted groupings: examples may be "issuebased"—focused on the environment, child labor, or AIDS; or they may be

---

5   J. Habermas, *Legitimation Crisis*, T. McCarthy, trans., Boston: Beacon, 1975.
6   M. E. Keck and K. Sikkink, *Activists beyond Borders: Advocacy Networks in International Politics*, Ithaca: Cornell University Press, 1998.

"identity-based"—feminist, indigenous, gay, diasporic. The Mumbai-based movement discussed here is also a site of such cross-border activism.

Together, these three points of entry allow me to describe the Mumbai Alliance of urban activists as part of an emergent political horizon, global in its scope, that presents a post-Marxist and post-developmentalist vision of how the global and the local can become reciprocal instruments in the deepening of democracy.

THE SETTING: MUMBAI IN THE 1990S

Chapter 7 offers a lengthy examination of the transformation of Mumbai's cultural economy since the 1970s, with an emphasis on the brutal ethnic violence of December 1992–January 1993. That chapter contains a relatively detailed analysis of the relationships between the politics of right-wing Hindu nationalism—seen mostly in the activities of India's major urban xenophobic party, the Shiva Sena—the political economy of deindustrialization, and the spectral politics of housing in Mumbai. I analyze the steady expansion of anti-Muslim politics by the Shiva Sena, the radical inequality in access to living space in the city, and the transformation of its industrial economy into a service economy. I argue that Mumbai became a perfect site for the violent rewriting of national geography as urban geography through a paroxysmal effort to eliminate Muslims from its public sphere and its commercial world.

I will not retell that story here, but I will review some major facts about Mumbai in the 1990s that are not widely known. Mumbai is the largest city in a country, India, whose population has just crossed the 1 billion mark (one-sixth of the world's population). The city's population is at least 12 million (and more, if we include the growing edges of the city and the population of a twin city, New Mumbai, that has been built across Thane Creek). This means a population totaling 1.2 percent of one-sixth of the world's population. Not a minor case, even in itself.

Here follow some facts about housing in Mumbai on which there is a general consensus. About 40 percent of the population (about 6 million persons) live in slums or other degraded forms of housing. Another 5 to 10 percent are pavement dwellers. Yet according to one recent estimate, slum dwellers occupy only 8 percent of the city's land, which totals about 43,000 hectares. The rest of the city's land is either industrial land, middle- and high-income housing, or vacant land in the control of the city, the state (regional and federal), or private owners. The bottom line: 5 to 6 million poor people living in substandard conditions in 8 percent of the land area of a city smaller than the two New York City boroughs of Manhattan and Queens. This huge and constricted population of insecurely or poorly housed people has negligible access to essential services, such as running water, electricity, and ration cards for food staples.

Equally important, this population—which we may call *citizens without a city*—is a vital part of the urban workforce. Some of them occupy the respectable low end of white-collar organizations and others the menial low end of industrial and commercial concerns. But many are engaged in temporary, physically dangerous, and socially degrading forms of work. This latter group, which may well comprise 1 to 2 million people in Mumbai, is best described, in the striking phrase of Sandeep Pendse,[7] as Mumbai's "toilers" rather than as its proletariat, working class, or laboring classes—all designations that suggest more stable forms of employment and organization. These toilers, the poorest of the poor in the city of Mumbai, work in menial occupations (almost always on a daily or piecework basis). They are cart pullers, rag pickers, scullions, sex-workers, car cleaners, mechanic's assistants, petty vendors, small-time criminals, and temporary workers in petty industrial jobs requiring dangerous physical work, such as ditch digging, metal hammering, truck loading, and the like. They often sleep in (or on) their places of work, insofar as their work is not wholly transient in character. While men form the core of this labor pool, women and children work wherever possible, frequently in ways that exploit their sexual vulnerability. To take just one example, Mumbai's gigantic restaurant and food-service economy is almost completely dependent on a vast army of child labor.

Housing is at the heart of the lives of this army of toilers. Their everyday life is dominated by ever-present forms of risk. Their temporary shacks may be demolished. Their slumlords may push them out through force or extortion. The torrential monsoons may destroy their fragile shelters and their few personal possessions. Their lack of sanitary facilities increases their need for doctors to whom they have limited access. And their inability to document their claims to housing may snowball into a general invisibility in urban life, making it impossible for them to claim any rights to such things as rationed foods, municipal health and education facilities, police protection, and voting rights. In a city where ration cards, electricity bills, and rent receipts guarantee other rights to the benefits of citizenship, the inability to secure claims to proper housing and other political handicaps reinforce each other. Housing—and its lack—set the stage for the most public drama of disenfranchisement in Mumbai. In fact, housing can be argued to be the single most critical site of this city's politics of citizenship.

This is the context in which the activists I am working with are making their interventions, mobilizing the poor and generating new forms of politics. The next three sections of this chapter address various dimensions of this politics: its vision, its vocabularies, and its practices.

---

7   S. Pendse, "Toil, Sweat and the City," in S. Patel and A. Thorner, eds., *Bombay: Metaphor for Modern India*, Bombay: Oxford University Press, 1995.

THE POLITICS OF PATIENCE

In this section, I give a sketch of the evolving vision of the Alliance of SPARC, Mahila Milan, and the National Slum Dwellers Federation as it functions within the complex politics of space and housing in Mumbai. Here, a number of broad features of the Alliance are important.

First, given the diverse social origins of the three groups that are involved in the Alliance, their politics awards a central place to negotiation and consensus-building. SPARC is led by professionals with an Anglophone background, connected to state and corporate elites in Mumbai and beyond, with strong ties to global funding sources and networking opportunities. However, SPARC was born in 1984 in the specific context of work undertaken by its founders—principally a group of women trained in social work at the Tata Institute for the Social Sciences—among poor women in the neighborhood of Nagpada. This area has a diverse ethnic population and is located between the wealthiest parts of South Mumbai and the increasingly difficult slum areas of Central and North Mumbai. Notable among SPARC's constituencies was a group of predominantly Muslim ex–sex trade workers from Central Mumbai who later became the cadre of another partner in the Alliance, Mahila Milan. The link between the two organizations dates to around 1986, when Mahila Milan was founded, with support from SPARC.

The link with the NSDF, an older and broader-based slum dwellers' organization, was also made in the late 1980s. The leadership of the three organizations cuts across the lines between Hindus, Muslims, and Christians and is explicitly secularist in outlook. In a general way, SPARC contributed technical knowledge and elite connections to state authorities and the private sector. NSDF, through its leader, Arputham Jockin (who himself has a background in the slums), and his activist colleagues, brought a radical brand of grassroots political organization in the form of the "federation" model, to be discussed later in this essay. Mahila Milan brought the strength of poor women who had learned the hard way how to deal with police, municipal authorities, slumlords, and real estate developers on the streets of Central Mumbai but had not previously had a real incentive to organize politically.

These three partners still have distinct styles, strategies, and functional characteristics. But they are committed to a partnership based on a shared ideology of risk, trust, negotiation, and learning among their key participants. They have also agreed upon a radical approach to the politicization of the urban poor that is fundamentally populist and anti-expert in strategy and flavor. The Alliance has evolved a style of pro-poor activism that consciously departs from earlier models of social work, welfarism, and community organization (an approach akin to that pioneered by Saul Alinsky in the United States). Instead of relying on the model of an outside organizer who teaches local communities how to hold the state to its normative obligations to the poor, the Alliance is committed to methods of organization, mobilization, teaching, and learning that build on what poor persons already know and understand. The first principle of this approach is that no one knows more about how to survive poverty than the poor themselves.

A crucial and controversial feature of this approach is its vision of politics without parties. The strategy of the Alliance is that it will not deliver the poor as a vote bank to any political party or candidate. This is a tricky business in Mumbai, where most grassroots organizations, notably unions, have a long history of direct affiliation with major political parties. Moreover, in Mumbai, the Shiva Sena, with its violent, street-level control of urban politics, does not easily tolerate neutrality. The Alliance deals with these difficulties by working with whoever is in power, at the federal and state level, within the municipality of Mumbai, or even at the local level of particular wards (municipal subunits). Thus the Alliance has elicited hostility from other activist groups in Mumbai for its willingness, when deemed necessary, to work with the Shiva Sena. But it is resolute about making the Shiva Sena work for its ends, not vice versa. Indeed, because it has consistently maintained an image of nonaffiliation with all political parties, the Alliance enjoys the double advantage of appearing nonpolitical while retaining access to the potential political power of the poorer half of Mumbai's population.

Instead of finding safety in affiliation with any single party or coalition in the state government of Maharashtra or in the Municipal Corporation of Mumbai, the Alliance has developed a complex political affiliation with the various levels of the state bureaucracy. This group includes civil servants who conduct policy at the highest levels in the state of Maharashtra and run the major bodies responsible for housing loans, slum rehabilitation, real estate regulation, and the like. The members of the Alliance have also developed links with quasi-autonomous arms of the federal government, such as the railways, the Port Authority, and the Bombay Electric Supply and Transport Corporation, and with the municipal authorities who control critical elements of the infrastructure, such as the regulations governing illegal structures, the water supply, and sanitation. Finally, the Alliance works to maintain a cordial relationship with the Mumbai police—and at least a hands-off relationship with the underworld, which is deeply involved in housing finance, slum landlordism, and extortion as well as in the demolition and rebuilding of temporary structures.

From this perspective, the politics of the Alliance is a politics of accommodation, negotiation, and long-term pressure rather than of confrontation or threats of political reprisal. This *realpolitik* makes good sense in a city like Mumbai, where the supply of scarce urban infrastructure—housing and all its associated entitlements—is entangled in an immensely complicated web of slum rehabilitation projects, financing procedures, legislative precedents, and administrative codes which are interpreted differently, enforced unevenly, and whose actual delivery is almost always attended by an element of corruption.

This pragmatic approach is grounded in a complex political vision about means, ends, and styles that is not entirely utilitarian or functional. It is based on a series of ideas about the transformation of the conditions of poverty by the poor in the long run. In this sense, the figure of a political horizon is meant to point to a logic of patience, of cumulative victories and long-term asset building, that is wired into every aspect of the activities of the Alliance. The Alliance maintains that the mobilization of the knowledge of the poor into methods driven by the poor and for the poor is a slow and risk-laden process; this premise informs the group's strong bias against "projects" and "projectization" that underlies almost all official ideas about urban change. Whether the World Bank, most Northern donors, the Indian state, or other agencies, most institutional sources of funding are strongly biased in favor of the "project" model, in which short-term logics of investment, accounting, reporting, and assessment are regarded as vital. The Alliance has steadfastly advocated the importance of slow learning and cumulative change against the temporal logics of the project. Likewise, their other strategies and tactics are also geared to long-term capacity building, the gradual gaining of knowledge and trust, the sifting of more from less reliable partners, and so on. This open and long-term temporal horizon is a difficult commitment to retain in the face of the urgency, and even desperation, that characterize the needs of Mumbai's urban poor. But it is a crucial normative guarantee against the ever present risk, in all forms of grassroots activism, that the needs of funders will gradually obliterate the needs of the poor themselves.

Patience as a long-term political strategy is especially hard to maintain in view of two major forces. One is the constant barrage of real threats to life and space that frequently assail the urban poor. The most recent such episode was the massive demolition of shacks near the railroad tracks, which, since April 2000, has produced an intense struggle for survival and political mobilization in the midst of virtually impossible political circumstances. In this sense, the strategies of the Alliance, which favor long-term asset building, run against the same "tyranny of emergency," in the words of Jérôme Bindé,[8] that characterizes the everyday lives of the urban poor.

The other force that makes patience hard to maintain is the built-in tension within the Alliance about different modes and methods of partnership. Not all members of the Alliance view the state, the market, or the donor world in the

8   J. Bindé, "Toward an Ethics of the Future," *Public Culture,* 2000, 12(1), 51–72.

same way. Thus, every new occasion for funding, every new demand for a report, every new celebration of a possible partnership, every meeting with a railway official or an urban bureaucrat can create new sources of debate and anxiety within the Alliance. In the words of one key Alliance leader, negotiating these differences, rooted in deep diversities in class, experience, and personal style, is like "riding a tiger." It would be a mistake to view the pragmatic way in which all partnerships are approached by the Alliance as a simple politics of utility. It is a politics of patience, constructed against the tyranny of emergency.

To understand how this broad strategic vision is actually played out as a strategy of urban governmentality, we need to look a little more closely at some critical practices, discursive and organizational, by which the Alliance has consolidated its standing as a pro-poor movement in Mumbai.

WORDS AND DEEDS

As with all serious movements concerned with consciousness-changing and self-mobilization, there is a conscious effort to inculcate protocols of speech, style, and organizational form within the Alliance. The coalition cultivates a highly transparent, nonhierarchical, antibureaucratic, and antitechnocratic organizational style. A small clerical staff conscientiously serves the needs of the activists, not vice versa; meetings and discussions are often held with every-one sitting on mats on the floor. Food and drink are shared during meetings, and most official business (on the phone or face to face) is held in the midst of a tumult of other activities in crowded offices. A constant undercurrent of bawdy humor runs through the members' discussions of problems, partners, and their own affairs. Conversation is almost always in Hindi, Marathi, or Tamil, or in English interspersed with one of these Indian languages. The leadership is at pains to make its ideas known among its members and to the residents of the actual slum communities who are, in effect, the coalition's rank and file. Almost no internal request for information about the organization, its funding, its planning, or related matters is considered out of order. Naturally, there are private conversations, hidden tensions, and real differences of personality and strategy at all levels. But these are not validated or legitimated in bureaucratic protocols or organizational charts.

This style of organization and management produces constant tensions among members of the Alliance and various outside bodies—donors, state institutions, regulators—which frequently demand more formal norms of organization, accounting, and reporting. To a very considerable extent the brunt of this stress is borne by SPARC, which has an office in Central Mumbai where the formal bureaucratic links to the world of law, accountancy, and reporting are largely centralized. This office serves partly to insulate the other two partners, NSDF and Mahila Milan, from the needs of externally mandated bookkeeping, fund management, reporting, and public legal procedures. The latter two organizations have their own headquarters in the compound of a municipal dispensary in Byculla. This office is in the heart of a slum world where many of the core members of Mahila Milan actually live, an area in which Muslims are a major presence, and the sex trades, the criminal world, and petty commerce are highly visible. The office is always filled with men and women from the communities of slum dwellers that are the backbone of the Alliance. There is constant movement among key personnel between this office, the SPARC office in Khetwadi, and the outlying new suburbs where the Alliance is building transit facilities or new houses for its members—Dharavi, Mankhurd, and Ghatkopar.

The phones are in constant use as key members of the Alliance exchange information about breaking crises, plans, and news across these various locations in Mumbai—and also across India and the world. Every few hours during an average day, a phone rings at one of these offices and turns out to be one of the members of the Alliance checking on or tracking down something—a call is as likely to come from Phnom Penh or Cape Town as from Mankhurd or Byculla. Because everyday organizational life is filled with meetings with contractors, lawyers, state officials, and politicians as well as among Alliance members, spatial fixity is not valued and the organization functions in and through mobility. In this context, the telephone and e-mail play an increasingly vital role. The key leaders of the Alliance, with a few significant exceptions, either use e-mail or have access to it through close colleagues. The phones are constantly ringing. Schedules shift at the drop of a hat as travel plans are adjusted to meet emergent opportunities or to address the presence or absence of key members. The general impression is of a fast game of ice hockey, with players constantly tumbling in and out of the most active roles in response to shifting needs and game plans.

Nevertheless, through experiences and discussions that have evolved over fifteen years (and in some cases, more), there is a steady effort to remember and reproduce certain crucial principles and norms that offset organizational fluidity and the pressures of daily crises. These norms and practices require a much more detailed discussion than I can give here, but some impression of them is vital to understanding the political horizon of this form of deep democracy.

Possibly the central norm is embodied in a common usage among the members of the Alliance and its partners around the world. It is the term *federation*, used as a noun, or *federate* and *federated*, used as verbs. This innocuous term from elementary political science textbooks has a special meaning and magic for the Alliance. At its foundation is the idea of individuals and families self-organizing as members of a political collective to pool resources, organize lobbying, provide mutual risk-management devices, and confront opponents, when necessary. Members of the Alliance often judge the effectiveness of other

NGOs, in India and elsewhere, by reference to whether or not they have learned the virtues of federating. The National Slum Dwellers Federation is clearly their own model of this norm. As an image of organization, it is significant in two ways. It emphasizes the importance of political union among already preexisting collectives (thus federating, rather than simply uniting, joining, and lobbying). And it mirrors the structure of the Indian national state, which is referred to as the Indian Union, but is in fact a federal model whose constituent states retain extensive powers.

In the usage of the Alliance, the idea of federation is a constant reminder that groups (even at the level of families) that have a claim to political agency on their own have chosen to combine their political and material power. The primacy of the principle of federation also serves to remind all members, particularly the trained professionals, that the power of the Alliance lies not in its donors, its technical expertise, or its administration, but in the will to federate among poor families and communities. At another level, the image of the federation asserts the primacy of the poor in driving their own politics, however much others may help them to do so. There is a formal property to membership in the federation, and members of the Alliance maintain ongoing debates about recruiting slum families, neighborhoods, and communities in Mumbai (and elsewhere in India) that are not yet part of the federation. For as long as the latter remain outside, they cannot participate in the active politics of savings, housing, resettlement, and rehabilitation that are the bread and butter of the Alliance.

Savings is another term that takes on a special meaning in Alliance usage. Creating informal savings groups among the poor—a process that the donor establishment has recognized under the term *microcredit*—is a current technique for improving financial citizenship for the urban and rural poor throughout the world. Often building on older models of revolving credit and loan facilities that are managed informally and locally, outside the purview of the state and the banking sector, microcredit has its advocates and visionaries in India and elsewhere. But in the life of the Alliance, savings has a profound ideological, even soteriological, status. The architect of the Alliance philosophy of savings is the NSDF's Jockin, who has used savings as a principal tool for mobilization in India and as an entry point to relationship building in South Africa, Cambodia, and Thailand. He sees daily savings as the bedrock of all federation activities; indeed, it is not an exaggeration to say that in Jockin's organizational exhortations, wherever he goes, federation equals savings. When Jockin and his colleagues in the Alliance speak about savings, it becomes evident that they are describing something far deeper than a simple mechanism for meeting daily monetary needs and sharing resources among the poor. Seen as something akin to a spiritual practice, daily savings—and its spread—is conceived as the key to the local and global success of the federation model.

In this connection, it may be noted that Mahila Milan, the women's group within the Alliance, is focused almost entirely on organizing small savings circles. By putting savings at the core of the politics of the Alliance, its leaders are making the work of poor women fundamental to what can be achieved in every other area. It is a simple formula: Without poor women joining together, there can be no savings. Without savings, there can be no federating. Without federating, there is no way for the poor themselves to enact change in the arrangements that disempower them. What is important to recognize here is that when Alliance leaders speak about a way of life organized around the practice of saving—in Jockin's words, it is like "breathing"—they are framing saving as a moral discipline. The practice builds a certain kind of political fortitude and commitment to the collective good and creates persons who can manage their affairs in many other ways as well. Daily savings, which do not generate large resources quickly, can therefore form the moral core of a politics of patience.

A final key term that recurs in the writing and speech of the leaders of the Alliance is *precedent-setting*. Underlying its bland, quasi-legal tone is a more radical idea: that the poor need to claim, refine, and define certain ways of doing things in spaces they already control and then use these practices to show donors, city officials, and other activists that their "precedents" are good ones and encourage such actors to invest further in them. This is a politics of show-and-tell, but it is also a philosophy of do first, talk later. The subversive feature of this principle is that it provides a linguistic device for negotiating between the legalities of urban government and the "illegal" arrangements to which the poor almost always have to resort, whether the illegality in question pertains to structures, living strategies, or access to water, electricity, or anything else that has been successfully siphoned out of the material resources of the city.

Precedent-setting moves practices such as these, along with new techniques for accessing food, health services, police protection, and work opportunities, into a zone of quasi-legal negotiation. By invoking the concept of precedent as enshrined in English common law, the linguistic device shifts the burden for municipal officials and other experts away from a dubious whitewashing of illegal activities to a building on "legitimate" precedents. The linguistic strategy of precedent-setting thus turns the survival tactics and experiments of the poor into sites for policy innovations by the state, the city, donor agencies, and other activist organizations. It is a strategy that moves the poor into the horizon of legality on their own terms. Most important, it invites risk-taking activities by bureaucrats within a discourse of legality, allowing the boundaries of the status quo to be pushed and stretched—it creates a border zone of trial and error, a sort of research and development space within which poor communities, activists, and bureaucrats can explore new designs for partnership.

But the world is not changed through language alone. These key words (and many other linguistic strategies not discussed here) can be positioned as the nervous system of a whole body of broader technical, institutional, and representational practices that have become signatures of the Alliance's politics. Here, I will briefly discuss three vital organizational strategies that illustrate the ways in which technical practices are harnessed to the Alliance's political horizon. They are: self-surveys and enumeration; housing exhibitions; and toilet festivals.

Contemporary scholars, led by Michel Foucault, have drawn attention to the use of censuses and other techniques of enumeration by political regimes from the seventeenth century onward. Foucault and others have indeed observed that the modern state and the idea of a countable population are historical co-productions, premised alike on distinctively modern constructions of governance, territory, and citizenship. Censuses are salient among the techniques identified by Foucault[9] as lying at the heart of modern governmentality. Tied up by their nature with the state (note the etymological link with statistics) and its methods of classification and surveillance, censuses remain essential instruments of every modern state archive. They are highly politicized processes, whose results are usually available only in packaged form and whose procedures are always driven from above, even when many members of the population are enlisted in the actual gathering of data. Given this background, it seems all the more remarkable that, without adherence to any articulated theory of governmentality—or opposition to it—the Alliance has adopted a conscious strategy of self-enumeration and self-surveying. Alliance members are taught a variety of methods of gathering reliable and complete data about households and families in their own communities. Codifying these techniques for ease of use by its members in the form of a series of practical tips, the Alliance has created a revolutionary system that we may well call governmentality from below.

Not only has it placed self-surveying at the heart of its own archive, the Alliance is also keenly aware of the power that this kind of knowledge—and ability—gives it in its dealings with local and central state organizations (as well as with multilateral agencies and other regulatory bodies). The leverage bestowed by such information is particularly acute in places like Mumbai, where a host of local, state-level, and federal entities exist with a mandate to rehabilitate or ameliorate slum life. But none of them knows exactly who the slum dwellers are, where they live, or how they are to be identified. This fact is of central relevance to the politics of knowledge in which the Alliance is perennially engaged. All state-sponsored slum policies have an abstract

---

9   M. Foucault, "Governmentality," in G. Burchell, C. Gordon, and P. Miller, eds., *The Foucault Effect: Studies in Governmentality,* Chicago: University of Chicago Press, 1979.

slum population as their target and no knowledge of its concrete human components. Since these populations are socially, legally, and spatially marginal—invisible citizens, as it were—they are by definition uncounted and uncountable, except in the most general terms.

By rendering them statistically visible to themselves, the Alliance comes into control of a central piece of any actual policy process—the knowledge of exactly which individuals live where, how they make their livelihood, how long they have lived there, and so forth. Given that some of the most crucial pieces of recent legislation affecting slum dwellers in Mumbai tie security of tenure to the date from which occupancy of a piece of land or a structure can be demonstrated, such information collection is vital to any official effort to relocate and rehabilitate slum populations.

At the same time, self-surveys are powerful tools for the practice of democracy internally, since the principal form of evidence used by the Alliance to support slum dwellers' claims to space is the testimony of neighbors, as opposed to forms of documentation such as rent receipts, ration cards, electric meter readings, and other civic insignia of occupancy that can be used by the more securely housed classes in the city. The very absence of these amenities opens the door to radical techniques of mutual identification in the matter of location and legitimacy for slum dwellers. For, as Alliance leaders are the first to admit, the poor are not immune to greed, conflict, and jealousy, and there are always slum families who are prepared to lie or cheat to advance themselves in the context of crisis or new opportunities. Such problems are resolved by informal mechanisms in which the testimony of neighbors is utterly decisive, since the social life of slums is in fact characterized by an almost complete lack of privacy. Here, perpetual social visibility within the community (and invisibility in the eyes of the state) becomes an asset that enables the mechanisms of self-monitoring, self-enumerating, and self-regulation to operate at the nexus of family, land, and dwelling that is the central site of material negotiations in slum life.

To those familiar with Foucault's ideas, this may seem to be a worrisome form of auto-governmentality, a combination of self-surveillance and self-enumeration, truly insidious in its capillary reach. But my own view is that this sort of governmentality from below, in the world of the urban poor, is a kind of counter-governmentality, animated by the social relations of shared poverty, by the excitement of active participation in the politics of knowledge, and by its own openness to correction through other forms of intimate knowledge and spontaneous everyday politics. In short, this is governmentality turned against itself.

Housing exhibitions are the second organized technique through which the structural bias of existing knowledge processes is challenged, even reversed, in the politics of the alliance. Since the materialities of housing—its cost, its durability, its legality, and its design—are of fundamental concern to slum life, it is no surprise that this is an area where grassroots creativity has had radical effects. As in other matters, the general philosophy of state agencies, donors, and even NGOs concerned with slums has been to assume that the design, construction, and financing of houses require the involvement of various experts and knowledge professionals, ranging from engineers and architects to contractors and surveyors. The Alliance has challenged this assumption by a steady effort to appropriate, in a cumulative manner, all the knowledge required to construct new housing for its members. This has involved some extraordinary negotiations in Mumbai, involving private developers and contractors, the formation of legal cooperatives by the poor, innovations in urban law pushed by the Alliance, new types of arrangements in housing finance between banks, donors, and the poor themselves, and direct negotiations over housing materials, costs, and building schedules. In effect, in Mumbai, the Alliance has moved into housing development, and the fruits of this remarkable move are to be seen at three major sites, in Mankhurd, Dharavi, and Ghatkopar. One of these, the Rajiv-Indira Housing Cooperative in Dharavi, is a major building exercise that stands as a decisive demonstration of the Alliance's ability to put the actual families who will occupy these dwellings at the center of a process where credit, design, budgeting, construction, and legality come together. It is difficult to exaggerate the complexity of such negotiations, which pose a challenge even for wealthy developers because of the maze of laws, agencies, and political interests (including those of the criminal underworld) that surrounds any housing enterprise in Mumbai.

Housing exhibitions are a crucial part of this reversal of the standard flows of expert knowledge. The idea of housing exhibitions by and for the poor goes back to 1986 in Mumbai and has since been replicated in many other cities in India and elsewhere in the world. The exhibitions organized by the Alliance and other likeminded groups are an example of the creative hijacking of an upper-class form—historically developed for the display of consumer goods and high-end industrial products—for the purposes of the poor.

Not only have these exhibitions enabled the poor, especially poor women, to discuss and debate designs for housing that suit their own needs, they have also allowed the poor to enter into conversations with various professionals about housing materials, construction costs, and urban services. Through this process, slum dwellers' own ideas of the good life, of adequate space, and of realistic costs were foregrounded, and they began to see that professional housing construction was only a logical extension of their own area of greatest expertise—namely, building adequate housing out of the flimsiest of materials and in the most insecure of circumstances. Poor families were enabled to see that they had always been architects and engineers and could continue to play these roles in the building of more secure housing. In this process, many technical and design innovations were made, and continue to be made. Perhaps more significantly, the exhibitions have been political events bringing together poor families and activists from different cities in order to socialize, share ideas, and simply have fun. State officials also are invited, to cut the ceremonial ribbon and give speeches in which they associate themselves with these grassroots exercises, thus simultaneously gaining points for hobnobbing with "the people" while giving poor families in the locality some legitimacy in the eyes of their neighbors, civic authorities, and themselves.

As with other key practices of the Alliance, housing exhibitions are deep exercises in subverting the existing class cultures of India. By performing their competencies in public, by addressing an audience of their peers and of representatives of the state, other NGOs, and sometimes foreign funders, the poor families involved enter a space of public sociality, official recognition, and technical legitimation. And they do so with their own creativity as the main exhibit. Thus technical and cultural capital are generated collaboratively by these events, creating leverage for further guerrilla exercises in capturing civic space and areas of the public sphere hitherto denied them. At work here is a politics of visibility that inverts the harmful default condition of civic invisibility that characterizes the urban poor.

Running through all these activities is a spirit of transgression and bawdiness expressed through body language, speech styles, and public address. The men and women of the Alliance are involved in constant banter with one another and even with the official world (although with some care for context). Nowhere is this carnivalesque spirit displayed more clearly than in the toilet festivals (*sandas mela*) organized by the Alliance, which enact what we may call the politics of shit.

Human waste management, as it is euphemistically termed in policy circles, is perhaps the key issue where every problem of the urban poor arrives at a single point of extrusion, so to speak. Given the abysmal housing, often with almost no privacy, that most urban slum dwellers endure, shitting in public is a serious humiliation for adults. Children are indifferent up to a certain age, but no adult, male or female, enjoys shitting in broad daylight in public view. In rural India, women go to the fields to defecate while it is still dark; men may go later, but nevertheless with some measure of protection from the eyes of the public (with the exception of the railway passengers, inured to the sight of the squatting bodies in the fields, whose attitude is reciprocated). But the fact is that rural shitting is managed through a completely different economy of space, water, visibility, and custom from that prevailing in cities, where the problem is much more serious.

Shitting in the absence of good sewerage systems, ventilation, and running water—all of which, by definition, slums lack—is not only humiliating, it also enables the conditions under which waterborne diseases take hold and thus is potentially life-threatening. One macabre joke among Mumbai's urban poor is that they are the only ones in the city who cannot afford to get diarrhea. Lines at the few existing public toilets are often so long that the wait is an hour or more, and of course medical facilities for stemming the condition are also hard to find. In short, shitting and its management are a central issue of slum life. Living in an ecology of fecal odors, piles, and channels, where cooking water, washing water, and shit-bearing water are not carefully segregated, adds material health risks to the symbolic risks incurred by shitting in public view.

The toilet festivals organized by the Alliance in many cities of India are a brilliant effort to resituate this private act of humiliation and suffering as the scene of technical innovation, collective celebration, and carnivalesque play with officials from the state, the World Bank, and middle-class officialdom in general. The toilet festivals feature the exhibition and inauguration not of models, but of functioning public toilets designed by and for the poor, incorporating complex systems of collective payment and maintenance with optimal conditions of safety and cleanliness. These facilities are currently small scale and have not yet been built in anything like the large numbers required for India's slum populations. But they represent another performance of competence and innovation in which the politics of shit is (to mix metaphors) turned on its head, and humiliation and victimization are transformed into exercises in technical initiative and self-dignification.

This is nothing less than a politics of recognition[10] from below. When a World Bank official has to examine the virtues of a public toilet and discuss the merits of this form of shit management with the shitters themselves, the condition of poverty moves from abjection to subjectivation. The politics of shit—as Gandhi showed in his own efforts to liberate the lowest castes, whom he called Harijans, from the task of hauling upper-caste ordure—presents a node at which concerns of the human body, dignity, and technology meet, a nexus the poor are now redefining with the help of movements like the Alliance. In India, where distance from one's own excrement can be seen as the virtual marker of class distinction, the poor, for too long having lived literally in their own shit, are finding ways to place some distance between their waste and themselves. The toilet exhibitions are a transgressive display of this fecal politics, itself a critical material feature of deep democracy.

In June 2001, at a major meeting held at the United Nations to mark the five years that had passed since the 1996 Conference on Human Settlements in Istanbul, the Alliance and its international partners built a model house as well as a model children's toilet in the lobby of the main UN building. The

---

10   C. Taylor, *Multiculturalism and the Politics of Recognition: An Essay*, Princeton: Princeton University Press, 1992.

models—which were erected only after considerable internal debate within the Shack/Slum Dwellers International (SDI) and official resistance at the UN—were visited by Secretary-General Kofi Annan in a festive atmosphere that left an indelible impression on the officials of the UN and other NGOs who were present. Annan was surrounded by poor women from India and South Africa who sang and danced as he walked through the model house and toilet that had been placed in the heart of his own bureaucratic empire. It was a magical moment, full of possibilities for the Alliance, and for the secretary-general, as they engage jointly with the politics of global poverty. This event is discussed in more detail in chapters 9 and 10. Housing exhibitions and toilets, too, can be built, moved, refabricated, and deployed anywhere, thus sending the message that no space is too grand—or too humble—for the spatial imagination of the poor.

These organized practices sustain one another. Self-surveys form the basis of claims to new housing and justify its exhibition; model housing built without due attention to toilets and fecal management makes no sense. Each of these methods uses the knowledge of the poor to leverage expert knowledge, redeems humiliation through a politics of recognition, and enables the deepening of democracy among the poor themselves. And each of them adds energy and purpose to the others. They enact public dramas in which the moral directives to federate, to save, and to set precedents are made material, refined, and revalidated. In this way, key words and deeds shape one another, permitting some leveling of the field of knowledge, turning sites of shame into dramas of inclusion, and allowing the poor to work their way into the public sphere and visible citizenship without resort to open confrontation or public violence.

THE INTERNATIONAL HORIZON

Transnational advocacy networks and associations of grassroots NGOs are in the process of internationalizing themselves, thus creating networks of globalization from below. Such networks have mobilized most recently in Seattle, Prague, Göteborg, and Washington, D.C., but they have been visible for some time in global struggles over gender issues, the environment, human rights, child labor, and the rights of indigenous cultures. More recently, there has been a renewed effort to link grassroots activists in such diverse areas as violence against women, the rights of refugees and immigrants, the employment of sweatshop labor by multinational corporations, indigenous peoples' claims to intellectual property, the production and consumption of popular media, mediation between combatants in civil conflicts, and many other issues. The underlying question for many of these movements is: How can they organize transnationally without sacrificing their local projects? When they do build transnational networks, what are their greatest assets and their greatest handicaps? At a deeper political level, can the mobility of capital and new information technologies be contained by, and made accountable to, the ethos and purpose of local democratic projects? Put another way, can there be a new design for global governance that mediates the speed of capital, the power of states, and the profoundly local nature of actually existing democracies?

These questions go beyond the scope of this chapter, and a detailed analysis of the efforts to globalize from below of this activist network, and others like it, must be left for another occasion. But a brief account of this global context is certainly in order. For more than a decade the Alliance in Mumbai has been an active part of a transnational network concerned with "horizontal learning," sharing, and exchanging. Given official form as the Shack/Slum Dwellers International, or SDI, in 1996, the network includes federations in fourteen countries on four continents. The process that led to this formalization goes back to the mid 1980s. Links among federations of the poor in South Africa, India, and Thailand appear to have been the most vital in the gradual building of these grassroots exchanges and, to a considerable extent, still are. Key to these exchanges are visits by groups of slum or shack dwellers to one another's settlements in other countries to share in ongoing local projects, give and receive advice and reactions, share in work and life experiences, and exchange tactics and plans. The mode of exchange is based on a model of seeing and hearing rather than of teaching and learning; of sharing experiences and knowledge rather than seeking to impose standard practices, with key words being *exposure*, *exploration*, and *options*. By now, a large body of practical wisdom has accrued about how and when these exchanges work best, and this knowledge is constantly being refined. Visits by small groups from one city to another, either within the same or to another region, usually involve immediate immersion in the ongoing projects of the host community. These range from scavenging in the Philippines and sewer digging in Pakistan to women's savings activities in South Africa and housing exhibitions in India.

These horizontal exchanges now function at four levels. First, they provide a circulatory counterpart to the building of deep democracies locally. By visiting and hosting other activists concerned with similar problems, communities gain a comparative perspective and provide a measure of legitimation for external efforts. Thus, activist leaders struggling for recognition and space in their own localities may find themselves able to gain state and media attention for their local struggles in other countries and towns, where their presence as visitors carries a certain cachet. The fact that they are visiting as members of some sort of international federation further sharpens this image. In fact, local politicians feel less threatened by visitors than by their own activists and sometimes open themselves to new ideas because they come from outside.

Second, the horizontal visits arranged by the federations increasingly carry the imprimatur of powerful international organizations and funders such as the

World Bank, state development ministries, and private charities from the Neth-erlands, England, the United States, and Germany, and increasingly involve political and philanthropic actors from other countries as well. These visits, designed and organized by the poor in their own communities and public spaces, become signs to local politicians that the poor themselves have cosmo-politan links—a factor that increases their prestige in local political negotiations.

Third, the occasions that these exchanges provide for face-to-face meetings between key leaders in, for example, Mumbai, Cape Town, and Bangkok actu-ally allow them to progress rapidly in making more long-term strategic plans for funding, capacity building, and what they call *scaling up*, which is now perhaps their central aim. That is, having mastered how to do certain things on a small scale, they are eager to expand onto a broader canvas, seeking collective ways of making a dent in the vast range of problems shared by slum dwellers in different cities. In a parallel movement, they are also exploring ways of *speeding up*, by which they mean shortening the times involved in putting strategies into practice in different national and urban locations.

There is some evidence that speeding up through horizontal learning is somewhat easier than scaling up. In support of the latter goal, the core SDI leadership is working on ways to build a transnational funding mechanism that will reduce the federations' dependence on existing multilateral and private sources, putting even long-term funding in the hands of the SDI so as to free its members further from the agendas of project planners, donors, states, and other actors, whose aims can never be quite the same as those of the urban poor. Elements of such a mechanism exist among the South African and Thai members of the SDI, but the structure is yet to be realized on a fully global scale. That will require the current leadership of SDI to proceed with a demanding mixture of political cooperation, willingness to negotiate, and stubbornness of vision in their dialogues with the major funders of the battle against urban poverty worldwide. The objective of creating a worldwide fund controlled by a pro-poor activist network is the logical extension of a politics of patience combined with a politics of visibility and self-empowerment. It is directly pitched against the politics of charity, training, and projectization long recog-nized as the standard solution. As such, it represents a formidable wager on the capacities of the poor to create large-scale, high-speed, reliable mechanisms for the change of conditions that affect them globally. The proposal for a coordi-nated funding mechanism inaugurates a new vision for equalizing material resources and knowledge at one stroke. The self-organization of this network is very much in process and constitutes an ongoing experiment in globalization from below and in deep democracy.

The fourth, and most important, level at which the traffic among local and national units functions within the Shack/Slum Dwellers International is that of the circulation of internal critical debate. When members of the SDI meet in one another's localities (as well as on other occasions, such as meetings in London, New York, or the Hague), they have the occasion to raise hard questions about inclusion, power, hierarchy, and political risk or naïveté in their host's local and regional organizations. This is because their role as outsiders allows for frank questions, based on real or rhetorical ignorance—questions that would frequently be regarded as unacceptable coming from closer quarters.

Who handles the money? Why are there not more women at the meeting? Why are you being so nice to the city officials who oppress you? How do you deal with defaulters on small loans? Who is doing the real work? Who is getting the perks of foreign travel? Why are we staying in one kind of hotel and you in another? Why are some poor people in your city for you and others against you? Why did your savings group start falling apart? Are you happy with this or that leader? Is someone getting too big for his boots? Are we beginning to take up partnerships that might fail us in the long run? When we agree to a global agenda, which national partner is really setting it? How far should we go in trusting each other's intuitions about partners, strategies, and priorities?

These are some of the tough questions that are asked by friendly but skeptical visitors, and usually answered frankly by the local hosts. And when the answers are weak or unsatisfying, they continue to reverberate in the locality, long after the visitors have returned to their home communities. This critical exchange is a long-term asset, a vital part of globalization from below. The visits—and the e-mails that sustain them in the interim—incorporate a crucial dimension through which the challenge of facing internal criticism can be mediated: distance. The global network of poor communities turns out to be, among other things, a constant source of critical questions about theory and practice, a flow of irritating queries, doubts, and pauses. But coming from a distance, they sound less harsh than the same queries when they come from local opponents. At the same time, coming from communities equally poor, their moral urgency cannot be ignored.

It is this last consideration that now allows us to return to the relations among risk, creativity, and depth in the democratic experiments of the Alliance and its global network, the SDI. The Alliance and the transnational network of which it is a part belong to a group of nongovernmental actors that have decided to opt for various sorts of partnerships with other, more powerful actors—including the state, in its various levels and incarnations—to achieve its goals: to gain secure housing and urban infrastructure for the urban poor, in Mumbai, in other parts of India, and beyond. In opting for the politics of partnership, such movements consciously undertake certain risks. One is the risk that their partners may not hold even some moral goals in common with them. Another is that the hard-won mobilization of certain groups of the urban poor may not be best invested as political capital in partnership arrangements, as opposed to confrontation or violence.

And there is an even larger gamble involved in this strategy. This is the gamble that the official world of multilateral agencies, Northern funders, and Southern governments can be persuaded that the poor are the best drivers of shared solutions to the problems of poverty. What is at stake here is all the energy that has been invested in setting precedents for partnership at all levels, from the ward to the world. The hoped-for pay-off is that, once mobilized and empowered by such partnerships, the poor themselves will prove more capable than the usual candidates—the market, the state, or the world of development funding—of scaling up and speeding up their own disappearance as a global category. In the end, this is a political wager on the relationship between the circulation of knowledge and material equalization, and about the best ways to accelerate it.

In making this wager, activist groups like the Alliance in Mumbai and its global counterparts are also striving to redefine what governance and governmentality can mean. They approach their partners on an ad hoc basis, taking advantage in particular of the dispersed nature of the state as an apparatus of local, regional, and national bodies to advance their long-term aims and form multilateral relationships. Moreover, in a country like India, where poverty reduction is a directive principle of the national constitution and the tradition of social reform and public service is woven into nationalism itself, the Alliance can play the politics of conscience to considerable effect. But even then, it hedges its bets through practices of building on, sharing, and multiplying knowledge—strategic practices that increase its hold on public resources.

CONCLUSION: DEEP DEMOCRACY

One of the many paradoxes of democracy is that it is organized to function within the boundaries of the nation-state—through such organs as legislatures, judiciaries, and elected governments—to realize one or another image of the common good or general will. Yet its values make sense only when they are conceived and deployed universally, which is to say, when they are global in reach. Thus, the institutions of democracy and its cardinal values rest on an antinomy. In the era of globalization, this contradiction rises to the surface as the porousness of national boundaries becomes apparent and the monopoly of national governments over global governance becomes increasingly embattled.

Efforts to enact or revive democratic principles have generally taken two forms in the period since 1970, which many agree marks the beginning of globalization (or of the current era of globalization, for those who wish to write globalization into the whole of human history). One form is to take advantage of the speed of communications and the sweep of global markets to force national governments to recognize universal democratic principles within their own jurisdictions. Much of the politics of human rights takes this form. The second form, more fluid and quixotic, is the sort that I have described here. It constitutes an effort to institute what we may call "democracy without borders," after the analogy of international class solidarity as conceived by the visionaries of world socialism in its heyday. This effort is what I seek to theorize in terms of deep democracy.

In terms of its semantics, *deep democracy* suggests roots, anchors, intimacy, proximity, and locality. And these are important associations. Much of this chapter has been taken up with values and strategies that have just this quality. They are about such traditional democratic desiderata as inclusion, participation, transparency, and accountability, as articulated within an activist formation. But I want to suggest that the lateral reach of such movements— their efforts to build international networks or coalitions of some durability with their counterparts across national boundaries—is also a part of their "depth."

This lateral or horizontal dimension, which I have touched upon in terms of the activities of the Shack/Slum Dwellers International, seeks direct collaborations and exchanges among poor communities based on the "will to federate." But what gives this cross-national politics its depth is not just its circulatory logic of spreading ideas of savings, housing, citizenship, and participation "without borders" and outside the direct reach of state or market regimes. Depth is also to be located in the fact that, where successful, the spread of this model produces poor communities able to engage in partnerships with more powerful agencies—urban, regional, national, and multilateral—that purport to be concerned with poverty and citizenship. In this second sense, what these horizontal movements produce is a series of *stronger* community-based partners for institutional agencies charged with realizing inclusive democracy and poverty reduction. This in turn increases the capability of these communities to perform more powerfully as instruments of deep democracy in the local context. The cycles of transactions—both vertical (local/national) and horizontal (transnational/global)—are enriched by the process of criticism by members of one federated community, in the context of exchange and learning, about the internal democracy of another. Thus, internal criticism and debate, horizontal exchange and learning, and vertical collaborations and partnerships with more powerful persons and organizations together form a mutually sustaining cycle of processes. This is where depth and laterality become joint circuits along which pro-poor strategies can flow.

This form of deep democracy, the vertical fulcrum of a democracy without borders, cannot be assumed to be automatic, easy, or immune to setbacks. Like all serious exercises in democratic practice, it is not automatically reproductive. It has particular conditions of possibility and conditions under which it grows weak or corrupt. The study of these conditions—which include such contingencies as leadership, morale, flexibility, and material enablement—requires many more case studies of specific movements and organizations. For those concerned with poverty and citizenship, we can begin by recalling that one crucial condition of possibility for deep democracy is the ability to meet emergency with patience.

CHAPTER NINE

The Capacity to Aspire: Culture and the Terms of Recognition

THE ARGUMENT

This chapter seeks to provide a new approach to the question: why does culture matter? Or let us revise the question and ask why culture matters for development and for the reduction of poverty. This both narrows and deepens the question. The answer is that it is in culture that ideas of the future, as much as of those about the past, are embedded and nurtured. Thus, in strengthening the capacity to aspire, conceived as a cultural capacity, especially among the poor, the future-oriented logic of development could find a natural ally, and the poor could find the resources required to contest and alter the conditions of their own poverty. This argument runs against the grain of many deep-seated images of the opposition of culture to economy. But it offers a new foundation on which policymakers can base answers to two basic questions: why is culture a capacity (worth building and strengthening), and what are the concrete ways in which it can be strengthened?

GETTING PAST DEFINITIONS

We do not need one more omnibus definition of culture any more than we need one of the market. In both cases, the textbooks have rung the changes over the long century in which anthropology and economics have taken formal shape as academic disciplines. And not only have the definition mongers had ample say, but there has been real refinement and academic progress on both sides. Today's definitions are both more modest and more helpful. Others are better equipped to tell the story of what we really ought to mean when we speak of markets. Here I address the cultural side of the equation.

General definitions of culture rightly cover a lot of ground, ranging from general ideas about human creativity and values, to matters of collective identity and social organization, matters of cultural integrity and property, and matters of heritage, monuments, and expressions. The intuition behind this capacious net is that what it gains in scope, it loses in edge. In this chapter, I do not deny the broad humanistic implications of cultural form, freedom, and expression. But I focus on just one dimension of culture—its orientation to the future—that is almost never explicitly discussed. Making this dimension explicit could have radical implications for poverty and development.

In taking this approach to culture, we run against some deeply held counter-conceptions. For more than a century, culture has been viewed as a matter of one or other kind of pastness—the keywords here are habit, custom, heritage, tradition. On the other hand, development is always seen in terms of the future—plans, hopes, goals, targets. This opposition is an artifact of our definitions and has been crippling. On the anthropological side, in spite of many important technical moves in the understanding of culture, the future remains a stranger to most anthropological models of culture. By default, and also for independent reasons, economics has become the science of the future, and when human beings are seen as having a future, the keywords such as wants, needs, expectations, calculations, have become hardwired into the discourse of economics. In a word, the cultural actor is a person of and from the past, and the economic actor a person of the future. Thus, from the start, culture is opposed to development, as tradition is opposed to newness, and habit to calculation. It is hardly a surprise that nine out of ten treatises on development treat culture as a worry or a drag on the forward momentum of planned economic change.

It is customary for anthropologists to pin the blame for this state of affairs on economists and their unwillingness to broaden their views of economic action and motivation and to take culture into account. And economics is hardly blameless, in its growing preoccupation with models of such abstraction and parsimony that they can hardly take most real-world economics on board, much less the matter of culture, which simply becomes the biggest tenant in the black box of aggregate rationality. But anthropologists need to do better by their own core concept. And this is where the question of the future comes in.

In fact, most approaches to culture do not ignore the future. But they smuggle it in indirectly, when they speak of norms, beliefs, and values as being central to cultures, conceived as specific and multiple designs for social life. But by not elaborating the implications of norms for futurity as a cultural capacity, these definitions tend to allow the sense of culture as pastness to dominate. Even the most interesting recent attempts, notably associated with the name of Pierre Bourdieu,[1] to bring practice, strategy, calculation, and a strong agonistic dimension to cultural action have been attacked for being too structuralist (that is, too formal and static) on the one hand, and too economistic on the other. And what is sometimes called "practice" theory in anthropology does not directly take up the matter of how collective horizons are shaped and of how they constitute the basis for collective aspirations that may be regarded as cultural.

---

1   P. Bourdieu, *Outline of a Theory of Practice*, R. Nice, trans., Cambridge: Cambridge University Press, 1977.

There have been a few key developments in the anthropological debate over culture, which are vital building blocks for the central concern of this chapter. The first is the insight, incubated in structural linguistics as early as Saussure, that cultural coherence is not a matter of individual items but of their relationships, and the related insight that these relations are systematic and generative. Even those anthropologists who are deeply unsympathetic to Lévi-Strauss and anything that smacks of linguistic analogy in the study of culture now assume that the elements of a cultural system make sense only in relation to one another, and that these systematic relations are somehow similar to those which make languages miraculously orderly and productive. The second important development in cultural theory is the idea that dissensus of some sort is part and parcel of culture and that a shared culture is no more a guarantee of complete consensus than a shared platform in the democratic convention. Earlier in the history of the discipline, this incomplete sharing was studied as the central issue in studies of children and of socialization (in anthropology, of "enculturation"), and was based on the obvious fact everywhere that children become culture bearers through specific forms of education and discipline. This insight became deepened and extended through work on gender, politics, and resistance over the last three decades, notably through the work of scholars such as John and Jean Comaroff, James Scott, Sherry Ortner, and a host of others, now so numerous as to be invisible.[2] The third important development in anthropological understandings of culture is the recognition that the boundaries of cultural systems are leaky, and that traffic and osmosis are the norm, not the exception. This strand of thought now underwrites the work of some of the key theorists of the cultural dimensions of globalization,[3] who foreground mixture, heterogeneity, diversity, heterogeneity, and plurality as critical features of culture in the era of globalization. Their work reminds us that no culture, past or present, is an island unto itself, except in the imagination of the observer. Cultures are and always have been interactive to some degree.

Of course, each of these developments in anthropology is accompanied by a host of footnotes, debates, and ongoing litigations (as must be the case in any serious academic discipline). Still, no serious contemporary understanding of culture can ignore these three key dimensions: relationality (between norms,

2   J. Comaroff and J. Comaroff, *Of Revelation and Revolution,* Chicago: University of Chicago Press, 1991; J. C. Scott, *Domination and the Arts of Resistance: Hidden Transcripts,* New Haven: Yale University Press, 1990; S. B. Ortner, "Resistance and the Problem of Ethnographic Refusal," *Comparative Studies in Society and History,* 1995, 37(1), 173–93.

3   U. Beck, *What is Globalization?* London: Blackwell, 2000; U. Hannerz, *Cultural Complexity: Studies in the Social Organization of Meaning,* New York: Columbia University Press, 1992; *Transnational Connections: Culture, People, Places,* London: Routledge, 1996; A. Mbembe, *On the Postcolony: Studies on the History of Society and Culture,* Berkeley: University of California Press, 2001; S. Sassen, *Globalization and its Discontents,* New York: New Press, 1998; *Guests and Aliens,* New York: New Press, 1999.

values, beliefs, etc.); dissensus within some framework of consensus (especially in regard to the marginal, the poor, gender relations, and power relations more generally); and weak boundaries (perennially visible in processes of migration, trade, and warfare now writ large in globalizing cultural traffic).

This chapter builds on and returns to these important developments. They are of direct relevance to the recovery of the future as a cultural capacity. In making this recovery, we will also need to recall some of these wider developments within anthropology. But my main concern here is with the implications of these moves for current debates about development and poverty reduction.

BRINGING THE FUTURE BACK IN

The effort to recover, highlight, and foreground the place of the future in our understandings of culture is not a matter where anthropology has to invent the wheel. Allies for this effort can be found in a variety of fields and disciplines, ranging from political theory and moral philosophy to welfare economics and human rights debates. My own thinking on this project builds on and is in dialogue with three important sets of ideas that come from outside anthropology, and others from within it. These ideas inform the argument about the capacity to aspire in this chapter and also those of the last part of this book, especially of its final chapter, and are an important inspiration of the title of this book.

Outside anthropology, the effort to strengthen the idea of aspiration as a cultural capacity can build on Charles Taylor's path-breaking concept of "recognition," his key contribution to the debate on the ethical foundations of multiculturalism.[4] In this work, Taylor showed that there is such a thing as a "politics of recognition," in virtue of which there was an ethical obligation to extend a sort of moral cognizance to persons who shared worldviews deeply different from our own. This was an important move, which gives the idea of tolerance some political teeth, makes intercultural understanding an obligation, not an option, and recognizes the independent value of dignity in cross-cultural transactions apart from issues of redistribution. The challenge today, as many scholars have noted, is how to bring the politics of dignity and the politics of poverty into a single framework. Put another way, the issue is whether cultural recognition can be extended so as to enhance redistribution.[5]

I also take inspiration from Albert Hirschman's now classic work[6] on the

---

4   C. Taylor, *Multiculturalism and the Politics of Recognition: An Essay*, Princeton: Princeton University Press, 1992.

5   See especially N. Fraser and A. Honneth, *Redistribution or Recognition?: A Political-Philosophical Exchange*, London: Verso, 2003; N. Fraser, *Redistribution, Recognition and Participation: Toward an Integrated Conception of Justice*, World Culture Report 2, Paris: UNESCO Publications, 2001.

6   A. O. Hirschman, *Exit, Voice and Loyalty: Responses to Decline in Firms, Organizations, and States*, Cambridge, MA: Harvard University Press, 1970.

relations between different forms of collective identification and satisfaction, which enabled us to see the general applicability of the ideas of "loyalty," "exit," and "voice," terms that Hirschman used to cover a wide range of possible responses that human beings have to decline in firms, organizations, and states. In Hirschman's terms, I would suggest that we have tended to see cultural affiliations almost entirely in terms of loyalty (total attachment) but have paid little attention to exit and voice. Voice is a critical matter for my purposes since it engages the question of dissensus. Even more than the idea of exit, voice is vital to any engagement with the poor (and thus with poverty), since one of their gravest lacks is the lack of resources with which to give "voice," that is, to express their views and get results directed at their own welfare in the political debates that surround wealth and welfare in all societies. So, a way to put my central question in Hirschman's terms would be: how can we strengthen the capability of the poor to have and to cultivate "voice," since exit is not a desirable solution for the world's poor and loyalty is clearly no longer generally clear-cut?

My approach also responds to Amartya Sen, who has placed us all in his debt through a series of efforts to argue for the place of values in economic analysis and in the politics of welfare and well-being. Through his earlier work on social values and development,[7] to his more recent work on social welfare (loosely characterized as the "capabilities" approach)[8] and on freedom,[9] Sen has made major and overlapping arguments for placing matters of freedom, dignity, and moral well-being at the heart of welfare and its economics. This approach has many implications and applications, but for my purposes, it highlights the need for a parallel internal opening up in how to understand culture, so that Sen's radical expansion of the idea of welfare can find its strongest cultural counterpoint. In this chapter, I am partly concerned to bring aspiration in as a strong feature of cultural capacity, as a step in creating a more robust dialogue between "capacity" and "capability," the latter in Sen's terms. In more general terms, Sen's work is a major invitation to anthropology to widen its conceptions of how human beings engage their own futures.

Within anthropology, in addition to the basic developments I addressed already, I regard this chapter as being in a dialogue with two key scholars. The first, Mary Douglas, in her work on cosmology,[10] and later on commodities and budgets, and later still on risk and nature,[11] has repeatedly argued for seeing ordinary people as operating through cultural designs for anticipation and risk

7   A. K. Sen, *Resources, Values and Development*, Oxford: Blackwell, 1984.
8   A. K. Sen, *Commodities and Capabilities*, Amsterdam: Elsevier, 1985.
9   A. K. Sen, *Development as Freedom*, New York: Knopf, 1999.
10   M. Douglas, *Natural Symbols: Explorations in Cosmology*, New York: Pantheon Books, 1970.
11   M. Douglas and A. B. Wildavsky, *Risk and Culture: An Essay on the Selection of Technical and Environmental Dangers*, Berkeley: University of California Press, 1983.

reduction. This is a line of thought that helps us to investigate the broader problem of aspiration in a systematic way, with due attention to the internal relations of cosmology and calculation among poorer people, such as those members of the English working classes studied by Douglas in some of her best work on consumption.[12]

Finally, James Fernandez has had a long-term interest in the problem of how cultural consensus is produced. In this exercise, he has reminded us that even in the most apparently "traditional" cultures, such as the Fang of West Africa, about whom Fernandez has written extensively, we cannot take consensus for granted. His second major contribution is in showing that through the specific operations of various forms of verbal and material ritual, through "performances" and metaphors arranged and enacted in specific ways, real groups actually produce the kinds of consensus on first principles that they may appear to take simply for granted.[13] This work opens the ground for me, in my own examinations of activism among the poor in India and elsewhere, to note that certain uses of words and arrangements of action that we may call cultural may be especially strategic sites for the production of consensus. This is a critical matter for anyone concerned with helping the poor to help themselves, or in our current jargon, to "empower" the poor. With Fernandez, we can ask how the poor may be helped to produce those forms of cultural consensus that may best advance their own collective long-term interests in matters of wealth, equality, and dignity.

I turn now to asking why such a revitalized tool kit is called for to make real progress on the relationship between culture, poverty, and development. What exactly is the problem?

THE CAPACITY TO ASPIRE

Poverty is many things, all of them bad. It is material deprivation and desperation. It is lack of security and dignity. It is exposure to risk and high costs for thin comforts. It is inequality materialized. It diminishes its victims. It is also the situation of far too many people in the world, even if the relative number of those who are escaping the worst forms of poverty is also increasing. The number of the world's poor, their destitution, and their desperation now seem overwhelming by most measures.

The poor are not just the human bearers of the condition of poverty. They are a social group, partly defined by official measures but also conscious of

---

12   M. Douglas and B. Isherwood, *The World of Goods: Towards an Anthropology of Consumption*, New York: Basic, 1979.

13   J. Fernandez, "Symbolic Consensus in a Fang Reformative Cult," *American Anthropologist*, 1965, 67(4), 902–27; *Persuasions and Performances: The Play of Tropes in Culture*, Bloomington: Indiana University Press, 1986.

themselves as a group, in the real languages of many societies. Just as ordinary human beings have learned to think of themselves as "people" and even as "the people" in most human societies, in the wake of the democratic revolution of the last three centuries, poor people increasingly see themselves as a group, in their own societies and also across these societies. There may not be anything that can usefully be called a "culture of poverty" (anthropologists have rightly ceased to use this conceptualization), but the poor certainly have understandings of themselves and the world that have cultural dimensions and expressions. These may not be easy to identify, since they are not neatly nested with shared national or regional cultures, and often cross local and national lines. Also, they may be differently articulated by men and women, the poorest and the merely poor, the employed and the unemployed, the disabled and the able-bodied, the more politically conscious and the less mobilized. But it is never hard to identify threads and themes in the worldviews of the poor. These are strikingly concrete and local in expression but also impressively general in their reach. The multi-volume World Bank–sponsored study of the "Voices of the Poor" is a major archive of these threads and themes.[14]

This archive and other close observations of poor populations in different parts of the world reveal a number of important things about culture and poverty. The first is that poor people have a deeply ambivalent relationship to the dominant norms of the societies in which they live. Even when they are not obviously hostile to these norms, they often show forms of irony, distance, and cynicism about these norms. This sense of irony, which allows the poor to maintain some dignity in the worst conditions of oppression and inequality, is one side of their involvement in the dominant cultural norms. The other side is compliance, not mere surface compliance but fairly deep moral attachment to norms and beliefs that directly support their own degradation. Thus, many untouchables in India comply with the degrading exclusionary rules and practices of caste because they subscribe in some way to the larger order of norms and metaphysical propositions which dictate their compliance: these include ideas about fate, rebirth, caste duty, and sacred social hierarchies. Thus the poor are neither simple dupes nor secret revolutionaries. They are survivors. And what they often seek strategically (even without a theory to dress it up) is to optimize the terms of trade between recognition and redistribution in their immediate local lives. Their ideas about such optimization may not be perfect, but do we have better optima to offer to them?

I refer to this ambivalence among the poor (and by extension the excluded, the disadvantaged, and the marginal groups in society more generally) about

---

14 D. Narayan, R. Chambers, M. K. Shah, and P. Petesch, *Voices of the Poor: Crying Out for Change*, New York: Published for the World Bank by Oxford University Press, 2001; D. Narayan, R. Patel, K. Schafft, A. Rademacher, and S. Koch-Schulte, *Voices of the Poor: Can Anyone Hear Us?* New York: Published for the World Bank by Oxford University Press, 2001.

the cultural worlds in which they exist in terms of the idea of the terms of recognition (building on Taylor's ideas). In speaking about the terms of recognition (by analogy with the terms of trade, or the terms of engagement), I mean to highlight the conditions and constraints under which the poor negotiate with the very norms that frame their social lives. I propose that poverty is partly a matter of operating with extremely weak resources where the terms of recognition are concerned. More concretely, the poor are frequently in a position where they are encouraged to subscribe to norms whose social effect is to further diminish their dignity, exacerbate their inequality, and deepen their lack of access to material goods and services. In the Indian case, these norms take a variety of forms: some have to do with fate, luck, and rebirth; others have to do with the glorification of asceticism and other forms of material deprivation; yet others connect social deference to deference to divinity; yet others reduce major metaphysical assumptions to simple and rigid rules of etiquette that promise freedom from reprisal. When I refer to operating under adverse terms of recognition, I mean that in recognizing those who are wealthy, the poor permit the existing and corrupt standing of local and national elites to be further bolstered and reproduced. But when they are recognized (in the cultural sense), it is usually as an abstract political category, divorced of real persons (Indira Gandhi's famous slogan *garibi hatao*—remove poverty—and many other populist slogans have this quality). Or their poverty is perversely recognized as a sign of some sort of worldly disorder that promises, by inversion, its own long-term rectification. The poor are recognized, but in ways that ensure minimum change in the terms of redistribution. So, to the extent that poverty is indexed by weak terms of recognition for the poor, intervention to positively affect these terms is a crucial priority.

In other terms, returning to Hirschman, we need to strengthen the capacity of the poor to exercise "voice," to debate, contest, and oppose vital directions for collective social life as they wish, and not only because this is virtually a definition of inclusion and participation in any democracy. There is a stronger reason for strengthening the capacity for voice among the poor: it is the only way in which the poor might find locally plausible ways to alter what I am calling the terms of recognition in any particular cultural regime. Here I treat voice as a cultural capacity, not just as a generalized and universal democratic virtue, because for voice to take effect, it must engage social, political, and economic issues in terms of ideologies, doctrines, and norms that are widely shared and credible, even by the rich and powerful. Furthermore, voice must be expressed in terms of actions and performances that have local cultural force. Here, Gandhi's life, his fasting, his abstinence, his bodily comportment, his ascetical style, his crypto-Hindu use of non-violence and of peaceful resistance, were all tremendously successful because they mobilized a local palette of performances and precursors. Likewise, as the poor seek to strengthen their voices as a cultural capacity, they will need to find those levers of metaphor, rhetoric, organization, and public performance that will work best in their cultural worlds. And when they do work, as we have seen with various movements in the past, they change the terms of recognition, indeed the cultural framework itself. So, there is no shortcut to empowerment. It has to take some local cultural form to have resonance, mobilize adherents, and capture the public space of debate. And this is true in the efforts that the poor make to mobilize themselves (internally) and in their efforts to change the dynamics of consensus in their larger social worlds.

The complex relationship of the poor and the marginalized to the cultural regimes within which they function is clearer still when we consider a specific cultural capacity, the capacity to aspire. I have already indicated that this is a weak feature of most approaches to cultural processes and frequently remains obscure. This obscurity has been especially costly for the poor, and in regard to development more generally.

Aspirations certainly have something to do with wants, preferences, choices, and calculations. And because these factors have been assigned to the discipline of economics, to the domain of the market, and to the level of the individual actor (all approximate characterizations), they have been largely invisible in the study of culture.

To repatriate them into the domain of the culture, we need to begin by noting that aspirations form parts of wider ethical and metaphysical ideas that derive from larger cultural norms. Aspirations are never simply individual (as the language of wants and choices inclines us to think). They are always formed in interaction and in the thick of social life. As far back as Émile Durkheim and George Herbert Mead, we have learned that there is no self outside a social frame, setting, and mirror. Could it be otherwise for aspirations? And aspirations about the good life, about health and happiness, exist in all societies. Yet a Buddhist picture of the good life lies at some distance from an Islamic one. Equally, a poor Tamil peasant woman's view of the good life may be as distant from that of a cosmopolitan woman from Delhi, as from that of an equally poor woman from Tanzania. But in every case, aspirations to the good life are part of some sort of system of ideas (remember relationality as an aspect of cultural worlds) that locates them in a larger map of local ideas and beliefs about: life and death, the nature of worldly possessions, the significance of material assets over social relations, the relative illusion of social permanence for a society, the value of peace or warfare. At the same time, aspirations to the good life tend to quickly dissolve into more densely local ideas about marriage, work, leisure, convenience, respectability, friendship, health, and virtue. More narrowly still, these intermediate norms often stay beneath the surface and emerge only as specific wants and choices: for this piece of land or that, for that marriage connection or another one, for this job in the bureaucracy as opposed to that job overseas, for this pair of shoes over that pair of trousers. This last, most immediate and visible inventory of wants has often led students of consumption and of poverty to lose sight of the intermediate and higher-order normative contexts within which these wants are gestated and brought into view. And thus decontextualized, they are usually downloaded to the individual and offloaded to the science of calculation and market economics.

The poor, no less than any other group in a society, do express horizons in choices made and choices voiced, often in terms of specific goods and outcomes, often material and proximate, like doctors for their children, markets for their grain, husbands for their daughters, and tin roofs for their homes. But these lists, apparently just bundles of individual and idiosyncratic wants, are inevitably tied up with more general norms, presumptions, and axioms about the good life, and life more generally.

But here is the twist with the capacity to aspire: it is not evenly distributed in any society. It is a sort of meta-capacity, and the relatively rich and powerful invariably have a more fully developed capacity to aspire. What does this mean? It means that the better off you are (in terms of power, dignity, and material resources), the more likely you are to be conscious of the links between the more and less immediate objects of aspiration. Because the better off, by definition, have a more complex experience of the relation between a wide range of ends and means, because they have a bigger stock of available experiences of the relationship of aspirations and outcomes, because they are in a better position to explore and harvest diverse experiences of exploration and trial, because of their many opportunities to link material goods and immediate opportunities to more general and generic possibilities and options. They too may express their aspirations in concrete, individual wishes and wants. But they are more able to produce justifications, narratives, metaphors, and pathways through which bundles of goods and services are actually tied to wider social scenes and contexts, and to still more abstract norms and beliefs. This resource, unequally tilted in favor of the wealthier people in any society, is also subject to the truism that "the rich get richer," since the archive of concrete experiments with the good life gives nuance and texture to more general norms and axioms; conversely, experience with articulating these norms and axioms makes the more privileged members of any society more supple in navigating the complex steps between these norms and specific wants and wishes.

The capacity to aspire is thus a navigational capacity. The more privileged in any society simply have used the map of its norms to explore the future more frequently and more realistically, and to share this knowledge with one another more routinely than their poorer and weaker neighbors. The poorer members, precisely because of their lack of opportunities to practice the use of this navigational capacity (in turn because their situations permit fewer experiments and less easy archiving of alternative futures), have a more brittle horizon of aspirations.

This difference should not be misunderstood. I am not saying that the poor cannot wish, want, need, plan, or aspire. But part of poverty is a diminishing of the circumstances in which these practices occur. If the map of aspirations (continuing the navigational metaphor) is seen to consist of a dense combination of nodes and pathways, relative poverty means a smaller number of aspirational nodes and a thinner, weaker sense of the pathways from concrete wants to intermediate contexts to general norms and back again. Where these pathways do exist for the poor, they are likely to be more rigid, less supple, and less strategically valuable, not because of any cognitive deficit on the part of the poor but because the capacity to aspire, like any complex cultural capacity, thrives and survives on practice, repetition, exploration, conjecture, and refutation. Where the opportunities for such conjecture and refutation in regard to the future are limited (and this may well be one way to define poverty), it follows that the capacity itself remains relatively less developed.

This capacity to aspire—conceived as a navigational capacity that is nurtured by the possibility of real-world conjectures and refutations—compounds the ambivalent compliance of many subaltern populations with the cultural regimes that surround them. This is because the experiential limitations in subaltern populations, on the capacity to aspire, tend to create a binary relationship to core cultural values, negative and skeptical at one pole, over-attached at the other. Returning to Hirschman's typology, this may be part of the reason that the less privileged, and especially the very poor, in any society, tend to oscillate between "loyalty" and "exit" (whether the latter takes the form of violent protest or total apathy). Of course, the objective is to increase the capacity for the third posture, the posture of "voice," the capacity to debate, contest, inquire, and participate critically.

The faculty of "voice" in Hirschman's terms, and what I am calling the capacity to aspire, a cultural capacity, are reciprocally linked. Each accelerates the nurture of the other. And the poor in every society are caught in a situation where triggers to this positive acceleration are few and hard to access. Here empowerment has an obvious translation: increase the capacity to aspire, especially for the poor. This is by definition an approach to culture, since capacities form parts of sets, and are always part of a local design of means and ends, values and strategies, experiences and tested insights. Such a map is always a highly specific way of connecting what Clifford Geertz long ago called the "experience-near" and the "experience-distant" aspects of life and may thus rightly be called cultural or, less felicitously, a "culture."[15] This is the map that needs to be made more real, available, and powerful for the poor.

---

15   C. Geertz, "Thick Description: Toward an Interpretative Theory of Culture," in C. Geertz, *The Interpretation of Cultures: Selected Essays*, New York: Basic Books, 1973.

Having suggested that the capacity to aspire requires strengthening among poor communities, it is vital to note that examples of such efforts are already available in a variety of new social movements, many driven from and by the poor themselves. In these movements, we can see what can be accomplished when the capacity to aspire is strengthened and tested in the real world, the world in which development can either fail or succeed. In looking closely at one such movement, we are also able to see how mobilization can expand and enrich the capacity to aspire within a specific social and cultural milieu.

CHANGING THE TERMS OF RECOGNITION: ON THE GROUND IN MUMBAI

In chapters 7 and 8, I have offered a detailed ethnographic account of the pro-poor Alliance of housing activists based in Mumbai who are building a global coalition to serve their vision. This movement forcefully represents what happens when a group of poor people begins to mobilize its capacity to aspire in a specific political and cultural regime. The Alliance allows me to say something about the lived experience of poverty but also about a specific set of ways in which a specific pro-poor activist movement is changing the terms of recognition for the urban poor and enriching the cultural capacity to aspire among its members through a strategy that creates a double helix between local activism and global networking.

For instead of finding safety in affiliation with any single ruling party or coalition in the state government of Maharashtra or in the municipal corporation of Mumbai, the profoundly localized Alliance has developed a complex political affiliation with various levels and forms of the state bureaucracy. Its strategy—in Mumbai and beyond—is based on a series of ideas about the transformation of the conditions of poverty by the poor in the long run. In this sense, the idea of a political horizon implies an idea of patience and of cumulative victories and long-term asset building that is wired into every aspect of the activities of the Alliance. The Alliance believes that the mobilization of the knowledge of the poor into methods driven by the poor and for the poor is a slow and risk-laden process that informs the strong bias of the Alliance against "projects" and "projectization" that underlies almost all official ideas about urban change.

Yet this resistance to externally defined time frames (driven by donor schedules, budgets, and economies) is a critical part of the way in which the Alliance cultivates the capacity to aspire among its members. It is played out in tough negotiations (both internal to the Alliance and with external agencies) about how plans are made, risks taken, commitments solidified, and accountability defined. For example, the Alliance succeeded in getting a major contract to build a large number of community toilets in Mumbai, on a scale previously reserved for private contracts and developers, or for government organizations and experts. By acquiring this major contract, the Alliance set itself the challenge of relating its long-term visions of dignity, health, and sanitary self-sufficiency to its short-term capacities for handling contractors, builders, suppliers, engineers, and banks in Mumbai. In this ongoing exercise (which is a textbook case of what "empowerment" could really mean), important segments of Mumbai's slum dwellers are collectively exercising the sinews of the capacity to aspire, while testing their capacities to convince skeptics from the funding world, the banking world, the construction industry, and the municipality of Mumbai that they can deliver what they promise, while building their capacities to plan, coordinate, manage, and mobilize their energies in a difficult and large-scale technical endeavor.

The idea here is that the poor need to claim, capture, refine, and define certain ways of doing things in spaces they already control and then use these to show donors, city officials, and other activists that these "precedents" (see chapter 8) are good ones, and encourage other actors to invest further in them. Strategies of precedent setting also constitute spaces for exploring the capacity to aspire and for testing the possibilities for change in the terms of recognition. For in every discussion about precedent setting, what is involved is a map of a journey into the future, whether in the matter of relocating homes (after demolition of temporary homes by the police) or of arrangements with contractors to provide services for building toilets, or of dealings with funders about deadlines, reports, and accountability. In each of these instances, activists and the poor communities they answer to (or come from) have to practice the arts of aspiration, lending vision and horizon to immediate strategies and choices, lending immediacy and materiality to abstract wishes and desires, and struggling to reconcile the demands of the moment against the disciplines of patience. In short, the Alliance practices a set of evolving rituals that borrows the legitimacy of precedent while introducing important elements of improvisation, exploration and aspiration.

A creative repertoire of rituals and performances, both linguistic and technical, creates the sort of feedback loop between general principles and specific goals that is at the heart of all active social change. It applies both to the partnerships that the Alliance seeks and to its internal dynamics. These performances increase the density, variety, and frequency of the loops between nodes and pathways that I discussed when I described the capacity to aspire as a navigational capacity. The more it is exercised, the more its potential for changing the terms of recognition under which the poor must operate. The Alliance has palpably changed these terms of recognition, both internally (for example, in how the men in the movement treat and regard the women) and externally (for example, in how funders and multilaterals now treat members of the Alliance and other similar activists today—less as objects than as partners).

CONSENSUS, CAPACITIES, CAPABILITIES

I have tried to show that specific forms of self-governance, self-mobilization, and self-articulation are vital to changing the conditions under which activists among the poor are changing the terms of recognition, globally and locally, for the poor. The first is the transformation of core norms that surround the poor in any particular socio-cultural regime. The second is that internal consensus is produced through what the Alliance, including Shack/Slum Dwellers International (SDI) activists, themselves refer to as their own "rituals" of practice and procedure. In both cases, existing forms of consensus are changed and new forms of consensus are built, as James Fernandez would have predicted, by the deliberate orchestration of forms of language and special social performances that we could loosely refer to as "ritualized."

Ritual here should not be taken in its colloquial sense, as the meaningless repetition of set patterns of action, but rather as a flexible formula of performances through which social effects are produced and new states of feeling and connection are created, not just reflected or commemorated. This creative, productive, generative quality of ritual is crucial to consensus building in popular movements, and it is a quintessential window into why culture matters for development.

For many pro-poor movements, such as the Alliance of housing activists I described in detail (see chapters 7 and 8), the capacity to aspire (what I referred to earlier as a meta-capacity) is especially precious in the face of the peculiar forms of temporality within which they are forced to operate. In this, they are not different from many other poor groups, especially in cities, but also in the countryside in many societies. The paradox of patience in the face of emergency has become a big feature of the world of globalization as many poor people experience it. The world as a whole operates increasingly in the mode of urgency, of emergency, of dangers that require immediate reaction and attention. The poor, as refugees, as migrants, as minorities, as slum dwellers, and as subsistence farmers, are often at the center of these emergencies. Yet their biggest weapon is often their patience as they wait for relief to come, rulers to die, bureaucrats to deliver promises, government servants to be transferred, or drought to pass. This ability to hurry up and wait (an American joke about life in the army) has much more serious meaning in the life of the poor.

In helping the poor to negotiate emergency with patience, the capacity to aspire guarantees an ethical and psychological anchor, a horizon of credible hopes, with which to withstand the deadly oscillation between waiting and rushing. Here, too, the capacity to aspire is a cultural capacity whose strengthening addresses some of the most peculiar cruelties of economic exclusion.

This meta-capacity, the capacity to aspire, is also a collective asset that is clearly linked to what Amartya Sen[16] has referred to as capabilities. They are two sides of the same coin, much as recognition and redistribution recall and require one another. The capacity to aspire provides an ethical horizon within which more concrete capabilities can be given meaning, substance, and sustainability. Conversely, the exercise and nurture of these capabilities verifies and authorizes the capacity to aspire and moves it away from wishful thinking to thoughtful wishing. Freedom, the anchoring good in Sen's approach to capabilities and development, has no lasting meaning apart from a collective, dense, and supple horizon of hopes and wants. Absent such a horizon, freedom descends to choice, rational or otherwise, informed or not.

What does this mean for those engaged in the active work of development, as planners, lenders, philanthropists? What does it mean to nurture the capacity to aspire?

NUTS AND BOLTS

I began by noting that culture is many things, and I have by no means addressed them all. The capacity to aspire is one important thing about culture (and cultures), and it has been given too little attention so far. Since the work of development and poverty reduction has everything to do with the future, it is self-evident that a deeper capacity to aspire can only strengthen the poor as partners in the battle against poverty. This is the only way that words like *participation*, *empowerment*, and *grassroots* can be rescued from the tyranny of cliché. But even if this seems intuitively right and true, what exactly can lenders, planners, and managers in an institution like the World Bank actually do?

Here I make a few suggestions, not to provide a detailed blueprint, but to provide a guide to further deliberation about making the argument of this chapter into an actual method of intervention and a principle of partnership between the poor and those who subscribe to the view that the poor must have an active role in changing their situations for the better.

The premise is that the capacity to aspire, as a cultural capacity, may well be a capacity (that is, a meta-capacity) whose fortification may accelerate the building of other capacities by the poor themselves. If so, it ought to be a priority concern of any developmental effort and a priority component of any project with other substantive goals (such as health, food security, or job provision) directed to the reduction of poverty. How can this recommendation be concretely explored?

Some general principles appear relevant.

---

16   Sen, *Commodities and Capabilities*.

First, whenever an outside agent enters a situation where the poor (and poverty) are a major concern, he or she should look closely at those rituals through which consensus is produced both among poor communities and between them and the more powerful. This process of consensus production is a crucial place to identify efforts to change the terms of recognition. And any consistent pattern in internal efforts to positively tilt the terms of recognition of and for the poor should be supported, either as a side-benefit or as a major target of the exercise. Such support can take the form of encouragement to report, record, and repeat such efforts, wherever possible.

Second, every effort should be made to encourage exercises in local teaching and learning that increase the ability of poor people to navigate the cultural map in which aspirations are located and to cultivate an explicit understanding of the links between specific wants or goals and more inclusive scenarios, contexts, and norms among the poor.

Third, all internal efforts to cultivate voice among the poor (rather than loyalty or exit) in the context of any debated policy or project should be encouraged rather than suppressed or ignored. It is through the exercise of voice that the sinews of aspiration as cultural capacity are built and strengthened, and conversely, it is through exercising the capacity to aspire that the exercise of voice by the poor will be extended.

Fourth, any developmental project or initiative, however grand or modest in its scope, should develop a set of tools for identifying the cultural map of aspirations that surround the specific intervention that is contemplated. This requires a method of placing specific technologies or material inputs in their aspirational contexts for the people most affected by them. This will require careful and thoughtful surveys, which can move from specific goods and technologies to the narratives within which they are understood and thence to the norms that guide these narratives. This last proposal also recognizes that aspirations connect to much of the rest of what we may regard as beneficial about culture, including the lifestyle, values, morals, habits, and material life of any community. And this brings us back to culture more generally.

CODA ON CULTURE

I began by noting that we need a sea change in the way we look at culture in order to create a more productive relationship between anthropology and economics, between culture and development, in the battle against poverty. This change requires us to place futurity, rather than pastness, at the heart of our thinking about culture. I have tried to draw out the implications of such a revision and have argued that it is of more than academic interest. It has direct implications for increasing the ability of the poor to truly participate in the aims (and debates) of development.

This does not mean that we need to forget about culture in its broader sense, as the sense of tradition, the fabric of everyday understandings, the archive of memory and the producer of monuments, arts, and crafts. Nor do we need to slight the idea that culture is the fount of human expression in its fullest range, including the arts, music, theatre, and language. Culture is all of these things as well. But culture is a dialogue between aspirations and sedimented traditions. And in our commendable zeal for the latter at the cost of the former, we have allowed an unnecessary, harmful, and artificial opposition to emerge between culture and development. By bringing the future back in, by looking at aspirations as cultural capacities, we are surely in a better position to understand how people actually navigate their social spaces. And in terms of the relationship between democracy and development, this approach gives us a principled reason to build the capacity to aspire in those who have the most to lose from its underdevelopment—the poor themselves. The social materials and scholarly protocols for such an approach are considered in greater detail in the final part of this book, and especially in its closing chapter.

CHAPTER TEN

Cosmopolitanism from Below: Some Ethical Lessons from the Slums of Mumbai

THE FIELD OF DEBATE

When cosmopolitanism is debated in scholarly circles, as it has intensely been in the last decade, slums, urban poverty, and global deprivation rarely enter the picture, except to remind us that cosmopolitanism is an elite privilege, and debating it is likewise an elite luxury. There are reasons for this bias, and they are to be found in our common understandings about what cosmopolitanism actually is. Most definitions of cosmopolitanism, either directly or indirectly, assume that it is a certain cultivated knowledge of the world beyond one's immediate horizons and is the product of deliberate activities associated with literacy, the freedom to travel, and the luxury of expanding the boundaries of one's own self by expanding its experiences. For this reason, cosmopolitanism is usually contrasted with various forms of rootedness and provincialism—the latter being associated with attachment to one's own friends, one's own group, one's own language, one's own country, and even one's own class, and a certain lack of interest in crossing these boundaries. The cosmopolitan is often identified with the exile, the traveler, the seeker of the new, who is not content with his or her historically derived identity, biography, and cultural values. In today's world, cosmopolitanism is loosely associated with post-national sensibilities, a global ethos, multicultural politics and values and a generalized openness to cultural experimentation, hybrid identities, and international cultural transfers and exchanges. This set of associations is hardly the same as the universalism of the Enlightenment, but it has some affinities with it, in its common interest in an expanded idea of humanity that transcends the boundaries of nation and ethnos.[1]

---

1 For a discussion of some vital debates surrounding the relationships between patriotism, cosmopolitanism, nationalism, and multiculturalism see: B. Robbins, *Feeling Global: Internationalism in Distress*, New York: New York University Press, 1999; M. C. Nussbaum and J. Cohen, *For Love of Country: Debating the Limits of Patriotism*, Boston: Beacon Press, 1996; P. Cheah and B. Robbins, eds., *Cosmopolitics: Thinking and Feeling beyond the Nation*, Minneapolis: University of Minnesota Press, 1998. To get a sense of how far the distance is between those who would identify cosmopolitanism with transnational movements and visions, and those who are eager to restore the image of the nation as the favored space of all true cosmopolitanism, see C. A. Breckenridge, S. Pollock, and H. K. Bhabha, eds., *Cosmopolitanism*, Durham: Duke University

Here I wish to suggest that a rather different sort of cosmopolitanism can be discerned in the world of internally generated forms of activism which are incubated among the world's poorest populations, more or less independent of advanced education and privileged access to the means of travel, leisure, and informed self-cultivation. Nevertheless, what I call "cosmopolitanism from below" has in common with the more privileged form of cosmopolitanism the urge to expand one's current horizons of self and cultural identity and a wish to connect with a wider world in the name of values that, in principle, could belong to anyone and apply in any circumstance. This vernacular cosmopolitanism also resists the boundaries of class, neighborhood, and mother-tongue, but it does so without an abstract valuation of the idea of humanity or of the world as a generally known or knowable place. This is a variety of cosmopolitanism that begins close to home and builds on the practices of the local, the everyday, and the familiar, but is imbued with a politics of hope that requires the stretching of the boundaries of the everyday in a variety of political directions. It builds toward global affinities and solidarities through an irregular assortment of near and distant experiences and neither assumes nor denies the value of its universality. Its aim is to produce a preferred geography of the global by the strategic extension of local cultural horizons, not in order to dissolve or deny the intimacies of the local, but in order to combat its indignities and exclusions. It is thus closely tied to the politics of hope and the promise of democracy as a space of dignity as well as of equality. It is indeed correct to call this style of life cosmopolitan, but it is cosmopolitanism driven by the exigencies of exclusion rather than by the privileges (and ennui) of inclusion.

URBAN HOUSING AS A WINDOW TO THE WORLD

The different organizations comprising the Mumbai housing movement, as we have seen already, have all developed links (since the early 1990s) with an important movement of slum dwellers in South Africa, as well as in Nepal, the Philippines, and Thailand. These global links, steadily fortified by shared strategies of internal mobilization (such as daily savings), internal discipline (such as self-surveys and censuses), and house-building techniques and strategies, have gradually evolved into the most important global alliance of community-based housing activists, all of whom share a common commitment to local organization, internal financial savings, and community-based toilet- and house-building strategies. Their main organizational methods are global exchanges for learning and knowledge-sharing and a coordinated strategy for educating and

---

Press, 2000, and P. Cheah, *Inhuman Conditions: On Cosmopolitanism and Human Rights*, Cambridge, MA: Harvard University Press, 2006. The debates in these widely varied writings cannot conceal their general lack of attention to the ways in which poor people generate their own visions and strategies.

pressuring city and state governments, international funders and multilateral agencies, and national governments. This international network, the Shack/Slum Dwellers International (SDI), has also evolved its own funding capacity, based on a sustained commitment to gain independence from the vagaries of global funding agencies and fashions, and has played a major part in global campaigns to oppose slum demolition, achieve secure tenure for the urban poor, and build credit and finance capacities for member communities of the network by cooperating across almost thirty countries, primarily in Asia and Africa, but also in Latin America and the Middle East. The SDI today is recognized as a major global voice for the urban poor by a variety of major multilateral organizations, including the UNCHS (United Nations Center for Human Settlements), the World Bank, the World Urban Forum, and numerous other formal and informal groupings concerned with urban futures and the rights of the urban poor.

The striking successes of this global network cannot be attributed to any single circumstance, factor, or historical trend. The global spread of the ideology of human rights since the middle of the twentieth century is certainly one factor. The recognition that democracy, as a worldwide value, is not just a matter of votes and representation but also of dignity and livelihood is another major factor. The worry about the relationship between extreme poverty, disease, disenfranchisement, and terror (especially in recent decades) is also relevant. The worry that the world's increasingly networked financial growth engines, and its exploding service economy, cannot subsist in a world of impoverished cities, angry slums, and rotten urban cores ("a planet of slums," in Mike Davis's colorful phrase) is also a contributing element. Last, but hardly least, the increased availability of the internet, especially to the more socially active among the world's poor, has created a galactic growth in what has been called "activism without borders,"[2] a remarkable efflorescence of popular efforts to harness the energies of the very poor, both in cities and in the countryside, to unite across national boundaries. In so doing, they have been able to influence national and multilateral policies in regard to the environment, human rights, labor rights, trade equities, intellectual property correctives to excess elite power, opposition to mega-projects (such as big dams) perceived as damaging the lives and livelihoods of the poor, and a host of smaller but no less significant matters of consequence to the world's bottom 50 percent. In general, the knowledge and democracy revolutions of the last few decades, powered by the spread of new information technologies, have combined to encourage the greatest diversity of popular and transnational civil society movements that we have witnessed in the history of mankind.

---

2   M. E. Keck and K. Sikkink, *Activists beyond Borders: Advocacy Networks in International Politics*, Ithaca: Cornell University Press, 1998.

The Alliance of Mumbai housing activists that is my focus here and the global network of which it is a part can only be seen in the context of this world-wide widening of the boundaries of civil society and the parallel broadening of the range of issues with which poor people have come to be politically concerned. It also true that each of these movements has a specific history and geography, which is deeply connected to its special focus, be it housing or AIDS, pollution or big dams, agricultural prices or women's rights, intellectual property or sexual traffic. And so it is with housing activism among the very poor, which has its own special characteristics and historical sources.

Here I am not concerned to tell the story of the broad global profile of such transnational activisms or of their range and variety, a story that is now beginning to attract widespread scholarly attention.[3] Rather, I want to focus on a cultural dimension of these movements, one that can be captured in the idea of "cosmopolitanism from below." To get a close look at this sort of cosmopolitanism, I start with the shape it takes in Mumbai.

MUMBAI AS A COSMOPOLITAN SPACE

Cosmopolitanism is, in some ways, Mumbai's self-governing cliché. Both rich and poor emphasize the ability of people who live in Mumbai ("Mumbaikars") to live with, and even enjoy, cultural and linguistic difference. And cosmopolitanism in Mumbai is rarely identified with self-cultivation, universalism, or with the ideals of globalism with which it is historically linked in Enlightenment Europe. Rather, it is primarily identified with cultural co-existence, the positive valuation of mixture and intercultural contact, the refusal of monoculturalism as a governing value, and a strong sense of the inherent virtues of rubbing shoulders with those who speak other languages, eat other foods, worship other gods, and wear their clothes differently.

This proposal could reasonably be greeted with the objection that Mumbai has also been the home of India's most powerful movement for linguistic monoculturalism and the dominance of a single regional culture, the culture of Maharashtra, especially after the linguistic reorganization of states, which allowed regional politicians to claim a separate state for Maharashtrians in 1956 and to claim Bombay for this state rather than for the adjoining state of Gujarat. The political party called the Shiva Sena was an urban byproduct of this linguistic separatism and has been a major force in Mumbai politics since at least the late 1960s, and it is still a force to be contended with. Much has been written about the rise of the Shiva Sena, its success in killing socialist consciousness among Mumbai's Marathi-speaking working class, its ability to capture the

3   See, for example, S. Batliwala and L. D. Brown, *Transnational Civil Society: An Introduction*, Bloomfield, CT: Kumarian Press, 2006.

attention of Mumbai's lumpen Maharashtrian youth, of large parts of its police force and lower-level government bureaucracy, and of its success in linking neighborhood social service functions with rabid Hindu nationalism and Marathi chauvinism. The Shiva Sena has rightly been seen as the single major force behind the Hindu-Muslim riots of the last three decades, and especially of the brutal pogroms that followed the destruction of the Babri Masjid mosque in December 1992 by Hindu fundamentalism cadres (see chapter 7 for more detail). But the Shiva Sena is increasingly internally divided and weakened, as its aging leader and supreme ideologue, Bal Thackeray, loses his charismatic force and control, and it shows every sign of being in a struggle for its very political life. The Marathi-speaking working and poor classes of Mumbai showed remarkable restraint after two major flashpoints in Mumbai's more recent political history: the burning of a train coach, which resulted in the death of a group of Hindu activists in February 2002 near Godhra in Gujarat, and the coordinated carnage of a series of train bombs, which paralyzed the city in July 2006. In both cases, there were strong allegations of the involvement of Muslim radical activists, possibly in cahoots with extra-national Islamic forces and support, but Mumbai's working classes refused to be drawn into major retaliatory violence against Muslims. Thus, it is important to understand the broad sources of Mumbai's cosmopolitanism before we return to examining how it relates to the strategies of the housing activists of the Alliance.

Mumbai is a city with a history built around contact, commerce, and conquest. The presence and struggles of the British and the Portuguese around the set of islands that later became the island city of Mumbai makes Mumbai a city of "outsiders" from the start. Apart from its few coastal fishing communities, virtually every community in Mumbai has a relatively short local history, and the variety of these communities, which includes Jews, Muslims, Parsis, Christians (both foreign and local), and many dozens of communities that might loosely be considered Hindu and Muslim, gave the city a character that was inherently cross-cultural, negotiated and built on brokerage and translation. Many of these groups were tied up with trade and commerce between themselves, with various local and foreign rulers, with various inland empires and, above all, with the wider world of commerce in the Indian Ocean, and especially in the Persian Gulf. This made Mumbai, from the very beginnings of its modern history, as much a part of the maritime world of the Arabian Sea as a part of the Indian subcontinent.

In general, Mumbai's cosmopolitanism has long been tied up with its commercial fortunes, and until the 1980s, the textile manufacturing world of Mumbai was built on a working social contract between the largely Marathi-speaking factory labor force of the mills and the largely Gujarati-speaking class of textile mill owners. Yet the working class of Mumbai was never entirely Marathi-speaking, since it was always also populated by poorer farmers and others who migrated to Mumbai from the south, from the Hindi heartland, from tribal Gujarat, and in smaller numbers from virtually every other part of India. In addition, the petty moneylenders of Mumbai were often Pathans from the northwest provinces, the guards and watchmen of many homes and office buildings were often from Nepal, and some of the most important buildings on the regal Marine Drive were owned by the ruling families of Kuwait. The railway staff in Mumbai, as throughout India, always had a significant number of Anglo-Indians, and the Catholic population of Mumbai retained strong links with their Portuguese ancestors and rulers in their native Goa. As Mumbai evolved into a major commercial and financial center in the twentieth century, with a powerful industrial base in the thriving textile industry, its ruling classes included wealthy Gujaratis, Marwaris, Parsis, Sindhis, Bohras, and Ismailis, as well as a small number of Marathi-speaking entrepreneurial families such as the Garwares, the Kirloskars, and the Dahanukars. No major social class in Mumbai, from the financial elites to the toiling classes of the Mumbai docks, was monolingual or monoreligious.

I described Mumbai as the "city of cash" in chapter 7, where the flow of money—liquid and abstract, in coins and checks, as gold and shares, as loans and debts, as pay-offs and commissions, as bribes and gifts—is virtually the circulatory substance that holds the entire economy of the city together. Of course, such cash flows are important in all major cities, especially in financial centers like Mumbai. But Mumbai's mythology and its everyday life places an especially heavy emphasis on the centrality of cash, as an object of desire, of worship, of mystery, and of magical properties that far exceed its mere utility. And Mumbai's defining industry, the film industry known globally as Bollywood, is the major engine through which the cosmopolitanism of enterprise, hustling, and cash is kept alive and magical. And Bollywood is, in various other ways, a key to Mumbai's cosmopolitanism and special in this context.

From its very beginnings, the Bombay film industry was the primary business in which Mumbai's many linguistic groups and religious communities learned to collaborate in a machinery of money-making and a mythology of celebrity, prosperity, and pleasure that retains its distinctive signature today. Gujarati financiers and producers, Bengali singers and scriptwriters, Maharashtrian editors, singers, and cinematographers (harking back to the film industry of Kolhapur and the Prabhat studios) came into contact with the great courtesanal families of the Muslim north, which yielded stars like Nargis and singers like Noor Jehan, as well as poets and scriptwriters like the great Saadat Hasan Manto. In a slightly later period, the Urdu progressive movement of the Gangetic heartland created an exile class of songwriters and scriptwriters (such as Kaifi Azmi, Sahir Ludhianvi, Majrooh Sultanpuri, Hasrat Jaipuri, and others) who permanently infused the film-going public with their version of Hindustani, deeply steeped in the Urdu and Persian traditions of the small royal courts of north India. Their songs, which became the hallmark of Hindi films and the primary source of popular music throughout India in the 1950s, 1960s, and until the present (along with the small printed chapbooks on which the lyrics were printed for those who wished to know them well), infused Bombay film fans with a deep appreciation of a certain lyric Hindustani vocabulary and style, which lives in street Hindi even today. At the same time, the great radio song shows, such as the Binaca Geet Mala of the 1950s and 1960s, played and replayed these songs while the movies were being shown in theaters and long after, so that the soundscape of Mumbai's streets literally echoed with the poetic lyrics of these songs, often derived from courtly northwestern poetic and lyric traditions such as the *ghazal*.[4] On the other hand, the news on the radio was in a form of Hinduized Hindi, shorn of its Persian and Urdu elements and heavily infused with Sanskrit roots and neologisms. Thus Bombay's film-viewers and radio-listeners grew up in a strangely bifurcated Hindi world, absorbing the courtly words and lyrics of Urdu and Persian poetry through the songs and scripts of the Hindi popular film, and the very different, classicized and de-Islamicized Hindi of the radio news and the major Hindi newspapers and magazines.

Thus, what is sometimes lampooned as Bambaiyya Hindi (especially by the educated gentry of Delhi) is a fascinating linguistic formation, of which the most noted fact is its penetration by lexemes, grammatical forms, and various minor grammatical and syntactic features derived primarily from Marathi—such as the famous *kayko* instead of *kyon* for the English "why," or the equally famous *khali-pili* meaning roughly "for no good reason"—as well as various less noticed semantic and syntactic features from the Gujarati of Mumbai, itself drawn into the language stereotype comic voice of Parsis in many Hindi films. The "unmarked" ethnicities of Hindi cinema during its golden decades (from 1950 to about 1980) were always vaguely North Indian (Panjabi peasants, Rajput princes and warriors, Mughal emperors, Lucknow courtesans, cow-belt landlords, and the like) while the "marked" ethnicities (often figures of humor) were often Catholic, Anglo-Indian, Tamil, Sikh, or ostentatiously Baniya (Gujarati or Marwari), and were frequently associated with their stereotypical occupations. The great Johnny Walker played almost every one of these "marked" comic ethnicities in his illustrious career. In an odd way, the figure of the Maharashtrian was frequently absent—neither figure nor background—indexing the strange absence of any linguistic hinterland for Bombay, except of course in the small but interesting Marathi film industry that never dominated the imagination of the city as the Hindi film industry did. Thus the films and songs produced by Bollywood created the basic idiom of Bombay Hindi,

---

4 P. Manuel, *Cassette Culture: Popular Music and Technology in North India*, Chicago: University of Chicago Press, 1993.

something that has itself changed in subtle ways through the six decades after 1950, but was always a more interesting hybrid than has been conceded by Hindi speakers from the north, who tend to lampoon Bombay Hindi from the point of view of some absurd idea of the authenticity of their own forms of Hindi. The latter, of course, are serial hybrids of Urdu, Hindustani, numerous varieties of *khari-boli*, and the numerous earlier spoken languages of North India, ranging from Marwari in Rajasthan to Maithili in Bihar.

The idea of some sort of "standard" North Indian Hindi, by comparison with which Bambaiyya Hindi is a proletarian and ridiculous hybrid, is a fatuous act of regional chauvinism parading as high linguistic propriety. It ignores not only the complex ways in which various North Indian forms of Hindustani have helped to form Bombay Hindi, but also assigns to the *khari-boli* of the north a privilege that is denied to languages such as Marathi and Gujarati. The irony, of course, is that both Marathi and Gujarati owe a much larger lexical debt to Urdu and Persian in the pre-colonial period than do many folk languages of the Hindi heartland. But that history is not critical to my argument.

Today, the combination of commerce, cash, and cinema, along with other forms of industry, manufacture, and enterprise, creates an enormously complicated multilingual universe, unified by a constantly evolving form of Bombay Hindi, which both shapes and is shaped by the songs and scripts of Bollywood. At the same time, Mumbai's Marathi is hardly simple, single, or homogenous, as path-breaking ground-level research on the enormous variety of Marathi dialects in the greater Mumbai area has recently shown.[5]

One final observation returns us to the tension between Mumbai's film-centered linguistic cosmopolitanism and the power of the Shiva Sena, which has historically emphasized the ownership of Mumbai by Maharashtrians, the cultural dominance of Marathi as a language, and the priority of the history of Maharashtra as a region in the textbooks, street names, and religious life of the city nowhere better expressed than in the cult of the warrior-king Shivaji in the political theology of the Shiva Sena. Even this Marathi chauvinist party has been forced to make concessions to the linguistic diversity of Mumbai by publishing Hindi and Gujarati versions of its main propaganda newspaper,

---

5 A careful survey conducted by the Marathi Public Sphere Project of a Bombay research group called PUKAR (Partners for Urban Knowledge Action and Research), discussed in chapter 14, has done fascinating work to document the growing variety of Marathi dialects and speech varieties that are proliferating in new neighborhoods in the expanding metropolis as new groups of Marathi speakers migrate to Mumbai and as new groups of quasi-rural populations are simply absorbed into the physical expansion of Bombay city into the Marathi-speaking mainland. These newly urbanized forms of Marathi gradually also make their way into the consciousness of Mumbai's elite Marathi-speakers, who dominate its Marathi theatre, magazine, and newspaper world, so that the relationship between high Marathi and popular forms of Marathi is also increasingly complex and evolving. Thus the idea that a proper North Indian Hindi is corrupted by a static Mumbai Marathi is an absurd proposition at both ends.

Saamna, to reach audiences that may be susceptible to Shiva Sena ideologies in their nationalist Hindu fundamentalist aspects but have no interest in abandoning their own linguistic loyalties.[6] It is in this extremely interesting and layered linguistic world that we need to place the specific cosmopolitan strategies of the communities and organizations that compose the Alliance of housing activists in Mumbai and their global networks.

THE COSMOPOLITANISM OF THE URBAN POOR

We return now to the cultural strategies of the urban poor who have mobilized themselves: by organizing themselves into federations, primarily through the work of the National Slum Dwellers Federation (NSDF); by building on the street experiences of the women who formed Mahila Milan in the aftermath of their earlier struggles as sex-workers in the variety of neighborhoods that fan out from Bombay Central, one of Bombay's two major railway stations; and by taking advantage of the middle-class resources of the women who built up the nongovernmental organization (NGO) known as SPARC (Society for the Promotion of Area Resource Centers). The story of this collaboration, which begins the early 1980s in Bombay through a series of accidental encounters, has also been told in numerous published accounts.[7]

To date, the poor women and men of Mahila Milan and NSDF have come a long way from their beginnings as self-organizing urban activists struggling to gain secure housing, minimal civil rights, and minimal protection from the depredations of police, criminals, and the municipal authorities in Mumbai. They have learned to speak directly to banks, engineers, architects, developers, politicians, academics, and multinational celebrities. They have learned to document, survey, monitor, and regulate their own communities, through techniques of surveying, enumeration, and mutual information. They have evolved sophisticated forms for articulating their own savings circles and assets with official and quasi-official banking and credit institutions. They have become the principals in a major construction company (an independent private company called NIRMAAN) through which they handle capital, loans, and the planning and execution of building projects centered on housing and sanitation in Mumbai and in many other Indian cities. They have vastly improved their capacity to deliver built infrastructure up to the standards of municipal and private lending authorities and have been asked by state and federal authorities to extend their experiences and strategies to cities in India that have been

---

6   I am grateful to Rahul Srivastava for bringing these facts to my attention.

7   D. Mitlin and D. Satterthwaite, *Empowering Squatter Citizen: Local Government, Civil Society and Urban Poverty Reduction*, London: Earthscan, 2004; S. Patel, S. Burra, and C. D'Cruz, "Slum/Shack Dwellers International (SDI): Foundations to Treetops," *Environment and Urbanization*, 2001, 13(2), 45–59, among others.

struggling with housing and infrastructure for the poor for decades without success. They have learned to deal with the constant movement and transfers of civil servants working for city and state agencies whose support they have learned to cultivate and husband over decades. They have mastered the art of presenting their numerical strength as an asset for the support of often cynical and corrupt politicians without conceding to the constant pressure to become passive vote-banks for specific politicians or political parties. They have earned the envy (and the respect) of commercial builders and land developers for whom all housing markets in Mumbai are a zone for unhindered profit-making; and they have earned the grudging regard of politicians and quasi-criminal interests who tend to dominate the real estate and development world of Mumbai. Above all, they have had steady and growing success in eroding the view that the street- and slum-dwelling poor are non-citizens and parasites on the economy of Mumbai, and in forcing politicians, bureaucrats, planners, and various urban elites to recognize that the poor cannot be treated as a cancer on the body of the city, but are citizens who deserve the same rights as all others and are in numerous ways vital to the service and production economies of Mumbai. In short, the various communities and leaders who are at the core of the Alliance have created an irreversible dynamic of "recognition" (in Charles Taylor's sense) that today makes it impossible to ignore their massive numerical presence and their legitimate rights to housing, to infrastructure, and to political voice in the life of the city.

The cosmopolitan practices of the Alliance have much to do with these hard-won successes. And it can be seen in the most humble as well as the most dramatic of forms. It can be seen in the housing and toilet exhibitions that I have discussed earlier in this volume. In these events, which combine festivity, learning, dialogue, and solidarity-building, women (and men) from different cities and regions encounter each other and make the effort to encompass some of India's linguistic and cultural diversities. They discuss their hopes about domestic space, their experiences with different building materials and techniques, their practices of savings and credit, and more generally their hopes for permanent housing and political security in their streets and cities. Friendships are formed, tragedies are shared, stories are exchanged, and experiences of urban struggle are framed to be understood by women for other women who come from different worlds of poverty. Often these exchanges involve linguistic negotiation, as when women from Nepal or Orissa talk to women from Pune or Tamil Nadu, often through the bridging efforts of the polyglot women of Mahila Milan from Mumbai. A single extended collective conversation could involve the use of several varieties of Hindi and Marathi, or Kannada and Oriya and Tamil, and even some English (if visitors from overseas funding networks are present). Translation is a continuous background activity, as participants gloss and explain exchanges to each other, and older and less literate members are told about new social and technical issues. Language in these settings is both medium and message, background and foreground, tool and horizon. It is rarely articulated as a site of conscious negotiation or effort. *Yet language is the first and most critical site of the effort to stretch the cultural horizons of these poor women and men.* It cannot be underestimated as the basis for all other forms of translation, learning, and exchange in the work of the global network.

These inter-city occasions within the Indian framework cannot be seen as the main context in which the membership of the Alliance learns the strategies of cosmopolitanism. In fact, the daily struggles to self-organize in Mumbai over the decades from the early 1980s to the present cannot be seen outside the context of the steady will of the poorest members of the Alliance to negotiate and transcend a variety of critical cultural boundaries and thus to create an expanded sense of their own cultural selves. For example, the poorest women who constitute the senior core of Mahila Milan are largely Muslim women from the Telugu-speaking region of Andhra Pradesh, who entered the sex-trade as sex-workers in Nagpada and the adjoining areas of Central Mumbai. Their already complex linguistic and cultural worlds (quite different from the world of the quasi-courtesans of the Muslim North) encountered in Mumbai the brutal world of multilingual male sex-shoppers, corrupt Marathi-speaking policemen, and toilers and brokers speaking many varieties of Hindi, Tamil, and Gujarati and various other Indian languages. As they organized themselves into the self-help group called Mahila Milan to escape their previous professions, learn other modes of livelihood, and achieve housing security, they remained for decades confined to pavement dwellings in their original working neighborhoods. But they also learned to work and cooperate with the largely male membership of the NSDF, many of whom are Tamil-speakers from Dharavi and its nearby Tamil-dominated neighborhoods far to the north of Nagpada. These Tamil-speaking men represented a different set of histories and trajectories, often less than sympathetic to the sex-workers (as most Mumbai males would be), and were also further advanced in the strategies of Mumbai housing politics and civic survival. Emerging from the complex occupational and political world of Dharavi and its environs, they were already fairly skilled in dealing with their own Tamil underworld, with its Muslim extensions (since some of the most prominent members of Mumbai's underworld in the period from 1950 to 1980 were Tamils, both Hindu and Muslim). They were likewise deeply experienced in operating in the fringe world constituted in the nexus of ward politics, crime, police, and slum landlords, and thus brought a more sophisticated set of political assets to the Alliance. The transactions between these two microcultures in Mumbai (the Muslim female ex-sex-workers of Mahila Milan and the largely male, Tamil-speaking, working-class membership of the NSDF) already required more than a modest negotiation of cultural styles and gaps in the mosaic of Mumbai's class, language, and sexual politics. This ongoing negotiation, which has direct implications for the overall strategies of the Alliance in Mumbai, is one example of the daily struggles to negotiate cultural differences among the poorest of the urban poor in Mumbai. Such cosmopolitanism is hard won, unsupported as it is by the apparatus of literacy and cultural privilege or by the practices of leisure and self-cultivation.

This microcosmopolitanism of the urban poor underwrites and supports numerous wider arenas and contexts for the practice of cosmopolitanism. Perhaps the most important of these pertains to the periodic and catastrophic episodes of violence between Hindus and Muslims in Mumbai, notably in December 1992 and January 1993. In these bloody riots, which largely resulted in death and destruction among the poorest members of Mumbai's Hindu and Muslim slums, the areas dominated by the defeated communities of the Alliance were able to minimize street violence and harm to the Muslim minority, were active in distributing aid and support to riot victims from both communities, and were vital contributors in the efforts to resist inflammatory propaganda and cool the embers of intercommunal enmity. This remains a marked strength of the Alliance in a city that has grown increasingly susceptible to the volatile nexus that links urban poverty, local fundamentalist politics, nationalist Hindu politics, anti-Pakistan hysteria, and the constant stimulation of the global "war on terror." This grassroots secularism, documented by many observers, means more in a city in which almost half the population of almost 16 million lives in slums composed of Hindus and Muslims, living cheek by jowl, than all the high-level hand-wringing of theorists of Indian secularism. For such theorists, secularism has less to do with the struggles of the urban poor for daily survival in India's cities than it has to do with constitutional values and modernist respectability, not easily graspable by India's poor and illiterate masses in their abstract forms.

Nor does local cosmopolitanism among the urban poor begin and end with grassroots secularism. It also extends to public rallies, political oratory, and linguistic traffic with local, national, and international elites. When Hilary Clinton, Colin Powell, and Prince Charles have paid visits to the homes and offices of NSDF and Mahila Milan in Mumbai, they have been drawn into the spaces and discourses of the poor, and though linguistic translation is an ever-present activity, the terms of this traffic have been so designed as to foreground the voices of the poor in preference to the voices of experts and other mediators. These encounters, which have been numerous over the years, have brought leaders of every variety into contact with the poorest men and women of the Alliance, to discuss their plans, their hopes, their strategies, and their list of real needs for support and assistance. These encounters build on the experiences of the microcosmopolitanism of daily life in Mumbai that I have briefly described, and on the confidence developed in the efforts of these men and women to negotiate their own diversity of worlds in Mumbai.

But these encounters also build on another form of encounter that is vital to the transnational politics of the global network of urban communities to which the Alliance belongs. These are the learning exchanges between members of these communities, in small groups, who travel to each other's communities across Africa, Asia, and even England, united by a common concern with homelessness and urban housing security. In these encounters, the urban poor of immensely diverse communities (from Cape Town and Johannesburg to Mumbai, Manila, and Bangkok) share stories, songs, strategies, and public oratory with each other, sometimes in intimate and informal contexts and sometimes in large-scale political and public events, in which politicians, policymakers, and urban elites are drawn into a space of cross-national cosmopolitanism, *which they neither define or control.* The cultural politics of these large-scale events is subtle and multilayered, for they combine local, national, regional, and global traffic, and creative negotiation. Speeches and songs might switch across two or three local languages or dialects; dances might celebrate three or four countries or continents; cultural performances might present slum dwellers' interpretations of high cultural dance or song forms (such as Zulu dances in Durban or Koli fishing community dances in Mumbai). These public dramas always foreground the presence of leaders from the poor communities themselves, thus pulling various middle-class elites, global celebrities, or civil society intelligentsia (such as myself) into a completely non-theorized, non-elite form of cultural imagination, performance, and negotiation.

Many elements of these practices of microcosmopolitanism and transnational cultural bridge-building were caught in an extraordinary event in 2001, in which I was privileged to participate.[8] The context was a major meeting about global urban housing hosted by the United Nations at its global headquarters in New York, in the heart of the most sophisticated cosmopolis in the world. The world of nongovernmental organizations was not granted much space in this event, which was dominated by official country delegations and recognized multilateral bodies such as the UNCHS. Yet the members of Shack/Slum Dwellers International managed to stage an extraordinary piece of guerrilla theater by securing permission to build a model house and a set of model toilets right in the lobby of the United Nations building, with informal materials and their own labor, in the presence of the hundreds of official delegates from many countries. The core participants from the Alliance were a group of fifteen or so men and women from the India and South African nodes of the network and a handful of civil society activists associated with them. The small model house and the children's toilets attracted so much attention from everyone who

---

8 For a detailed report and documentation of this extraordinary event (Istanbul + 5), see the publication called "Istanbul + 5: Creating a Space for All Voices," 2001.

passed through the lobby of the UN that in the midst of the conference there was a tidal movement from the corridors of the UN. All of a sudden, Kofi Annan, the former secretary-general of the UN, and Anna Tibaijuka, the former executive director of UNCHS, were in the midst of the informal exhibits surrounded by a dancing, singing, ululating group of women from South Africa and India, and an even larger crowd of curious delegates and visitors in suits, who followed this spontaneous political drama through the lobby of the UN. Some short speeches were delivered, and the luminaries were swept away if only for a few brief moments. The political power and magic of the UN had been drawn into the space of the urban poor, and the highest representatives of the United Nations were surrounded by the voices, the songs, the dances, and the physical exhibits of the poorest of the poor—their true constituency. They knew it was a magical moment and so did everyone else. It was a fully cosmopolitan moment, staged by the poorest women and men from slum communities in Africa and India, who had the long experience of their own microcosmopolitanisms to draw on when the opportunity presented itself—however briefly—to capture the charisma of the United Nations on their own terms. And in such events can be found the significance of cosmopolitanism from below, the topic of my concluding reflections.

COSMOPOLITANISM AND THE POLITICS OF HOPE

In the preceding chapters of part 2, I stressed the local practices and values that underlie what I called the "deep democracy" of this movement, and subsequently of the ways in which the Alliance was able to build among the urban poor what I called "the capacity to aspire." In this concluding section, I connect my account of "cosmopolitanism from below" to the structures of deep democracy and the conditions for developing the capacity to aspire, since together these are the raw materials of the politics of hope for the world's urban poor.

Cosmopolitanism tends to be seen as a practice relevant to cultural identity and individual self-enhancement. Consequently, it is not often tied to the broader political economy of rights, resources, and recognition. This is an impoverished view of cosmopolitanism, for among the many ways in which the poor are excluded from the benefits of participation, especially in multicultural democracies, is by their exclusion from the institutions of education, career-building, expertise, and the opportunities to expand their sense of their own possibilities for self-development. This deficit has, of course, long been recognized in national and global policies of development and modernization, especially those associated with the movements for economic modernization in the new nations that emerged after World War II. Similar impulses to draw the poor into mass politics through the mechanisms of mass education also had some precedents in the great social revolutions of Russia and China in the twentieth century, and in a more modest way in the social revolutions of the eighteenth century in England, France, and the United States, all of which helped to deepen the links between popular sovereignty and the elimination of poverty. But this historical trend toward mass education, itself certainly a product of the Enlightenment emphasis on the link between the ideals of knowledge, education, and social equality, has generally involved a greater emphasis on technical skills, basic literacy, and formal educational capacities at various levels as the keys to democratization. This emphasis is not in itself mistaken, but it tends to underestimate the political significance of cosmopolitanism as a tool of enfranchisement in its own right.

Let us think again about the kinds of practice through which the urban slum dwellers I have described struggle to extend their cultural worlds, starting near their own worlds in (and even within) Mumbai. These practices require them to imagine their everyday worlds, and the conditions of their own daily survival and security, initially and always, in a multilingual and multicultural space. That is because, in a city like Mumbai, it is never easy to separate language, caste, and religion from matters of class, power, and spatial privilege. Nor is it that these differences map neatly onto one another, so that one's peers are cultural familiars (in one way or another) while the powers that be are one's cultural others. Difference of some sort is both horizontal and vertical, and the poor (some 8 million strong, one must recall) are as divided from one another in terms of language, religion, and caste as they might be from the 8 million citizens of Mumbai who are better off than they are. *Thus all cultural transactions require negotiation, and all negotiation has a cultural dimension.* Language is the most visible (and audible) arena for this negotiation, but it also serves as an example for other sites of difference, such as region of origin, religion, or caste, none of which are without relevance to the urban poor, however destitute they may be.

Thus the struggle to extend one's cultural horizons, linguistically and otherwise, is *non-optional* in two regards: it is compulsory in the effort to build horizontal solidarities, for example, between the Muslim women of Mahila Milan and the Tamil men of the NSDF; but it is also compulsory in efforts to deal with the police, the banks, the municipal authorities, and the middle classes that dominate urban policy. But most importantly, the extension of one's cultural horizons in a democratic society is compulsory for the urban poor because the language of mass democratic politics is rarely singular across all political parties, candidates, and constituencies, especially in cities like Mumbai, but to some extent even in cities in more linguistically homogeneous areas (such as Bangalore in Karnataka or Hyderabad in Andhra Pradesh). Even in a city like Surat in Gujarat, the closer one gets to the political reality of actual neighborhoods, wards, and political constituencies, the greater the variety of dialects and languages, even in a broadly monolinguistic world. To some extent, this is the nature of large cities, which frequently grow through migrations over large distances and over long periods of time.

The compulsory nature of cosmopolitanism for the urban poor also makes it a more reliable resource for the practices of deep democracy. Deep democracy is democracy near at hand, the democracy of neighborhood, community, kinship, and friendship, expressed in the daily practices of information-sharing, house- and toilet-building, and savings (seen as the foundation of federation-building all across this global network). Deep democracy is the democracy of suffering and of trust; of work and of slum defense (against demolition and displacement); of small-scale borrowings and repayments; and above all, of the daily recognition in every organized activity of these communities that women are the most vital sources of continuity, community, patience, and wisdom in the struggle to maintain everyday security in the face of constant crisis and threat from many directions. Deep democracy precedes what happens at the ballot-box, the political rally, and the government office, though it supports and energizes all of these. Deep democracy—and especially in India, where poverty is mostly expressed in the form of abjection, subordination, and mechanical deference to all and sundry, especially to the rich and the powerful—is the transformation of constitutional bourgeois ideals into daily forms of consciousness and behavior, in which debate can be respectfully conducted; in which the voices of the weak, the very poor, and particularly women are accorded full regard; and in which transparency, in the conduct of disputes and other differences, becomes a habitual practice. Deep democracy is public democracy as it is internalized into the lifeblood of local communities and made into a part of the local habitus, in the sense made famous by Pierre Bourdieu.

All these practices and expressions of deep democracy rest on new habits of communication, and since even the smallest communities of the urban poor involve accidents that bring people with different cultural backgrounds and regional histories into the same pavements or informal settlements, compulsory cosmopolitanism is the absolute condition for keeping deep democracy alive. For without the daily extension of one's linguistic and cultural horizons, how can an organized group of poor men and women debate the choice of a Hindu woman and neighbor to spend some of the money she borrowed from community savings on saris for her daughter's wedding? Or the pressure on a Muslim grandmother with an early history as a sex-worker to celebrate her grandson's wedding with as much pomp and public expenditure as possible, in the drive for respectability? Or the merits of a railway construction worker's claim on community small-group savings to support travel to his father's funeral? In every case, compulsory cosmopolitanism and deep democracy require and sustain one another, since the stretching of one's cultural and linguistic horizons is the *sine qua non* of engaged debate on these vital matters of trust, scarce collective resources, and obligations. Such democratic debate also reinforces the virtues of cultural self-extension, in the harsh, often emergency conditions of slum life.

And this leads us to the topic of the capacity to aspire. In chapter 9, I referred to this capacity as a navigational one, unequally distributed among wealthier and poorer communities, that allows people to make their way from more proximate needs to more distant aspirational worlds. I argued also that this capacity was less developed among poor communities (both rural and urban) because the archive of experiences and stories through which wealthier communities were able to build the sinews of the imagination that underlie the capacity to aspire is precisely what the poor lack, this experiential deficit being virtually the hallmark of poverty. Thus, I proposed that the struggle between individuals and communities over the terms of recognition, an essential part of the effort of poor families to improve their place in local economies of dignity, could only be improved by enhancing the capacity to aspire. This set of connected arguments about the capacity to aspire rested on the view that for any durable change to occur in the distribution of resources, the poor needed to be empowered to gain and exercise "voice," a fact that has been widely recognized by development scholars and practitioners. What has not been adequately recognized is that for "voice" to be regularly and effectively exercised by the poor, in conditions of radical inequalities in power and dignity, requires permanent enhancements of their collective capacity to aspire. The daily organizational work and public rituals of the Alliance are excellent examples of organized communities of the poor that have discovered numerous ways to strengthen their own capacity to aspire and, in the process, have found ways to draw those in power into various formal and informal agreements to cooperate with them.

If we can retain the idea that changes in the distribution of the capacity to aspire could dramatically affect the terms of recognition for poor communities of every type, then compulsory cosmopolitanism becomes a vital source of energy for this objective. For both the microcosmopolitanism of the federated communities of the urban poor, which I have discussed above, and the practices that enhance the capacity to aspire draw on the habit of imagining *possibilities*, rather than giving in to the *probabilities* of externally imposed change (see also chapter 15). Imagining possible futures, concrete in their immediacy as well as expansive in their long-term horizons, inevitably thrives on communicative practices that extend one's own cultural horizons. As these horizons are extended by poor families and communities, they gain plausible access to the stories and experiences of others—and not just of adversity and suffering, but also of movement and accomplishment. In a multilingual and multicultural world, the expansion of this archive, through the dynamics of compulsory cosmopolitanism, adds speed and depth to the strengthening of the capacity to aspire, whose main fuel lies in credible stories (from one's own life-world) of the possibility to move forward, outward, and upward, even as one tends a leaking roof or a sick child in a fragile pavement dwelling on the streets of Nagpada.

Part III

MAKING THE FUTURE

CHAPTER ELEVEN

The Spirit of Weber

DISCOVERING MAX WEBER

I was introduced to a certain brand of social science at the University of Chicago before aggregation and explanation became more or less completely captured by largely quantitative techniques and before rational choice models of decision making swept much of social science. In 1970, my first year of graduate school, in an obscure interdisciplinary entity called the Committee on Social Thought, a peculiarly University of Chicago department, I took two courses with Edward Shils, both revolving around Max Weber. After that year, I abandoned Shils and embraced Weber. Such are the vagaries of graduate school.

In this important year in my own training, I was exposed to the ways in which Max Weber's ideas were translated into American sociology by Talcott Parsons, Edward Shils, and a few others like Reinhard Bendix, Hans Gerth, and C. Wright Mills. These efforts became the underpinning of what is still called modernization theory. Modernization theory was the main framework in which American social science looked at the great nineteenth- century problematic of the movement from *Gemeinschaft* to *Gesellschaft*, from community to society. It also became the principal way in which three other intellectual projects were handled: the general project of comparison for the study of modern societies; the study of induced development, now simply called development studies; and what is still called area studies. Anthropology was especially affected by area studies—as a paradigm—and important anthropologists like Charles Wagley, Milton Singer, and others were crucial in making the journey from the Kroeberian idea of "culture area" to the more strategic locution of area studies. In any case, the general project of comparison, at least in the principal social sciences, as well as the fields of development and of area studies, was more or less built on Weberian foundations via modernization theory.

Thus the 1980s and 1990s, the era of post-everything, was a rude awakening for modernization theory and not prime time for Max Weber. Marx limped on, however battered; Durkheim was salvaged by sub-currents of French post-structuralism, even as recent as Bourdieu; but poor Weber was largely abandoned, seen as the keystone cop of charisma, the iron cage, and the poor man's *verstehen*. Jürgen Habermas was a notable exception to this negative chorus, though even he gradually moved away from his preoccupation with the Marx-Weber dialectic. The other giants of the Frankfurt School did not care that much about Weber. Many younger scholars pointed the finger at Weber, blaming him for too much typologizing, too weak a grasp of the sexy capitalisms of the non-European world, too much focus on bureaucracy and law, too little attention to the exception, the emergency, and the emergent.

For those of the faithful doubters, who, like me, lived in the iron cage of area studies, our disenchantment took the form of a strong reaction against modernization theory. We blamed the messenger and the message, and the first messenger was Max Weber. In short, Weber quickly became too sociological for the culturalist, too comparative for the localists, too Germanic for the Francophiles, too statist for the subalterns, too interpretive for the priests of rational choice. These were bad times for Weber.

Well, the world has changed since then, and we are now desperate for any hint of law, rationality, or procedure in a world drunk on charisma, brutalized by illegality, savaged by exception. Max Weber does not look like the source of all our troubles anymore. Perhaps we need to look back at his most important genealogical product in the United States and ask what lessons it might hold for the century we have entered. What follows are a retrospect and a rethinking of modernization theory, and Max Weber's place in it.

IS MODERNIZATION THEORY ALL BAD?

Let me give away the punch line, which is that I do not now think that modernization theory is all bad. If not, what is good about it? To answer this question requires a bit more work, which is to decide what is good about it and what is bad, or less good. This has one other entailment, which is to look back at the theory in the light of subsequent history, which is to say with hindsight. Normally, we say that hindsight is not a good way to look at theories, but in the case of modernization theory it is even trickier, since the theory was a theory of the future—that is, a theory based on foresight and prediction about the course of human welfare. Thus, there is no option but to ask whether modernization was ever a good theory, but also whether, insofar as it was good, it was good in some general way, or whether it was good or bad in regard to where it expected the world to go.

One more tricky point: is it the same thing to judge whether modernization theory is good (and if so to what extent) and whether modernization itself is good (and if so to what extent)? Let me state my methodological position, since ambiguity here could skew my whole message and have us all barking up two trees when we could be barking up one. Here too I have bad news. Since modernization theory clearly rests on normative grounds (which I will discuss in a minute), it is virtually impossible to separate the virtues of the theory from the virtues of the state (process) it purports to analyze. In this regard, modernization theory is more like the theory of the welfare state than like the theory of evolution, the latter being an example of a theory in which the virtues of the process have little to do with the virtues of the theory.

Still, let us pretend for a moment that we can assess modernization theory as theory, independent of our views of modernization (or even of modernity or its various new cousins, such as late, early, and too-late modernity, as well as another branch that involves multiple modernities, alternative modernities, counter-modernities, and the like).

Let us now recite the standard litany of criticisms of the theory. Modernization theory was and is unilinear, evolutionary, Eurocentric, and prescriptive while pretending to be descriptive or analytic. Sub-critiques would lead us into hidden forms of racism, developmentalism, colonialism, scientism, elitism, technocratism, and other bad isms. Yet other criticisms took such forms as: What about Japan? What about hiccups in the Western story itself? What about rationalities that require irrationalities to make them work (such as Weberian calculation standing on the hidden shoulders of Calvinist predestination ethics)?

And what about prediction? Here modernization theory fares even worse: do elections produce full democracy? Does an increase in entrepreneurship (today more frequently associated with free markets and open trade) guarantee greater general freedom? Does the increase in education regularly mean more enlightenment, more tolerance, more respect for human rights? Well, the record on these predictions is mixed, to say the least.

But the real predictive failures of modernization theory are deeper. Here history has been harsh. All of modernization theory rested on the model of independent states and national economies that could be made to converge at certain levels of welfare and freedom through selective social and political inducements (collectively gathered under the categories of development and foreign aid). Modernization theory, in its heyday, roughly measured by the bookends of Daniel Lerner's *The Passing of Traditional Society* and Lloyd and Susanne Rudolph's *The Modernity of Tradition*, did not come anywhere near predicting the relative shrinkage of the autonomy of national markets in relation to the formation of regional and national markets that drive national development in key regards. Nor did modernization theory predict that the production of highly educated national elites would produce global knowledge classes that encouraged brain drain and regional disparities rather than building up the human capital of the societies that invested in their own educational institutions. Likewise, modernization theory did not anticipate that the newest financial instruments would create a growing disconnect between manufacture and finance capital, which would produce growing gaps between the investor classes and all varieties of industrial labor.

I will now rightly be accused of blaming modernization theory for being a child of its times and not a crystal ball. After all, which social science theory predicted the fall of the Berlin Wall, the collapse of the Soviet Union, the rise of the internet and the *worldwide* democratic revolutions of the 1990s (or for that matter, the events of the Arab Spring in 2011)? So perhaps we are angry with modernization theory because it promised cultural convergence, political stability, worldwide economic growth, and a universal replacement of violence by the combined rationalities of science, market, and education, while the world has turned out to have grown culturally divergent and deeply unstable, with its educated elites becoming either global arbitrage players or arms dealers and corporate predators.

THE WORLD AND THE THEORY

This raises the question whether the world failed modernization theory or the reverse. This is not an idle question for a theory whose robustness was closely tied to its capacity to produce social policies that would prove the predictions of the theory to have been correct. On the one side, we could simply say that modernization theory could not win the race against corporate greed, climactic disaster, the outsourcing of the state, and the double death of nationalism by global forces on the one hand and pathological xenophobias on the other. And neither could the policy instruments of modernization theory (such as international aid, technology transfer, and agricultural revolution) keep pace with global depredation. Nor, finally, could the hope that modernization theory placed in universal education (at the true core of the Enlightenment values of modernization theory) keep pace with changes in the very nature of basic knowledge itself, represented by the growth of machine languages, cyber-technologies for communication, and new technical possibilities for vision and translation. Above all, modernization theory did not understand that education and information would come radically apart in the world of "the web" and "the net," making it possible for messages of hate and suspicion to circulate at vastly greater speeds than those of hope and compassion. In all these regards, it may fairly be said that the world (or history) failed modernization theory, rather than vice versa.

But the reverse argument is often made, so it is worth reviewing. This argument, best articulated by such important and different theorists as Michel Foucault and Ashis Nandy, is that there is a canker at the very core of modernity, one which produces an early and unholy alliance between science, market, and state, whose foundation is so deeply embedded in the foundational grammar of the Renaissance and the Enlightenment that modernization theory was dead on arrival. In this view, a vivisectionist science, allied to a panoptical capacity to see like a state,[1] meets a bankrupt secularist worldview and a banal

---

1   J. C. Scott, *Seeing Like a State: How Certain Schemes to Improve the Human Condition Have Failed*, New Haven: Yale University Press, 1998.

form of commodity worship, to produce not just the "iron cage" that Max Weber came to dread but something worse. They produced a charnel house of destructive technologies and a host of repressive and invasive technological devices, allied to fundamentally deadening governmentalities through which states, statistics, capillary repressions, and various new technologies helped to produce what Slavoj Žižek called "a plague of fantasies."[2]

In this view, modernization theory was the latest incarnation of a false social science that did not recognize its own debt to repression and governmentalist assumptions and then sold this misrecognition as a utopia of education, economic growth, and democratic participation. In the extreme versions of this view, not only did modernization theory fail the world, but it was doomed to do so, because it was always compromised by its dependence on false universalisms, cynical ideas about the relation of science to freedom, and a shameless pact with the state, which it both relied on and allowed to grow against the forces of civil society. The weaker versions of this view, which I touched on earlier, base their critique on evolutionism, unilinearity, the naïve faith in progress, and the shallow scientism of the theory.

Moderate versions of the critique of modernization theory, which nevertheless criticize the theory rather than the world that refused to rise to its standards, take a lapsarian view of the theory, in which the offspring fails to rise to the grandeur of its parents. On this view, the great forebears of modernization theory—typically Auguste Comte, Ferdinand Tönnies, Émile Durkheim, and, of course, Max Weber (and some even more antique forebears going back to Kant and, via Kant, to Descartes and Aristotle at the very beginning)—had the right ideas about Enlightenment as achievable through careful observation, rational explanations, tolerant arguments, and transparent political fora. Their descendants were portrayed as wrong, not in arguing for a great divide between traditional and modern societies, and the journey from one to the other, but on more technical counts, including careless generalization, weak attention to peculiar cases (usually Japan), incomplete data, or some other problems of methodology or design.

In this view, modernization as a theory has the right lineages, but its fall begins when it becomes tied to social science proper, which in the United States can be dated to the birth of political science in the 1920s or shortly thereafter. In cruder versions of this critique, the failure of modernization theory is strictly associated with the descent of grand European social theory to crass American empiricism (and later to behaviorism).

So let me return to the question: did modernization theory fail the world or vice versa? My own position is that modernization theory failed the world. My reasons for coming down on this side are not the usual ones. In my view,

---

2   S. Žižek, *The Plague of Fantasies*, London: Verso, 1997.

modernization theory failed the world not so much because of its generic qualities (such as its evolutionism, its unilinearity, and its faith in progress and
convergence under the stimuli of education and democratic institutions in "the
new states"), nor because of its premature reliance on specific ideologies of
development, aid, and technology transfer (although these too were certainly
flawed). So if these two flaws—unilateral optimism and bad technologies of
change inducement—were not modernization theory's most serious ones,
where did its biggest flaw lie? In my view, the biggest flaw lay on the predictive
side. Let me lay out this argument a bit more carefully before returning to
Weber.

MODERNIZATION AND PREDICTION

Modernization theory is nothing if it is not predictive. It is fundamentally a
theory about the conditions under which social changes on a worldwide basis
may be expected to converge in the direction of increased levels of a key set of
public goods, such as freedom, equality, productivity, and prosperity, assured by
the thoughtful dissemination of specific tools of technology, productivity,
entrepreneurship, and education. But the world turned out to react poorly to
these inducements, these transfers, and these exogenous pressures to change,
for reasons that are still hotly debated. Some blame the patient, saying that the
unmodernized countries could not free themselves from the prison house of
primordialism, and its cousins such as nepotism, patrimonialism, risk aversion,
authority fetishism, and the like. Others, more cosmopolitan and more technocratic, blame the technologies of inducement, notably the Bretton Woods
institutions, and their incapacity to crack the technical problems of poverty
reduction. But whatever the apparent relationship between bread and circuses
in these criticisms, they converge on the observation that the world that
modernization produced turned out to be full of surprises.

The main surprises, in my view, were the following: the refusal of religion
to become etherized upon the table of developmentalism and modern science;
the paradoxical proclivity of new communication technologies to encourage
cultural difference instead of a rush to sameness; and the tendency of the voice
of the people to demand blood, revenge, war, and ethnocide as it was drawn
more fully into the technologies of modernity, thus giving the lie to the expected
relationships between democratic institutions and the growth of tolerance and
patience as political virtues. The story of the recent democratic elections in Iraq,
Bolivia, Palestine, Egypt, and Nepal, to name the most striking examples, is that
elections are not necessarily the friends of moderation. The final surprise was
the rise of a new communicative technology, organized around the internet and
allied tools, which made free and fast communication a resource for the
strengthening of highly specific and non-cosmopolitan communities of

interest, including terrorists, hackers, and child pornographers. In its failure to recognize these dangers, no doubt modernization theory fell into the well-known traps of scientific arrogance, teleological thinking, crude evolutionism, and even some versions of Orientalism.

THE TRAP OF TRAJECTORISM

But there are traps, and then there are meta-traps. I would like to discuss one such meta-trap, and that is the trap of thinking within the optic of "trajectories," or what we may call, in a rather inelegant way, the meta-trap of "trajectorism." Trajectorism has an old history in the West, traceable at least to the Bible, with its ideas about the journey from sin to salvation, from this world to the other, from blindness to redemption, all exemplified in the life of Jesus at one level, and in the road to Damascus at another level. The Greeks were not exempt from this way of thinking, and Plato's famous allegory of the Cave is an early version of the journey from darkness to light, from shadow to substance. And ever since, the idea of a trajectory has formed and framed Western thought, even to the extent of creating a retrospective narrative of the inevitability of the West itself, constructed out of the bits and pieces of Greek philosophy, Biblical mythology, Roman law, Gothic architecture, Renaissance humanism, and many more minor elements, constantly composed into a retrospect story of "rise and fall," of progress and stasis, of dark and bright episodes, all framed in a grand trajectory that we still see, with remarkable lack of distance, as the story of the West. But the story of the West is no more than one version of our deep bias toward what I call trajectorism. And this is the meta-trap that social science inherited most powerfully from its great ancestors in religion and pre-industrial humanism.

I should add that trajectorism is not the same as evolutionism, triumphalism, predestinationism, the myth of progress, growth, or convergent modernization, though each of these relies on the hidden ontology of trajectorism. Trajectorism is a deeper epistemological and ontological habit, which always assumes that there is a cumulative journey from here to there, or more exactly from now to then, in human affairs, as natural as a river and as all-encompassing as the sky. Trajectorism is the idea that time's arrow inevitably has a telos, and in that telos are to be found all the significant patterns of change, process, and history. Modern social science inherits this telos and turns it into a method for the study of humanity.

In other places, such as China, India, Africa, and the Islamic Belt—not to speak of the islands and forests of anthropology—the trap of the trajectory never became the framing conceptual trap, although its presence can sometimes be detected, especially in Islam. These places have their own meta-traps, such as the idea of the nothingness of the world, or the myth of eternal return, or the idea of multiple births, or some other driving meta-narrative. But "trajec-torism" is the great narrative trap of the West and is also, like all great myths, the secret of its successes in industry, empire, and world conquest.

TRAJECTORIES IN TIME AND SPACE

So far, I have perhaps conveyed the assumption that trajectorism is mainly an episteme about time's arrow and has to do with sequence, cause, duration, and chronology—the normal hallmarks of our current scientific assumptions about temporality. This is true, but it is not the most important truth for my purposes.

Let me back up. One of the persistent puzzles about the European world journey has been the question of the link between the universalism of the Enlightenment (which argued for the necessity of worldwide equality through the spread of knowledge, among its other key arguments) and the European imperial project, a project of spatial dominion that ended up also as a project of world conquest. In spite of many efforts to cast light on this inner affinity between the project of *Aufklärung* (Enlightenment) and the project of world dominion—by authors like Edward Said, Valentin Mudimbe, Terence Hopkins, Immanuel Wallerstein,[3] and many others—we have made no real progress on this problem. Foucault, who might have had something to say on this matter, did not speak much of the French imperial project, and even the great Max Weber did not elect to link the global journey of capitalist ethics to the project of empire.

Suffice it to say that it does not seem likely that the journey from Renais-sance humanism to Kantian universalism, roughly from the sixteenth to the eighteenth centuries in Europe, could not have been connected to the project of Vasco da Gama and his many maritime successors to find the New World in searching for the Old World (and vice versa). Well before the age of industrial capitalism and the imperial adventure of Europe in the nineteenth century, the Iberian sailors and conquistadors had connected the projects of conquest, conversion, and economic plunder in the New World, a connection touched upon in the work of writers like Anthony Pagden and Peter Hulme.[4]

Perhaps this is not the first time in human history that a project of ethical universalism was tied to a project of conversion and conquest: two earlier exam-ples are the Roman Empire and the early history of Islamic expansion. But there

---

3   E. W. Said, *Orientalism*, New York: Pantheon Books, 1978; V. Y. Mudimbe, *The Idea of Africa*, Bloomington: Indiana University Press, 1994; T. K. Hopkins and I. M. Wallerstein, *World-Systems Analysis: Theory and Methodology*, Beverly Hills: Sage Publications, 1982.

4   A. Pagden, *The Fall of Natural Man: The American Indian and the Origins of Comparative Ethnology*, Cambridge: Cambridge University Press, 1983, and P. Hulme, *Colonial Encounters: Europe and the Native Caribbean, 1492–1797*, New York: Methuen, 1986.

is something special about the European understanding of its ethical universalism (rooted in Enlightenment ideas of knowledge, education, and common humanity) and the urge to world exploration and global expansion that characterizes the Dutch, English, and French projects after 1800 and later the German, Belgian, and Italian adventures, especially in Africa. What is this special quality?

I propose that this quality has something to do with the post-Renaissance European idea of modernity, which requires *complete global expansion for its own inner logic to be revealed and justified*. In both the Roman and Islamic examples, the ethical project was self-standing and conquest was a secondary extension of this project. But European modernity could not regard itself as complete without covering the surface of the globe. Naturally, this proposal does not pretend to address the myriad ways in which ethical visions seeped into mercantile, military, and political ambitions, sometimes of the most violent and greedy varieties. Another way to put this proposition is that the idea of the cosmopolis as it took shape in the seventeenth century in Europe[5] was in some ways integrally linked to the imperial vision.

Till very recently, European cosmopolitan impulses, whether expressed in travel, adventure, mapping, surveying, trading, or warfare, were characterized by an inner contradiction between the urge to translate and interpret other worlds, and the urge to colonize and to convert, often by means of violence.

What I have called trajectorism is thus not only a parochial vision of temporal processes; it is in addition a problematic ideology of spatial expansion. Empire, specifically the European imperialism of the last three centuries, is a transverse spatial enactment of a defective vision of temporality in which time's arrow always has a single direction and a known destination. That destination is the world written in the image of Europe. Europe, in this mode of thinking, is unthinkable except as the singular expression of time's arrow, and this arrow is so conceived as to require its dominion over the globe. Thus, the world and the globe become one and the same, and each is seen as Europe's tomorrow and Europe's elsewhere.

THE INNER DIALECTIC OF EUROPEAN COSMOPOLITANISM

The inner problem of European cosmopolitanism in the past three centuries has something to do with its contradictory and alternative genealogies. We must recognize, to start with, that contrary to the dominant meta-narrative of Western modernity, it is not itself a cumulative, predictable, or inevitable outcome of any discernable history. This meta-narrative is itself an expression

---

5   See, for example, Toulmin's useful overview of this process: S. Toulmin, *Cosmopolis: The Hidden Agenda of Modernity*, New York: Free Press, 1990.

of a trajectorist ideology, which tends to see Europe itself as a logical outcome of ideas that led from one phase or idea to the next, in some sort of destined manner.

The fact is that the self-construction of Europe, itself a selective later image of certain possibilities in the idea of Western Christendom, is a product of continuous triage and selective retrospective historicization. Part of Europe's special mix of confidence, ethnocentrism, and world adventure comes surely out of the modern debt to the missionizing logic of Western Christendom, a genealogy that is still visible in current debates over the future of secularization. Other parts owe themselves to a conscious orientation to the Roman vision of the world, which centers on law, technology, and military force as key elements of the relevant past. Yet other parts favor the classical Greek heritage, notably those modern self images of Europe in which reason and its empire take precedence over all other forms of argument and imagination. Still other images are deliberately shortsighted, and see in modern Europe a history that most importantly begins in the Renaissance and its ideas of humanism, individual expression, and a highly aestheticized vision of what is properly Europe's real past. There are, of course, many other streams of European self-fashioning, which stress more obscure referents in the past, ranging from its early scientific traditions to more obscure poetic, mystical, and political moments and texts in its past. Thus, the idea of Europe, in the modern period, always builds the meta-narrative of the European trajectory from a varied and sometimes contradictory archive, a rearview mirror that is continuously adjusted as different classes, estates, and regions seek to see in their own claims a larger unfolding of the European story.

Thus, when the Enlightenment becomes the dominant ideology of the political present in Europe, it never fully displaces alternative images of the European trajectory. The battle between the variety of trajectorist meta-narratives never really abates, and we can see this in a series of debates, sometimes strictly intellectual and sometimes bloody struggles for power and place among groups and classes in Europe. Thus, when the idea of the cosmopolis takes shape in Europe after the seventeenth century, what it exports to the rest of the world is less a unified value system or world-picture and more a series of efforts to paper over the cracks in the European meta-narrative, the struggle between its contradictory trajectorist narratives. The battle between church and state, the struggle between private property and various visions of collective ownership, the tension between the rule of law and the rule of the masses, the opposition of this and otherworldly impulses in European religiosity—these are all examples of the unresolved contradictions that Europe played out in the imperial project, in which these deep conflicts encountered societies and ideologies that contained their own, often very different visions of these very matters. For cosmopolitanism is ultimately a matter of ideas, and what Europe exported in its imperial projects was its own demons, divisions, and unresolved anxieties, this time on a global terrain.

This is the most serious problem with European ethnocentrism as it played out in the colonies of Africa, Asia, and the Islamic world in the age of empire: not its clarity or arrogance, but its numerous contradictions, all of which found their genealogies in different versions of trajectorism. In a word, European cosmopolitanism—as spread throughout the world through books, speeches, icons, images, and narratives—imposed profound European conflicts onto an unpredictable series of colonial spaces, each of which had its own forms of intellectual culture and world imaging. In short, European cosmopolitanism was not primarily an effort to impose some European consensus on the rest of the world; it was an effort to find consensus by the staging of unresolved European debates on a world which had not invited this engagement. What do we do with this troubled project of cosmopolis?

A RISK WORTH TAKING

What we have today is an opportunity for Europe to take risks of a different type than those entailed by the Enlightenment project in its eighteenth century form or its imperial project of world dominion. To continue on that model in today's world of global dependencies, mass migration, democratization, and mass mediation leads directly to the policies of "Fortress Europe," a direction that is as far from any cosmopolitan ideal as we are likely to get.

The risk that Europe, and Europeans, might better be advised to take has two sides. One is the risk of re-examining the sources of Europe's trajectorist ideologies—from missionization to modernization and development—so as to achieve a deeper and more critical understanding of Europe's self-formation in the mirror of a mistaken imperial project. This risk, the downside of which is self-flagellation normally followed by self-congratulation, has an upside, which is the potential of discovering alternative sources of the always evolving European self, sources that might be more congenial to dialogue rather than dominion as a world strategy. The other, even more worthy of risk, is to make a more sympathetic effort to explore the alternative ways in which other societies and civilizations have imagined cosmopolis,[6] since these other images and imaginaries might yield deeper grounds for exchange, criticism, and political conviviality in the realities of European society today. The downside risk here is that we may discover that the European archive has indeed, after a thousand years of world ascendancy, finally run dry and has nothing new to offer in our

6   A monumental example of such an alternative cosmopolis is to be found in Sheldon Pollock's path-breaking study of the politics and poetics of the Sanskrit cosmopolis in pre-modern South and Southeast Asia, *The Language of the Gods in the World of Men: Sanskrit, Power and Culture in Premodern India,* Berkeley: University of California Press, 2006.

struggles to achieve equity, sustainability, and conviviality in our cities and countries. But the upside is also clear, and this is the possibility that in separating cosmopolis from empire and seeking an actual encounter between alternative images of cosmopolis, Europe might discover untold riches in its own multiple genealogies.

THE ARGUMENTS FOR REDEMPTION

So let us return to the virtues of modernization theory. If it is Eurocentric, based on a naïve idea about rational discourse, allied to bad technical ideas about poverty reduction and wealth production, and permanently hobbled by its evolutionism, what are its merits? The *first* merit of modernization theory is that it is inseparably connected with a social project, namely the project of modernization, which it both underpins and predicts. In this regard, it marks a sharp tension within the legacy of Max Weber, in regard to value-free social science. Modernization is a value-laden theory, intimately tied up with a project of induced social change. In this regard it harks back to Marx rather than to Weber, in spite of its deep reliance on other aspects of Weber's heritage. This is a reminder that the boldest, strongest, and most wide-ranging social theories are those that are not ashamed of their relationship to values, indeed their saturation by values, and more specifically values that endorse general and generalizable social change.

The *second* virtue of modernization theory is that it is—at heart—a theory of justice. By placing the possibility of access to equity, rationality, freedom, and participation in all hands and in all societies, it avoids the sort of a priori racism that characterizes such theories as those of the "clash of civilizations." In this respect, the charge of Eurocentrism is somewhat off the mark. Modernization theory is substantively but not formally Eurocentric, to make another important Weberian distinction. That is, the theory elevates certain historically specific virtues, such as punctuality, the need for achievement, and the spirit of enterprise, to the level of general possibilities. But it does not formally exclude anyone from the orbit of its application. It is thus not formally culturalized or racialized in any marked way.

The *third* virtue of modernization theory as a general theory of induced change is that it unashamedly recognizes the importance of ideas, dispositions, orientations, and ideologies in the building of viable social actors and communities. The Weberian inspiration of much modernization theory encourages attention to the complexity of ethics (such as the Protestant ethic) in the generation of collective action. Seen this way, modernization theory is far more historically and culturally sensitive than theories that might seem otherwise more progressive. It has been difficult to recognize this virtue of modernization theory as a result of its low-brow applications.

The *fourth* virtue of modernization theory is perhaps the most important. In its utopian dimensions, in its conviction that dynamic changes can follow from certain social investments and policies, modernization theory is still the strongest single precursor of contemporary efforts to reduce widespread harms, to assert capacities for planned change in all human communities, and to mobilize different movements based on the politics of hope. Thus, modernization theory, even with all its king-size disabilities, has significant relevance for ideas about social justice, such as my own ideas about the "capacity to aspire" (see chapter 9), which might help us to tackle the still fundamental issue of the relationship between recognition and redistribution.

Finally, and *fifthly*, because modernization theory is a theory of endogenously induced social change, it is remarkably free of the current bias toward one or another variety of rational choice theory as explanatory of all significant interested human action. Modernization theory, depending as it does on the force of such factors as planned social investment, large-scale developmental forces, and on the power of broad psycho-social dispositions to risk, collective well-being, and justice, is not strictly about rational choice. It is about something markedly different, which Max Weber discussed under the rubric of calculation (see chapter 12). This is a fine distinction, but a distinction nevertheless. The rational calculation of the Weberian actor—which underpins all modernization theory—is a peculiar mix of what Weber called *Wertrationalität* and *Zweckrationalität*, roughly "value rationality" and "instrumental rationality." Modernization theory rarely hives the two off completely from one another, and in this regard it is very different from more recent rational choice models. What is more, the sort of rationality presumed by modernization theory has room for the ethics of risk, salvation, and freedom wired into its inner workings, whereas most varieties of rational choice theory work hard to evacuate themselves of the temptation to take these dispositions seriously. And finally, while rational choice theory is fundamentally individualistic and agonistic (hence its proximity to market models as well as to game theoretic models), modernization theory leaves a large amount of room for collective ideas of welfare, planning, and rights as sources of political change.

These five virtues of modernization theory may not be enough to absolve its very real flaws and its failure to predict very much about the world we live in today, yet they are worth bearing in mind when we examine competitive theories of induced social change, whether they issue from Foucault or the Frankfurt School. We can, based on the five virtues I have identified, at very least rediscover the more interesting Weberian features of modernization theory, rather than judging it by its least attractive applications and exemplars. This requires us to return to Max Weber.

BACK TO MAX WEBER

Let me conclude with a thought experiment or a sort of séance to see how Max Weber might have engaged with the world of globalization, the world of planetary ecological crises, of volatile financial flows disconnected from manufacture and labor, of eroding economic sovereignties and worldwide experiments in the building of real democracies. Of course, this is not an effort to ask Weber to rise from the grave and help us one more time, nor is it an effort to project what he may have thought or felt about the world a century after his most important contributions. Rather, where are the ideas in Weber's great corpus to which we might fruitfully return to tackle some critical issues of our day?

Weber was deeply preoccupied with charisma, and both in his typology of leaders and of authority, charisma played a vital role. How can we return to Weber's idea about charisma to cast light on such issues as leadership, stardom, celebrity, and tyranny today? We may look back to his ideas about the "routinization" of charisma, which Shmuel Eisenstadt[7] explored in an important edited collection, and note that the problem with charisma today is not its routinization but its ephemerality, its vulnerability to high-speed fame, short reputations, and brief moments of credibility for elected leaders. Thus, we may want to reflect on the volatility of charisma, rather than its routinization, as its major vulnerability.

On Weber's lifelong preoccupation with the ethical sources of capitalist selfhood and his ideas about discipline and what he called "methodicality," how can we extend these ideas to the great entrepreneurs of our electronically and informationally driven world? We know that what Weber found in Calvinism alone, of all the world religions, was the capacity to make a methodical life the proof of divine election, and thus he thought that something about the ethics of predestination was the missing ingredient in the other great religions that might otherwise also have given birth to the spirit of capitalism. In today's world, the spirit of capitalism seems dominated by the ethics of risk, chance, and gambling—not by the methodicality of the Calvinist merchant. But if we think a bit more carefully, it may be that the new bearers of the capitalist spirit are also methodical, though their methodicality may be keyed to the technologies of uncertainty such as the stock market, the poker table, the high-cost acquisition or merger. So, as I argue in detail in chapter 12, there may be a future for the deeper study of methodicality in Weber's sense.

Weber also had some very interesting ideas about what he called "status groups" or *stande*, groups defined by lifestyle and consumption rather than by

---

7   M. Weber, *On Charisma and Institution Building*, introduction by S. N. Eisenstadt, Chicago: University of Chicago Press, 1968.

their relationships to the means of production. A part of his long debate with Marx, this aspect of Weber's thought has plenty of room for creative recovery, connecting as it does to Thorstein Veblen, Georges Bataille, Jean Baudrillard, and others who have helped us see that consumption is a socially productive sphere in itself, creating inequalities, solidarities, and ideological hegemonies independent of what is produced by the relations of production. This aspect of Weber's thinking has the potential for helping us to enrich our theories about class, and to go further on the journey that Pierre Bourdieu began in his work *Distinction*.[8]

So though Weber was a master of historical and regional comparison, he never paid serious attention to the logics of connectivity that connected the great civilizations and their religions and economies, a methodological challenge that was addressed in chapter 2. Nobody is perfect. So, in the end, we must all make our own journeys to Europe—and away from it—for the masters, like Max Weber, cannot be treated as prophets, who knew in advance how to understand the worlds that would emerge after their passing.

---

8 P. Bourdieu, *Distinction: A Social Critique of the Judgement of Taste*, Cambridge, MA: Harvard University Press, 1984.

CHAPTER TWELVE

The Ghost in the Financial Machine

This chapter lays out an argument that leads back from some debates in contemporary social studies of finance to arguments that re-engage with the ideas of Max Weber, which were the subject of the previous chapter. My starting point here is Jacques Derrida's[1] famous argument about the "impossibility" of the gift, which annuls itself by its implicit expectation (a negative performative) of a return. I focus here on the idea of the "return" as one entry into a new approach to contemporary financial devices.

Derrida's argument about the logical impossibility of the pure gift is in fact anticipated in the very first pages of Mauss's classic essay "The Gift," in the perception by Mauss of the inner contradiction between the voluntary and the compulsory as well as the disinterested and the self-serving elements of the gift. Two facts about Mauss's study have become lost from view. One is that his entire and fundamental interest throughout this essay is in the question of the force behind *the obligation to return*. The second point is that Mauss's thorough archaeology of the gift (in both primitive and archaic societies) was wholly motivated by his interest in the moral force behind the modern contract (legal, impersonal, obligatory, etc.). Bearing these two points in mind allows us to understand better what may have been Mauss's rich and only partial answer to his own question, that is, that the obligation to return lay in the spirit of the thing given (the famous *hau* of Polynesia), which in turn provided a dynamic and forceful connection between giver and receiver, and the first giver and the second giver/returner, and so forth.

I draw two conclusions from this reading of Mauss. The first is that Mauss was quite aware of the inner affinity between archaic and modern forms of binding obligation to return. And he was especially interested in the "spirit" behind the archaic gift, which he was also convinced was the "spirit" behind the modern contract. He found this spirit in a series of cosmologies (themselves dramatically different), all of which see some things as imbued with the spirit of the giver and thus as capable of exercising a moral force on the receiver. This spirit is what animates the specific devices or forms taken by the gift. Notice here that his sociological strategy is to induce the spirit not from the device but from some other nonmechanical source. This sense of spirit closely resembles Weber's notion of the "spirit" of capitalism, by which usage Weber sought to

---

1   J. Derrida, *Given Time: I. Counterfeit Money*, P. Kamuf, trans., Chicago: University of Chicago Press, 1994.

capture the spirit, the *anima*, behind specific capitalist forms and devices (such as double-entry bookkeeping and the rational calculation of profit).

Both Mauss and Weber stand on one side of a great divide that we also see before us today. On the one side, we have Michel Callon, and many others,[2] who argue that the best way to understand new economic devices, especially the devices of the market, is to account for their performativity as devices. On the other side stand thinkers like Mauss and Weber,[3] whose contributions dispose me to think that there is something akin to a Gödel-type problem in inducing the spirit that animates a particular set of mechanisms from within the properties of the device itself. The rest of this chapter is an extension of this "animistic" argument and its relevance to modern financial markets.

THE SPIRIT IN WEBER

Weber's use of the word "spirit" (*Geist*), most famously in his work *The Protestant Ethic and the Spirit of Capitalism*, has nowhere clearly been analyzed. It belongs to a family of Weberian terms, which include "ethic," "ethos," and "habitus." This last word, most often seen as part of our debt to Pierre Bourdieu, has been noticed by Jean-Pierre Grossein,[4] whose translations into French of some of Weber's important writings might be one key to the relationship between Weber and the work of Bourdieu and his collaborator Jean-Claude Passeron. The other (discussed later in this chapter) is Bourdieu's explicit debt to Mauss, who was the first modern to use the term "habitus."

Weber's discussion of the "spirit" of capitalism in chapter 2 of his famous essay demands a close rereading. "Spirit" in Weber's usage is most often taken as belonging to the nineteenth-century sense of the German *Geist*, and is thus assumed to refer to the worldview of an epoch or historical age. This assumption is not wholly wrong, and Weber's own use of the word "ethos," which is

2 M. Callon, ed., *The Laws of the Markets*, Malden: Blackwell, 1998; "An Essay on the Growing Contribution of Economic Markets to the Proliferation of the Social," *Theory, Culture and Society*, 2007, 24(7–8), 139–63; M. Callon, Y. Millo, and F. Muniesa, eds., *Market Devices*, Malden: Blackwell, 2007; M. Callon and F. Muniesa, "Economic Markets as Calculative Collective Devices," *Reseaux*, 2003, 21(122), 189–233; and Callon's many other colleagues and collaborators: D. Beunza and D. Stark, "Tools of the Trade: The Socio-Technology of Arbitrage in a Wall Street Trading Room," *Industrial and Corporate Change*, 2004, 13(2), 369–401; B. Latour, *Reassembling the Social: An Introduction to Actor-Network-Theory*, Oxford: Oxford University Press, 2005; D. MacKenzie, *An Engine, Not a Camera*, Cambridge: MIT Press, 2007; D. MacKenzie, F. Muniesa, and L. Siu, eds., *Do Economists Make Markets? On the Performativity of Economics*, Princeton: Princeton University Press, 2007.

3 See also J. A. Schumpeter, *Capitalism, Socialism, and Democracy*, New York: Harper Perennial, 2008 (1942) and A. O. Hirschman, *The Passions and the Interests: Political Arguments for Capitalism*, Princeton: Princeton University Press, 1977.

4 M. Weber, *The Sociology of Religion*, J. P. Grossein, ed. and trans., with an introduction by Jean-Claude Passeron, Paris: Gallimard, 1996.

related to his use of the word "spirit," refers to a cultural sensibility associated with a group, class, profession, or sect and is more diffuse than a mere ideology or doctrine in that it conveys a sense of a bodily disposition, a sensibility, a moral style, and elements of a cultural psychology. In this sense, when Weber speaks of the "spirit of capitalism," he does not mean its explicit doctrines, or its ideology, or even less specific technical orientations to market, profit, and calculation. He means something less formal, more dispositional, and moral, something that also makes sense of its crystallization in a particular "ethic."

As Weber, in *The Protestant Ethic*, sets out to describe the spirit of capitalism, he embarks on an interesting methodological exercise, in which the key elements of the "spirit" of capitalism lie outside its technical or professional expressions and speak to a disposition that is somehow anterior (both logically and historically) to its concrete calculative expressions in nineteenth-century capitalist behavior. This anterior "ethos" begins to anticipate Bourdieu's use of the term "habitus." Various scholars have touched on the links among the ideas of style, deportment, disposition, and spirit in Weber's corpus.

If we look at Weberian "spirit" in this way, as a matter of disposition rather than of worldview, it comes closer to an embodied moral sensibility, which precedes action or organization and amounts to a collective psycho-moral disposition. In this sense, the "spirit" of capitalism, in Weber's argument, is external to and prior to any and all of its distinctive devices, both technological and institutional. The content of this spirit is what will lead us back to Mauss's thoughts on the gift.

ANIMATING MODERN CAPITALISM

After a close reading of a series of extracts from two famous works of Benjamin Franklin, Weber[5] notes that "in fact, the *summum bonum* of this ethic, the earning of more and more money, combined with the strict avoidance of all spontaneous enjoyment of life, is above all completely devoid of any *eudaemonistic*, not to say, hedonistic, admixture." Weber goes on to suggest that all varieties of avarice, of adventurism, of reckless pursuit of profit, are not part of the Franklin ethos. He further goes on to say that the most plausible answer (before his own) to what inspired true capitalist discipline (if it was not simple greed) was that of Werner Sombart, who argued that the spirit of modern capitalism lay in the gradual emergence of rationalization.

Weber gives Sombart much credit but argues, in a few closely reasoned pages,[6] that rationalization is by itself an inadequate source for the modern

5   M. Weber, *The Protestant Ethic and the Spirit of Capitalism*, T. Parsons, trans., New York: Charles Scribner's Sons, 1958, 53.
6   Ibid., 75–8.

spirit of systematic, even ascetical, commitment to money-making. In fact, he suggests that the spirit of modern capitalism actually has something "irrational" about it that requires historical sourcing, and that this irrationality is in fact expressed in the hostility of the Franklin ethic to the eudaemonistic motive for money-making. This irrational component is what leads Weber to the Protestant conception of the "calling" as the key to the modern spirit of capitalism. In chapter 3 of *The Protestant Ethic*, he gives a close reading of Martin Luther's conception of *Beruf* (calling) and shows that it is in fact too traditionalistic to be the source of the spirit of Franklin; that is, Luther's *Beruf* was still an attitude to worldly activity that was cautious and qualified, because of his antipathy to any disposition that might lead back to the doctrine of "salvation through works." This step leads Weber to argue that to truly find the source of Franklin's irrational restraint apropos of money-making, we must turn to Calvin and his ideas about election, proof, and salvation.

Weber's reading of Calvin, which is the pivot of *The Protestant Ethic*, is contained in chapter 4, "The Religious Foundations of This-Worldly Asceticism." Every line of this chapter has been read and debated, both in Weber's own lifetime and up to the present day. So I will note just one critical element of what Weber found in Calvin, what he thought distinguished Calvin from Luther, which served as the key to Weber's argument about the "spirit" of modern capitalism. This is the spirit of "methodicality." Chapter 4 of *The Protestant Ethic* is virtually a thriller, a heart-stopping effort to trace a key distinction, to get to the heart of a mystery, to catch a great idea in its germinal form. It has a breathtaking urgency about it, a breakneck attention to the trail, and a remarkable lateral attention to possible alternative paths that need to be rejected or avoided.

We see here a series of careful efforts by Weber, mainly to distinguish Calvin's views on grace, works, election, and proof, both from earlier Catholic views and from Luther's views, which come close to the later Calvinist position and then retreat from it. The drift here is toward taking the ascetical (monastic) model of systematic ethical action and moving it into a model for the systematic ethical organization of the totality of a man's life. Weber points out that the plight of Calvin's believer is that as a consequence of his belief in God's power, grace, and foreordained plan for man's salvation, there is no way whatsoever for man to alter (whether by prayer, by confession, or by works) God's decision about who is saved and who is not. Furthermore, there is no way to *distinguish* (by their behavior or by any other sign) those who are saved from those who are not. This produces an immense form of loneliness (here Weber is very much in the line of Søren Kierkegaard), and the systematic and methodical dedication of one's life to the accumulation of wealth is only as a sign to oneself of a life that resembles the sort of life that can enhance God's glory, regardless of whether one is numbered among the elect. This pattern of life is not intended as an effort to influence God in any way (for that is absurd in Calvin's theology), nor is it a sign of inner certainty about one's own status. It is in fact a *gamble on God's grace*. But it is a special sort of gamble. It is not a gamble on an outcome. It is a *derivative gamble*; that is, it is a gamble *on a gamble*. The primary gamble is a gamble on the possibility that one is elect (already predetermined, but absolutely unknowable); the second is the gamble that in performing *as if* one were elect, one is likely to be acting to enhance the glory of God (felicitously, one might say in J. L. Austin's terms) rather than infelicitously, that is, as one who is not elect but is nevertheless performing as if "saved."

One could make a cruder reading of Weber's interpretation of Calvin to the following effect. I can never know if I am one of the elect. This makes me feel lonely and anxious. So I will act as if I were one of the elect, by dedicating my *worldly* life to a methodical ethical plan. This will change nothing. But it will make me feel better because, at the very least, I am acting so as to celebrate God's grace in my own way. A more nuanced reading would be that the Calvinist approach to profit-making in this world—absent any possibility of certainty about one's status as saved or damned—is a derivative gamble in the face of radical uncertainty about the eternal disposition of God's grace. That is, Calvinist economic methodicality in the pursuit of worldly wealth (ascetical rationality) is a gamble on the felicity of a performative.

RISK AND GRACE IN WEBER

The stage is now set to discuss the biggest puzzle in looking at Weber's work on the entrepreneurial ethic and indeed his work on economic history more generally: it contains virtually no references to the problem of "risk," except in some brief asides on medieval shopping and commerce in his famous essay on "general economic history."[7] This is a bit surprising, since Weber's ideas about the emergence of modern capitalism remain among the major arguments about the "entrepreneurial" spirit in the nineteenth and twentieth centuries.

A close reading of *The Protestant Ethic* and Weber's other writings on what he often called "ascetical capitalism" reveals two things that cast light on this puzzle. The first is that Weber's primary ideas about uncertainty were expressed in his account of Calvin's ideas about grace, election, and salvation, and the profound uncertainty (hence the loneliness) of the Calvinist believer, who could never look into the black box of divine providence to ascertain whether he was one of the elect. This radical uncertainty, which leads to the doctrine of *certitudo salutis* (the certainty of salvation), was at the very heart of Weber's account of the Calvinist ethos. When it comes to modern capitalism and its spirit, Weber puts his entire stress on the linked ideas of methodicality, rationalization,

---

7 M. Weber, *General Economic History*, New Brunswick: Transaction, 1981 (1923).

calculation, and sober business practice. Nowhere in his account of ascetical capitalism is risk mentioned, not even when he focuses on profit as the critical driver of double-entry bookkeeping and capital accounting in modern commercial organizations. Weber's quintessential Calvinist is not a risk taker. Or more precisely, it was not the risk-taking side of modern business enterprises that most interested Weber.

Prima facie, this fact seems to disqualify Weber from being invoked in any discussion of the contemporary financialization of capitalism, since this process has risk at its very heart. What then can we take from Weber, given his complete disinterest in risk as a feature of the modern entrepreneurial enterprise? To answer this question, we must take a page out of Weber's own book and note that he said that the Calvinist spirit was crucial not to the ongoing, routinized evolution of capitalism, but only to its originary moment (that moment which he identified more in the eighteenth than in the nineteenth century). After that moment, capitalism becomes a self-propelling machine that no longer requires the ascetical spirit of capitalism for its key players to be animated and motivated. The Calvinist spirit, in this later phase, has been fully incorporated into the capitalist machine. This methodological division between the founding moment and later moments is a distinction I will return to in regard to risk.

I would argue that the period since the early 1970s, which might be seen as the beginning of the thoroughgoing financialization of capitalism (especially and initially in the United States), is not in fact a moment of unbridled risk taking, as so many analysts and media observers have been prone to say, especially in the wake of the 2008 global meltdown. I would suggest rather that it is a period when the *spirit of uncertainty* has been reawakened in relation to the unprecedented formalization/abstraction/commercialization of the machinery of risk itself.

So here is the proposition that I think is worthy of careful further development and critique: over the course of the last forty years, the machinery for measuring, modeling, managing, predicting, commoditizing, and exploiting risk has become the central diacritic of modern capitalism. Financial markets lead and shape other markets, financial capital vastly outstrips manufacturing or industrial capital, financial policymakers dominate global economic policy, and major economic crises are produced and prolonged by the runaway growth of risk instruments, markets, and creative legal and accounting devices. The careful sociological analysis of these devices is the greatest accomplishment of the major scholars working on the sociology of finance.[8] The bulk of this work, and corresponding technical work within the finance field itself, comes out of the path-breaking essay by Frank H. Knight on "risk and uncertainty."[9] Knight

---

8   See Callon, MacKenzie, Stark, and their numerous colleagues and collaborators.
9   F. H. Knight, *Risk, Uncertainty and Profit*, Boston: Houghton Mifflin Co., 2009 (1921).

was the first to make a fundamental distinction between risk and uncertainty, arguing that situations with risk were those where decision making was faced with unknown outcomes but known ex-ante probability distributions. In Knight's view, these situations, where decision-making rules such as maximizing expected utility can be applied, differ in a deep way from those where the probability distribution of a random outcome is unknown. Although there is some emerging work in economics on "Knightian uncertainty," it is not yet easily available or widely discussed in the literature on the sociology of finance, which is largely preoccupied with risk-based measures and practices.[10] I look forward to an emerging future dialogue in which work on Knightian uncertainty (as opposed to risk) can provide a new platform for conversations among sociologists, economists, and anthropologists concerned with modern finance.

Meanwhile, it is interesting to note that Knight, the father of all subsequent work on the economics of risk, was also a major American translator and mediator of Weber and that he saw much to commend in Weber's work in economic history. Absent any explicit discussion (of which I am aware) by Knight of Weber's views of the capitalist spirit, I propose the following argument.

Risk is now part and parcel of the machinery of contemporary capitalism, and the "devices" that measure, model, and forecast risks are central to the financialization of modern capitalism. What has happened to Knightian uncertainty (apart from the famous Rumsfeldian formulation about "known unknowns")? We might say that while some actors in the field of finance do know what they do not know, and perhaps also what they would like to know, they certainly have no good way to measure what they do not know, and even more, they do not know how to measure it probabilistically. Thus uncertainty remains outside of all financial devices and models. So what do we, as analysts, do about uncertainty in the current financial world? I suggest that a set of attitudes, dispositions, and intuitions, in short, an ethos (or what we might today call an imaginary) about uncertainty is certainly discernible, although it cannot be directly deduced from any social or technical study of practices in which risk devices are embedded. In what does this imaginary consist?

---

10   An interesting exception is Daniel Beunza and Raghu Garud's paper, "Calculators, Lemmings or Frame-Makers? The Intermediate Role of Securities Analysts," in M. Cullon, Y. Millo, and F. Muniesa, eds., *Market Devices*, Malden, MA: Blackwell, 2007. In this paper the authors seek to make a strong argument about the importance of calculative "frame-making" as the key to analysts' valuations of companies in conditions of Knightian uncertainty. They are critical of Bayesian approaches (which dominate the financial literature) and the "imitation" approach, which dominates behavioral economics. The frame-making approach of Beunza and Garud, derived from Erving Goffman's analysis of "frames," is reasonable and adequate for analyzing the rhetoric, diversity, and differential uptake of analysts' reports, but it leaves open the question of what more general intuitions about the economy determine large-scale decisions by major institutional players, such as short sellers and hedge-fund managers, who are more direct reflections of decisions in the face of Knightian uncertainty. This latter group is of primary relevance to my argument in this chapter.

THE UNCERTAINTY IMAGINARY

Weber found the ethos of rational capitalist action in the Calvinist mindset, in a specific set of ideas about God's grace, human salvation, the nature of proof about election to the company of the saved, and the bourgeois virtues that this set of ideas engendered, which he labeled "ascetical capitalism." Plainly, when we look at the heroes (and demons) of the past forty years in global finance, especially in the United States (individuals such as Michael Milken, Ivan Boesky, and Bernard Madoff), we cannot see in them much of the spirit of the ascetical Calvinist businessman, who was deeply opposed to greed, excess, exuberance, and worldly pleasure in almost any form. Rather, the typical "master" of the financial universe is not a dull or nerdy accountant or lawyer but a gaudy, adventurous, reckless, amoral type, who embodies just the sort of avarice, adventurism, and charismatic self-motivation that Weber saw as the absolute enemy of systematic capitalist profit making.

It is not hard to see, especially in the past year or two, when we look at the extraordinary incomes, extravagant lifestyles, and swashbuckling heroics of the major bankers, hedge-fund managers, arbitrageurs, swappers, insurers, and their imitative juniors, that we are in the presence not of sober risk managers but of individuals who have chosen to define—without any models, methods, or measurements to guide them—the space of financial uncertainty as such. In this regard, these heroes of the financial imaginary are precisely not about the taming of the "passions" by the "interests" (in Hirschman's famous formulation), but rather are about the animation of the interests by the passions.

That is, the world of financial risk, and its numerous emerging instruments and devices, is in fact nothing other than an enormous set of tools, a technology, for the mapping and measuring of risk, not to manage it but rather to *exploit* it. However, the exploitation of risk, by definition, cannot be animated within the boundaries of the information provided to any player by his devices alone. It is of course clear that financial players also use information gathered from their peers, their social networks, the media, and, not least, their prior worldly experiences. But the availability of such extra-technical information is a truism. What is important is the ethos, the spirit, the imaginary through which the world of the screen, the floor, the office, and even the invisible collegial network is valued, assessed, and shaped. Markets may be about efficiency, but financial actors are not. Nor will individualistic psychological theories of expectation, preference, and utility (which constitute 99 percent of the foundation of behavioral economics) take us any further, if we are interested in collective orientations and dispositions.

I propose that the primary feature of the ethos of financial players in the past few decades, those who have both played and shaped the financial game, is to be found in a working (though not consciously theorized or articulated) disposition toward exploiting uncertainty as a legitimate principle for managing risk. In other words, those players who define the strategies through which financial devices are developed and operated (as opposed to those who simply react or comply with these strategies) use their own intuitions, experiences, and sense of the moment to outplay other players who might be excessively dominated by their tools for handling risk alone. In short, these key players (the contemporary incarnations of, say, Benjamin Franklin and John Baxter, in Weber's argument) are those who are not just bold enough and wealthy enough to "sell short" (for example), like John Paulson and George Soros, but also those who are in one way or another skeptical of the reliability of devices. This group includes, but is not confined to, short sellers.

The ethic of these key players in today's financial world is not yet easy to glean, even with the plethora of narrative accounts of the great players and dramas in the financial markets of recent years.[11] Still, we can suggest some possibilities for characterizing this type of actor. First, they are not afraid to be pessimistic about the possibilities of certain markets, economies, and even nations. Second, they are "contrarian" in their approach to most general opinions about investment and stock appreciation. Third, they are willing to take large bets on their pessimistic assessment of weak corporations, bad underwriting, and current credit-rating consensus. The common structural property of each of these dispositions is simple: their sense of the environment of relevant uncertainties inclines them to be more confident about their reading of downside rather than of upside risks. If it is true that whatever rises must fall, and that whatever falls must rise (virtually the founding axiom of the financial markets), the short-sell ethic or imaginary is more comfortable with the inevitability of fall. This might be described as the core of the contrarian imaginary of uncertainty. We might suggest that those financial players who are inclined to sell short, owing to a sort of structural pessimism, are more confident about downside than upside risk. This is clearly tied to the major feature that distinguishes short sellers who make money (even fortunes) rather than lose money: their confidence in their capacity to be right about the *timing* of the downturn, which is the key to large profits on the short sell. Thus, these are players who are not only contrarians but are also actors willing to infuse their reading of

11   See W. D. Cohan, *House of Cards: A Tale of Hubris and Wretched Excess on Wall Street*, New York: Anchor Books, 2010; M. Lewis, "In Nature's Casino," *New York Times*, 2007; C. R. Morris, *The Two Trillion Dollar Meltdown: Easy Money, High Rollers, and the Great Credit Crash*, New York: Public Affairs, 2009; A. R. Sorkin, *Too Big to Fail: The Inside Story of How Wall Street and Washington Fought to Save the Financial System—and Themselves*, New York: Viking, 2009; G. Tett, *Fool's Gold: How the Bold Dream of a Small Tribe at J. P. Morgan Was Corrupted by Wall Street Greed and Unleashed a Catastrophe*, New York: Free Press, 2009; and D. Wessel, *In Fed We Trust: Ben Bernanke's War on the Great Panic*, New York: Crown Business, 2009.

uncertainties (doubtless hard to quantify) into their reading of the timing of the downturn as measured on the screens that reflect risk.[12]

Here I am not trying to privilege "bears" over "bulls" or pessimists over optimists in the financial markets. I am interested in those who are willing to recognize that the main brute fact about uncertainty is that it might not favor you in the management of risk. Their pessimism is at least as exemplary of the imaginary of uncertainty as the ethos of those who consistently bet on short- or long-term upswings in any financial market. Contrarians define a tendency to wager on uncertainty rather than on risk as such. This hypothesis about the spirit of those actors that defines the financialization of contemporary capitalism requires a closer look at the relations among uncertainty, calculation, and market analysis in this ethos, and is the subject of the following two sections.

UNCERTAINTY AND CALCULATION

As I have already suggested, the idea of uncertainty has been almost completely forgotten both by practitioners and by analysts who study contemporary capitalism. Hence we need to look more closely at the process—which is simultaneously discursive, technical, institutional, and ideological—by which risk has pushed uncertainty out of the picture, though not entirely successfully. Here Weber can once again come to our assistance.

Weber's entire corpus, especially in those writings concerned with the comparative history of capitalism, turned on his particular understanding of the idea of "magic." For Weber, magic was the main obstacle to the birth of Protestant capitalism, the capitalism of methodicality, sobriety, thrift, and discipline. In his lifelong efforts to study why other major world religions, such as Hinduism, ancient Judaism, Confucianism, and Taoism, did not have the ethical ingredients to kick-start modern capitalism, the culprit for Weber is "magicality." There have been few thorough efforts to examine how Weber used the word "magic," but my own preliminary study suggests that for Weber magic meant some sort of irrational reliance on any sort of technical procedure, in the effort to handle the problems of evil, justice, and salvation. Magic is a kind of coercive proceduralism. Weber, of course, was a great believer in the importance of procedure and associated formalisms in the emergence of modern law, politics, and bureaucracy. But proceduralism in the realm of salvation or ethics

---

12 I owe to my son, Alok Appadurai, the refinement that just timing is not what sets the short sellers apart from those on the "long" side. It is actually their awareness that the downturn has much greater velocity than the uptick, the latter being usually a more gradual and cumulative process. Both short sellers and long sellers must be attuned to timing, but short sellers have much more to fear from the sheer velocity of the decisive downturn on which they have wagered. This also sets these contrarians apart from the bulk of those who "hedge" their investments, since the latter are always trying to balance incompatible expectations about the timing of downturns.

was for him a vestige of magical thinking and an obstacle to ethical rationality and methodicality. It is true that Weber did not have a chance to study Catholicism and Islam carefully in his magnificent tour through the world religions, but his passing observations on these cases confirm that he also regarded them as failures in the elimination of magical thinking and the achievement of the clean ethical slate on which Calvinist methodicality might have taken shape.

Today, however, it is possible to identify a series of magical practices (by which I mean both coercive and divinatory performative procedures) at the heart of global capitalism and, in particular, of the financial sectors. These practices are premised on a general, absolute, and apparently transcendent faith in the market, which appears in both the daily discourses of traders in the financial markets of the United States[13] and in the plaintive wailings of George W. Bush, as when he begged us all to remain loyal members of what might be called "the faith-based economy." Reversing the Weberian logic that leads from doubts about salvation to ascetical discipline, to ethical methodicality, to thrift, and to rational profit making, the new religion of the market treats the market as the source of certainty, as the reward for disciplined focus on its messages and rhythms, and as the all-embracing power that rewards its own elect, so long as they obey its ethical demands. The magical practices that flow from this faith cover a range of terrains, including (1) the varieties of what Callon[14] and his colleagues call "formatting," which allow no products to be qualified, classified, and made legitimate without necessarily being visible; (2) the role of "framing" in the practices of securities analysts, in the face of Knightian uncertainty;[15] (3) the role of finding "likenesses" or similarities in the efforts of investment banks to provide contact languages of valuation for new financial products among sectors of the bank, and between the bank and its clients; (4) the multiplex

---

13   For a vivid documentation, see C. Zaloom, *Out of the Pits: Traders and Technology from Chicago to London*, Chicago: University of Chicago Press, 2006. Zaloom's work belongs to an important set of recent studies that includes the work of Keith Hart, *The Memory Bank: Money in an Unequal World*, London: Texere, 2000; Karen Ho, *Liquidated: An Ethnography of Wall Street*, Durham: Duke University Press, 2009; Edward LiPuma and Benjamin Lee, *Financial Derivatives and the Globalization of Risk*, Durham: Duke University Press, 2004; Bill Maurer, "Repressed Futures: Financial Derivatives' Theological Unconscious," 2002, *Economy and Society*, 31(1), 15–36; Hirokazu Miyazaki, "Between Arbitrage and Speculation: An Economy of Belief and Doubt," 2007, *Economy and Society*, 36(3), 397–416; and Annelise Riles, "Real Time: Unwinding Technocratic and Anthropological Knowledge," 2004, *American Ethnologist*, 31(3), 392–405, which forms the core of the emerging field of cultural studies of finance. This field is ethnographic, context-sensitive, actor-oriented, and meaning-driven in its approach to financial practices and stands in clear contrast to the more visible space of the sociology of finance. I do not engage with it at length in this chapter, given my rather narrow focus, but it should be clear that I see my work as deeply sympathetic to the cultural approach.

14   M. Callon, *The Laws of Markets*, Malden: Blackwell, 1998; M. Callon, Y. Millo, and F. Muniesa, eds., *Market Devices*, Malden: Blackwell, 2007.

15   D. Beunza and R. Garud, "Calculators, Lemmings or Frame-Makers? The Intermediary Role of Securities Analysts," in Callon, et al., *Market Devices*.

sociosemantic manipulations involved in the evolution of the large class of financial products called "derivatives," all of which have in common the sequences of metonym and metaphor identified long ago as primary properties of magical action; and (5) the logic of what has been called financial chartism[16] in the technical analysis of financial securities, which explicitly eschews any analysis of fundamentals, that is, of cause-and-effect relationships between prices and other fundamental economic data, and instead relies entirely on financial charts of prior price movements, which are used as the basis for predictions of the future. These detailed charts, which are regarded by others as entirely unscientific, have very good standing in financial markets and are in reality no different from the charts of astrologers, psychics, or tarot card operators or other diagrammatic formats for prognostication. In short, they are mechanical techniques of prediction with no interest in causal or explanatory principles. Such examples of magical thinking could be multiplied and detailed across the financial markets in great variety and detail. Some outcomes of the new magicalities that undergird the global financial system and especially its speculative institutions are discussed below.

The *techniques of calculability* (and hence its domain) have far exceeded the organizations and tools for its management, hence opening a new distance between expert and popular understandings of risk. I believe that this space is the new location of Knightian uncertainty and is therefore a magnet for exotic financial products, whose effects on the bottom lines of financial businesses is virtually impossible to measure.

Probability and *possibility* have become dangerously confused in many popular understandings, thus opening the door to myriad schemes, scams, and distortions based on emergent forms of personal charisma (see also chapter 15). From the now infamous hard-luck letters from dictators' widows in West Africa to the charismatic confidence game of Bernie Madoff and Allen Stanford, it is evident that widespread uncertainty is leading to wholesale predation by users of numerical strategies on the gullibility of luck- or fortune-oriented thinkers of every variety. The most important space in which to examine the confusion of possibility and probability as ethics, which absorb mass aspirations for change into the space of the official financial sphere, is the burgeoning world of microcredit. I believe that microcredit, in its many global incarnations, can be shown to be a space where small-scale savings among the poor are potentially drawn into large-scale financial profit-making spaces, using the ethicizing discourses of empowerment, trust, and social capital.

The external or transcendent sources of ethics identified by Weber (such as the Calvinist ethic) have been replaced in the corporate world in general, and the financial sector in particular, by various forms of *immanent corporate ethics*,

---

16   A. Preda, "Where Do Analysts Come From?" in Callon, et al., *Market Devices*.

indexed by terms like *transparency, accountability, corporate social responsibility, good governance,* and so forth, thus making the justification of calculative actions immune from broader ethical images and doctrines.

The single best example of the complexities of immanent corporate ethics is the entire doctrine of *conflict of interest,* which is deserving of much closer study by social scientists. This incarnation of older ideas of corruption, nepotism, and misuse of public office, all of which are offshoots of the modern division between personal and professional interest, are fascinating because of their recursive ethical impossibility. So if you take a close look at Sarbanes-Oxley, the locus classicus of recent legislation calculated to protect individuals and corporations from fraud, you can see that it suffers from the fundamental problem of all ethical voluntarism. It requires self-regulation and self-revelation as the guardians against improper business activity and, more specifically, improper profit-making strategies. Close examination of the problems of the voluntaristic nature of the doctrine will show that the entire edifice of professional ethics as conceived by Weber and others has been exposed as impossible by the financial professions. This opens up a space for a new sort of debate about moral regulation from outside the professional sphere.

Finally, in spite (or perhaps because) of the growth in highly technicized models of prediction, forecasting, and risk management in the financial sphere, there has been a steady *hybridization of the ideologies of calculative action,* so that the casino, the racetrack, the lottery, and gambling in general have infused the world of financial calculation and vice versa, thus confusing the spheres of chance and risk as technical features of human life. Such processes of hybridization have also been remarked in recent studies in the sociology of accounting itself.[17]

ACCOUNTING FOR UNCERTAINTY

The relationship between accounting practices and uncertainty in the financial markets has not been much analyzed or developed. I believe that a close redeployment of Weber's key ideas could be of much use in this sphere, if we accept that the major bridge between economic theories and economic instruments in the contemporary financial world is in the area of uncertainty. Knightian uncertainty remains the major challenge for both theorists and practitioners in the field of finance and accounts for debates within economics and between theorists in economics departments and in business schools.

To address the importance of accounting practices in a world of Knightian uncertainty, it is important to return to Weber's analysis of the importance of new accounting practices in the emergence of the modern capitalistic

17   P. Miller, L. Kurunmaki, and T. O'Leary, "Accounting, Hybrids and the Management of Risk," *Accounting, Organizations and Society,* 2008, 33(7–8), 942–67.

enterprise. In particular, we need to revisit Weber's idea of "capital accounting," one of the most lucid expositions of this fundamental innovation in the history of capitalism.

This analysis of the historical role of capital accounting permits us to make a critical link between Weber and Knight, on the matter of uncertainty. Weber's analysis of capital accounting shows that without an innovative accounting device, which permitted capital accounting, there could be a growth in the *wealth* of an actor, but there could be no *profit*. Let me quote Weber[18] on the idea of profit:

> There is a form of monetary accounting which is peculiar to rational economic profit-making; namely, "capital accounting." Capital accounting is the valuation and verification of opportunities for profit and of the success of profit-making activity by means of a valuation of the total assets (goods and money) of the enterprise at the beginning of a profit-making venture, and the comparison of this with a similar valuation of the assets still present and newly acquired, at the end of the process; in the case of a profit-making organization operating continuously, the same is done for an accounting period.

This observation leads Weber[19] to go on to say that "an economic enterprise [*Unternehmen*] is autonomous action capable of orientation to capital accounting." Furthermore, Weber[20] observes, in a crucial passage, that in a market economy "every form of rational calculation, especially of capital accounting, is orientated to expectations of prices and their changes," and this form of calculation depends critically on double-entry bookkeeping. Thus accounting is a precondition to the very idea of profit and is very far from a mere method of recording or measuring something that exists prior to the practice of double-entry bookkeeping. Here Weber has already identified the primary idea behind the entire corpus of MacKenzie and Callon on economic performativity, in spite of their later debates and refinements of this insight.

Nevertheless, as I have already noted, Weber barely paid any attention to risk, and his interest in uncertainty was wholly focused on the soteriological uncertainty of the Calvinist Protestant believer. This is where Knight's classic work on "risk and uncertainty"[21] is of social importance. A recent essay by a distinguished economist and financial practitioner is a strong reminder that we will all fail to explain the current financial crisis until we face Knight's brutal observations about uncertainty, to the effect that "profit arises out of the inherent, absolute unpredictability of things, out of the sheer, brute fact that the

---

18   M. Weber, *Economy and Society: An Outline of Interpretive Sociology*, G. Roth and C. Wittich, eds., Berkeley: University of California Press, 1978, 91.

19   Ibid., 92.

20   Ibid., 92.

21   Knight, *Risk, Uncertainty and Profit*.

results of human activity cannot be anticipated and then only in so far as even a probability calculation in regard to them is impossible and meaningless."[22]

William H. Janeway[23] goes on to make a strong argument to the effect that no amount of manipulation of current models and strategies for managing or forecasting risk will solve the problem of Knightian uncertainty and reminds us that Knight was deeply aware that the problem of uncertainty was a product of the fact that the economy was a forward-looking process and that, in the words of Paul Davidson,[24] the economy was a nonergodic system. We also need to notice that Knight was the first major thinker to recognize that uncertainty was the critical site in which profit-making activity found its success or failure, rather than in the sober methodicality of the Weberian businessman.

In a brilliant essay in a volume edited by J. Stan Metcalfe and Uwe Cantner,[25] Maria Brouwer juxtaposes the ideas of Weber, Schumpeter, and Knight on the role of entrepreneurship in economic development and in demonstrating both the dialogue and the differences among these three major thinkers distinguishes the Weberian entrepreneur, Schumpeter's innovator, and Knight's risk-financing capitalist, who is the only one who selects among alternative innovative ideas *in the face of uncertainty*. Brouwer is thus able to show the direct linkage of profits to uncertainty, the brilliance of Knight's insight that it is finance that makes the crucial difference in determining which innovations will actually come to market, and how the capacity of the financier to take risks on specific innovations actually depends on the capacity to face uncertainty, rather than to manage risk. Profit is the reward for facing uncertainty, not for managing risk or even less, as in Weber's analysis, for methodical business practice.

What Brouwer misses is that if we go back to Weber's ideas about the centrality of capital accounting to profit making, as opposed to his picture of the sober Puritanical businessman, we can see that Weber did understand the relationship of profit making (as opposed to wealth acquisition) to the instruments of accounting, which were in fact designed to measure the relationship between current and future asset value. In this sense, Weber did see that accounting was a tool for managing expectations. What has confounded many later analysts, including myself, is our tendency to confuse the charismatic confidence of Calvin himself (in his certainty of grace and thus in his endorsement of the organization of all of life to the glory of God, outside the confines of a monastic

22   Knight, quoted in W. H. Janeway, "Risk versus Uncertainty: Frank Knight's 'Brute' Facts of Economic Life," retrieved from SSRC website: ssrc.org, 2006.

23   Janeway, "Risk versus Uncertainty."

24   P. Davidson, *Post Keynesian Macroeconomic Theory: A Foundation for Successful Economic Policies for the Twenty-First Century*, Cheltenham: Edward Elgar, 1994.

25   M. Brouwer, "Weber, Schumpeter and Knight on Entrepreneurship and Economic Development," in J. S. Metcalfe and U. Cantner, eds., *Change, Transformation and Development*, Heidelberg: Physica Verlag, 2003.

life) with the more systematic, methodical, rationalized profile of his Puritan followers.[26] The inner certainty, the ecstatic confidence, and the irrational sense of election are all characteristic of Calvin and are what, suitably recontextualized and articulated, is the key to today's short sellers and "bears" that have no risk-managing devices on which to rely.

So where does this leave a new approach to the relationship among accounting, uncertainty, and the financial market? If the entire apparatus of probabilistic devices for financial forecasting cannot be the final guide to profit making in the face of uncertainty (or wagering on one's own sense of the direction and the timing of the downturn in the case of short sellers), we might need to look again at the innovations on the accounting side of the financial markets as the key devices that have now become guides for the exploitation of uncertainty. This possibility has been touched on in recent studies of the performativity of new accounting protocols.

My own (still to be fully developed) intuition is that the spirit that informs today's heroic, charismatic players at the very high ends of the financial market lies *not* in an as yet undiscovered set of proprietary databases, screens, tools, or models, to which lesser players in the market do not have ready access. Rather, these are players who have a different strategy of divination, of reading the signs, charts, trends, flows, patterns, and shifts in the market, than those who are less willing to take their outsized bets on the certainty and timing of market downturns. The sources of this divinatory confidence might lie—this is a working intuition, not a fully developed hypothesis—in the capacity of some players to link innovations in financial *accounting* to gray areas in financial *accountability*. This intuition needs exploration and debate in the future.

One further question that remains to be asked is what exactly we can currently surmise might be the spirit (ethos, ethic) that underpins these "bears." Here I turn to the recent work by Jackson Lears[27] on the historical tension between the culture of chance and the culture of control in American history. In this brilliant work, Lears documents the deep interconnections between religion, commerce, and leisure in American life, as well as the multiple historical sources of this tension. He suggests that today's speculators and day traders represent the still powerful yearning among Americans for the undeserved victory, the lucky gamble, which animates parts of the American economy, and argues that this ethos is part of the deep belief in grace, outside of all human efforts, which still animates many Americans.

I see much of merit in Lears's argument, not least in his readings of Mauss

---

26   I am especially grateful to several conversations with Benjamin Lee, the co-director of the Cultures of Finance Group of New York University, for helping me see the importance of splitting the charismatic and supremely confident Calvin from his methodical and anxious Puritan followers.

27   J. Lears, *Something for Nothing: Luck in America*, New York: Viking, 2003.

and Weber. However, I propose one significant modification of his account. In my view, the masters of the financial universe, particularly those who have the confidence in their own capacity to be lucky in the timing of the short sell, are not really acting on their faith in the workings of chance to offset the working of systems of control. Rather, they believe in their capacity to channel the workings of chance to win in the games dominated by cultures of control. More precisely, they believe in their capacity to channel the workings of uncertainty to be winners in games of risk. All the instruments of risk that characterize today's financial markets (most important, modern derivatives such as over-the-counter derivatives, unregulated by any clearinghouse) are "devices" whose buying and selling are available to anyone with the resources to purchase them. But selling them short requires a deep confidence in the realm of Knightian uncertainty, where there are, by definition, no tools for either modeling or forecasting the timing of the downturn. This confidence, whatever its sources, is the "grace" that the most powerful bears believe they possess.

It is not at all obvious that this sort of belief in the grace that allows one to infuse the machinery of risk with the spirit of chance among today's leading bears is a matter of religion, culture, or class, in any simple sense. Such individuals come from many religious, cultural, and national backgrounds and indeed do not have even common political values (note the contrast between Soros and Paulson, for example). So it does not make sense to replicate the Weberian answer and identify some sort of religious ethos as the distinctive feature of the disposition of these actors. It remains an important ethnographic challenge to identify the contours of this ethic of grace, which in these players takes the form of a capacity to channel uncertainty so as to tame the machinery of risk.

One possible objection to my proposal needs to be addressed: my approach to the ethic that animates the machinery of today's financialized capitalism takes as its quintessential players the bears, the contrarians, and the short sellers. Does this not put players who are by definition against the herd at the center of the sociology of finance?[28] Can outliers be modal social types? My tentative answer is that in a historical moment when the exploitation of risk for the maximization of profit is the central feature of the reigning game, those who are willing to bet against the majority are even better exemplars of the general ethos than those who are fully committed to the general wisdom about growth, upticks, secular improvements, and eternal self-correction in a market that comes closer and

<hr>

28   I should qualify this position by proposing that the "ideal type" of today's financial risk taker may in fact be a composite of several kinds of players. I am stressing in this chapter the profile of the short seller and, more generally, the "bear." Others may include the "proprietary trader," the arbitrageur, and other specialized traders. In this context, the forthcoming work of Robert Wosnitzer on the emergence and significance of proprietary trading in the early 1970s promises to shed important light on this composite social type.

closer to complete efficiency. The players who are most revealing of the foundational ethos in such a context are not those who wish to "tame chance" but those
who wish to use chance to animate the otherwise deterministic play of risk.

MAUSS AND THE PROBLEM OF RETURN

This long Weberian reading of the ethos of today's financialized capitalism was
initiated by some reflections on Mauss. I now return to these reflections. Mauss's
key idea—which was intended to explain not just the logic of gifts in archaic
and primitive economies but also the spirit of the contract in modern societies—was that the obligation to return was animated by the spirit of the gift,
which was in turn produced by the entwinement of giver, gift, and receiver in
the spirit of the thing. In Mauss's analysis, one form of this logic was to be found
in Polynesia, and the other form—much more competitive, political, and
aggressive—was to be found in the potlatch ceremonies of the American Northwest, as richly analyzed by Boas. Mauss's analysis of the North American
potlatch viewed it as an intermediate form between the entirely reciprocal,
collective, and totalizing spirit of the gift economy and the individualizing, utilitarian, and impersonal ethos of the modern contractual economy. Hence the
potlatch tended to revolve around themes of honor and credit, which were less
marked in the gift economies of Polynesia. The high-status players in the
potlatch were willing to spend, give away, and burn great amounts of property
(e.g., blankets, food, and coppers) in efforts to make the reciprocal gift a difficult
one and to create temporary status inferiority for the recipients of their excessive gifts. The ethos of the potlatch is the ethos of the destructively large wager,
the aggressively exorbitant gift. In gambling terms, this is a wager of "everything." The expectation of return in the potlatch is predicated on a downward
spiral of excessive gifts, a kind of mutually assured destruction over time that
binds all players in the game.

    This form of agonistic giving is also part of the spirit of those short sellers
who bet on the size and timing of major downturns in the market. While such
short sellers are often criticized for betting on failure in specific corporations,
markets, and even national economies, they are also lauded for a diligence that
identifies weak assets and overvalued corporations well before the general
population. Such short sellers are also taking large bets predicated on a series of
downturns, in which their chance of big returns is based on placing big bets on
a downward spiral. When Paulson buys insurance on large bundled sets of toxic
subprime mortgages (through Goldman Sachs and others), he is betting on the
obligation of return to him when the inevitable downturn occurs. Those who
buy his bundles of subprime mortgages are also compelled by the obligation to
return.

    Thus there is a simple way to get from Mauss's ideas about the potlatch to today's contrarians and short sellers: the players in the traditional Northwest American potlatch are classical examples of a willingness to bear high risks for high returns; so are their counterparts who specialize in the short sell. The difference is that today's financial players are able to take advantage of Knight's work and use their sense of grace (in regard to uncertainty) to animate their manipulation of derivative markets and their risk devices. They too rely on being successful beneficiaries of the power of the devices they operate to guarantee returns that are quite disproportionate to the amounts they wager to begin with. Especially in the world of today's hedge funds, what is at stake— exactly as Mauss pointed out for the potlatch—is the interlinked nature of honor and credit.

THE GHOST IN THE MACHINE

It remains now to explain the title of this chapter. A serious effort to look at various critical breaks, shifts, or innovations (such as double-entry bookkeeping, subprime mortgages, or credit default swaps, among others) presents evidence for the hypothesis, directly derived from Weber, that the "spirit" of capitalism can exist without any clear institutional, technical, or organizational expression for it and that, conversely, practical forms of capitalism can be identified absent the "spirit" of capitalism, as Weber described it.[29] Relaxed somewhat, this line of thinking suggests that the multitude of today's market devices (in Callon's sense) can be hypermethodical (quantified, monitored, external, impersonal, etc.), while the spirit of their operators can be avaricious, adventurous, exuberant, possessed, charismatic, excessive, or reckless in the manner that Weber argued was exactly *not* the spirit of modern capitalism. In other words, if "spirit" and "system" change over time but often without reference to each other, today's financial world might be a moment of maximum disjuncture (or torque) between hypercharismatic leaders and hypermethodical devices. There are, of course, other less simple combinations and conjunctures, but to explore any of them requires us to admit the gap between the "ghost" and the "machine," each of which might change relatively independently, but which together define the nature of the "system" as an empirical complex at any given place/time.

In a sense, this hypothesis opens an internal tension in that tradition of

---

29   See Knight, *Risk, Uncertainty and Profit*, especially chapter 2. I must note here why I do not directly engage the important work by Luc Boltanski and Eve Chiapello (L. Boltanski and E. Chiapello, *The New Spirit of Capitalism*, London: Verso, 2007) on the "spirit of capitalism," which also owes a great deal to Weber. I do not engage it directly because it focuses on management rather than on finance and is not much interested in the problem of tools, machines, or devices. In this sense my problematic shares more with Callon and Latour than with Boltanski, though I am deeply sympathetic to his efforts to restore Weberian approaches to the contemporary economic world.

science and technology studies that was massively shaped by Latour and Callon and evolved into the general form of Actor Network Theory (ANT) (see chapter 13 for further discussion). This powerful theory itself contains two contradictory impulses. One is brilliantly formulated by Latour[30] in his book on the dynamic role of "assemblages" in the constitution of the social. The other is expressed in many of Callon's important writings on the nature and sociology of devices.[31] If we are to seriously consider the complex process through which the contingent, emergent, and unpredictable associational logics of certain assemblages emerge, this process must involve something of a habitus, disposition, ethic, or spirit that infuses *some* associational forms and precipitates into actual existing crystallizations of the social. This is exactly how I see the spirit of the "bear" entering into the devices (instruments) of the financial market. Absent such a proposal, the world of the device—so brilliantly portrayed by Callon and his colleagues and interlocutors—can seem to be a self-animating device, a static crystallization of just the sort that Latour urges us not to assume as constituting the social a priori. In proposing that my Weberian approach to the spirit of capitalism might allow us to account for how the Latourian assemblage comes to animate the Callonian device, I am, in one sense, doing no more than recovering an idea that first occurred to me (albeit in a highly primitive form) when I wrote the introduction to *The Social Life of Things*.[32]

---

30   Latour, *Reassembling the Social*.
31   See, Callon et al., *Market Devices*.
32   This 1986 essay, in slightly abbreviated form, appears here as chapter 1.

CHAPTER THIRTEEN

The Social Life of Design

THE DESIGN OF EVERYDAY LIFE

Most ordinary people do not experience their social worlds as either planned or designed. They experience these worlds as given, as external to them, as relatively fixed, and as largely indifferent to their own preferences or desires. In reality, however, daily order is produced by social actors who elect to comply with certain rules, fulfill certain obligations, meet certain expectations, and make various deliberate social efforts. Of course, others choose to contest or violate these expectations, but that is a part of the subtlety of human social life.

Social scientists have looked at these activities in a variety of interesting ways. Some, usually anthropologists, have stressed the force of culture and the local understanding of a world that people are brought into as very young children and whose prejudices they quickly take to be part of ordinary life itself. Others, more sociologically inclined, stress the place of roles, statuses, interactions, and institutional rules, which are likewise learned in the process of what is tautologically called socialization. For some great thinkers, like Émile Durkheim, God was just another name for the moral force of society, experienced as so powerful, abstract, and unquestionable by individuals that they projected it into the cosmos as the sacred. Others, like Charles Cooley, George Herbert Mead, and Erving Goffman, were more matter-of-fact, and saw self and society as engaged in a perpetual give-and-take in which actions and reactions acted as a generative mirror, both teaching individuals how to behave and producing social order in its institutional forms. More critical thinkers, like Nietzsche, Marx, and Freud, saw in the dramas of ordinary social life the workings of deeper machineries of class, psyche, and power. But none of them quite characterized the production of daily life as an endeavor that requires effort and imagination as well as an uncommon amount of deliberate investment. Those social scientists who today work in the idiom of rational choice come closest to this recognition, but they suffer from the dogma that all the world's a market and that those ordinary actions that assure and create social order are largely comparable to those that govern the behavior of economic actors transacting in the marketplace. This is the irrational narrowness of rational choice theory.

My own view of the design of social forms took shape in the mid 1990s, when I was trying to understand globalization and found myself forced to ponder its antonym—the local.[1] I saw then that locality itself was a creation that required effort, imagination, deliberation, and persistence, and that it was quite the opposite of a default state or condition. To capture this insight, I coined the phrase "the production of locality,"[2] which I took to refer to the imaginative work that ordinary persons, throughout history, have engaged in to assure that today was as near to yesterday as it was possible to make it. This insight led me to see that the local was as much of a deliberate human construction as the global, and that the differences were differences of scale, texture, volatility, and participation rather than of kind. More important, this was the beginning of my own understanding that even the simplest societies, the ones that looked most stable, traditional, unreflective, and unquestioned, were products of continuous effort on a daily basis. Ordinary life was in fact the product of unrelenting efforts to make sure that catastrophic change, entropy, disenchantment, and weak attachment did not take the toll they so easily could. Thus, daily life in even the simplest societies must be seen as an outcome of design.

From this point of view, design is only partly a specialist activity, confined to an artisanal or digital class, and is better seen as a fundamental human capacity and a primary source of social order. This claim is not as farfetched as it may appear. In most social sciences, social order is not treated as a primary product, but rather as a byproduct of established systems of etiquette, law, religion, or some combination thereof. And byproducts are not usually seen as results of design.

If we change our perspective and view social order as a primary product, it becomes easier to see it as the most important result of design and as a capacity that we all exercise, all the time. In building our careers; in fine-tuning our dealings with our parents, children, and peers; in deciding how hard to party or how selflessly to work; in how to save and how to spend: we are daily engaged in deploying our energies, our resources, our ideas, and our bodies so as to accomplish results that meet our aspirations. These may include hard bodies, good wines, and long vacations as well as such social ends as strong friendships, fruitful careers, and social change. These design processes are the backdrop and social ground from which professional design, the making of iPods and glassware and houses and book covers and toys and watches, actually takes off.

DESIGN IN THE *LONGUE DURÉE*

Human history, from this perspective, could be re-written as a history of design. The ethnographic story of small, pre-state societies is primarily the story of habitation, hunting and gathering, marriage and reproduction, all done with

---

1   A. Appadurai, *Modernity at Large: Cultural Dimensions of Globalization*, Minneapolis: University of Minnesota Press, 1996.

2   Ibid.

enormous attention to the relationship between habitat, technology, climate, and social priorities. The story of pre-state societies is never only a matter of simple survival (and survival is hardly ever simple); it is also the story of intricate forms of tool making, body art, ritual creativity, storytelling, and mythmaking of which we might well be envious today. True, not all pre-state societies were successful, and many succumbed to disease, internal conflict, or massive environmental catastrophe. But that is no reason for us to be contemptuous of the immense range of design solutions found by low-tech societies throughout human history, any more than global warming today leads us to despise silicon chips or the genome project. And early state societies, which preceded the colonial, imperial expansion of Europe—whether in Latin America, Africa, Asia, or the Islamic world—were veritable treasure houses of design, both quotidian and spectacular. Mayan calendars, Chinese silk garments, Islamic calligraphy, and Benin sculpture existed simultaneously with Australian aboriginal kinship systems (that still defy our ability to analyze their intricacy), South Asian mathematical and philosophical systems (which rival any the world has seen), Pacific systems for trade and exchange (that showed exquisite calibrations of status and reciprocity across large distances), circumpolar adaptations to sub-zero temperatures (which required human beings to buttress sociality against the harshest possible climactic conditions), and so on.

Such examples can be indefinitely multiplied from the anthropological record. They show us that long before industrial capitalism, human beings designed sociologies and cosmologies of immense intricacy and did so with an infinite sensitivity to the ever-changing equilibrium between habitat, environment, technology, and social forms. Like all designs, the social designs of these pre-industrial societies were neither perfect nor unchanging. They sometimes led to dysfunctional outcomes, harsh environmental consequences, brutal forms of warfare and gender exploitation and institutions of oppression including corvée labor, slavery, domestic abuse, and tyrannical exploitation. But these are still part of the story of human social life.

With the first signs of the industrial revolutions of the West and the closely allied ventures of Western sailors, merchants, and warriors in search of wealth and power across the globe, a new chapter unfolds in the history of social design, one in which the capacity of new machines to speed up manufacture, trade, and transport inaugurates a new relationship between design, fashion, and the market. This change, which has a variety of tributary histories, is not wholly or solely a product of changes internal to the Atlantic world. It picks up great speed in the seventeenth, eighteenth, and nineteenth centuries, which witness the largest comprehensive world systems known to human history, powered largely by the incessant demands of industrial capitalism. Many of the massive technologies for the production, distribution, and consumption of commodities on a global basis were tied to human interests in new tastes (sugar, pepper, tobacco, tea, to name a few) and to the search for cheaper ways to fulfill basic needs, like textiles in England in the nineteenth century. This period, roughly from the seventeenth to the nineteenth centuries, inaugurates the birth of fashion in its contemporary form, and thus also of "design" in its current sense.

As design and fashion become quasi-independent forces closely connected to the movements of capital and the rapid growth of specialized technologies for manufacture, the world of commodities undergoes a galactic expansion. Starting in about the seventeenth century in Europe, we may properly begin to speak of the "birth of the consumer" and the worldwide reign of the commodity. Over the last four centuries or so, the design of social forms has grown gradually separate from the world of professional design, the latter becoming connected to markets, money, and merchandising with the former becoming substantially the province of rulers, administrators, and armies.

What is relevant to this context is that this period witnessed the gradual emergence of design, fashion, and merchandising as forces with a life of their own, a change which tends to obscure the fact that ordinary human beings continue to be designers of social forms, especially of those forms that define and reproduce the everyday. This is also the period, roughly the epoch of industrial capitalism, in which we can begin to observe a double gap: first a gap between professional design and the quotidian design of everyday life; and second, the subject of a later part of this chapter, a growing gap between design, as substantially confined to the realm of the marketed commodity, and *planning*, an activity connected with cities, states, and empires.

OBJECTS AS AGENTS

The relationship between objects offers a different angle on the tension between fashion, style, and rapid change, on the one hand, and old wealth, status, and lifestyle conservatism, on the other; it is full of paradoxes. At the heart of this tension is our commonsense view of the relationship between the things that surround us and the objects that we design. To refine this commonsense view requires a deeper understanding of the grammar of objects, a topic to which I will return.

It may help to recall the broad argument of chapter 1 about the relationship between things, values, and knowledge (originally formulated in 1986). That argument helped to reshape certain key ideas in the cultural analysis of material life; and among these, now fairly well absorbed into our commonsense, are the following propositions. The first was the idea that things are hard to classify, for example, as being gifts rather than commodities because they are ever-changing. The second idea was that this shape-shifting quality was both cultural, in the sense that objects could be seen to have biographies, lives, and trajectories;

and social, insofar as these biographies were themselves products of long-term shifts in regimes of value. The third perhaps had the most widespread traction, and that was the idea that things could usefully be regarded as having not just itineraries, but also intentionalities, projects, and motives independent of their human handlers.

Now, twenty-five years after these observations have been refined and extended in numerous directions, and across a broad range of disciplines, we are all suffering some degree of object fatigue. And just as we seem to have rung the changes on every canonic problem of this field, from iconography to garba-gology, we are also faced with changes in the spaces of technology, sociality, and media that appear to challenge the very commonsense of our previous under-standings of materiality. Among these are virtualities of every type: mediations without distance, memories without time, clones without originals, and ersatz socialities beyond our pre-cybernetic imaginations. Furthermore, the big ideas of the 1980s and 1990s, loosely gathered together under the label of "post-modernism," seem themselves to have been old-fashioned humanist efforts to contain the coming anarchy of things. So it seems like a good time to revisit the matter of materiality, so as to open up a new line of thinking that leads from the social life of things to the connected issues of fashion, design, and planning. None of these topics had played much of a role in my earlier thinking, and one of them—namely, fashion—had come to interest me in relation to the subject of consumption, which I partially addressed in *Modernity at Large*.

Let us revisit the idea of the social life of things. My starting point here is Bruno Latour's argument, developed over the last decade or so, which amounts to a playful and damning critique of social science, based on his earlier readings of the archive of sociology and anthropology. The critique is simple: if the things that surround us, especially the machinic things, can be shown to have entelechies of their own (swinging doors, subway trains, and the like), may it not be said that social science has committed a huge anthropomorphic sin by omitting nonhu-man actors from its consideration, what Latour called "the missing masses"?[3] And if the confusion of human sociality with all sociality was a huge oversight, what must we do about it? The broad answer shared by Latour and Michel Callon was to announce and exemplify the practice of what they call "Actor Network Theory" (ANT), their major claimant to being the next big idea in social science.

I offer here some thoughts about my unease with the Latourian dispensa-tion about the sociality of things. I have no objection to that part of Actor Network Theory that overlaps with important arguments from Gilles Deleuze and Felix Guattari,[4] extends the insights of *The Social Life of Things*, and

3   B. Latour, "Where are the Missing Masses? Sociology of a Few Mundane Artifacts," in W. Bijker and J. Law, eds., *Shaping Technology, Building Society: Studies in Sociotechnical Change*, Cambridge, MA: MIT Press, 1992.

4   G. Deleuze and F. Guattari, *A Thousand Plateaus: Capitalism and Schizophrenia*,

seeks to develop the idea that the things around us make claims upon us that are not mere ventriloqual socialities, reflecting our own claims upon them. But Actor Network Theory takes a huge sociological tax on earlier ideas of sociality in order to extend the idea of sociality to the empire of things. The tax is this: like all pendulums, ANT has now fixed itself at the other end of the pendulum, and, in its preoccupation with the agency of the device, has evacuated from its accounts of sociality all the things that make human sociality so fascinating in the first place. These occluded elements include: ethical anguish, irrational exuberance, self-fulfilling prophecies (or failed ones), hypocrisy, sour grapes, rising expectations, bottomless wants, and selective receptivity to propaganda, to name just a few. In other words, the cost of extending the idea of sociality in this manner to the empire of things has been to require a truly narrow picture of sociality, shorn of those things that make human sociality worth studying. Some of these criticisms have been raised by other critics of ANT.

The key site of the occlusion of the properly human—or the interestingly and distinctly human—in ANT is to be found in its massive dependence on the idea of the "network," which has now spread from the physical and biological sciences to anthropology, economics, epidemiology, geography, and a host of other social sciences over the last fifty years or so. The image of the network has doubtless had many positive effects on a social science that tended to be atomistic on various scales ranging from individuals to nations. But this benefit has come with a cost, which is the view of the nodes in any network as being relatively passive points of transfer and connectivity. This view has had its own problematic effects because it predisposes us to ignore the possibility that the materiality of nodes makes its own active demands.

The primary problem with images of object agency, network, and the device is not just that they tend to lose the soul of objects, in spite of their intention to reanimate the object, but that they have no real grip on the deepest problem of objects, which is their capacity to generate contexts. The problem of context is one of the black holes of current social science, and this black hole opens new possibilities for thinking about design processes from a social and cultural point of view. This argument about context is what I turn to next.

OBJECTS AND CONTEXTS

We might begin by adapting John Donne's famous line: no object is ever an island, entire unto itself. But here we need to make a small definitional rule. Objects are not things; objects are *designed* things. Or more loosely, objects are

Minneapolis: University of Minnesota Press, 1987; W. J. T. Mitchell, *What Do Pictures Want?: The Lives and Loves of Images*, Chicago: University of Chicago Press, 2005; J. Bennett, *Vibrant Matter: A Political Ecology of Things*, Durham: Duke University Press, 2010.

things as humans have brought them into the orbit of social life. Thus, some trees are objects, while others are just things. To recollect the philosopher George Berkeley, who famously discussed trees falling without anyone hearing them, we may say that such falling trees, outside the human gaze, are merely things. But other trees—the objects of logging, painting, dreaming, pruning— are indeed objects, in the double sense of being objects of a human interest and objects in some sort of social milieu.

If this distinction makes sense, it is not hard to see that objects, due to their long association with human projects and contexts, rarely present themselves in isolation. In this regard, they are like words. They appear in sets, and those sets have some sort of logic. The reason for this is that design is essentially about making categories, sets, and sequences. Design is not about isolated objects.

Before I elaborate on this observation, let me note that the single biggest error in designer thinking is to imagine that the designer works over a single type of object: a watch, a building, a shirt, a video game. This may be called the illusion of singularity, produced by a mistaken overemphasis on the idea of the designer as an artist. It is not, of course, that there is no connection between design and art; it is rather that design mediates the relationship between art, engineering, and the market, with the last two stressing repetition and commodification, the first stressing singularity. The slippage here is from designing a category of object to designing a truly singular member of that category—for example, a watch that is one, and *just* one, of a kind. The extreme step in this "one of a kind" thinking is that it can lead to an interest in producing not just a brilliant new brand, but an object that is truly singular, which only one consumer can buy, own, and enjoy. At this point, the designer has become totally identified with the artist, and has lost his or her links to merchandising and engineering, which are the hallmarks of design as a vocation.

For now, let us simply observe that all objects are designed and that design always implies sets and sequences. Think of an object—any object—and try to think of it all by itself. This is a very hard mental exercise. Objects invariably call forth associations with other objects, sooner or later. A shirt evokes a tie. And then a tie evokes a collar, a collar evokes a bone, a bone evokes muscle, a muscle evokes yet other things. Start somewhere else. Consider the moon, the subject of so much poetry, music, and human observation. Can you think the moon without thinking sooner or later about stars, and once stars enter the picture, can the rest of the visible cosmos be far behind? Or consider something more ordinary, but nevertheless the product of human intervention, like salt or steel. These dumb objects, lumps of materiality, also come with their links, their associations, their sequences, their trajectories, their families of affinity and affiliation.

At this point, it might be objected that I am reinventing Freud and simply suggesting that all objects have associations and that associations, being free, are also arbitrary human creations that have nothing to do with what objects want or how they seek meaning. In fact, Freud's real insight was that what looked like free association to the patient on the couch was the key to underlying patterns, signs, and repressions that were anything *but* free in the realm of the unconscious. The sets and sequences of which objects as designed things are the elementary units, the products of association, are—like linguistic forms— both arbitrary and predictable. That is, they are cultural and conventional. And, as with language, our job is to find out how these sets connect into larger sets and systems. Though conventional, these sets and systems are not simply the product of individual fantasy or whim, any more than a grammatical sentence in English is.

Nor am I simply offering a remix of Proust, who with his celebrated "madeleine" reminded us that objects can evoke moments, periods, and entire biographies through their sensory properties. What Proust neglected to do was to observe that this sensory fact is partly owed to the first loyalty of objects, which is to their own kind, that is, to other objects. As the chain of what I would call "object memories" multiplies, their role as apertures for more abstract recollections kicks in. We do not likely go directly from our response to a "madeleine" to the moment we first tasted of them, but rather through some more obscure chain of material associations that mushroom into the sensation of nostalgia, loss, or melancholy, which object memories sometimes induce.

Since design is surely a part of culture (seen as some sort of local, historical, generative system for producing meaningful actions and legible social forms), we need to be careful not to commit the mistakes of an earlier social science by making the linguistic analogy too mechanical or literal. As far back as the 1970s, linguistically oriented anthropologists showed that language and culture (words and meanings) did not behave in parallel ways and that the point of real connection between language and culture may lie, not in the dictionary (or in one-to-one correspondences between words and meanings), but in the way that words point to or signify things that cannot be deduced from their meaning alone.[5] Since then, anthropologists have tried to look at language less as a model for culture and more as a partial and irregular guide to how cultural systems actually mobilize meaning, affect, and behavior. This has led to a fairly stable consensus that meaning lies less in semantics (the dictionary) and more in pragmatics (what is actually supposed to be accomplished by saying or doing something in a particular way).

So far the relationality of objects has found a loose echo in the idea that objects, like words, also have a grammar. But what sort of grammar are we talking about? How is it related to the meanings of individual things? How do

---

5   M. Silverstein, "Shifters, Linguistic Categories, and Cultural Description," in K. Basso and H. Selby, eds., *Meaning and Anthropology*, New York: Harper & Row, 1976.

people in a particular historical moment recognize proper sequences of objects, meaningful arrangements as opposed to nonsensical ones? The beginnings of an answer to these questions lie in recognizing that the search for grammar in this realm is not well served by looking for the smallest possible unit we can find—unlike, say, in physics, where the quantum revolution showed that the laws of nature were truly built on the behavior of extremely small particles and elements. Today's nanotechnology is based on this strategy. Likewise, in social thought, Claude Lévi-Strauss (building on the insights of the great linguist Ferdinand de Saussure) argued for the importance of very small units (morphemes) whose relationship (through contrast, opposition, etc.) laid the foundation for those distinctions that could be extended to bigger contrasts (night and day, white and black, good and evil, etc.). This was the elementary genius of European structuralism.

This formal miniaturism held sway for some period in anthropology and literary criticism, but gradually came under fire, in the first place because it tended to have difficulties with change and history, and secondly because it tended to ignore the vast range of distinctions that were not oppositions in the structuralist sense. Most important, the erosion of confidence in structuralism as a method came from the growing attention to context among socio-linguists, literary critics, and others (some of them structuralists themselves). Once we concede that all linguistic elements require context for their animation, structuralism becomes inverted and upended. In Jonathan Culler's aphorism, "Meaning is context bound, but context is boundless." What this means is that even in regard to linguistic forms, especially those that compress meaning in the way that poetry typically does, interpretation requires the widening of context and not its reduction to ever smaller elements.

Thus, applied to objects (defined as designed things), we need to ask how objects demand contexts for people to enjoy them, buy them, use them, and interpret them. In human history, for the most part, these contexts were relatively slow to change and thus were fairly straightforward to build and to interpret. Take one well-studied, low-technology context, the world of Melanesia, which till recently experienced little dramatic change in basic technologies of survival, reproduction, and communication. In this world, there was a great deal of long-distance traffic in bird's feathers, which played an important role in the aesthetic and political lives of quite small, isolated societies. These feathers were a kind of luxury good, but they ended up nesting into fairly stable cosmetic and personal patterns in particular kin-based localities. Context, in this case, was relatively stable and relatively legible, both for the people in these communities and for those who now study them.

Once the world of sumptuary laws begins to break down and the relationship between groups of objects and groups of people is no longer tightly controlled by law or public opinion, fashion and design come properly into play as essential elements of social life. Design and fashion, in this changing world, become the infrastructure through which the demand of objects for contexts becomes channeled and stabilized to some extent. This is a vital point, for it allows us to recognize that objects (designed things, by definition) demand contexts that can never be rigidly derived or deduced in advance from any inherent property of the object.

And in a post-sumptuary world, objects have an indefinite multiplicity of possible contexts. A designer tie might suggest a shirt to accompany it. But it may also suggest the fabric for a suit, or for a hat, or for shoes, to take a very simple example. Consider a more nuanced example. An expensive Jaguar may suggest an expensive mountaintop home (as in the popular TV advertisement where a corporate high-flyer says goodbye to his wife at the door of their designer home and skydives off his front porch to the bottom of a canyon, brushes himself off and gets into his car). Thus, a sexy car could also segue into a scene of physical adventure and prompt associations with travel, adventure, conflict, and war. Likewise, diamonds are indeed "forever," but they can support all sorts of ensembles of lifestyle, romance, discretion, or display, in combination with carefully selected scenes involving furs, tiaras, glass and steel lobbies, flowers, and men attired in their own ensembles of context-seeking objects. It is design that renders this potential infinity of contexts into something finite, grammatical, and seductive.

So here is an unconventional answer to how objects demand contexts (and therefore seek meaning). They do so through the regulative and selective work of design, which reduces the range of possibilities and makes a particular designed possibility appear both credible and grammatical. In other words, unlike with language, the grammar of objects is emergent, improvised, and indeed constantly designed and redesigned. This is why we cannot get carried away by the linguistic analogy, so far as objects are concerned.

In the world of design and fashion (which is roughly coterminous with the world after the breakdown of sumptuary societies in many parts of the world after the seventeenth century), objects can seek the company of other objects in a promiscuous and relatively unlimited way. This is even truer in the last thirty years, in what could be called the age of "designer humanity." What I mean by this—following the proposal that we live in a world in which objects and humans are not sharply opposed, but loosely different—is that the combinations of company in which objects (designed things) find themselves has become indefinitely open. And design comes into being to police this infinite variety and bring it into the realm of the possible—and the plausible. Design exists to tame the endless arrangements into which objects may find their way, and to police the imagination of fashion, which is the high-octane force to which design is opposed. So here is an idea worth pausing over: *design exists not to serve fashion, but to limit its infinitude.*

The point is to question the cliché that design as a social practice multiplies material possibilities. Fueled by fashion, in the industrial and post-industrial world, design is seen as producing infinite combinations and contexts for things, marrying colas to perfumes, cars to carnivals, foods to designer homes, drugs to retirement resorts, and so on without limit. In fact, it may be more useful to see design as trying to regulate fashion by slowing down the infinite play of combinatorial possibilities, the dizzying vista of new arrangements of bodies, materials, forms, and functions that advertising daily puts before us.

And this insight may lead us closer to the logic connecting design and context than the conventional idea that design, being the loyal servant of fashion, simply adds technique to the lust for change that defines fashion. Design certainly involves the imagination, but it is defined by the imagination as a source of discipline and not imagination merely as a source of new possibilities for combination and cohabitation among objects. The contemporary joke about the "fashion police" in fact disguises from us the subtler reality of the "design police." To understand the discipline behind design we need to reopen the ways in which designers typically handle objects.

THE CONTEXT AS OBJECT

I have already argued that designers most often think of themselves as having to design a single—and sometimes singular—object: a building, a shirt, a city, a drug, a façade, an interior. But this is a professional illusion that has no future in the age of designer humanity. The fact is that designers—makers of designed things—design contexts for objects which are subsequently sold as self-standing objects. In order to see how designers construct contexts, let us more closely examine a field that is, on first glance, all about context: the field of interior design. Interior design is an interesting field, because it refers to an implicit context—the house or the home—which is already an object, a designed thing. So, the "interior" is a designed object in two senses. First, it is the interior of another object; and secondly, it is itself an object, though a peculiar object, being simultaneously an object and a context. As a context, it contains other objects: lighting, painted surfaces, fabrics, furnishings, fixtures of all sorts, more or less exposed utilities, and instruments. At its outer shell or skin—the house— interior design meets another discipline, architecture. This shell is an object for architects, since it is the thing on which they operate their design intentions. But for interior designers, it serves as a container or context for other objects.

In fact, I want to suggest that this dual identity pertains to all objects of design, not in the literal scalar logic of Chinese boxes or Russian dolls, neatly contained within one another, but in the less literal sense that all objects are simultaneously objects of design and contexts or partial contexts for other objects. The difficulty at the heart of design is how to balance these two aspects of the identity of any designed thing. If you will permit me a hypothesis, I would suggest that great designers know how to blend and balance these two aspects of any object.

The explicit knowledge that underlies design education tends to focus on the property of the object in itself—the lamp, the wine glass, the watch, the room, the house, the gated community, even the city. Younger fields focus on different sorts of objects, such as the logo, the font, the image, the screen, the signal, or other digital objects. But in all cases, the context tends to fall into the unconscious of design education and is rarely consciously discussed by designers themselves. This is natural, since the context in itself looks empty, as if it were not any sort of thing, but merely the blank space between things. It is not a random space, however. Context is a space that generates meanings by generating real and possible relationships and intended and unintended effects for viewers and users. But because contexts cannot be fully anticipated, they fall out of the conscious thinking of designers.

The challenge for designers is that the market does not organize itself through the principle of assemblage, and neither do the methods of industrial and post-industrial manufacture. Both manufacture and merchandising typically tend to concentrate on single categories and reward virtuoso design of the single object, leaving it to a different class of tastemakers to assist customers with making the right assemblage. However expert the advice, the tastemaker (such as Martha Stewart or any number of lesser lifestyle gurus) is swimming uphill against the object, which is usually designed as a competitor with its own kind (watches against watches, fabrics against fabrics). The brilliant impulse behind the Martha Stewart empire, which few have been able to fully imitate, is the insight that one design intellect needs to design all the objects and all the contexts, including the biggest context of all, a lifestyle of glamour for the entire global middle class. The challenge with this sort of ambition to produce a species of "designed humanity" is that it requires intense personal charisma to adhere to the brand, which in this case is the person himself or herself.

Thus, if we closely examine the three-way relationship between design, context, and fashion, we could make the following interim conclusion. Fashion provides the force that stirs the pot by unsettling contexts, just as design defines contexts for objects by defining what objects can relate to each other in a plausible, legible, teachable way. The secret of the great design empires is that they discovered how to keep this cycle of stimulation going for long periods, without much friction in the machine and without allowing the impulses of fashion and design to confuse each other. This is the key to the designer names with long lives: Chanel, Bill Blass, and Christian Dior are only three examples of this genius.

But the problem with fashion, which is also its seduction, is that it is by definition ephemeral. It is made for supersession and obsolescence. Hence my observations about fashion, design, and context cannot be mechanically applied to design in relation to social planning—the building of habitations, streets, cities, and those products which are the tools of community at all levels. So the question I pose today is this: if fashion is the imaginative fuel against which design exercises creative discipline in the realm of consumer products, thus creating new forms of designer humanity, how does this work with buildings, streets, elevators, engines, pipes, parks, cities, highways, and other material tools for social life? What fuel can social design draw on for making our world healthier, more equitable, and more peaceful, if fashion is not quite right for this job? For an answer to this question, we have to reexamine what happens when we replace the joys of ephemerality, which are the key to fashion, with the imperatives of durability, which are the key to social sustainability in design. This brings us to the subject of planning.

PLANNING AND THE FUTURE OF DESIGN

I argued initially that design and fashion define their relationship through a creative tension. Where fashion opens infinite possibilities for the combination of bodies, spaces, and objects, design limits this infinitude by providing a system for making some possible arrangements more credible than others. How, then, is design different from planning?

As with design, it could also be said that planning is as old as humanity, combining as it does the elementary need to predict and forecast and the long and varied history of such techniques as astrology, divination, and seasonal rites with other modes of foresight and calculation involved in migration, settlement design, and marital alliances between groups. At a more abstract conceptual level, all planning carries with it the magic of its roots in the universal inclination to utopias, to images of future perfection, which are to be found in all societies, including the simplest. Likewise, planning can also be seen as a modern solution to the fear of disaster and dislocation that has haunted all human societies, to some degree. So we should not take too short a view of the long-term human practices out of which planning emerges.

But unlike design, which primarily emerges from the explosion of industrial techniques, machines, and social systems, and their direct link to the growth and expansion of world markets through the workings of empire and capital, planning emerges in the early twentieth century mainly under the sponsorship of the state. The intimate connection between planning and the state has been richly discussed by James Scott in his important work, *Seeing Like a State*.[6] Others have made rich contributions to this tradition of analysis, by

6   J. C. Scott, *Seeing Like a State: How Certain Schemes to Improve the Human Condition Have Failed*, New Haven: Yale University Press, 1998.

looking at the general relationship of states to statistics[7] and the links of nationalism to the birth and flourishing of many fields of social inquiry, from geography to literary criticism. Especially important for our purposes is the relationship between colonial governments in Asia and Africa, and the birth of the fields of demography, planning, and development economics. Of these, the closest attention has been paid to the field of development economics, and how it evolved in the wake of the Depression and World War II as the United States began to define a massive role in applying Keynesian economics to the task of reconstruction in Europe, and soon after, in the less developed world. Today, development economics has been encompassed by a wider field of development studies, which includes an interest in health, governance, infrastructure, education, and conflict resolution, as well as in primarily economic subjects like technology transfer, savings, investment, and commerce. Yet planning, as a field, is in an uneasy space, partly claimed by schools of architecture and design, partly by schools of public policy and administration, and partly by departments and programs in applied and development economics. This is because planning, as a field, has not yet achieved an independent disciplinary status, with an independent set of core ideas and texts, methods and techniques, data and hypotheses. It is a hybrid space. This is not a bad thing, and it is indeed an opportunity, since some of the most exciting developments in the natural sciences are occurring across traditional fields, in fields like materials science, biomedicine, nanotechnology, and molecular biology, which do not worry much about recombining the traditions of physics, chemistry, and biology.

The divorce of planning from design has some good justifications. Design has tended to be oriented to objects, to consumers, and to markets. It is built on the triangle between art, engineering, and merchandising. Planning is about collective goals, long-term benefits, and bigger contexts than the individual product, consumer, or household. Planning is more explicitly concerned with sustainability—both social and environmental—than design, and so it has a regulatory relationship to design, just as design has a regulatory relationship to fashion. Where design can be caught up in an immediate need, trend, or material opportunity, planning aspires to be design with a social conscience and to connect the world of goods to the world of politics, justice, and long-term resource constraints.

Thus, the key word that brings design and planning together in this sense is the word "sustainability," a vexed word for which we nevertheless have no good substitute. The main doubts about sustainability arise from two sources. The first is internal, based on the paradox that sustainability is about the long-term,

---

7   J. Brewer, *The Sinews of Power: War, Money, and the English State, 1688–1783*, Cambridge, MA: Harvard University Press, 1990; I. Hacking, "Biopower and the Avalanche of Printed Numbers," *Humanities in Society*, 1982, 5(3–4), 279–95.

but not about eternal life, the latter being God's business. So sustainability is always about social designs that might work for a relatively long time, and this relativity opens up much room for high-stakes debates about costs, priorities, and uncertainties. The second source of doubt about sustainability is that it confuses two different matters, namely the market and our relationship to nature. Those who believe in the market as a natural regulator of all human transactions and as a somewhat magical source of perfect solutions to most social problems worry that sustainability introduces nonmarket issues into social choice, thus putting glue in the engine of the market rather than high-octane fuel. Market-oriented policymakers believe that desirable long-term outcomes are the likely cumulative result of desirable short-term outcomes, and that the market is best on short-term outcomes in regard to anything that involves scarce resources. The fact is that markets fail quite regularly, and their capacity to deliver desirable social outcomes, even in the short run, has convincingly been shown to be doubtful. Hence, we need to think through how planning, sustainability, and design can best work together, both as correctives to market failure and as sources of social policy that do not rely entirely on efficiencies measured by price and consumer demand.

If we recognize that ordinary human beings have significant capacities to plan and design their own futures, we will find stronger connections between our ideas and the values and motives of those whom we actually claim to serve and to represent. We need to make better designs for planning and improve the planning context for our social designs, so that these two activities become more fruitfully meshed in developing solutions for the short- and long-terms. In both regards, we would do well to recognize that ordinary people are already involved in both planning and design as part of their efforts to achieve dignity and equity in their lives in hard cities like Mumbai (see part 2 in this volume). Neither of these goals can be achieved without addressing two subjects, which are the subjects of the following two chapters. In chapter 14, in an effort to place ordinary human beings back at the center of the project of future-building, since humans have always been both planners and designers, we need to build a different model of research as a democratic activity, one which is not restricted to the sphere of high science, policy experts, or other elites. We also need to revisit the project of anthropology, which has so far focused too much on humans as bearers of the force of history, custom, and habit. If anthropology is to make a true contribution to the ways in which human beings can flourish as future-makers, it needs to make the future as a cultural fact an equally important part of its mission. This latter project, which is in many ways the main ethical impulse behind this book, is the topic of the last chapter.

CHAPTER FOURTEEN

Research as a Human Right

This chapter argues that research should be recognized as a right of a special kind—that it be regarded as a more universal and elementary ability. It suggests that research is a specialized name for a generalized capacity to make disciplined inquiries into those things we need to know but do not know yet. I maintain that knowledge is both more valuable and more ephemeral in the age of globalization, and that it is vital for the exercise of informed citizenship. I am concerned here with that portion of the world's population that may get past elementary education to the bottom rung of secondary and post-secondary education, and argue that one of the rights that this group ought to claim is the right to research—to gain strategic knowledge—as this is essential to their claims for democratic citizenship. I then explore the democratization of the right to research, and the nexus between research and action, using the Mumbai-based Partners for Urban Knowledge Action and Research (PUKAR) as an example.

DEPAROCHIALIZING RESEARCH

Research is normally seen as a high-end, technical activity, available by training and class background to specialists in education, the sciences, and related professional fields. It is rarely seen as a capacity with democratic potential, much less as belonging to the family of basic rights. All human beings are, in a sense, researchers, since all human beings make decisions that require them to make systematic forays beyond their current knowledge horizons.

This is especially the case in a world of rapid change, where markets, media, and migration have destabilized secure knowledge niches and have rapidly made it less possible for ordinary citizens to rely on knowledge drawn from traditional, customary, or local sources. Further, as the institutions and values of democracy sweep the world, knowledge (both abstract and empirical) is the coin of the realm, and the capacity to distinguish knowledge from rumor, fact from fiction, propaganda from news, and anecdote from trend, is vital for the exercise of informed citizenship.

Globalization makes knowledge—of whatever type—simultaneously more valuable and more ephemeral. Thus, thinkers like Robert Reich[1] recognized the

---

1 R. B. Reich, *The Work of Nations: Preparing Ourselves for 21st-Century Capitalism*, New York: A. A. Knopf, 1997.

importance of knowledge workers, and many industrial societies are constructing policies for lifelong training and education as essential tools for the economic survival of nations and the economic security of individuals. In this environment, the bulk of the world's ordinary people find themselves in one of three categories. The lower 50 percent are not even in the knowledge game, because they are starving, dispossessed, or economically marginalized. Another category, perhaps another 30 percent of the world's population, have the means and wish to expand their horizons and improve their lives, but they are often pushed into degree factories of one type or another and rapidly channeled into professional or vocational fields where they may get jobs, but rarely get the chance to change jobs, much less to change careers. The top 20 percent (arguably) have the privilege of choosing among career options, examining their options critically, establishing educational preferences, placing bets on different knowledge paths, and changing careers as a consequence of their capacity to benefit from high-end knowledge about knowledge. Such meta-knowledge is the true mark of the global elite.

My argument is addressed to the bottom portion of the upper half of the typical population in poorer countries, the 30 percent or so of the total population who have a shot at getting past elementary education to the bottom rungs of secondary and post-secondary education. This group (which consists of perhaps 1.5 billion people in the world today) is within the framework of global knowledge societies. But their existence in this category is insecure for many reasons, including partial education, inadequate social capital, poor connectivity, political weakness, and economic insecurity. I would suggest that among the rights that this group is capable of claiming—and ought to claim—is the right to research. By this I mean the right to the tools through which any citizen can systematically increase the stock of knowledge that they consider most vital to their survival as human beings and to their claims as citizens.

This rights-based definition of research is hardly conventional. My reasons for proposing it as a starting point for this chapter are partly substantive and partly rhetorical. The substantive part is based on the view that full citizenship today requires the capacity to make strategic inquiries—and gain strategic knowledge—on a continuous basis. Knowledge of AIDS, knowledge of riots, knowledge of labor market shifts, knowledge of migration paths, knowledge of prisons, knowledge of law—all of these are now critical to the exercise of citizenship or the pursuit of it for those who are not full citizens. The rhetorical reason for viewing research from a rights-based perspective is to force us to take some distance from the normal, professionalized view of research and derive some benefit from regarding research as a much more universal, elementary, and improvable capacity.

THE MODERN RESEARCH ETHIC

In much recent discussion about the internationalization of research, the problem term is taken to be "internationalization." I propose that we focus first on research, before we worry about its global portability, its funding, and about training people to do it better. The questions I wish to raise here are: What do we mean when we speak today of research? Is the research ethic, whatever it may be, essentially the same thing in the natural sciences, the social sciences, and the humanities? By whatever definition, is there a sufficiently clear understanding of the research ethic in the academic world of North America and Western Europe to justify its central role in current discussions of the internationalization of academic practices?

Such a deliberately naïve, anthropological reflection upon the idea of research is difficult. Like other cultural keywords, it is so much part of the ground on which we stand and the air we breathe that it resists conscious scrutiny. In the case of the idea of research, there are two additional problems. First, research is virtually synonymous with our sense of what it means to be scholars and members of the academy, and thus it has the invisibility of the obvious. Second, since research is the optic through which we typically find out about something as scholars today, it is especially hard to use research to understand research.

Partly because of this ubiquitous, taken-for-granted, and axiomatic quality of research, it may be useful to look at it not only historically—as we might be inclined to do—but anthropologically, as a strange and wonderful practice that transformed Western intellectual life perhaps more completely than any other single procedural idea since the Renaissance. What are the cultural presumptions of this idea and thus of its ethic? What does it seem to assume and imply? What special demands does it make upon those who buy into it?

Today, every branch of the university system in the West, but also many branches of government, law, medicine, journalism, marketing, and even the writing of some kinds of fiction and the work of the armed forces, must demonstrate their foundation in research in order to command serious public attention or funds. To write the history of this huge transformation of our fundamental protocols about the production of reliable new knowledge is a massive undertaking, better suited to another occasion. For now, let us ask simply what this transformation in our understanding of new knowledge seems to assume and imply.

Consider a naïve definition. Research may be defined as the systematic pursuit of the not-yet-known. It is usually taken for granted that the machine that produces new knowledge is research. But the research ethic is obviously not about just any kind of new knowledge. It is about new knowledge that meets certain criteria. It has to plausibly emerge from some reasonably clear grasp of relevant prior knowledge. The question of whether someone has produced new knowledge, in this sense, requires a community of assessment, which is usually preexistent, vocational, and specialized. This community is held to be competent to assess not just whether a piece of knowledge is actually new, but whether its producer has complied with the protocols of pedigree: the review of the literature, the strategic citation, the delineation of the appropriate universe—neither shapelessly large nor myopically small—of prior, usually disciplinary, knowledge. In addition, legitimate new knowledge must somehow strike its primary audience as interesting. That is, it has to strike them not only as adding something recognizably new to some predefined stock of knowledge, but, ideally, as adding something interesting. Of course, boring new knowledge is widely acknowledged to be a legitimate product of research, but the search for the new-and-interesting is always present in professional systems of assessment.

Reliable new knowledge, in this dispensation, cannot come directly out of intuition, revelation, rumor, or mimicry. It has to be a product of some sort of systematic procedure. This is the nub of the strangeness of the research ethic. In the history of many world traditions (including the Western one) of reflection, speculation, argumentation, and ratiocination, there has always been a place for new ideas. In several world traditions (although this is a matter of continuing debate) there has always been a place for discovery, and even for discovery grounded in empirical observations of the world. Even in those classical traditions of intellectual work, such as those of ancient India, where there is some question about whether empirical observation of the natural world was much valued, it is recognized that a high value was placed on careful observation and recording of human activity. Thus, the great grammatical works of Panini (the father of Sanskrit grammar) are filled with observations about good and bad usage that are clearly drawn from the empirical life of speech communities. Still, it would be odd to say that Panini was conducting research on Sanskrit grammar, any more than that Augustine was conducting research on the workings of the will, or Plato on tyranny, or even Aristotle on biological structures or politics. Yet these great thinkers certainly changed the way their readers thought, and their works continue to change the way we think about these important issues. They certainly produced new knowledge, and they were even systematic in the way they did it. What makes it seem anachronistic to call them researchers?

The answer lies partly in the link between new knowledge, systematicity, and an organized professional community of criticism. What these great thinkers did not do was to produce new knowledge in relation to a prior citational world and an imagined world of specialized professional readers and researchers. But there is another important difference. The great thinkers, observers, discoverers, inventors, and innovators of the pre-research era invariably had moral, religious, political, or social projects, and their exercises in the production of new knowledge were therefore, by definition, virtuoso exercises. Their protocols could not be replicated, not only for technical reasons but because their questions and frameworks were shot through with their political projects and their moral signatures. Once the age of research (and its specifically modern ethic) arrives, these thinkers necessarily become confined to the proto-history of the main disciplines that now claim them or to the footnotes of the histories of the fields into which they are seen as having trespassed. But in no case are they seen as part of the history of research, as such. This is another way to view the much discussed growth of specialized fields of inquiry in the modern research university in the course of the nineteenth and twentieth centuries.

These considerations bring us close to the core of the modern research ethic, to something that underpins the concern with systematicity, prior citational contexts, and specialized modes of inquiry. This is the issue of replicability, or, in the aphoristic comment of my colleague George Stocking, the fact that what is involved here is *not search but re-search*. There is of course a vast technical literature in the history and philosophy of science about verifiability, replicability, falsifiability, and the transparency of research protocols. All of these criteria are intended to eliminate the virtuoso technique, the random flash, the generalist's epiphany, and other private sources of confidence. All confidence in this more restricted ethic of new knowledge reposes (at least in principle) in the idea that results can be repeated, sources can be checked, citations can be verified, calculations can be confirmed by one or many other researchers. Given the vested interest in showing their peers wrong, these other researchers are a sure check against bad protocols or lazy inferences. The fact that such direct crosschecking is relatively rare in the social sciences and the humanities is testimony to the abstract moral sanctions associated with the idea of replicability.

This norm of replicability gives hidden moral force to the idea, famously associated with Max Weber, of the importance of value-free research, especially in the social sciences. Once the norm of value-free research successfully moves from the natural sciences into the social and human sciences (no earlier than the late nineteenth century), we have a sharp line not just between such "ancients" as Aristotle, Plato, and Augustine on the one hand and modern researchers on the other, but also a line between researchers in the strict academic sense and such modern thinkers as Goethe, Kant, and Locke. The importance of value-free research in the modern research ethic assumes its full force with the subtraction of the idea of moral voice or vision and the addition of the idea of replicability. It is not difficult to see the link of these developments to the steady secularization of academic life after the seventeenth century.

Given these characteristics, it follows that there can be no such thing as individual research, in the strict sense, in the modern research ethic, though of course individuals may and do conduct research. Research in the modern, Western sense, is through and through a collective activity, in which new knowledge emerges from a professionally defined field of prior knowledge and is directed toward evaluation by a specialized, usually technical, body of readers and judges who are the first sieve through which any claim to new knowledge must ideally pass. This fact has important implications for the work of "public" intellectuals, especially outside the West, who routinely address nonprofessional publics. I will address this question below. Being first and last defined by specific communities of reference (both prior and prospective), new knowledge in the modern research ethic has one other crucial characteristic that has rarely been explicitly discussed.

For most researchers, the trick is how to choose theories, define frameworks, ask questions, and design methods that are most likely to produce research with a plausible shelf life. Too grand a framework or too large a set of questions and the research is likely not to be funded, much less to produce the ideal shelf life. Too myopic a framework, too detailed a set of questions, and the research is likely to be dismissed by funders as trivial, and even when it is funded, to sink without a bubble in the ocean of professional citations. The most elusive characteristic of the research ethos is this peculiar shelf life of any piece of reliable new knowledge. How is it to be produced? More important, how can we produce institutions that can produce this sort of new knowledge predictably, even routinely? How do you train scholars in developing this faculty for the lifelong production of pieces of new knowledge that function briskly but not for too long? Can such training be internationalized?

I have already suggested that there are few walks of modern life, both in the West and in some other advanced industrial societies, in which research is not a more or less explicit requirement of plausible policy or credible argumentation, whether the matter is child abuse or global warming, punctuated equilibrium or consumer debt, lung cancer or affirmative action. Research-produced knowledge is everywhere, doing battle with other kinds of knowledge (produced by personal testimony, opinion, revelation, or rumor) and with other pieces of research-produced knowledge.

Though there are numerous debates and differences about research style among natural scientists, policymakers, social scientists, and humanists, there is also a discernible area of consensus. This consensus is built around the view that the most serious problems are not those to be found at the level of theories or models, but those involving method: data gathering, sampling bias, reliability of large numerical data sets, and comparability of categories across national data archives, survey design, problems of testimony and recall, and the like. To some extent, this emphasis on method is a reaction to widespread unease about the multiplication of theoretical paradigms and normative visions, especially in the social sciences. Furthermore, in this perspective, method, translated into research design, is taken to be a reliable machine for producing ideas with the appropriate shelf life. This implicit consensus and the differences it seeks to manage take on special importance for any effort to internationalize social science research.

In a paper published in 2000, I argued that the very idea of research has not been sufficiently reflected on, though many adjacent subjects, such as the history of scientific inquiry, the history of the university, the history of education as a field or even sub-practices within it, and of course the history of teaching, have been the subject of much discussion.[2] But these topics surrounded the idea of research, on which there was little critical reflection. My conclusion then was that research was so much a part of the natural vocabulary of contemporary critical thought that there was either no distance or insufficient distance from it. Research is so vital to our academic common sense that it is not a surprise that there is not a lot of direct reflection on it. I remain deeply interested in what research is, and how research as an idea has evolved in the West, what its meanings are, what people think they are doing when they say they are "doing research" or when they are teaching others to do research. And how do people who are entering the world of research, from outside its Western historical home, try to do so? What are the conditions of entry to that world? Why is it so hard to teach people how to "do" research, or what a good research proposal is? Why do some research proposals seem weak or even if they seem strong, why do they later not work, or not seem to produce some significant result? Depending on whether it is in the empirical sciences—social or natural—or in the humanities fields, there is still much to be said about the peculiarity of the activity itself. I continue to be interested in thinking about why research is a strange activity, and above all where its strangeness lies, and I hope to build on the observation that its fundamental mystery is that it purports to be a systematic means for discovering the not-yet-known. How can you have a systematic means for getting to what you do not know? For example, what you do not know might be so profoundly unsystematic that systematically getting to it is logically impossible. Or it may be that your systematic way is not suited to the most important object that you do not know, but ought to be thinking about. So there remains a paradox deep inside the idea of research, and this paradox might explain why it is such a hot-house activity.

I have also become interested in how one teaches about research. If one accepts that there is some element of mystery, paradox, and strangeness about research, how is one going to teach it as part of a pedagogic activity that can be seen as adjacent to research, as in "research and teaching"? Later, in my Mumbai example, I will attempt to flesh out the question, "What does it mean to engage in a pedagogy about research?" in a context where lots of people have no

---

2 A. Appadurai, "Grassroots Globalization and the Research Imagination," 2000, *Public Culture* 21(1), 1–19.

familiarity with that world, and where others (within the university system) who do are not doing so well by the standard criteria. For example, sociology, which used to be a very strong field in Mumbai, is today a weak field by conventional standards. Again, one might question the standards, but by normal standards, the university system in Mumbai would not be considered a healthy system in the sense in which it was healthy in the first century of its existence. And like many other parts of the world, Mumbai's strengths are now in engineering, due to the strong presence of the Indian Institute of Technology (IIT), which is part of a national group of schools, and also in architecture, in design, in business, and of course, in computer programming of every variety. But the classical university system that issues BAs, MAs, PhDs in all the standard fields of humanities, and the social and life sciences, is in poor shape. I will return to the relation of pedagogy to research itself—teaching people to be researchers, as opposed to pedagogy as a whole. This argument requires a prior engagement with one aspect of the link between research and human rights.

THE CRISIS OF RIGHTS

There is a broad and growing literature on the relationship of civil and political human rights (conceived as pertaining to freedom, justice, and equality of some sort) to social and economic rights of many kinds. A parallel discussion in political theory seeks to connect problems of dignity and recognition to discussions of equity and redistribution. These debates grow out of a broader historical context in which the vocabulary and institutions of human rights were formalized as universal values and policy aims after the formation of the United Nations in the middle of the twentieth century. The spread of the values and assumptions of human rights thinking is arguably one of the fastest instances of the globalization of a social ideology. Today, although there is strenuous resistance among various states to particular interpretations of human rights, and of their records in regard to human rights, very few states or political elites openly eschew or dismiss the principle of human rights as such. This is a revolution in consciousness, which has been accompanied by many specific initiatives and dramas at an institutional and personal level. These initiatives often involve previously marginal or invisible harms, such as those affecting children, refugees, guest workers, as well as citizens of different kinds.

The problem with this worldwide ascendancy of the ideology of human rights is that it occurs at the same time as a series of other sweeping changes, some of which also seem to be crises, in the life of national economies, societies, and cultures. As a consequence, there is pressure on human rights laws, courts, and advocates to solve problems of human rights on a larger scale and on a more volatile canvas than at any prior moment in human history. There is a paradox here, since some of these crises of equity, citizenship, and justice are produced by the increased acceptance and endorsement of the idea of human rights itself. Others have independent origins but come to roost in the sites where the values of human rights take national, legal, and political shape. In both cases, the language of human rights is asked to stretch itself beyond elementary and abstract freedoms to include more subtle and material ones. To understand this process, we need a brief survey of the broader turbulence produced by the process of globalization.

Some crises are produced by the rapid, irregular movement of capital as, for example, produced the famous "Asian crisis" of the late 1990s, and are not gone by any means. The divorce of finance capital from other kinds of capital, its rapid movement in forms that are very poorly understood—derivatives and the like—continues with full force (see chapter 12). This movement has produced, worldwide, a deep tension between economic sovereignty, at the locus of the nation state, and cultural sovereignty. I believe that this is the source of a lot of large-scale violence, state violence, as well as other kinds of violence (as I argue in chapters 3 and 4). Few nation states, including the wealthiest, can claim real economic sovereignty, which is a very important basis of the classical nation state. Take the US for example. It is common knowledge that the US consumer economy is financially in hock to mainland China. In broader economic terms, the US is intimately linked with Chinese money, Chinese trade, Chinese goods, and so on. Here is the world's largest and most powerful economy, but it is hardly in control of its own destiny, and of course, smaller economies face the same predicament. This tension produces a certain amount of international conflict, and it also produces a large amount of intranational conflict, especially about minorities or groups who are perceived to be minor, numerically or otherwise.[3] These conflicts are frequently articulated as human rights struggles.

The lag between globalization and the knowledge of globalization is more acute than ever before. For example, in India there is a very vigorous privatization of education, in every sphere, and aggressive overseas players—notably from Australia, but also from the UK, Canada, and to some extent the US—are increasingly involved with the Indian educational market. But now the state is waking up, and paying very close regulatory attention, and is beginning to create elaborate procedures for what are called foreign educational providers, which cannot be ignored by these actors except at the risk of being in noncompliance with the law. India, for all the serious talk about deregulation, privatization, and the open market, is a state-saturated society. The state has recently realized that a significant part of its control over education is being lost, both to private operators inside who have no outside partners, and to educational entrepreneurs from the outside. The field of education shows its

3   Appadurai, *Fear of Small Numbers*.

own version of the new tensions between state sovereignty and the play of the market. The market encourages collaboration, acquisition, mergers, and so on to catch the growing demand (largely located in the 30-percent population segment I discussed earlier) for various new sorts of degrees, diplomas, and certificates for some vocational purpose. Many of these new credentials are about success in a globalized world, and many involve some association with an overseas institution.

This rush to credentialize can be seen, for example, in the field of art and design in India, which is currently being vigorously explored by non-Indian educational ventures. Some of the most aggressive players in the Indian design education market are barely certified or legitimate in their home countries. They are often completely new players. What we see here is a growing diploma market in countries with large populations whose members aspire to "global" certification, and a struggle by recognized universities and their home states to find the right blend of protection and market exploitation. In both India and China, there is a burgeoning field of educational activities that involve major overseas collaborations sanctioned by the official state and university system on the one hand (Harvard, Yale, and Columbia, for example, are among at least fifty American universities with major collaborative agreements in India and China), and a much more seamy bottom end, where barely qualified entrepreneurs, both indigenous and foreign, peddle dubious degrees to the more desperate and the less discriminating. This transformation of the educational sphere complicates the broader traditional history of student traffic between countries (as measured in "international" students in various countries, for example).

The point about this messy space of global educational entrepreneurship, for the purposes of this chapter, is that it reveals that the process of globalization forces states and professional educators to open their markets, offer new kinds of certification, and engage in new forms of market regulation, because the capacity to produce globally useful knowledge is not evenly distributed.

This gap is where "the right to research" can become important. These new educational degrees and institutions are rarely concerned with research. More importantly, they rely on two major distinctions. They thrive on the distinction between teaching and training, and on the distinction between training and research. Thus, they have two effects. The first is to deepen the gap between vocational training and the capacity of the individual to make independent inquiries about their own lives and worlds. The second is to confine research increasingly to high-end inquiries in a handful of capital-intensive settings (usually connected to the natural sciences and technology), while the bulk of the citizenry is pushed into the credentialing machines (if they are in the lucky upper half of their societies that have made it to the post-secondary level).

DEMOCRATIZING THE RIGHT TO RESEARCH: AN EXAMPLE FROM INDIA

What about research that is not confined to the university or the professional elites, but which can be part of the lives of ordinary people? Here I move to a more personal mode, which is nevertheless not just anecdotal.

About ten years ago, sometime before I began to think about grassroots globalization,[4] I decided to do research on Mumbai, the city in which I had grown up, and on which I had done very little research before. I began with an interest in ethnic violence—violence against Muslims in the early 1990s—which quickly expanded to include subjects such as housing, crime, cinema, and other subjects that could not easily be isolated from the issue of collective violence. I also began to see that the official university system was close to bankrupt. The main older Mumbai universities and colleges were, at best, official degree factories where good faculty were often demoralized, coffers were empty, and people were often not getting paid on time. This seemed strange for a university that was well established in India, a country where universities have been very well established for a long time. So I began to think—especially in connection to my own research on grassroots activism in relation to housing (see part 2 of this volume) that I should make an intervention in Mumbai, designed to bring together youth and globalization in a forum for cross-disciplinary debate oriented to extend beyond the upper middle classes of the city. With neither official support nor private backing, and just a small amount of my own research monies, my late spouse and colleague Carol A. Breckenridge and a few other people I knew in India helped to create a small organization called PUKAR, which in Hindi means "to call," and is also an acronym for Partners for Urban Knowledge Action and Research. PUKAR is about ten years old and is registered as a charitable trust, which is the equivalent of a non-profit organization in the US. It involves bringing together what we call "early career researchers," people in their early thirties, with architects and journalists as well as with teachers and social activists. PUKAR also has an older generation of advisors, people who have no stake in it other than to mentor others, who come from the worlds of journalism, business, and film, not just from the university. The idea was to place knowledge and action—specifically creative action, artistic action, political action—in some common framework and to do so with an eye to a number of ambitious goals for any place, but certainly for Mumbai. One goal was to insist that research and action in what we would call the arts, humanities, film, media, should not be separate from research on the economy, infrastructure, and planning. The second aim was to have a local constituency, but to recognize that Mumbai, like

4 Appadurai, "Grassroots Globalization and the Research Imagination."

many other cities, is embedded in global processes, and thus to develop a cadre of younger people who were not only academics, but who shared an interest in the city's future, and in locating the city in the world. Today, this particular aim is the active principle behind a major PUKAR initiative called the Youth Fellowship Project, named for its funders, the Sir Ratan Tata Trust, one of India's most distinguished philanthropies. The SRTT Project currently employs about two dozen senior fellows, each of whom trains between ten and fifteen junior fellows in the techniques of documentation discussed below.

PUKAR (on which more information is available at pukar.org.in) is still fragile because it is not connected to any larger organization, to the state, to the university system, or even to any big NGO or civil society entity. It is funded from small charitable contributions and a few major grants. The distinctive ambition of PUKAR is to find a space in which English speakers—younger English speakers of college age, and their counterparts who are more comfortable in such languages as Marathi, Hindi, and Gujarati, among others—can enter a common dialogue about the city, themselves, and the future.

My honorary relationship to PUKAR is as president of the board of trustees. In Mumbai, we have a director, a small staff, and a group of colleagues we call associates—people who actually do funded research, who collaborate with other institutions in India and abroad—and a group of advisors who help to keep us alert about the larger environment. Our board of trustees helps make policies, runs our budgets, and assures that we are in full compliance with the law in all our activities.

DOCUMENTATION AS INTERVENTION

The organizing slogan (and signature) of PUKAR is the principle that "documentation is intervention." PUKAR owes this idea to one of our younger associates, Rahul Srivastava, who was teaching as a lecturer at Wilson College in Mumbai before he came to PUKAR. Rahul had developed a quite brilliant and unique technique for teaching non-English speakers, or people who had come to English pretty late, and who were not from the upper classes, about urban sociology in a manner that drew on their own knowledge and lives. He established a set of techniques whereby he got them to write essays about their buildings, their streets, and their families. He then encouraged them to take photographs of those things they knew about, and then make films in some cases, and envision more public forms of debate and communication. The idea was to produce a document about their world in the city, because they were all people who felt uncertain about how they belonged in the city, while they are actually crucial to it. Yet they felt as though they were outside the city, outside to some other more powerful, more urbane, more Anglophone citizen. This technique, which has subsequently been adopted by many other groups and organizations concerned with college-age youth, took the name of The Neighborhood Project under Rahul Srivastava, who served as director of PUKAR for three years (2002–2005).

In the last few years, the PUKAR community—its members, its leaders, its partners, and its supporters—have begun to evolve a better understanding of the relationship between the value of documentation as intervention, of grassroots globalization, and of the importance of bringing the capacity to research within the reach of ordinary citizens, especially college-age youth. In this process, we have scaled up our efforts to bring training to larger groups of teachers and students, through the principle of "documentation as intervention." We have also begun to clarify ways of teaching young people, often with humble educational backgrounds, the best ways to use documentation as a pathway into gathering information, entering official archives, doing certain forms of systematic analysis, and disseminating their results in speech, writing, and other media to various urban audiences. As we have scaled up and refined our projects, we have also had deeper confirmation of the potential of this approach to increase the motivation of young people to treat their city and their lives as objects of study, and as contexts susceptible to change. And finally, these experiments in documentation have opened a double path for many young people; one is a deepening of skills they desperately need; the other is the recognition that developing the capacity to document, to inquire, to analyze, and to communicate results has a powerful effect on their capacity to speak up as active citizens on matters that are shaping their city and their world.

Finally, as a knowledge-based organization in a complex urban environment, we are gradually discovering that our commitment to expanding the reach of the idea of research is a truly distinctive way that we can add value to the work of other organizations concerned with even more urgent material issues, such as housing, mortality, sanitation, and safety. Citizens' groups concerned with these other topics frequently need the capacity for research and documentation, but too often they are forced to buy this capacity at high cost or accept external studies and assessments that they cannot easily contest or replace. The detailed story of these experiments and partnerships in the Mumbai context is to be found in various reports and studies done by the PUKAR team.

WHY THE RIGHT TO RESEARCH?

The brief way to firm up the argument of this chapter is to reconnect the steps that link knowledge, globalization, citizenship, and research. The world in which we live is characterized by a growing gap between the globalization of knowledge and the knowledge of globalization. This gap is reflected in the rush for vocational credentials, the struggle to get job-related credentials, the growth in educational mergers, ventures, and collaborations worldwide, and the parallel decline in traditional university settings for teaching, research, and higher education. This gap is most noticeable in the social sciences and humanities, and less so in the professional and technological fields where teaching and training are virtually indistinguishable, and research is completely separated as a high-end laboratory-style activity. At the same time, even for modest jobs, businesses or careers of any kind, young people are faced with questions that transcend their own local experiences and are permeated by global forces and factors: call centers, specialized production techniques, new methods of borrowing and investing money, and new technologies for organizing information and expressing opinion all make it hard for people with strictly local knowledge to improve their circumstances. In a word, while knowledge of the world is increasingly important for everybody (from tourist guides to pharmaceutical researchers), the opportunities for gaining such knowledge are shrinking.

This is why it is important to deparochialize the idea of research and make it more widely available to young people with a wide range of interests and aspirations. Research, in this sense, is not only the production of original ideas and new knowledge (as it is normally defined in academia and other knowledge-based institutions). It is also something simpler and deeper. Research is the capacity to systematically increase the horizons of one's current knowledge, in relation to some task, goal, or aspiration. A Mumbai journalist trying to find out about an earthquake in a nearby town, a hotel manager seeking to make better use of the internet to facilitate bookings, a patient checking to see whether his or her medication is the cheapest or best one available for their condition, a student seeking to know whether a certain school or college is best for him or her, a family trying to find out whether a certain bank is the best one for the type of loan they need, an architect or designer trying to learn where the best possible materials for their project may be available: these are all examples of citizens who need to understand where the best information is available, how much information is enough for a sound decision, where such information is stored, and who might help them to extract what is most significant about it. This is research as a part of everyday life in the contemporary world.

PUKAR's commitment to college-age youth in Mumbai and to the doctrine of documentation as intervention seeks to open the door to this wider conception of research. It is one way in which young people who are entering a world of rapid change, new technologies, and volatile job markets can develop the triple capacity to inquire, to analyze, and to communicate. Research, in this sense, is an essential capacity for democratic citizenship.

The capacity to do research, in this broad sense, is also tied to what I have called "the capacity to aspire" (see chapter 9), the social and cultural capacities to plan, hope, desire, and achieve socially valuable goals. The uneven distribution of this capacity is both a symptom and a measure of poverty, and it is a form of maldistribution that can be changed by policy and politics. In the current context, I can only suggest that the capacity to aspire and the right to research are necessarily and intimately connected. Without aspiration, there is no pressure to know more. And without systematic tools for gaining relevant new knowledge, aspiration degenerates into fantasy or despair. Thus, asserting the relevance of the right to research, as a human right, is not a metaphor. It is an argument for how we might revive an old idea—namely, that taking part in democratic society requires one to be informed. One can hardly be informed unless one has some ability to conduct research, however humble the question or however quotidian its inspiration. This is doubly true in a world where rapid change, new technologies, and rapid flows of information change the playing field for ordinary citizens every day of the week.

Most of all, there is an additional urgency to regarding research as a human right and creating new institutions that enable building a capacity for research. If research is about anything, it is about the ability to create new knowledge. Without new knowledge there can be no new futures. And if anthropology itself is in urgent need of placing the future as a cultural fact at its center, as I shall argue in the next and final chapter of this book, then making the opportunity and capacity for conducting research more widely available to all human beings is the ethical and political counterpart to this intellectual project.

CHAPTER FIFTEEN

The Future as Cultural Fact

I end this book by contemplating a puzzle. Anthropology has had surprisingly little to say about the future as a cultural fact, except in fragments and by ethnographic accident. The historical reasons for this oversight are not hard to identify, but the costs have been high. As the social sciences took shape in the latter half of the nineteenth century, and as sociology took as its central problem the shift from societies of sentiment to societies of contract, anthropology elected a double burden: the study of societies of the past and the studies of societies that appeared immune to the arrival of Western modernity. The rest is history, as they say, and anthropology for most of the twentieth century has struggled to break out of this double confinement. In recent decades, the subjects of anthropology have increasingly been those of the present and of the world we live in: ethnographies of science, technology, state, law, markets, and finance show that anthropology has begun to bring the tools of cultural analysis to the interconnected problems of worldwide and globalizing processes.

Still, the intellectual infrastructure of anthropology, and of the culture concept itself, remains substantially shaped by the lens of pastness. In one or another way, anthropology remains preoccupied with the logic of reproduction, the force of custom, the dynamics of memory, the persistence of habitus, the glacial movement of the everyday, and the cunning of tradition in the social life of even the most modern movements and communities, such as those of scientists, refugees, migrants, evangelists, and movie icons. We maintain the voices of reproduction, durability, and resilience in human life, while the culture concept maintains an epistemology for the discovery of the variety of ways in which human beings absorb newness into frames that they always carry with them before the fact.

This does not mean that anthropology has ignored the many ways in which humanity has encountered, managed, and anticipated the future as a cultural horizon. But these moments, and these insights, have not been aggregated into a general point of view about humans as future-makers and of futures as cultural facts. Consequently, today, the systematic analysis of future-making remains the province of many fields in the social and natural sciences, but not of anthropology. Neoclassical economics (and its many derivative policy fields) is still the most important of these, having formed itself primarily around the study of needs, wants, estimates, calculation, and the projection of macro-outcomes from micro- actions and -choices.[1] In alliance with specialized techniques derived from statistics, and more recently from linear algebra, operations research, and the computational sciences, economics has consolidated its place as the primary field in which the study of how humans construct their future is modeled and predicted. Other fields, such as the environmental sciences and planning and disaster management, have built themselves on the confluence of sophisticated computational techniques and new techniques for mapping, visualization, and high-order information processing. These techniques have captured the dominant spaces in such debates as those surrounding global warming, population growth, long-term resource evaluation, and military/strategic scenario-building. Design, architecture, and planning have substantially dominated that dimension of the future that has to do with tools, ornaments, habitations, and infrastructures (see chapter 13). Anthropology still plays a relatively limited role in ethical debates surrounding such topics as animal rights, cloning, new forms of genetic engineering, and emergent forms of mechanical warfare, except as a site of valuable humanist resistance and critique. But such humanist critique, valuable as it may be, does not constitute a powerful intervention based on a deep understanding of the future as a cultural fact. So how can we build a more systematic and fundamental anthropological approach to the future?

THE FUTURE AS CULTURAL FACT: ASPIRATION, ANTICIPATION, IMAGINATION

We need to construct an understanding of the future by examining the interactions between three notable human preoccupations that shape the future as a cultural fact, that is, as a form of difference. These are imagination, anticipation, and aspiration. I have written elsewhere about the imagination as a social fact, as a practice and a form of work, trying to put the imagination back at the center of cultural activity.[2] The same can and must be done with anticipation and with aspiration.

As we refine the ways in which specific conceptions of aspiration, anticipation, and imagination become configured so as to produce the future as a specific cultural form or horizon, we will be better able to place within this scheme more particular ideas about prophecy, well-being, emergency, crisis, and regulation. We also need to remember that the future is not just a technical

1   T. C. Schelling, *Micromotives and Macrobehavior*, New York: W. W. Norton & Co., 1978.
2   A. Appadurai, *Modernity at Large: Cultural Dimensions of Globalization*, Minneapolis: University of Minnesota Press, 1996.

or neutral space, but is shot through with affect and with sensation. Thus, we need to examine not just the emotions that accompany the future as a cultural form, but the sensations that it produces: awe, vertigo, excitement, disorientation. The many forms that the future takes are also shaped by these affects and sensations, for they give to various configurations of aspiration, anticipation, and imagination their specific gravity, their traction, and their texture. Social science has never been good at catching these properties of human life, but it is never too late to improve.

THE WORK OF THE IMAGINATION

In *Modernity at Large*, I stated the case for looking at the imagination as a collective practice that played a vital role in the production of locality. This argument required me to revisit and revise the history of ethnography so as to observe that the massive archive of field ethnography, produced by anthropologists and their precursors since the late nineteenth century, was less a series of portraits of the local than a series of portraits of the production of locality as an active, sustained, and ongoing process, through which the local emerged against the forces of entropy, displacement, material hardship, and social corrosion faced by all human communities. The idea here was that the local, quite independent of the conditions of the recent phase of globalization, was always a sustained work in process, an emergent that required not only the resources of habit, custom, and history, but also the work of the imagination. In this context, I proposed that the imagination is a vital resource in all social processes and projects, and needs to be seen as a quotidian energy, not visible only in dreams, fantasies, and sequestered moments of euphoria and creativity—as Durkheim, for example, made famous in *The Elementary Forms of the Religious Life*. Anthropologists have frequently noted the power of the imagination in what Victor Turner famously called "liminal" moments,[3] usually special occasions in the lives of shamans, initiates, prophets, and other persons in special states. The ritual lives of these special categories of persons have produced a vast efflorescence of anthropological analyses of dreams, séances, shamanistic ecstasies, possessions, spirit-loss episodes, and other culturally orchestrated traumas. The analysis of myth and ritual in the history of anthropology is replete with testimony to the work of the imagination in small-scale societies, but it is rarely connected to the quotidian social labor of producing locality. Rather, it is typically part of a picture of the inversion, subversion, sublation, or transcendence of the social. As work on ritual grew in sophistication in the second half of the twentieth century, through the

---

3   V. Turner, *The Forest of Symbols: Aspects of Ndembu Ritual*, Ithaca: Cornell University Press, 1970.

work of anthropologists as different as Victor Turner, Clifford Geertz, and Claude Lévi-Strauss, there was a deeper convergence about the social productivity of ritual. Victor Turner's work on social dramas, Geertz's virtuoso piece on the Balinese cockfight, and Lévi-Strauss's meditations on totemic thinking did much to remind us that the imagination was part of the primary machinery of social reproduction. But this work did not produce a generalized rethinking of the production of everyday life, the dynamics of lived experience, or the production of locality as an always incomplete project in even the simplest of societies.

This can even be seen in Pierre Bourdieu's bold effort to place the workings of history, structure, agency, and calculation into a single framework, as early as *Outline of a Theory of Practice*, in which calculation, strategy, and improvisation were deployed as counterpoints to the logic of the habitus. But even here the weight of an earlier structuralist disposition was exorcised by a view of interest, agency, and tactics that seemed too narrow and economistic to be a fully satisfactory account of the complex spaces within which social improvisation actually occurs. Nevertheless, Bourdieu's contributions to what was later dubbed a "theory of practice" must not be underestimated, and they certainly constitute an important step forward in seeing futurity within a broadly cultural frame.

We need a general recuperation of the traces of the imagination in the anthropological record, as one vital element in building a robust anthropology of the future. This will require a new conversation between approaches to liminal moments and persons, to the production of the everyday, and to the linguistic and discursive processes by which violence, disaster, and emergency are made tolerable. One powerful, recent example of this conversation is to be found in Veena Das's major study of violence and its relationship to the everyday in the lives of men and women in Delhi who live in and through the memories of Partition.[4] In my own previous work, I have tried to show that, especially in the lives of ordinary people, the personal archive of memories, both material and cognitive, is not only or primarily about the past, but is about providing a map for negotiating and shaping new futures.[5] While state-generated archives may primarily be instruments of governmentality and bureaucratized power, personal, familial, and community archives—especially those of dislocated, vulnerable, and marginalized populations—are critical sites for negotiating paths to dignity, recognition, and politically feasible maps for the future.

---

4   V. Das, *Life and Words: Violence and the Descent into the Ordinary*, Berkeley: University of California Press, 2006.

5   A. Appadurai, ed., *Globalization*, Durham: Duke University Press, 2003.

ASPIRATION AND THE POLITICS OF HOPE

Hope, and its politics and ethics, now play an increasingly prominent part in philosophy and progressive social science. Ernst Bloch's grand work on hope[6] marked a transition in European social thought from a preoccupation with utopias, radical revolution, and millennial change to more nuanced engagements with hope as a feature of quotidian social life and with the conditions for its cultivation. Michael Hardt and Antonio Negri's ideas about "the multitude"[7] constitute a sketch of the conditions for the global politics of hope, and David Harvey,[8] speaking from a deep engagement with Marxism and geography, has offered us some panoramic thoughts on the spaces of hope.

As one element of my own work with a global network of housing activists, working on the problems of slums, housing, and eviction among the world's poorest urban citizens (see part 2 of this volume), I have argued that what may be called "the capacity to aspire" is unequally distributed and that its skewed distribution is a fundamental feature, and not just a secondary attribute, of extreme poverty (see chapter 9). In that context, I also suggested that in the dialogue between anthropology and economics, especially in the field of development studies, the future had been more or less completely handed over to economics, with anthropology providing a sort of Greek chorus about diversity, history, cultural values, and the dignity of local ways of living. I went on to suggest that it was not fruitful for anthropologists to make the well-known criticisms about neoclassical economics, its abstractions, its indifference to moral frameworks, and its excessive reliance on market models and solutions in regard to the challenges of poverty. The central place for a new dialogue between anthropology and economics is the space in which a variety of social theorists are discussing the relationship between recognition and redistribution, seeking to reconcile the apparently competing claims of dignity with those of elementary access to material needs. The exchanges between Nancy Fraser and Axel Honneth[9] belong to this field of debate.

My own view is that we need to see the capacity to aspire as a social and collective capacity without which words such as "empowerment," "voice," and "participation" cannot be meaningful. In conversation with Charles Taylor, Amartya Sen, and Albert Hirschman, I see the capacity to aspire as a navigational capacity, through which poor people can effectively change the "terms of

6   E. Bloch, *The Principle of Hope*, Cambridge: MIT Press, 1986.
7   M. Hardt and A. Negri, *Multitude: War and Democracy in the Age of Empire*, New York: Penguin Press, 2004.
8   D. Harvey, *Spaces of Hope*, Berkeley: University of California Press, 2000.
9   N. Fraser and A. Honneth, *Redistribution or Recognition?: A Political-Philosophical Exchange*, London: Verso, 2003.

recognition" within which they are generally trapped, terms which severely limit their capacity to exercise voice and to debate the economic conditions in which they are confined. Changing the terms of recognition and strengthening the capacity to aspire is already a strategy of many grassroots social movements, including the housing movement which I study and support, namely, the Shack/ Slum Dwellers International (SDI).

For the purpose of the current argument about the future, it is important to see that the capacity to aspire is a cultural capacity, in the sense that it takes its force within local systems of value, meaning, communication, and dissent. Its form is recognizably universal, but its force is distinctly local and cannot be separated from language, social values, histories, and institutional norms, which tend to be highly specific. Both in the specific context of debates over development, and in the broader context of the conditions of future-making, it is important to show in what sense the capacity to aspire is a cultural capacity, though it belongs to a family of capacities which is recognizably universal.

The best way to do this is by examining the significance of ideas of the good life in different societies. It is true that today, as a consequence of the widespread impact of global media, the speed of cyber-communication and the multiplication of travel circuits (ranging from sex tourism and humanitarian intervention to foreign wars and labor migration), there is a generalized growth in shared images of the good life, some commercial and wealth centered (as evidenced in the rush to trade in stocks among Japanese housewives and Chinese men) and others more political, such as the global growth in popular ideas of democracy, even in places as isolated as Burma and Nepal. Yet these global convergences in the search for prosperity, mobility, and voice still take their force from configurations of value, ethics, and religion that are strikingly local and variable. These configurations can be looked at in the variety of images of the good life that still characterize our world.

An obvious case of this specificity is the world of evangelical Christianity in the United States. For all its bewildering internal variety, it assembles a specific constellation of meanings surrounding the very idea of life, the afterlife, the Christian life, and the virtuous life. Today, especially in those sectors of this world that are heavily mediated through television and radio in the United States, there is a specific combination of values and messages that saturates the Christian fundamentalist world and tends to emphasize: a form of salvific self-help; a healthy dose of commercial enterprise; a powerful stress on "bearing witness" to those who are not "saved"; a strong tendency to enter debates on creation, abortion, and other scientific matters; and a longstanding bias toward the family as a moral oasis against the threats of homosexuality, divorce, and sexual freedom. At the same time, this evangelical world has a strong missionizing dimension, and through such organizations as World Vision has become deeply embedded in the world of transnational humanitarianism, especially in the context of worldwide natural disasters. The vision of the good life that underpins this worldview is Christian in a highly specific American way,[10] in which politics, commerce, and science are co-articulated into a highly particular image of what the Christian good life is about. This conception of the good life is necessarily connected to the highly specific picture of the afterlife, with the figure and person of Jesus being the central ethical presence that both redeems and represents life in the here and now.

This conception of the Christian good life is of course full of internal debates and variations, as is the case in the Islamic world, which also contains a rich variety of ideas of the good life, though they have largely been represented in the West through the lens of terror, jihad, and suicide bombing. This is a rather thin view of the Muslim sense of the good life, which combines a rather different picture of the relationship of authority to community, of commerce and profit to social values and solidarity, and of political warfare to self-reform (as thoughtful students of the concept of *jihad* have made very clear). As Faisal Devji has begun to show in his recent work[11] on the discourses of various Muslim radical thinkers, including the ideologues of Al-Qaeda, they too speak today in the language of humanity and humanism, and thus are not well understood if we see them as crudely anti-secular. They may well represent a powerful metaphysics of the virtuous Muslim life (and afterlife), but this does not prevent them from speaking in the idiom of a certain brand of modernist humanitarianism about suffering, justice, human rights, and human welfare. Yet the languages of the good life in quotidian Muslim practice, with its many variations across the Shia, Sunni and Ismaili worlds, and across the range of social classes from the slums of Cairo to the courts of the Persian Gulf, are marked by their own brands of sexual puritanism, religious fervor, and political aggressiveness. The 2007 pronouncements of the President of Iran at Columbia University, rambling and opportunistic as they might have been, also show that there is a special flavor to ideas about political autonomy, sexual freedom, military strength, and modern educational culture in the contemporary Shia world. The Islamic missionizing impulse also has its own forms of humanist intervention, and although the global spread of Islamic philanthropic money has been widely associated with the financing of terror, there is ample evidence that Islamic global philanthropy is also tied up with its own ideas of equity, social justice, and security for the poor of the Muslim world.

These examples could be multiplied in the pictures of the good life, the afterlife, and the just life in many societies. They are sometimes differentiated by religion, sometimes by history, geography, and language, and sometimes by

---

10   On this cultural specificity, see P. Guyer, *Kant's Groundwork for the Metaphysics of Morals: Reader's Guide*, London: Continuum, 2007.

11   F. Devji, *The Terrorist in Search of Humanity: Militant Islam and Global Politics*, New York: Columbia University Press, 2008.

292   MAKING THE FUTURE

powerful modernist national traditions. All societies contain traditions of messianism, millennialism, and radical change, and in the era of globalization, these have begun to produce unusual new foci of cultural conflict and ethical adventurism, as we witnessed recently in the crisis of a group of South Korean Protestant missionaries in Afghanistan, which has highlighted the rising importance of South Korea as a Protestant missionizing force second only to the United States in various Asian societies and beyond. Anthropology has a fairly strong record in the study of various forms of millennial eruption, notably in the studies of Pacific Island societies in the wake of contact with the West in the middle of the twentieth century and in Native American societies ravaged by white soldiers and colonists in North America in the nineteenth and early twentieth centuries.

Like other social science fields, however, the tendency within anthropology has been to oscillate between studies of utopian and millennial movements on the one hand and, more recently, studies of cultural trauma on the other. This has created a notable gap in the systematic study of the variability in visions of the good life, the afterlife, and the just life. The consequence has been to reinforce the sense that hope is a product of moments of exception and emergency and that the future is not a routine element of thought and practice in all societies. When attention has been paid to the ways in which the future is a part of how societies shape their practices, there has been a similar tendency to oscillate between the poles of metaphysics and abstraction on the one hand (one example of which is the work of the French ethnologist Geneviève Calame-Griaule,[12] on the worldview of the Dogon people of Africa), and on the other, to portray peasants and other non-Western peoples as hyper-rational decision makers, essentially operating from basically universal rational-choice propensities and algorithms.

The missing piece here has been a systematic effort to understand how cultural systems, as combinations of norms, dispositions, practices, and histories, frame the good life as a landscape of discernible ends and of practical paths to the achievement of these ends. This requires a move away from the anthropological emphasis on cultures as logics of reproduction to a fuller picture in which cultural systems also shape specific images of the good life as a map of the journey from here to there and from now to then, as a part of the ethics of everyday life. Such an approach to ideas of the good life as systematically variable and valuable would be a major step toward identifying what it means to assert, as I have done, that the capacity to aspire is a cultural capacity, albeit one that is everywhere the key to changing the terms of the status quo insofar as recognition and redistribution are concerned.

---

12   G. Calame-Griaule, *Ethnologie et Langage. La parole chez les Dogon*, Paris: Gallimard, 1965.

Another way in which to make the case for aspiration as a critical piece of the future as a cultural fact is to say that hope is the political counterpart to the work of the imagination. For it is only through some sort of politics of hope that any society or group can envisage a journey to desirable change in the state of things. It might be true that in some sort of abstract typology there are "hot" and "cold" societies (in Lévi-Strauss's famous distinction), societies which engage or deny change, but in the world we live in today it seems difficult to assert that any society or social group is entirely satisfied with the state of things or that any society has dispensed with the need for a politics of hope. Yet imagination and aspiration, both of which can be shown to be everywhere features of the work of culture, are intimately connected with a third faculty, the faculty of anticipation, which has in some ways been given the greatest amount of play in the archive of anthropology. So let us turn to anticipation as a critical element in the study of the future as a cultural fact.

ANTICIPATION, RISK, AND SPECULATION

In a sense, the good life may be characterized as what, in any society, many people hope to achieve. Yet anthropology has been substantially preoccupied with what societies fear and therefore seek to avoid. At least as far back as the great ethnographic study by E. E. Evans-Pritchard, *Witchcraft, Oracles and Magic Among the Azande*, a major interest among anthropologists working in non-Western societies has been to understand such practices as witchcraft, sorcery, and divination, all linked by a common preoccupation with misfortune but also geared to the containment of the uncertainties in the future as represented by maleficent events in the present. In societies organized along more textual and numerical lines, this is the dynamic that underlies geomancy, astrology, and other technologies of prediction. Max Weber, to whom I shall return shortly, made a fundamental distinction in his gigantic comparative project on the birth of capitalism between magic and religion. Magic, in his view, is substantially characterized by what he considered to be irrational modes of predicting and controlling the religious unknown.

In the study of cultural approaches to risk, we have a rich variety of traditions on which we could draw in order to build a robust anthropology of the future. Perhaps the most familiar is to be found in the many contributions of Mary Douglas on cosmology, the social body, purity, and danger. Beginning with her classic argument about purity and danger,[13] Mary Douglas was perhaps the first major anthropologist to see that there were frequent categorical homologies between cultural maps of the human body, the social body, and the

---

13 M. Douglas, *Purity and Danger: An Analysis of Concepts of Pollution and Taboo*, New York: Praeger, 1966.

cosmos, and that many human societies located danger at those points where categorical distinctions ran the risk of blurring or mixture. This argument, which she famously made with regard to the rules of the Book of Leviticus, provoked much debate and some strong counter-arguments, but it remains a classic argument which can be captured in her brilliant aphorism to the effect that "dirt is matter out of place." In her subsequent work on "natural symbols,"[14] Douglas developed these ideas further and sought to deepen the relationship between bodily, social, and cosmological processes in order to illuminate where different societies located danger and sought to manage it by the avoidance of categorical confusion. But in her later work, explicitly oriented to modern Western societies, she moved from an interest in danger to an interest in risk. In these later writings, notably a major study done in collaboration with Aaron Wildavsky,[15] Douglas made an initial effort to extend her insights from the cosmologies of small-scale societies to the problem of risk and its management in contemporary industrial societies. This later work did bring in an explicit concern with the future as a culturally organized dimension of human life, but it was only a partial breakthrough, since she remained indebted to the concern with taxonomies and classification that she had partly derived from Evans-Pritchard and largely from Durkheim and Mauss. This prevented Douglas from taking on the aspect of risk in modern societies that had come to be dominated by an actuarial framework, itself derived from the birth of probabilistic thinking, the early modern history of insurance in the West, and the subsequent and sharp distinction between risk and uncertainty, first strongly theorized by Frank Knight (see chapter 12). One might say that Mary Douglas bequeathed to us a strong interest in risk, but only a weak understanding of probability, uncertainty, and the manipulation of large numbers in modern life.

That deficit has been recently addressed in a rich body of recent work on a variety of market processes, including modern monetary forms.[16] This specific body of ethnographic inquiries into risk as a managed feature of contemporary life fits into a broader stream of culturally oriented work on emergent neo-liberal forms of capitalism, including millennial capitalism, casino capitalism,

14   M. Douglas, *Natural Symbols: Explorations in Cosmology*, New York: Pantheon Books, 1970.

15   M. Douglas and A. B. Wildavsky, *Risk and Culture: An Essay on the Selection of Technical and Environmental Dangers*, Berkeley: University of California Press, 1983.

16   K. Hart, *The Memory Bank: Money in an Unequal World*, London: Texere, 2000; stock-exchanges: H. Miyazaki, "Between Arbitrage and Speculation: An Economy of Belief and Doubt," *Economy and Society*, 2007, 36(3), 397–416; A. Riles, "Real Time: Unwinding Technocratic and Anthropological Knowledge," *American Ethnologist*, 2004, 31(3), 392–405; new financial instruments: E. LiPuma and B. Lee, *Financial Derivatives and the Globalization of Risk*, Durham: Duke University Press, 2004; gambling as game and lifestyle: J. R. Cattelino, *High Stakes: Florida Seminole Gaming and Sovereignty*, Durham: Duke University Press, 2008; and related similar risk-related phenomena of modern global life: B. Maurer, "Repressed Futures: Financial Derivatives' Theological Unconscious," *Economy and Society*, 2002, 31(1), 15–36.

disaster capitalism, and other highly specific forms of risk-making and risk-taking, which connect the study of modern markets to other dimensions of speculation, crisis, and value in contemporary life.[17] While this is not the context for a detailed review or exegesis of this new body of work, it is worth noticing that it builds on earlier traditions of interest in entrepreneurial ethics (Weber), in commodity fetishism of many kinds (Marx), in spectacle and excess (Bataille),[18] and in cargo cults and various other economic hysterias. What is relevant in much of this work, for the purposes of an anthropology of the future, is a tension between what I call the *ethics of possibility* and the *ethics of probability*.

By the ethics of possibility, I mean those ways of thinking, feeling, and acting that increase the horizons of hope, that expand the field of the imagination, that produce greater equity in what I have called the capacity to aspire, and that widen the field of informed, creative, and critical citizenship. This ethics is part and parcel of transnational civil society movements, progressive democratic organizations, and in general the politics of hope. By the ethics of probability, I mean those ways of thinking, feeling, and acting that flow out of what Ian Hacking called "the avalanche of numbers,"[19] or what Michel Foucault saw as the capillary dangers of modern regimes of diagnosis, counting, and accounting. They are generally tied to the growth of a casino capitalism which profits from catastrophe and tends to bet on disaster. This latter ethics is typically tied up with amoral forms of global capital, corrupt states, and privatized adventurism of every variety.

I offer these two contrasting ethical styles to suggest that beneath the more conventional debates and contradictions that surround what we call globalization there is a tectonic struggle between these two ethics. One place in which we can examine what is at stake in this struggle between the ethics of possibility and the ethics of probability is in the recent attention that has been paid to systematic profiteering from disaster, insecurity, and emergency as a new branch of capitalist speculation.

Two authors in the public sphere offer sobering pictures of the new economy of catastrophe. Naomi Klein[20] draws a direct line from the

---

17   J. Comaroff and J. Comaroff, *Of Revelation and Revolution,* Chicago: University of Chicago Press, 1991; A. Mbembe, *On the Postcolony: Studies on the History of Society and Culture,* Berkeley: University of California Press, 2001; V. Rao, "Post-Industrial Transitions: The Speculative Futures of Citizenship in Mumbai," in R. Mehrotra and P. Joshi, eds., *The Mumbai Reader,* Mumbai: Urban Design Research Institute, 2006; J. L. Roitman, *Fiscal Disobedience: An Anthropology of Economic Regulation in Central Africa,* Princeton: Princeton University Press, 2005.

18   G. Bataille, *Visions of Excess: Selected Writings, 1927–1939,* A. Stoekl, ed., Minneapolis: University of Minnesota Press, 1985.

19   I. Hacking, "Biopower and the Avalanche of Printed Numbers," *Humanities in Society,* 1982, 5(3–4), 279–95.

20   N. Klein, "Disaster Capitalism: The New Economy of Catastrophe," *Harper's,* October

reconstruction profiteering in Iraq to the money that has been made by a variety of corporate interests in infrastructure, energy, security, and engineering in post-Katrina New Orleans. Klein shows that in many sites of disaster, both natural and manmade, throughout the world, we see a similar logic. In her analysis,

> not so long ago, disasters were periods of social leveling, rare moments when atomized communities put disasters aside and pulled together. Today they are moments when we are hurled further apart, when we lurch into a radically segregated future where some of us will fall off the map and others ascend to a parallel privatized state, one equipped with well-paved highways and skyways, safe bridges, boutique charter schools, fast-lane airport terminals, and deluxe subways.[21]

Klein's analysis of what she calls the disaster capitalism complex shows that it is more worrisome than the old military industrial complex, for it is not simply parasitic on the state and public resources, but actually seeks to gut and replace them until public infrastructure is thoroughly exhausted and these very private interests can rent public goods to the very society and state from which it originally hijacked them. Klein is able to show evidence from both the heart of the US government to well beyond it that we are entering a period where disaster apartheid is well on its way to producing a world of suburban green zones, a global version of Baghdad where middle-class suburbanites in guarded suburbs buy and provide their own infrastructure, energy, and security, in anticipation of widespread disaster and infrastructural breakdown. We are already seeing, in areas like suburban Atlanta, the birth of "contract cities"—that is, cities created from scratch by private contractors in order to create stand-alone cities for the suburbs, and to allow them to escape all tax responsibilities for their poorer neighbors and fellow citizens. Even more worrisome, analyses of global economic and political trends show that stock markets now greet news of major disasters with ebullient stock-price increases, thus suggesting that political disaster creates economic booms, *unlike* the steep crash in various markets after 9/11. The spectacular profits produced by the recent spate of disasters worldwide show the thin line between exploiting disasters and counting on them in the race for profits:

> An economic system that requires constant growth while bucking almost all serious attempts at environmental regulation generates a steady stream of disasters all on

---

2007, 47–58; see also N. Klein, *The Shock Doctrine: The Rise of Disaster Capitalism*, New York: Metropolitan Books/Henry Holt, 2007.
    21   Ibid., 50.

its own, whether military, ecological or financial. The appetite for easy, short-term profits offered by purely speculative investment has turned the stock, currency and real-estate markets into crisis-creation machines, as the Asian financial crisis, the Mexican peso crisis, the dot-com collapse, and the subprime-mortgage crisis demonstrate. . . . Disaster generation can therefore be left to the market's invisible hand. This is one area in which it actually delivers.[22]

Klein's analysis can be linked directly into the ethics of probability by referring to an essay by Michael Lewis that appeared in the *New York Times Sunday Magazine* on August 26, 2007, with the title, "In Nature's Casino."[23] Lewis's essay also focuses on disasters, catastrophes, and profits, but has a narrower aim, which is to illuminate the specific ways in which risk managers and analysts have developed new techniques for calculating the odds of catastrophe. Though it appeared a few weeks before Klein's, this essay can be read as an analysis of the technical weaponry generated by the disaster capitalism complex to handle the new risks from which it aims to profit.

Lewis's essay centers on the insurance industry and its relationship to other elements of the global market in risk, especially in the period after Katrina, during which many insurers took massive losses after decades of massive gains in disaster-prone regions of the United States. The center of Lewis's analysis is the growth in the role and respectability of a remarkable new financial instrument called the catastrophe bond, or "cat bond" for short. The catastrophe bond is an instrument calculated to produce profits and minimize losses for the insurance industry, but as a derivative device it also allows a variety of other players to play in what Lewis calls "nature's casino," the market in the calculation of the risks associated with extremely rare events (what quantitative traders call "tail risks" or financial cataclysms that are believed to have a 1 percent or less chance of occurring). Catastrophe bonds allow their buyers in effect to become sellers of catastrophe insurance: the buyer will lose all his or her money if a certain disaster event occurs within a certain number of years and the seller of the cat bond—usually an insurance company seeking to insure itself against extreme losses—pays the buyer a high rate of interest. Certain hedge funds are big players in catastrophe bonds, and an entirely new brand of companies, which are dominated by natural scientists and mathematicians, create models for valuing the risks of catastrophic events, on the basis of which the whole casino operates. In short, catastrophe has become an object not just of the profits from traditional insurance (and so-called re-insurance) but of new kinds of financial instruments that quantify risk in relation to events where the past is a highly imperfect guide to the future. This industry, built around a sophisticated

22   Ibid., 58.
23   M. Lewis, "In Nature's Casino," *New York Times*, 2007.

combination of probabilistic thinking, gambling, scientific modeling, pricing, and risk-assessment, captures almost perfectly what I am calling the ethics of probability and its ruthless approach to the problems of a world of (valuable) disasters. If we combine Naomi Klein's incisive analysis of the disaster capitalism complex (which directly promotes disaster as a source of windfall profits based on disaster apartheid and the gutting of public infrastructure) with Lewis's analysis of new financial instruments and protocols (which increase the ways of profiting from the risk associated with unlikely events), we can see that the ethics of probability takes risk to spaces of emergency and suffering which were unimagined by someone like Weber when he associated the spirit of entrepreneurship with certain Calvinist religious doctrines and psychologies.

The challenge for those who wish to study mechanisms for gambling, speculation, risk taking, and other forms of wager in the contemporary world is that we do not yet have a reliable way to connect vernacular understandings of uncertainty, risk, and forecasting as practices of everyday life in all societies, to the massive new technologies that have emerged to manage risk in its aggregate and catastrophic forms and to profit from it through sophisticated new financial markets and instruments. To be able to do this we need to examine, in a culturally informed way, the zones and practices through which the ethics of possibility come into contact with the ethics of probability in specific regional, historical, and cultural milieus. This will require the close study of whether and how those who sell their organs as part of an organ trade, or those who practice highly risky forms of sexual contact, or those who undertake dangerous journeys in order to cross national borders, or those who elect to work in extremely hazardous conditions (such as diamond mines) on the chance of striking it rich, or those who use *feng shui* to determine the logic of expensive new homes, or those who build homes in ecologically fragile settings against all warnings, see their actions in the complex negotiations between the ethics of possibility and the ethics of probability. Such ethnographic work is still in its infancy. To explore this space more carefully, we need to reopen the many meanings of the idea of "speculation," all of which have strong linguistic, religious, and vernacular inflections, so that we can gain a better picture of the ways in which the sciences of anticipation today interact with the quotidian strategies and practices of future-making.

For the large percentage of the world's population which may be said to function in the condition of "bare life,"[24] we have not yet found ways to articulate how anticipation, imagination, and aspiration come together in the work of future-making. For even "bare life" never lacks in moral shape and texture, and never operates outside a rich affective frame. As the world of the habitus has

---

24 G. Agamben, *Homo Sacer: Sovereign Power and Bare Life*, Stanford: Stanford University Press, 1998.

been steadily eroded by the pressures of improvisation, the future is certainly not a neutral or technical space for all those who occupy the space of possibility rather than of probability as their primary orientation to the world. To most ordinary people—and certainly to those who lead lives in conditions of poverty, exclusion, displacement, violence, and repression—the future often presents itself as a luxury, a nightmare, a doubt, or a shrinking possibility. For those societies and groups now faced by growing suffering, dislocation, disaster, or disease—roughly 50 percent of the world's population by any measure—the biggest affective reality is that the future is a trauma inflicted on the present by the arrival of crises of every description. Consequently, hope is often threatened by nausea, fear, and anger for many subaltern populations. This affective crisis, which also inhabits a geography that is not uniform, planetary, or universal, needs to be fully engaged by those who seek to design the future, or even to design *for* the future, taking account of the fact that the future is not a blank space for the inscription of technocratic enlightenment or for nature's long-term oscillations, but a space for democratic design that must begin with the recognition that the future is a cultural fact.

OUR DISCIPLINES, OURSELVES

These thoughts about the urgency of building a robust anthropology of the future bring me back to the journey I have undertaken in this book. I opened the book with a chapter that was first published in 1986, a chapter about how things circulate, about how such circulation both encounters and transforms different regimes of value, and about how these regimes can only be understood if we concede to objects some of the same forms of agency, energy, and biographical vicissitude that we attribute to ourselves.

The subsequent chapters of this book have explored ways in which the last few decades of globalization have complicated my initial thoughts about the social life of things. We can see now that the forms of circulation continue to interact with the circulation of forms to produce unexpected new cultural configurations in which locality always takes surprising new forms. And as the process of globalization continues to generate complex new crises of circulation, we need to commit ourselves to a partisan position, at least in one regard, and that is to be mediators, facilitators, and promoters of the ethics of possibility against the ethics of probability. I have alluded to this distinction at various points in the preceding chapters. Here I will simply say that this ethical commitment is grounded in the view that a genuinely democratic politics cannot be based on the avalanche of numbers—about population, poverty, profit, and predation—that threaten to kill all street-level optimism about life and the world. Rather, it must build on the ethics of possibility, which can offer a more inclusive platform for improving the planetary quality of life and can accommodate a plurality of visions of the good life.

For those of us who still work in and from the academy, this ethical argument cannot be applied abstractly or in those domains from which we are most distant or disconnected. It must begin at home: in our institutions, our disciplines, and our methods. This is why I have anchored this book around an argument about the importance of the anthropology of the future to the very future of anthropology. It is not that I believe in the divine election of anthropology to save the academy, and much less the world. Every field of expertise and inquiry can and must make its own versions of this critical journey. I foreground anthropology in recognition of the fact that it is my own medium, context, and formative ground. It is, furthermore, also a circulating form of thought that will continue to make its own global journeys. I believe that these global journeys in the future of anthropology are much more likely to strengthen the ethics of probability if they take serious account of the need for an anthropology of the future. In this regard, if in no other, we have nothing to lose but our chains.

Bibliography

Adams, F. G., and Behrman, J. R. (1982). *Commodity Exports and Economic Development*. Lexington, MA: Lexington Books.

Agamben, G. (1998). *Homo Sacer: Sovereign Power and Bare Life*. Stanford: Stanford University Press.

Alsop, J. W. (1982). *The Rare Art Traditions: The History of Art Collecting and its Linked Phenomena*. Princeton: Princeton University Press.

Alter, J. (2000). *Gandhi's Body: Sex, Diet, and the Politics of Nationalism*. Philadelphia: University of Pennsylvania Press.

Anderson, B. (1991 [1983]). *Imagined Communities: Reflections on the Origin and Spread of Nationalism*. London: Verso.

Anderson, B. (1998). *The Spectre of Comparisons: Nationalism, Southeast Asia, and the World*. New York: Verso.

Appadurai, A. (1978). "Understanding Gandhi." In P. Homans (ed.), *Childhood and Selfhood: Essays on Tradition, Religion, and Modernity in the Psychology of Erik H. Erikson*. Lewisburg, PA: Bucknell University Press.

Appadurai, A. (ed.). (1986). *The Social Life of Things: Commodities in Cultural Perspective*. Cambridge: Cambridge University Press.

Appadurai, A. (1996). *Modernity at Large: Cultural Dimensions of Globalization*. Minneapolis: University of Minnesota Press.

Appadurai, A. (1998). "Dead Certainty: Ethnic Violence in the Era of Globalization." *Public Culture* 10(2), 225–47.

Appadurai, A. (1998). "Full Attachment." *Public Culture* 10(2), 443–9.

Appadurai, A. (2000). "Grassroots Globalization and the Research Imagination." *Public Culture* 12(1), 1–19.

Appadurai, A. (ed.). (2003). *Globalization*. Durham: Duke University Press.

Appadurai, A. (2006). *Fear of Small Numbers: An Essay on the Geography of Anger*. Durham: Duke University Press.

Appadurai, A., and Holston, J. (1999). "Introduction: Cities and Citizenship." In J. Holston (ed.), *Cities and Citizenship*. Durham: Duke University Press.

Arendt, H. (1951). *The Origins of Totalitarianism*. New York: Harcourt, Brace & Co.

Arendt, H. (1958). *The Human Condition*. Chicago: University of Chicago Press.

Austin, J. L. (1962). *How to Do Things with Words*. Oxford: Oxford University Press.

Azoy, G. W. (1982). *Buzkashi, Game and Power in Afghanistan*. Philadelphia: University of Pennsylvania Press.

Balibar, E. (1991). "The Nation Form: History and Ideology." In E. Balibar and I. M. Wallerstein (eds.), *Race, Nation, Class: Ambiguous Identities*. New York: Verso.

Bataille, G. (1985). *Visions of Excess: Selected Writings, 1927–1939*. A. Stoekl (ed.). Minneapolis: University of Minnesota Press.

Batliwala, S., and Brown, L. D. (2006). *Transnational Civil Society: An Introduction*. Bloomfield, CT: Kumarian Press.

Baudrillard, J. (1968). *Le Système des Objets*. Paris: Gallimard.

Baudrillard, J. (1975). *The Mirror of Production*. St. Louis: Telos Press.

Baudrillard, J. (1981). *For a Critique of the Political Economy of the Sign*. St. Louis: Telos Press.

Bayly, C. A. (1983). *Rulers, Townsmen, and Bazaars: North Indian Society in the Age of British Expansion, 1770–1870*. Cambridge: Cambridge University Press.

Bayly, C. A. (1986). "The Origins of Swadeshi (Home Industry): Cloth and Indian Society, 1700–1930." In Appadurai, A. (ed.), *The Social Life of Things: Commodities in Cultural Perspective*. Cambridge: Cambridge University Press.

Beck, U. (1992). *Risk Society: Towards a New Modernity*. London: Sage Publications.

Beck, U. (2000). *What is Globalization?* London: Blackwell.

Benedict, B. (1983). *The Anthropology of World's Fairs: San Francisco's Panama Pacific International Exposition of 1915*. London: Scolar Press.

Benjamin, W. (1968). "The Work of Art in the Age of Mechanical Reproduction." In H. Arendt (ed.), *Illuminations*. New York: Harcourt, Brace & World.

Bennett, J. (2010). *Vibrant Matter: A Political Ecology of Things*. Durham: Duke University Press.

Beunza, D., and Garud, R. (2007). "Calculators, Lemmings or Frame-Makers? The Intermediary Role of Securities Analysts." In M. Callon, Y. Millo, and F. Muniesa (eds.), *Market Devices*. Malden, MA: Blackwell.

Beunza, D., and Stark, D. (2004). "Tools of the Trade: The Socio-Technology of Arbitrage in a Wall Street Trading Room." *Industrial and Corporate Change* 13(2), 369–401.

Bhabha, H. K. (1990). *Nation and Narration*. New York: Routledge.

Bindé, J. (2000). "Toward an Ethics of the Future." *Public Culture* 12(1), 51–72.

Bloch, E. (1986). *The Principle of Hope*. Cambridge, MA: MIT Press.

Bohannan, P. (1955). "Some Principles of Exchange and Investment among the Tiv." *American Anthropologist* 57(1), 60–70.

Boltanski, L. (1999). *Distant Suffering: Morality, Media, and Politics*. New York: Cambridge University Press.

Boltanski, L., and Chiapello, E. (2007). *The New Spirit of Capitalism*. London: Verso.

Bose, S. (2011). *His Majesty's Opponent: Subhas Chandra Bose and India's Struggle against Empire*. Cambridge, MA: Belknap Press of Harvard University Press.

Bourdieu, P. (1977). *Outline of a Theory of Practice*. R. Nice (trans.). Cambridge: Cambridge University Press.

Bourdieu, P. (1984). *Distinction: A Social Critique of the Judgment of Taste*. Cambridge, MA: Harvard University Press.

Braudel, F. (1982). *The Wheels of Commerce*. New York: Harper & Row.

Breckenridge, C. (1984). "The Subject of Objects: The Making of a Colonial High Culture." Unpublished paper.

Breckenridge, C. A., Pollock, S., and Bhabha, H. K. (eds.). (2000). *Cosmopolitanism*. Durham: Duke University Press.

Brewer, J. (1990). *The Sinews of Power: War, Money, and the English State, 1688–1783*. Cambridge, MA: Harvard University Press.

Brouwer, M. (2003). "Weber, Schumpeter and Knight on Entrepreneurship and Economic Development." In J. S. Metcalfe and U. Cantner (eds.), *Change, Transformation and Development*. Heidelberg: Physica Verlag.

Buford, B. (1993). *Among the Thugs*. New York: W. W. Norton & Co.

Burghart, R. (1978). "Hierarchical Models of the Hindu Social System." *Man* 13(4), 519–36.

Calame-Griaule, G. (1965). *Ethnologie et Langage. La parole chez les Dogon*. Paris: Gallimard.

Callon, M. (ed.) (1998). *The Laws of the Markets*. Malden, MA: Blackwell.

Callon, M. (2007). "An Essay on the Growing Contribution of Economic Markets to the Proliferation of the Social." *Theory, Culture and Society* 24(7–8), 139–63.

Callon, M., Millo, Y., and Muniesa, F. (eds.). (2007). *Market Devices*. Malden, MA: Blackwell.

Callon, M., and Muniesa, F. (2003). "Economic Markets as Calculative Collective Devices." *Reseaux* 21(122), 189–233.

Campbell, S. (1983). "Kula in Vakuta: The Mechanics of Keda." In J. W. Leach and E. R. Leach (eds.), *The Kula: New Perspectives on Massim Exchange*. Cambridge: Cambridge University Press.

Cassady, R. (1974). *Exchange by Private Treaty*. Austin: Bureau of Business Research, University of Texas at Austin.

Cassanelli, L.V. (1986). "Qat: Changes in the Production and Consumption of a Quasilegal Commodity in Northeast Africa." In Appadurai, A. (ed.), *The Social Life of Things: Commodities in Cultural Perspective*. Cambridge: Cambridge University Press.

Castells, M. (1996). *The Rise of the Network Society*. Cambridge, MA: Blackwell.

Cattelino, J. R. (2008). *High Stakes: Florida Seminole Gaming and Sovereignty*. Durham: Duke University Press.

Chapman, A. (1980). "Barter as a Universal Mode of Exchange." *L'Homme* 20(3), 33–83.

Chatterjee, P. (1986). *Nationalist Thought and the Colonial World: A Derivative Discourse.* Minneapolis: University of Minnesota Press.

Cheah, P. (2006). *Inhuman Conditions: On Cosmopolitanism and Human Rights.* Cambridge, MA: Harvard University Press.

Cheah, P., and Robbins, B. (eds.). (1998). *Cosmopolitics: Thinking and Feeling beyond the Nation.* Minneapolis: University of Minnesota Press.

Cochrane, G. (1970). *Big Men and Cargo Cults.* Oxford: Clarendon.

Cohan, W. D. (2010). *House of Cards: A Tale of Hubris and Wretched Excess on Wall Street.* New York: Anchor Books.

Collins, R. (1979). *The Credential Society.* New York: Academic Press.

Comaroff, J., and Comaroff, J. (1991). *Of Revelation and Revolution.* Chicago: University of Chicago Press.

Comaroff, J., and Comaroff, J. (2000). "Privatizing the Millenium: New Protestant Ethics and the Spirits of Capitalism in Africa, and Elsewhere." *Afrika Spectrum* 35(3), 293–312.

Curtin, P. D. (1984). *Cross-Cultural Trade in World History.* Cambridge: Cambridge University Press.

Dalton, G. (1978). "The Impact of Colonization on Aboriginal Economies in Stateless Societies." *Research in Economic Anthropology* 1(1), 131–84.

Damon, F. H. (1983). "What Moves the Kula: Opening and Closing Gifts on Woodlark Island." In J. W. Leach and E. Leach (eds.), *The Kula: New Perspectives on Massim Exchange.* Cambridge: Cambridge University Press.

Das, V. (2006). *Life and Words: Violence and the Descent into the Ordinary.* Berkeley: University of California Press.

Davenport, W. H. (1986). "Two Kinds of Value in the Eastern Solomon Islands." In Appadurai, A. (ed.), *The Social Life of Things: Commodities in Cultural Perspective.* Cambridge: Cambridge University Press.

Davidson, P. (1994). *Post Keynesian Macroeconomic Theory: A Foundation for Successful Economic Policies for the Twenty-First Century.* Cheltenham: Edward Elgar.

Davis, M. (2006). *Planet of Slums.* London: Verso.

de Boeck, F. (2001). "Garimpeiro Worlds: Digging, Dying and 'Hunting' for Diamonds in Angola." *Review of African Political Economy* 28(90), 549–62.

de Certeau, M. (1984). *The Practice of Everyday Life.* Berkeley: University of California Press.

Deleuze, G., and Guattari, F. (1987). *A Thousand Plateaus: Capitalism and Schizophrenia.* Minneapolis: University of Minnesota Press.

Derrida, J. (1994). *Given Time: I. Counterfeit Money.* P. Kamuf (trans.). Chicago: University of Chicago Press.

Derrida, J. (1994). *Specters of Marx: The State of the Debt, the Work of Mourning, and the New International*. New York: Routledge.

Devji, F. (2008). *The Terrorist in Search of Humanity: Militant Islam and Global Politics*. New York: Columbia University Press.

Dies, E. J. (1925). *The Wheat Pit*. Chicago: Argyle Press.

Dies, E. J. (1975). *The Plunger: A Tale of the Wheat Pit*. New York: Covici-Friede.

Dimaggio, P. (1982). "Cultural Entrepreneurship in Nineteenth-Century Boston: The Creation of an Organizational Base for High Culture in America." *Media, Culture & Society* 4(1), 33–50.

Diwakar, R. R. (1949). *Satyagraha in Action: A Brief Outline of Gandhiji's Satyagraha Campaigns*. Calcutta: Signet Press.

Douglas, M. (1966). *Purity and Danger: An Analysis of Concepts of Pollution and Taboo*. New York: Praeger.

Douglas, M. (1967). "Primitive Rationing: A Study in Controlled Exchange." In R. Firth (ed.), *Themes in Economic Anthropology*. London: Tavistock.

Douglas, M. (1970). *Natural Symbols: Explorations in Cosmology*. New York: Pantheon Books.

Douglas, M., and Isherwood, B. (1979). *The World of Goods: Towards an Anthropology of Consumption*. New York: Basic.

Douglas, M., and Wildavsky, A. B. (1983). *Risk and Culture: An Essay on the Selection of Technical and Environmental Dangers*. Berkeley: University of California Press.

Dumont, L. (1970). *Homo Hierarchicus: The Caste System and its Implications*. M. Sainsbury (trans.). Chicago: University of Chicago Press.

Dumont, L. (1980). *On Value (Radcliffe-Brown Lecture)*. Proceedings of the British Academy (Vol. LXVI). London: Oxford University Press.

Durkheim, É. (1965 [1912]). *The Elementary Forms of Religious Life*. New York: Free Press.

Dwivedi, S., Mehrotra, R., and Mulla-Feroze, U. (1995). *Bombay: The Cities Within*. Bombay: India Book House.

Edgerton, F. (trans.). (1972). *The Bhagavad Gita*. Cambridge, MA: Harvard University Press.

Engquist, J., and Lantz, M. (eds.). (2009). *Dharavi: Documenting Informalities*. New Delhi: Academic Foundation.

Erikson, E. H. (1969). *Gandhi's Truth: On the Origins of Militant Nonviolence*. New York: W. W. Norton & Co.

Evans-Pritchard, E. E. (1967 [1937]). *Witchcraft, Oracles and Magic among the Azande*. Oxford: Clarendon Press.

Fernandez, J. (1965). "Symbolic Consensus in a Fang Reformative Cult." *American Anthropologist* 67(4), 902–27.

Fernandez, J. (1974). "The Mission of Metaphor in Expressive Culture, with Comments and Rejoinder." *Current Anthropology* 15(2), 119–45.

Fernandez, J. (1986). *Persuasions and Performances: The Play of Tropes in Culture*. Bloomington: Indiana University Press.

Firth, R. (1983). "Magnitudes and Values in Kula Exchange." In J. W. Leach and E. Leach (eds.), *Kula: New Perspectives on Massim Exchange*. Cambridge: Cambridge University Press.

Fliegelman, J. (1993). *Declaring Independence: Jefferson, Natural Language and the Culture of Performance*. Stanford: Stanford University Press.

Foucault, M. (1979). "Governmentality." In G. Burchell, C. Gordon, and P. Miller (eds.), *The Foucault Effect: Studies in Governmentality*. Chicago: University of Chicago Press.

Fraser, N. (2001). *Redistribution, Recognition and Participation: Toward an Integrated Conception of Justice*. World Culture Report 2. Paris: UNESCO Publications.

Fraser, N., and Honneth, A. (2003). *Redistribution or Recognition?: and A Political-Philosophical Exchange*. London: Verso.

Geary, P. (1986). "Sacred Commodities: The Circulation of Medieval Relics." In Appadurai, A. (ed.), *The Social Life of Things: Commodities in Cultural Perspective*. Cambridge: Cambridge University Press.

Geertz, C. (1973). "Thick Description: Toward an Interpretative Theory of Culture." In C. Geertz, *The Interpretation of Cultures: Selected Essays*. New York: Basic Books.

Geertz, C. (1979). "Suq: The Bazaar Economy in Sefrou." In C. Geertz, H. Geertz, and L. Rosen (eds.), *Meaning and Order in Moroccan Society*. Cambridge: Cambridge University Press.

Geertz, C. (1980). "Ports of Trade in Nineteenth-Century Bali." *Research in Economic Anthropology* 3, 109–22.

Gell, A. (1986). "Newcomers to the World of Goods: Consumption among the Muria Gonds." In Appadurai, A. (ed.), *The Social Life of Things: Commodities in Cultural Perspective*. Cambridge: Cambridge University Press.

Ghassem-Fachandi, P. (2006). *Sacrifice, Ahimsa, and Vegetarianism: Pogrom at the Deep End of Non-Violence*. Ithaca: Cornell University Press.

Ghurye, G. S. (1964). *Indian Sadhus*. Bombay: Popular Prakashan.

Giddens, A. (2000). *Runaway World: How Globalization Is Reshaping Our Lives*. New York: Routledge.

Gingrich, A., and Banks, M. (eds.). (2006). *Neo-Nationalism in Europe and Beyond: Perspectives from Social Anthropology*. London: Berghahn Books.

Girard, R. (1977). *Violence and the Sacred*. Baltimore: Johns Hopkins University Press.

Gluckman, M. (1983). "Essays on Lozi Land and Royal Property." *Research in Economic Anthropology* 5(1), 1–94.

Goffman, E. (1969). *The Presentation of Self in Everyday Life*. London: Allen Lane.

Goffman, E. (1974). *Frame Analysis: An Essay on the Organization of Experience.* New York: Harper & Row.

Goldthwaite, R. (1983). "The Empire of Things: Consumer Culture in Italy." Paper presented at Ethnohistory Workshop, University of Pennsylvania, November 10, 1983.

Gourevitch, P. (1998). *We Wish to Inform You That Tomorrow We Will Be Killed With Our Families: Stories From Rwanda.* New York: Farrar, Straus and Giroux.

Graburn, N. H. H. (1976). *Ethnic and Tourist Arts.* Berkeley: University of California Press.

Gray, J. N. (1984). "Lamb Auctions on the Borders." *European Journal of Sociology* 25(1), 59–82.

Gregory, C. A. (1982). *Gifts and Commodities.* London: Academic Press.

Gudeman, S. (1984). "Rice and Sugar in Panama: Local Models of Change." Paper presented at the Ethnohistory Workshop, University of Pennsylvania, October 6, 1984.

Guyer, P. (2007). *Kant's Groundwork for the Metaphysics of Morals: Reader's Guide.* London: Continuum.

Habermas, J. (1975). *Legitimation Crisis.* T. McCarthy (trans.). Boston: Beacon.

Hacking, I. (1982). "Biopower and the Avalanche of Printed Numbers." *Humanities in Society* 5(3–4), 279–95.

Hannerz, U. (1992). *Cultural Complexity: Studies in the Social Organization of Meaning.* New York: Columbia University Press.

Hannerz, U. (1996). *Transnational Connections: Culture, People, Places.* London: Routledge.

Hansen, T. B. (1999). *The Saffron Wave: Democracy and Hindu Nationalism in Modern India.* Princeton: Princeton University Press.

Hardt, M., and Negri, A. (2004). *Multitude: War and Democracy in the Age of Empire.* New York: Penguin Press.

Hart, K. (1982). "On Commoditization." In E. Goody (ed.), *From Craft to Industry: The Ethnography of Protoindustrial Cloth Production.* Cambridge: Cambridge University Press.

Hart, K. (2000). *The Memory Bank: Money in an Unequal World.* London: Texere.

Harvey, D. (2000). *Spaces of Hope.* Berkeley: University of California Press.

Hebdige, D. (1983). "Travelling Light: One Route into Material Culture." *RAIN (Royal Anthropological Institute News)* 59, 11–13.

Heesterman, J. C. (1957). *The Ancient Indian Royal Consecration: The Rajasuya Described According to the Yajus Texts.* Gravenhage: Mouton.

Held, D. (1995). *Democracy and the Global Order: From the Modern State to Cosmopolitan Governance.* Stanford: Stanford University Press.

Hencken, H. (1981). "How the Peabody Museum Acquired the Mecklenburg Collection." In *Symbols* (Vol. 2–3). Peabody Museum, Harvard University.

Herzfeld, M. (1997). *Cultural Intimacy: Social Poetics in the Nation-State*. New York: Routledge.

Hirschman, A. O. (1970). *Exit, Voice and Loyalty: Responses to Decline in Firms, Organizations, and States*. Cambridge, MA: Harvard University Press.

Hirschman, A. O. (1977). *The Passions and the Interests: Political Arguments for Capitalism*. Princeton: Princeton University Press.

Ho, K. (2009). *Liquidated: An Ethnography of Wall Street*. Durham: Duke University Press.

Hobsbawm, E. J. (1990). *Nations and Nationalism since 1780: Programme, Myth, Reality*. Cambridge: Cambridge University Press.

Hodgson, M. G. S. (1974). *The Venture of Islam: Conscience and History in a World Civilization*. Chicago: University of Chicago Press.

Holston, J. (1991). "Autoconstruction in Working-Class Brazil." *Cultural Anthropology* 6(4), 447–65.

Honig, B. (1991). "Declarations of Independence: Arendt and Derrida on the Problem of Founding a Republic." *American Political Science Review* 85(1), 97–113.

Hopkins, T. K., and Wallerstein, I. M. (1982). *World-Systems Analysis: Theory and Methodology*. Beverly Hills: Sage Publications.

Hulme, P. (1986). *Colonial Encounters: Europe and the Native Caribbean, 1492–1797*. New York: Methuen.

Hyde, L. (1979). *The Gift: Imagination and the Erotic Life of Property*. New York: Random House.

Ignatieff, M. (1998). *The Warrior's Honor: Ethnic War and the Modern Conscience*. New York: Owl Books.

Janeway, W. H. (2006). "Risk versus Uncertainty: Frank Knight's 'Brute' Facts of Economic Life." Retrieved from SSRC website: www.ssrc.org.

Jockin, A., Patel, S., and Burra, S. (2005). "Dharavi: A View from Below." *Good Governance India Magazine* 2(1).

Keck, M. E., and Sikkink, K. (1998). *Activists beyond Borders: Advocacy Networks in International Politics*. Ithaca: Cornell University Press.

Khare, R. S. (1984). *The Untouchable as Himself: Ideology, Identity, and Pragmatism among the Lucknow Chamars*. Cambridge: Cambridge University Press.

Klein, N. (2007). "Disaster Capitalism: The New Economy of Catastrophe." *Harper's* (October), 47–58.

Klein, N. (2007). *The Shock Doctrine: The Rise of Disaster Capitalism*. New York: Metropolitan Books/Henry Holt.

Knight, F. H. (2009 [1921]). *Risk, Uncertainty and Profit*. Boston: Houghton Mifflin Co.

Kopytoff, I. (1986). "The Cultural Biography of Things: Commoditization as Process." In Appadurai, A. (ed.), *The Social Life of Things: Commodities in Cultural Perspective*. Cambridge: Cambridge University Press.

Latour, B. (1992). "Where Are the Missing Masses? Sociology of a Few Mundane Artifacts." In W. Bijker and J. Law (eds.), *Shaping Technology, Building Society: Studies in Sociotechnical Change*. Cambridge, MA: MIT Press.

Latour, B. (2005). *Reassembling the Social: An Introduction to Actor-Network-Theory*. Oxford: Oxford University Press.

Leach, E. (1983). "The Kula: An Alternative View." In J. W. Leach and E. Leach (eds.), *The Kula: New Perspectives on Massim Exchange*. Cambridge: Cambridge University Press.

Lears, J. (2003). *Something for Nothing: Luck in America*. New York: Viking.

Lears, T. J. J. (1981). *No Place of Grace: Antimodernism and the Transformation of American Culture, 1880–1920*. New York: Pantheon Books.

Lee, B. (1998). "Peoples and Publics." *Public Culture* 10(2), 371–94.

Lerner, D. (1958). *The Passing of Traditional Society: Modernizing the Middle East*. Glencoe: Free Press.

Lewis, M. (2007). "In Nature's Casino." *The New York Times*. Retrieved from http://www.nytimes.com/2007/08/26/magazine/26neworleans-t.html.

Lewis, M. (2010). *The Big Short: Inside the Doomsday Machine*. New York: W. W. Norton & Co.

LiPuma, E., and Lee, B. (2004). *Financial Derivatives and the Globalization of Risk*. Durham: Duke University Press.

Lomnitz, C. (2005). *Death and the Idea of Mexico*. Cambridge, MA: Zone.

Lopez, R. S. (1971). *The Commercial Revolution of the Middle Ages, 950–1350*. Englewood Cliffs, NJ: Prentice-Hall.

Lorenzen, D. N. (1978). "Warrior Ascetics in Indian History." *Journal of the American Oriental Society* 98(1), 61–75.

Lubin, T. (2001). "Veda on Parade: Revivalist Ritual as Civic Spectacle." *Journal of the American Academy of Religion* 69(2), 377–408.

MacKenzie, D. (2006). *An Engine, Not a Camera*. Cambridge, MA: MIT Press.

MacKenzie, D., Muniesa, F., and Siu, L. (eds.). (2007). *Do Economists Make Markets? On the Performativity of Economics*. Princeton: Princeton University Press.

Malinowski, B. (1978 [1922]). *Argonauts of the Western Pacific*. London: Routledge.

Malkki, L. H. (1995). *Purity and Exile: Violence, Memory, and National Cosmology among Hutu Refugees in Tanzania*. Chicago: University of Chicago Press.

Manuel, P. (1993). *Cassette Culture: Popular Music and Technology in North India*. Chicago: University of Chicago Press.

Marcus, G. (1985). "Spending: The Hunts, Silver, and Dynastic Families in America." *European Journal of Sociology* 26(2), 224–59.

Marriot, M. (1968). "Caste-Ranking and Food Transactions: A Matrix Analysis." In M. B. Singer and B. S. Cohn (eds.), *Structure and Change in Indian Society*. Chicago: Aldine.

Marx, K. (1971). *Capital: A Critical Analysis of Capitalist Production*. Moscow: Progress Publishers.

Marx, K. (1973). *Grundrisse: Foundations of the Critique of Political Economy*. New York: Vintage Books.

Maurer, B. (2002). "Repressed Futures: Financial Derivatives' Theological Unconscious." *Economy and Society* 31(1), 15–36.

Mauss, M. (1967). *The Gift*. New York: W. W. Norton & Co.

Mbembe, A. (2001). *On the Postcolony: Studies on the History of Society and Culture*. Berkeley: University of California Press.

Medick, H., and Sabean, D. (eds.). (1984). *Interest and Emotion: Essays on the Study of Family and Kinship*. Cambridge: Cambridge University Press.

Miller, D. (ed.). (1983). "Things Ain't What They Used to Be." Special section of *RAIN (Royal Anthropological Institute News)* 59, 5–7.

Miller, P., Kurunmaki, L., and O'Leary, T. (2008). "Accounting, Hybrids and the Management of Risk." *Accounting, Organizations and Society* 33(7–8), 942–67.

Mintz, S. W. (1979). "Time, Sugar and Sweetness." *Marxist Perspectives* 2(4), 56–73.

Mitchell, W. J. T. (2005). *What Do Pictures Want? The Lives and Loves of Images*. Chicago: University of Chicago Press.

Mitlin, D., and Satterthwaite, D. (2004). *Empowering Squatter Citizen: Local Government, Civil Society, and Urban Poverty Reduction*. London: Earthscan.

Miyazaki, H. (2007). "Between Arbitrage and Speculation: An Economy of Belief and Doubt." *Economy and Society* 36(3), 397–416.

Moffatt, M. (1979). *An Untouchable Community in South India: Structure and Consensus*. Princeton: Princeton University Press.

Morris, C. R. (2009). *The Two Trillion Dollar Meltdown: Easy Money, High Rollers, and the Great Credit Crash*. New York: Public Affairs.

Mudimbe, V. Y. (1994). *The Idea of Africa*. Bloomington: Indiana University Press.

Mukerji, C. (1983). *From Graven Images: Patterns of Modern Materialism*. New York: Columbia University Press.

Munn, N. D. (1977). "The Spatiotemporal Transformations of Gawa Canoes." *Journal de la Société des Océanistes* 33(54), 39–53.

Munn, N. D. (1983). "Gawan Kula: Spatiotemporal Control and the Symbolism of Influence." In J. W. Leach and E. Leach (eds.), *The Kula: New Perspectives on Massim Exchange*. Cambridge: Cambridge University Press.

Nappi, C. (1979). *Commodity Market Controls: A Historical Review*. Lexington, MA: Lexington Books.

Narayan, D., Chambers, R., Shah, M. K., and Petesch, P. (2001). *Voices of the Poor: Crying Out for Change*. New York: Published for the World Bank by Oxford University Press.

Narayan, D., Patel, R., Schafft, K., Rademacher, A., and Koch-Schulte, S. (2001). *Voices of the Poor: Can Anyone Hear Us?* New York: Published for the World Bank by Oxford University Press.

Nef, J. U. (1958). *Cultural Foundations of Industrial Civilization*. New York: Harper.

Neuwirth, R. (2004). *Shadow Cities: A Billion Squatters, a New Urban World*. New York: Routledge.

Nordstrom, C. (2007). *Global Outlaws: Crime, Money, and Power in the Contemporary World*. Berkeley: University of California Press.

Nussbaum, M. C., and Cohen, J. (1996). *For Love of Country: Debating the Limits of Patriotism*. Boston: Beacon Press.

Ortner, S. B. (1995). "Resistance and the Problem of Ethnographic Refusal." *Comparative Studies in Society and History* 37(1), 173–93.

Pagden, A. (1983). *The Fall of Natural Man: The American Indian and the Origins of Comparative Ethnology*. Cambridge: Cambridge University Press.

Patel, S., Burra, S., and D'Cruz, C. (2001). "Slum/Shack Dwellers International (SDI): Foundations to Treetops." *Environment and Urbanization* 13(2), 45–59.

Patel, S., and Thorner, A. (eds.). (1995). *Bombay: Mosaic of Modern Culture*. Bombay: Oxford University Press.

Pendse, S. (1995). "Toil, Sweat and the City." In S. Patel and A. Thorner (eds.), *Bombay: Metaphor for Modern India*. Bombay: Oxford University Press.

Perlin, F. (1983). "Proto-Industrialization and Pre-Colonial South Asia." *Past and Present* 98(1), 30–95.

Pinch, W. R. (1996). *Peasants and Monks in British India*. Berkeley: University of California Press.

Pinch, W. R. (2006). *Warrior Ascetics and Indian Empires*. New York: Cambridge University Press.

Pollock, S. I. (2006). *The Language of the Gods in the World of Men: Sanskrit, Culture, and Power in Premodern India*. Berkeley: University of California Press.

Powers, M. J. (1983). *Getting Started in Commodity Futures Trading*. Columbia: Investor Publications.

Preda, A. (2007). "Where Do Analysts Come From?" In M. Callon, Y. Millo, and F. Muniesa (eds.), *Market Devices*. Malden, MA: Blackwell.

Price, J. A. (1980). "The Silent Trade." *Research in Economic Anthropology* 3, 75–96.

Proctor, R. (1995). "The Destruction of 'Lives Not Worth Living.'" In J. Terry and J. Urla (eds.), *Deviant Bodies: Critical Perspectives on Difference in Science and Popular Culture, Race, Gender, and Science*. Bloomington: Indiana University Press.

Rao, V. (2006). "Post-Industrial Transitions: The Speculative Futures of Citizenship in Mumbai." In R. Mehrotra and P. Joshi (eds.), *The Mumbai Reader*. Mumbai: Urban Design Research Institute.

Reddy, W. M. (1986). "The Structure of a Cultural Crisis: Thinking About Cloth in France Before and After the Revolution." In Appadurai, A. (ed.), *The Social Life of Things: Commodities in Cultural Perspective*. Cambridge: Cambridge University Press.

Reich, R. B. (1992). *The Work of Nations: Preparing Ourselves for 21st-Century Capitalism*. New York: A. A. Knopf.

Renfrew, C. (1986). "Varna and the Emergence of Wealth in Prehistoric Europe." In Appadurai, A. (ed.), *The Social Life of Things: Commodities in Cultural Perspective*. Cambridge: Cambridge University Press.

Riles, A. (2004). "Real Time: Unwinding Technocratic and Anthropological Knowledge." *American Ethnologist* 31(3), 392–405.

Robbins, B. (1999). *Feeling Global: Internationalism in Distress*. New York: New York University Press.

Roitman, J. L. (2005). *Fiscal Disobedience: An Anthropology of Economic Regulation in Central Africa*. Princeton: Princeton University Press.

Rosenau, J. (1997). *Along the Domestic-Foreign Frontier: Exploring Governance in a Turbulent World*. Cambridge: Cambridge University Press.

Rothermund, I. (1963). *The Philosophy of Restraint: Mahatma Gandhi's Strategy and Indian Politics*. Bombay: Popular Prakashan.

Rudolph, L. I., and Rudolph, S. H. (1967). *The Modernity of Tradition: Political Development in India*. Chicago: University of Chicago Press.

Sahlins, M. D. (1972). *Stone Age Economics*. Chicago: Aldine.

Sahlins, M. D. (1976). *Culture and Practical Reason*. Chicago: University of Chicago Press.

Sahlins, M. D. (1981). *Historical Metaphors and Mythical Realities: Structure in the Early History of the Sandwich Islands Kingdom*. Ann Arbor: University of Michigan Press.

Sahlins, M. D. (1987). *Islands of History*. Chicago: University of Chicago Press.

Said, E. W. (1978). *Orientalism*. New York: Pantheon Books.

Sassen, S. (1998). *Globalization and its Discontents*. New York: New Press.

Sassen, S. (1999). *Guests and Aliens*. New York: New Press.

Sassen, S. (2000). "Spatialities and Temporalities of the Global: Elements for a Theorization." *Public Culture* 12(1), 215–32.

Schelling, T. C. (1978). *Micromotives and Macrobehavior*. New York: W. W. Norton & Co.

Schmidt, A. (1971). *The Concept of Nature in Marx*. London: New Left Books.

Schudson, M. (1984). *Advertising, the Uneasy Persuasion: Its Dubious Impact on American Society*. New York: Basic Books.

Schumpeter, J. A. (2008 [1942]). *Capitalism, Socialism, and Democracy*. New York: Harper Perennial.

Scott, J. C. (1990). *Domination and the Arts of Resistance: Hidden Transcripts*. New Haven: Yale University Press.

Scott, J. C. (1998). *Seeing Like a State: How Certain Schemes to Improve the Human Condition Have Failed*. New Haven: Yale University Press.

Seddon, D. (ed.). (1978). *Relations of Production: Marxist Approaches to Economic Anthropology*. London: Frank Cass.

Sen, A. K. (1984). *Resources, Values and Development*. Oxford: Blackwell.

Sen, A. K. (1985). *Commodities and Capabilities*. Amsterdam: Elsevier.

Sen, A. K. (1999). *Development as Freedom*. New York: Knopf.

Sharma, K. (2000). *Rediscovering Dharavi: Stories from Asia's Largest Slum*. New York: Penguin Books.

Siegel, J. T. (1997). *Fetish, Recognition, Revolution*. Princeton: Princeton University Press.

Silverstein, M. (1976). "Shifters, Linguistic Categories, and Cultural Description." In K. Basso and H. Selby (eds.), *Meaning and Anthropology*. New York: Harper & Row.

Simmel, G. (1957). "Fashion." *American Journal of Sociology* 62(6), 541–58.

Simmel, G. (1978 [1907]). *The Philosophy of Money*. London: Routledge.

Smith, F. M. (1987). *The Vedic Sacrifice in Transition: A Translation and Study of the Trikandamandana of Bhaskara Misra*. Poona: Bhandarkar Oriental Research Institute.

Sombart, W. (1967). *Luxury and Capitalism*. Ann Arbor: University of Michigan Press.

Sorkin, A. R. (2009). *Too Big to Fail: The Inside Story of How Wall Street and Washington Fought to Save the Financial System—and Themselves*. New York: Viking.

Spooner, B. (1986). "Weavers and Dealers: the Authenticity of an Oriental Carpet." In Appadurai, A. (ed.), *The Social Life of Things: Commodities in Cultural Perspective*. Cambridge: Cambridge University Press.

Sraffa, P. (1960). *Production of Commodities by Means of Commodities*. Cambridge: Cambridge University Press.

Srikrishna, B.N. (1998). *Damning Verdict: Report of the Srikrishna Commission*. Mumbai: Sabrang Communications and Publishing.

Stewart, S. (1984). *On Longing: Narratives of the Miniature, the Gigantic, the Souvenir, the Collection*. Baltimore: Johns Hopkins University Press.

Strathern, A. J. (1983). "The Kula in Comparative Perspective." In J. W. Leach and E. Leach (eds.), *The Kula: New Perspectives on Massim Exchange*. Cambridge: Cambridge University Press.

Swallow, D. (1982). "Production and Control in the Indian Garment Export Industry." In E. Goody (ed.), *From Craft to Industry: The Ethnography of Proto-Industrial Cloth Production*. Cambridge: Cambridge University Press.

Tambiah, S. J. (1984). *The Buddhist Saints of the Forest and the Cult of Amulets: A Study in Charisma, Hagiography, Sectarianism, and Millennial Buddhism*. Cambridge: Cambridge University Press.

Taussig, M. T. (1980). *The Devil and Commodity Fetishism in South America*. Chapel Hill: University of North Carolina Press.

Taylor, C. (1992). *Multiculturalism and the Politics of Recognition: An Essay*. Princeton: Princeton University Press.

Taylor, C. (1992). "The Politics of Recognition." In A. Gutmann and C. Taylor (eds.), *Multiculturalism and "The Politics of Recognition."* Princeton: Princeton University Press.

Tett, G. (2009). *Fool's Gold: How the Bold Dream of a Small Tribe at J. P. Morgan Was Corrupted by Wall Street Greed and Unleashed a Catastrophe*. New York: Free Press.

Thapar, R. (1989). "Syndicated Hinduism." In G.-D. Sontheimer and H. Kulke (eds.), *Hinduism Reconsidered*. New Delhi: Manohar Publications.

Thirsk, J. (1978). *Economic Policy and Projects*. Oxford: Clarendon Press.

Thompson, M. (1979). *Rubbish Theory: The Creation and Destruction of Value*. Oxford: Oxford University Press.

Toulmin, S. (1990). *Cosmopolis: The Hidden Agenda of Modernity*. New York: Free Press.

Turner, V. (1970). *The Forest of Symbols: Aspects of Ndembu Ritual*, Ithaca: Cornell University Press, 1970.

van der Veer, P. (1988). *Gods on Earth: The Management of Religious Experience and Identity in a North Indian Pilgrimage Centre*. London: Athlone Press.

van der Veer, P. (1994). *Religious Nationalism: Hindus and Muslims in India*. Berkeley: University of California Press.

Weber, M. (1958). *The Protestant Ethic and the Spirit of Capitalism*. T. Parsons (trans.). New York: Charles Scribner's Sons.

Weber, M. (1958). *The Religion of India: The Sociology of Hinduism and Buddhism*. Glencoe: Free Press.

Weber, M. (1978). *Economy and Society: An Outline of Interpretive Sociology*. G. Roth and C. Wittich (eds.). Berkeley: University of California Press.

Weber, M. (1978 [1922]). "Classes, Status Groups, and Parties." In W. G. Runciman (ed.), *Max Weber: Selections in Translation*. Cambridge: Cambridge University Press.

Weber, M. (1981 [1923]). *General Economic History*. New Brunswick: Transaction.

Weber, M., and Eisenstadt, S. N. (1968). *On Charisma and Institution Building.* Selected papers, edited and with an introduction by S. N. Eisenstadt. Chicago: University of Chicago Press.

Weber, M. (1996). *The Sociology of Religion,* J. P. Grossein, ed. and trans., with an introduction by Jean-Claude Passeron. Paris: Gallimard.

Weiner, A. B. (1983). "A World of Made is Not a World of Born: Doing Kula on Kiriwana." In J. W. Leach and E. Leach (eds.), *The Kula: New Perspectives on Massim Exchange.* Cambridge: Cambridge University Press.

Wessel, D. (2009). *In Fed We Trust: Ben Bernanke's War on the Great Panic.* New York: Crown Business.

Worsley, P. (1957). *The Trumpet Shall Sound: A Study of "Cargo" Cults in Melanesia.* London: MacGibbon & Kee.

Zaloom, C. (2006). *Out of the Pits: Traders and Technology from Chicago to London.* Chicago: University of Chicago Press.

Žižek, S. (1997). *The Plague of Fantasies.* London: Verso.

Index

accountability, 85, 128, 176, 190–1, 244, 248
accounting, 137, 161–2, 295
 "capital," in the work of M. Weber, 238, 245–7, 246n18–20
 sociology of, 245
 for uncertainty, 245–9
 See also numbers; statistics
activism, 61, 64, 115–16, 118, 201
 without borders, 156–7, 199
 See also Alliance, the housing; human right(s); nongovernmental organizations (NGOs)
Actor Network Theory (ANT), 251–2, 257–8
Adams, F. G., 53n136
advertising, 35, 58, 61, 262–3
aesthetics, 93, 226
 of commodity forms, 22, 29, 32–4, 44, 45, 51, 57, 117, 261
Agamben, G., 118, 118n3, 298n24
agency, 151, 164, 258, 288, 299
 See also Actor Network Theory (ANT); objects
ahimsa, 72, 74, 78, 82
Alliance, the housing, 123, 128–9
 consensus-building in, 159, 192–4
 federation model of, 159, 163–5, 171, 176, 212
 founding of, 154–55
 housing exhibitions of, 166–72, 206
 and the politics of knowledge, 161, 166–8, 171–3, 175, 190, 198–9
 and the politics of partnership, 128, 154, 159, 161–3, 165, 174–6, 191, 193
 and precedent–setting, 127–8, 165, 171, 175, 191
 realpolitik of, 160–1
 rituals of, 191–2, 194, 213
 and savings, 154, 164–5, 172, 174, 176, 198, 205–7, 212
 and self-surveys and enumeration, 166–7, 171, 194, 198, 205
 toilet festivals of (*sandas mela*), 166, 169–71, 206, 209–10
 See also nationalism; nongovernmental organizations (NGOs); Shack/Slum Dwellers International (SDI)
Alsop, J. W., 34n85
Alter, J., 72n2, 79n18
amputation. *See* surgery, political
Anderson, B., 64n6, 67, 67n8, 88–90, 89n10, 89n12, 101n1, 102n2
anomie, 98
anthropology, 2–3, 5–6, 9n2, 11, 19, 285–6, 292–3
 of India, 76

of nationalism, 88
and practice theory, 180
See also Actor Network Theory (ANT); area studies; comparative studies; culture; economics; future, the; globalization; good life, the; ritual; structuralism
anticipation, 183, 286–7, 293–9
anxiety of incompleteness, 91–3, 97
Appadurai, A., 72n2, 90n14, 91n16, 96n19, 121n5, 155n4, 275n2, 277n3, 279n4, 288n5
 and *Fear of Small Numbers*, 1, 63, 90–3
 and *Modernity at Large*, 1, 2n1, 63n2, 66n7, 68, 81n23, 82n25, 86n1, 91, 116n1, 155n1, 254n1–2, 257, 286n1, 287
 and *The Social Life of Things*, 2, 9n1, 65, 252, 256–8, 299
arbitrage, 220, 240, 249
architecture, 5, 115, 120, 223, 263, 266, 276, 286
area studies, 65–6, 217–18
Arendt, H., 48n122, 71–2, 73, 71n1, 104, 104n6, 118
art:
 auctions, 21, 27–8
 mechanical, 48–9
 tourist, 33, 34n86, 47, 50–1
asceticism, 117
 in Indic life and thought, 71–80, 86, 186
 militant or warrior, 71, 73, 75–80, 82–3, 86
 and capitalism, in M. Weber, 42, 236–8, 240, 243
aspiration(s), 110, 119, 213, 244, 254
 commercial, 77
 and culture, 180, 182–9, 194–5
 in economics, 187
 and the future as cultural fact, 286–7, 289–93, 298
 among housing activists, 117, 123, 191
 See also capacity to aspire, the; ethnography; research
attachment, full, 91, 91n16, 96n19
authenticity, 33, 34, 47–50, 59, 60, 86, 204
 See also expertise; technology
Azoy, G. W., 54n140

Babri Masjid, destruction of, 77, 133, 147–8, 150, 201
Balibar, E., 88–90, 89n11, 103, 103n3
Banks, M., 63n4
barter, 15–16, 19, 31
 See also finance
Bataille, G., 231, 295, 295n18

Batliwala, S., 200n3
Baudrillard, J., 14n19, 18n33, 27–8, 35, 37–8, 42, 48–52, 55n142, 231
Bauhaus, 34, 39
Bayly, C. A., 31n76, 36–9, 36n90, 76n13
Beck, U., 3, 3n2, 181n3
Behrman, J. R., 53n136
Benedict, B., 27n62, 51n131
Benjamin, W., 48–9, 48n122, 49n123
Bennett, J., 258n4
Berlin Wall, fall of the, 1, 3, 220
Beunza, D., 234n2, 239n10, 243n15
Bhabha, H. K., 67, 67n9, 197n1
Bhagavad Gita, 72–3
    Bindé, J., 161, 161n8
black or illegal markets, 61, 62, 97, 134, 136, 138, 141–2, 151
    See also market, the
Bloch, E., 289, 289n6
Bohannan, P., 20, 20n37, 26, 26n56, 33, 33n82
Bollywood. *See* India
Boltanski, L., 80n19, 251n29
Bombay. *See* Mumbai
Bose, S., 105–11
Bourdieu, P., 42, 52n134, 217, 231, 231n8
    and the gift, 17–18, 17n28, 18n30–32,
    and habitus, 81, 81n22, 212, 234–5, 288
    and taste, 38, 38n95, 48, 48n121, 57n147, 58n149,
    and theories of practice, 180, 180n1, 288
    See also gift, the; habitus
Braudel, F., 44, 44n108, 52n133, 145
Breckenridge, C., 51n131, 197n1, 279
Bretton Woods, 154, 156, 222
    See also International Monetary Fund; World Bank
Brewer, J., 266n7
Brouwer, M., 247–8, 247n25
Brown, L. D., 200n3
Buford, B., 103, 103n5
Burghart, R., 75, 75n10
Burra, S., 124n8, 205n7

Calame-Griaule, G., 292, 292n12
calculation, 11, 184, 273, 297
    in economics, 180, 187–8, 285–6
    and future making, 265
    political forms of, 95, 97
    spirit of, 31
    and tournaments of value, 27–8
    and uncertainty, 242–5
    and M. Weber, 42, 219, 229, 234, 235, 238, 242, 246
    See also gift, the
Callon, M., 234, 234n2, 238n8, 243, 243n14, 246, 251–2, 251n29, 252n31, 257–8
Campbell, S., 24n47, 25n48, 25n51, 26n55
capacity to aspire, the, 1, 126, 179, 184–95
    and communicative practices, 188, 194, 213
    and cosmopolitanism from below, 210, 213–14
    examples of, in social movements, 190–3

and future making, 179, 182–4, 188–9, 193–5, 289–90, 295
    and modernization theory, 229
    See also aspiration; citizenship; culture; democracy; development; imagination, the; research
capitalism, 86, 131, 224
    casino, 294–5
    and commodities, 21–2, 37–9, 46, 52–3, 56–8
    and design, 255–6
    disaster, 295–8
    millennial, 294
    in Mumbai, 134, 138, 143
    print, 67
    and M. Weber, 41, 52n133, 218, 224, 230, 233–52, 293
    See also asceticism; financialization; Marx, K.; United States
cargo cults, 52, 55–7, 295
cash, 115, 131–2
    and capital, 133
    as a guarante of cosmopolitanism, 137
    in Mumbai, as the city of, 134–8, 141, 142, 145–6, 151, 202, 204
    as a "signature of the visible," 137
cashocracy, 145
Cassady, R., 25n49
Cassanelli, L. V., 33–4, 33n83
Castells, M., 155n2
catastrophe bond ("cat bond"), 4, 297
Cattelino, J. R., 294n16
census, 80, 85, 90, 92, 117, 125, 166, 198
    See also governmentality
Chambers, R., 185n14
Chapman, A., 14, 14n18, 15–16, 15n21–2, 16n23
charisma, 105–6, 201, 210, 264
    contemporary forms of, in finance, 244, 247–8, 251
    and M. Weber, 2, 217–8, 230, 230n7, 240
Chatterjee, P., 101n1
Cheah, P., 197–8n1
Chiapello, E., 251n29
Chicago Grain Exchange, 52–3
China, 31, 64, 69, 118, 119, 210, 223, 278
    See also United States
cinema. *See* India; finance capital
circulation, 2, 9n1–2
    of commodities, objects, things, 9, 11–13, 16–18, 20, 24–5, 29, 41, 44–5, 47, 62
    versus connectivity, 65–6
    of currency, in Mumbai, 131, 135, 137
    the forms of, and the circulation of forms, 64–9, 71, 299–300
    mythologies of, 54–5, 57
    and the politics of value, 2, 299
    See also ethnography; Shack/Slum Dwellers International (SDI)
cities:
    of disposal, 125–6
    and global capital, 123–4, 131
    mega-, 1, 62, 82, 115, 120, 121, 123–4, 143

See also citizenship; economy, the; housing; Mumbai

citizenship, 61, 67, 86, 104, 166
  and the capacity to aspire, 126, 295
  efforts to reconstitute, among the urban poor, 155–6, 176–7
  in the public sphere, 171
  and research, 269–70, 276–7, 281–2
  uncertainty of, in cities, 131, 155, 158
  See also knowledge
citizenship, bare, 117–22, 126–9
  See also identity
citizenship, financial, 164
citizenship, spectral, 151
civil disobedience, 67, 78–9, 82
civil society, 1, 61, 123, 199–200, 209, 221, 280, 295
class-based internationalism, 153, 176
class, theories of, 41, 230–1, 253
cleansing:
  ethnic, 77, 86–99, 104
  urban, 146–51
  See also desire; ethnocide; genocide; violence
Cochrane, G., 56, 56n144
Cohan, W. D., 241n11
Cohen, J., 197n1
Collins, R., 52n135, 57n146
Comaroff, J., 181, 181n2, 295n17
Comaroff, J. L., 181, 181n2, 295n17
commodities, 2, 4, 9–12, 9n2, 61–2, 183, 221, 256
  biography of, 19, 23–4, 28–9, 39–41, 45, 256–7, 260
  enclaved, 22, 28–30, 32, 57–9
  life history of, 23, 29, 36, 39–41, 44, 49–50
  and knowledge, 12, 28, 33, 43, 45–60
  in motion, 11, 22, 30
  mythologies of, 51–2, 54–7
  paths and diversions of, 2, 12, 22–35, 44–5, 59–60, 64
  as signs, 42–3, 49, 55
  spirit of, 11–22, 29, 59
  See also aesthetics; capitalism; circulation; consumption; demand; desire; economy, the; fetish, the; gift, the; identity; Marx, K.; objects; ritual; speculation
commoditization, 21–3, 29–30, 36–7, 46, 56–7
  by diversion, 32–4
  of the fetish, 137
  of goods and services, 57–8
  of knowledge, 57
  speculative, 115
commodity chains, 62
commodity context, 19, 21, 28, 31, 54
commodity futures, 52–4, 57
commodity phase, 19, 21–3, 30
commodity situation, 19
communication, 37, 47, 64, 212, 280, 290
community-based organization (CBO), 123, 154
  See also nongovernmental organizations (NGOs)
comparative studies, 15, 18n31, 19, 28, 86

and the dilemmas of method, 65–6
and M. Weber, 2, 218, 231, 242–3, 293
consensus, 187, 227, 241
  and capacities and capabilities, 192–3
  in cultural theory, 181–2
  about research methods, 274–5
  rituals of producing, 184, 192, 194
consensus building. *See* Alliance, the housing; capacity to aspire, the
consumer(s):
  alienated, 51, 52, 56
  birth of the, 256
  democracy of the, 38
consumption, 9n2, 19, 29, 31, 33–58, 184, 188, 255, 257
  in Mumbai, 137–8, 144–6
  and M. Weber, 230–1
  See also demand; desire; fashion; luxury goods; sumptuary law
context. *See* demand; object(s)
corporations, multinational, 4, 61, 138, 171
corruption, 1, 61, 115, 118, 137, 161, 244
cosmopolis, 134, 209, 225–8, 227n6
cosmopolitanism, 1, 222–3
  from below, 198, 200, 210
  common understandings of, 197, 210
  inner dialectic of European, 225–7
  in Mumbai, 132–3, 137, 146, 152, 200–5
  and the politics of hope, 210–14
  as a tool of enfranchisement, 211
  of the urban poor, 173, 187, 205–10
  See also cash; decosmopolitanization; deep democracy; identity; nation, the
crime(s), 1, 115, 121, 131, 132, 207, 279
  against humanity, 120, 122
  organized, 62, 139, 148, 150–1
culture:
  anthropological theories of, 5, 63, 179–82, 189, 194, 217, 285, 292
  and the capacity to aspire, 179–95
  as a counterpoint to economy, 2, 179, 180, 187, 194
  and development or poverty reduction, 179, 180, 183–95
  and future making, 179, 180, 182, 194–5, 285, 293
  and language, 181, 260
  and meaning, 21
culture, material. *See* materiality
Curtin, P. D., 30n72, 39, 39n96

Dalton, G., 41n99
Damon, F. H., 25n53, 25n54, 26n55, 27n60
Das, V., 81n24, 288, 288n4
Davenport, W. H., 29–30, 29n68
Davidson, P., 247, 247n24
Davis, M., 199
D'Cruz, C., 205n7
De Boeck, F., 62n1
de Certeau, M., 81, 81n21
decosmopolitanization, 131–3, 151

deindustrialization, 142, 144, 152, 157
Deleuze, G., 257–58, 257n4
demand, 29–31, 34, 46, 56–60
    and desire, 12, 35–45
    mobilization or manipulation of, 35, 39, 58, 60
    of objects for contexts, 258, 261–2
    regulation of, 36–9, 43, 60
    and the force of the social, 16, 37–8
    supply and, 22, 25, 31, 39
    and value, 10, 36, 40
    See also consumption; price; sumptuary law
deep democracy, 155, 156, 163
    and compulsory cosmopolitanism, 210–14
    conditions of possibility for, 176–7
    norms and practices of, 163–71, 210
    and the politics of locality, 156–7, 169, 176
    and globalization, 153–4, 155, 173, 175–7
democracy, 1, 86, 91, 118, 198–9, 230, 269, 290
    without borders, 176
    and the capacity to aspire, 186–7, 195, 295
    and development, 120, 195
    circulating forms of, 67, 69
    and future making, 299
    in India, 77, 118–19, 124
    paradoxes of, 175
    See also consumer(s); deep democracy;
        modernization; people, the; research
democratization, keys to, 210–11
demography, 117, 266
derivatives, 61, 136, 243, 249, 251, 277, 297
    See also gambling
Derrida, J., 233, 233n1
design, 5, 17, 58, 260
    challenge of, 264
    of everyday life, 253–4, 256
    and fashion, 255–6, 257, 261–5
    and future making, 3, 265–7, 299
    as a fundamental human capacity, 254
    history of, 254–6
    and housing, 116–7, 123, 128–9, 168–9
    and the illusion of singularity, 259, 263
    and planning, 5, 256, 265–7, 286
    and social and environmental sustainability, 5,
        265, 266–7
    See also education; expertise; imagination, the;
        market, the; objects
designer humanity, 6, 262, 263–5
design, interior, 263
desire:
    for commodities, 9–10, 55, 59
    and demand, 12, 35–45
    for purification, 98
    See also consumption
detachment, the doctrine of, 72–4
    See also attachment, full
development, 2, 122, 165, 173, 175
    and the capabilities approach, 183, 192–3
    and the capacity to aspire, 187, 190, 193–4, 290
    future-oriented logic of, 179, 180
    and housing in urban spaces, 120, 123, 127,
        168, 206

role of entrepreneurship in, 247
    studies of, 117, 213, 217, 289
    See also culture; democracy; economics;
        modernization
developmentalism, 219, 222
Devji, F., 291, 291n11
dharma, 73–4
diaspora, 64, 154, 157
Dies, E. J., 54n138
Dimaggio, P., 52n135
disjunctures, 2, 68, 133, 251
diversity, 5, 19, 63, 162, 181, 204, 206, 208, 289
Diwakar, R. R., 79n17
Douglas, M., 18n33, 30–1, 37–8, 52n134, 88,
    94–5, 183–4, 293–4
Dumont, L., 10n8, 17n26, 18n31, 31n75, 75,
    75n9, 76n12, 93
Durkheim, É., 93, 98, 187, 217, 221, 253, 287,
    294

economics, 4–5, 187–8, 240, 258
    and anthropology, 179, 194, 289
    and Knightian uncertainty, 4, 239, 239n10,
        245
    neoclassical, 12–13, 57–8, 285–6, 289
    as a science of the future, 180, 186
    and sociology, 13
    welfare or development, 182, 183, 266
economy, the, 5, 68, 85, 239n10, 246
    alternative forms of, 16
    of catastrophe, 295
    and commodity exchange, 13, 20, 29, 36–8, 50,
        51, 54, 57
    faith-based, 243
    global cities in, including Mumbai, 121, 124,
        125, 132–8, 143, 155, 157, 202, 206
    in nineteenth-century thought, 14
    as the product of a forward looking process,
        247
    service sector of, 143, 157, 158, 199
    as a social form, 10
    and M. Weber, 246
    See also culture; gift, the; political economy;
        United States
education, 63, 266, 269–70, 280–1
    and design, 264, 278
    and modernization theory, 153, 219–22, 225
    of the poor, 1–2, 158, 198, 210–11, 270
    transformation of, 278
    See also entrepreneurship; privatization;
        university system, the
Eisenstadt, S. N., 230, 230n7
emergency, 80, 286, 288, 298
    as a branch of capitalist speculation, 295–8
    and the conditions of slum life, 121, 213
    ecological or as natural disaster, 116, 119, 220,
        291
    or the exception, 82–3, 118, 126, 218, 292
    "the tyranny of," 161–2
    See also patience
Engquist, J., 124n8

entrepreneurship, 32, 34, 46, 69, 219, 222
    in education, 277–8
    in Mumbai, 137–8, 143, 145, 202
    spirit of, 33, 298
    and M. Weber, 230, 237–8, 247, 295, 298
    See also development
Erikson, E. H., 72n2
ethics:
    corporate, 244–5
    of the everyday, 292
    See also asceticism; possibility, ethics of;
        research; risk; Weber, M.
ethnicity, 77, 134
ethnicization, 90, 92–3, 133, 153
ethno- or Euro- centrism, 18, 219, 226–8
ethnocide, 1, 77, 88, 91–2, 94, 98, 149, 152, 222
    See also cleansing; genocide; globalization;
        violence
ethnography, 22, 77, 87, 133, 190, 254, 285, 287
    of aspiration, 1
    of circulations, 155
    of anticipation, finance, risk, and/or
        speculation, 243n13, 249, 293–4, 298
    of tournaments of value, 20n38
Evans-Pritchard, E. E., 46, 46n110, 293–4
everyday, production of the, 80–1, 256, 288
    See also design
exchange, economic, 9–33, 9n2, 18n31, 20n38,
    36–44, 47, 52–9
    See also economy, the; gift, the; value
exchange value, 13–15, 21
exclusivity of commodity forms, 28, 48, 58
    See also luxury goods
exit. *See* Hirschman, A.; recognition
"experience-near" and "experience-distant," 189
expertise, 60, 118, 155, 267, 300
    anti-, 159
    and authenticity or credentialism in
        commodity flows, 47–51, 57
    in design and fashion, 38, 264
    technical, 153
    and the techniques of calculability, 244
    and the urban poor, 164–5, 168, 171, 191, 208,
        210

family, as a site of consanguinity, 102–4, 109–11
fashion, 31n76, 34, 49, 63
    politics of, 412, 43, 59–60
    and the regulation of consumption, 31, 38,
        43
    See also design; expertise; sumptuary laws
federation model of activism. *See* Alliance, the
    housing
Fernandez, J., 88n8, 184, 184n13, 192
fetishism, 222
    of commodities, 10, 14, 56–7, 137, 295
    of the consumer, 58
    methodological, 11
    See also commoditization; Marx, K.
fetishization, 53, 137
finance, 2, 115, 127, 129, 133, 251n29

barter as a response to barriers in
    international, 16
crisis or meltdown in, in the late 2000s, 4–5,
    62, 238, 246
and innovation, 247
as a means to exploit risk and uncertainty, 238,
    240–1, 248–9
social science of, 233, 238–9, 243n13, 245,
    249, 285
as a strategy of divination, 248
    See also citizenship; performativity;
        speculation
finance capital, 41, 62, 277
    and the disconnect between manufacture, 219
    and the film industry (*See also* India), 69, 136
    in Mumbai, 131, 133, 144
    See also globalization
financialization of contemporary capitalism, 61,
    238–9, 242, 249
Firth, R., 11, 11n10, 25, 25n50, 25n52
Fliegelman, J., 67, 67n12
flows, global cultural, 61–65
    See also circulation; disjunctures; identity;
        knowledge
Fordism, 132
Fordism, post, 131, 143
Foucault, M., 50, 85, 166–7, 166n9, 220, 224, 229,
    295
Frankfurt School, 217, 229
Fraser, N., 182n5, 289, 289n9
Freud, S., 81, 93, 98, 253, 259–60
future, the, 3, 5, 226, 191, 297
    as an affective reality, 287, 298–9
    anthropology of, 3, 5–6, 180, 182, 286, 288,
        292–3, 295, 299–300
    cities of, 129, 147
    as cultural fact, 267, 283, 285–7, 293, 299
    prediction of, 244, 293
    in the natural and social sciences, 180, 186,
        285–6, 287, 289, 292
    See also aspiration; calculation; capacity to
        aspire, the; culture; design; development;
        economics; imagination; knowledge;
        modernization; nation-state, the;
        research

gambling, 4, 230, 237, 245, 248, 250, 294n21,
    297–8
Gandhi, M., 36–7, 39, 67, 71–3, 77–82, 86,
    105–10, 170, 186
    See also asceticism; civil disobedience; public
        sphere, the; violence
Garud, R., 239n10, 243n15
Geary, P., 29–30, 29n70, 49, 49n127
Geertz, C., 18n31, 30n71, 37, 47, 47n115–16,
    189, 189n15, 288
Gell, A., 35, 35n89, 51, 51n130
gender, politics of, 63–4
    See also violence; women
genocide, 63, 91–2, 98
    See also cleansing; ethnocide; violence

Ghassem-Fachandi, P., 77n16
ghost in the machine, 251–2
Ghurye, G. S., 76n12
Giddens, A., 155n2
gift, the, 11, 18n31, 202
    and the commodity, 12, 15–19, 25, 28, 30–1,
        39, 57, 256
    "impossibility" of, 233
    in Indic thought, 75–7
    and sacrifice, 103
    spirit of, 17, 39, 233, 250
    See also Bourdieu, P.; Mauss, M.
Gingrich, A., 63, 63n4
Girard, R., 75n7, 87–90, 87n2–4, 88n5, 94–8
globalization, 1–5, 65, 67, 69, 116, 155, 175, 181,
        253, 287, 299
    anthropology of, 63, 155
    from below, 153–4, 171–4
    and finance capital, 62, 131
    and the modern nation-state, 86, 90
    violence in the era of, 91–2, 104, 292
    and M. Weber, 230–1
    See also activism; deep democracy;
        governance; knowledge
global warming, 5, 255, 274, 286
Gluckman, M., 28, 28n67, 30
Goffman, E., 81, 81n20, 238n10
Goldthwaite, R., 42n104
good life, the, 5, 168, 187–8, 290–3, 299
Gourevitch, P., 91, 91n17, 98, 98n20
governance, 86, 115, 166, 175, 244, 266
    and the crisis of redundancy, 156
    in the era of globalization, 3, 92
governance, global, 154, 156, 172, 175
governance, good, 244
governmentality, 3, 288
    from below, 167
    strategies of, in cities, 155, 162, 166–7, 175
Graburn, N. H. H., 22n42, 33n78, 47, 47n119, 51,
        51n129
Gray, J. N., 20n38
Gregory, C. A., 17n26, 57
Grossein, J.P., 234, 234n4
Guantanamo, 118
Guattari, F., 257–8, 257n4
Gudeman, S., 46, 46n113
Guyer, P., 291n10

Habermas, J., 156n5, 217
habitus, 81, 212, 234–5, 252, 285, 288, 298
Hacking, I., 266n7, 295, 295n19
Hannerz, U., 181n3
Hardt, M., 289, 289n7
Hart, K., 17, 17n25, 17n27, 22, 22n41, 243n13,
        294n16
Harvey, D., 289, 289n8
Hebdige, D., 58n149
hedge funds, 4, 239n10, 240, 251, 297
Heesterman, J. C., 75n8
Heidegger, M., 116, 124–5
Held, D., 155n2

Hencken, H., 33n79
Herzfeld, M., 88n6
Hindu nationalism. See nationalism
Hindu right, the, 77, 109, 133, 147
Hindutva, 133, 147–8, 150
Hirschman, A. O., 182–3, 182n6, 186, 189,
        234n3, 240, 289
histories make geographies, 66, 69
Ho, K., 243n13
Hobsbawm, E. J., 101n1
Hodgson, M. G. S., 34n84
Holston, J., 116, 116n2, 121n5, 155n4
Honig, B., 67, 67n11
Honneth, A., 182n5, 289, 289n9
hope, politics of, 124–9, 198, 210–14, 229,
        289–93, 295
    See also cosmopolitanism
Hopkins, T. K., 224, 224n3
housing:
    as dwelling, 116–17, 122, 124–6, 127, 129
    humanity, building locality, 115–17
    and sleep, 139–40, 146, 158
    urban, as a window to the world, 198–200
    See also Alliance, the housing; aspiration;
        activism; design; development; human
        right(s); Mumbai; scarcity; South Africa;
        speculation; warfare
housing exhibitions. See Alliance, the housing
housing, spectral, 138–46, 151–2, 157
Hulme, P., 224, 224n4
human right(s), 182, 219, 291
    discourses, ideologies, and politics of, 80, 61,
        63, 156, 176, 199
    housing as a, 118, 120–2
    and transnational advocacy, 171
    of women, 95
    See also research; rights, crisis of hybridization,
        67–8, 245
Hyde, L., 17n26

identity, 67, 86, 91, 98, 179
    and bare citizenship, 128
    -based advocacy, 156–7
    cards, 121
    cosmopolitan, 197, 198, 210
    marked through commodities, 25, 29, 36,
        63
    uncertainty about, produced by global flows,
        91
Ignatieff, M., 80n19
imaginary:
    of land in Mumbai, 144, 146–47
    of the nation, 89
    of uncertainty, 239, 240–2
imagination, the, 22, 88, 116, 151–2, 171, 181,
        203, 209, 226
    and the capacity to aspire, 213, 293, 295
    and design, 253–4, 257, 262–3
    and future making, 213–14, 286–7, 298
    and nationalism, 106, 154
    the work of, 66–8, 82, 287–8

imagined communities, 66–7, 89–90
information, role of, in economic activity, 47,
    54–5, 142, 240
India:
    cloth and textiles in, 36, 39, 78, 132, 134, 136,
        143, 201–2
    colonialism in, 78, 132, 134, 146, 204
    film industry of (Bollywood), 1, 69, 132, 134,
        136, 143, 202–4, 279
    independence of, 105–7, 110
    and kingship, 71, 75–6
    and Partition, 92, 111, 288
    practices of caste in, 74–5, 185
    Red Fort Trial in, 105
    Salt March in, 78, 79
    secularism in, 69, 108, 109, 147, 152, 159, 208,
        220
    See also asceticism; democracy; Gandhi, M.;
        gift, the; Japan; nongovernmental
        organizations (NGOs); urban poor, the;
        violence
India, political parties of:
    Bharatiya Janata Party (BJP), 126, 147
    Communist Party, the, 126
    Congress Party, the, 105–10, 126
    Sangh Parivar, 132–3
    Shiva Sena, the, 132–3, 146–52, 157, 160,
        200–1, 204–5
India, states, peoples and languages of:
    Andhra Pradesh, 207, 211
    Assam, 105, 108
    Gujarat, 77–8, 97, 133, 137, 200–5, 207, 211,
        280
    Maharashtra, 133, 141, 143, 147–8, 154, 160,
        190, 200–5
    Uttar Pradesh, 133
Indian National Army (INA), 105–11
Indian state, the (Indian Union), 106, 119, 161,
    164
indigenous groups or peoples, 115, 157, 171
insurance, 135–6, 250, 294, 297–8
internally displaced person (IDP), 119
International Monetary Fund, 156
    See also Bretton Woods
intimate nation, the, 101–3
Iraq, 68, 92, 222, 296
Isherwood, B., 18n33, 37, 37n91, 52n134, 184n12

Janeway, W. H., 246n22, 247, 247n23
Japan, 64, 69, 290
    and its historical connections to India, 105–6,
        108
    and modernization theory, 219, 221
Jockin, A., 124n8, 126, 159, 164–5

Keck, M. E., 156n6, 199n2
Khare, R. S., 75n11
Klein, N., 295–8, 295n20, 296n21, 297n22
Knight, F. H., 4, 4n3, 128, 128n9, 238–9, 238n9,
    239n10, 243–51, 246n21–2, 251n29, 294
    See also risk; uncertainty

knowledge, 65, 66, 256
    in the age of globalization, 219, 220, 269–70,
        277–8, 281
    for the exercise of citizenship, 270
    and the flow of forms, 64
    and future making, 283
    local, 282
    production of reliable new, 269, 271–4,
        282–3
    See also Alliance, the housing; commodities;
        commoditization; expertise; market, the;
        research
Koch-Schulte, S., 185n14
Kopytoff, I., 10n9, 19–20, 19n35, 23, 23n43, 28,
    28n66, 29n69, 33n81, 37, 40, 40n97
Kristeva, J., 42
kula system, 23–8, 32–3, 39, 41, 44, 47, 53–4,
    56
Kurunmaki, L., 245n17

Lantz, M., 124n8
Latour, B., 234n2, 251–2, 251n29, 252n30, 257–8,
    257n3
Leach, E., 23n45, 27, 27n63
Lears, J., 248, 248n27
Lears, T. J. J., 52n135
Lee, B., 67, 67n10, 243n13, 247n26, 294n16
Lerner, D., 219
Levinas, E., 116, 124–5
Lewis, M., 241n11, 297–8, 297n23
Liberia, 92, 95–6
LiPuma, E., 243n13, 294n16
locality, production of, 62–3, 66, 67–9, 81–2,
    116–17, 253–4, 287–8
Lomnitz, C., 88–9, 89n9
longue durée, 65, 103, 254–6
Lopez, R. S., 52n133
Lorenzen, D. N., 76n13
Lubin, T., 74n6
luxury goods, 41–4, 46, 48, 261

MacKenzie, D., 234n2, 238n8, 246
magic as prediction, 54–6, 242–4, 293
magicality, 242
maha arati, 149, 149n10
Mahila Milan. See nongovernmental
    organizations (NGOs); women
"majority," category of, 91–3
Malinowski, B., 24, 24n46
Malkki, L. H., 88, 88n7
Manuel, P., 203n4
Marcus, G., 52n135, 54n139
market, the, 4, 36, 69, 179, 187, 248, 278, 297
    cornering, 54–5
    and design, 255, 259, 264, 267
    free, 1, 43, 53, 141, 219
    knowledge of, 46
    manipulation of, 5, 243, 247, 251
    See also black markets; commodity futures;
        religion; short sellers
Marriot, M., 27n61

Marx, K., 3, 253
    and commodity fetishism, 10, 14–15,
        14n15–17, 15n20, 53, 56, 295
    critiques of, 11n10, 12, 16, 37
    and the early political economists, 12–13,
        12n12, 60
    and F. Engels, 14–15
    and M. Mauss, 17
    and the spirit of the commodity in capitalism,
        12–17, 19, 21, 23
    and M. Weber, 41, 217, 228, 231
Marxism, 131, 153, 289
    neo, 58
    post- ,157
materiality, 9n1, 11, 136, 191, 257–8, 259
Maurer, B., 243n13, 294n16
Mauss, M., 10–11, 17n29, 26, 103, 235, 294
    and K. Marx, 17
    and the modern contract, 233
    and the problem of return, 233, 250–1
    and M. Weber, 234, 248
    See also gift, the
maya, doctrine of, 73, 73n3
Mbembe, A., 103, 103n4, 181n3, 295n17
media, the, 1, 129, 240
    See advertising; finance capital; India; Mumbai
Medick, H., 18n31
Mehrotra, R., 295n22
memory, 2, 88, 90, 107–11, 195, 285
microcredit, 4, 164, 244
migration, 5, 64, 80, 96, 122, 182, 212, 227, 265,
        269, 270, 290
Miller, D., 11n11
Miller, P., 245n17
Millo, Y., 234n2, 243n14
"minority," category of, 91–3
Mintz, S. W., 44, 44n108
missionizing, 226, 227, 290–2
Mitchell, W. J. T., 258n4
Mitlin, D., 205n7
Miyazaki, H., 243n13, 294n16
modernity, 49, 66, 222–3, 285
    alternative, counter or multiple forms of, 2,
        219
    canker at the core of, 220
    European ideas of, 225–6
    tension of traffic in, 69
    See also research
modernization, 61, 132, 223
    and development, 153–4, 210–11, 227–8
    and prediction, 222–3
    theory of, 217–22, 228–9
    See also education; Japan; Weber, M.
Moffatt, M., 122n7
money, 10, 13, 15–17, 31, 35, 38, 241, 297
    in M. Weber, 235–6, 246
    See also cash; cashocracy; Mumbai; profit-
        making
morality of refusal, 78–80, 82–3
Morris, C. R., 241n11
Mudimbe, V. Y., 224, 224n3

Mukerji, C., 42–4, 42n102, 43n105, 44n109,
        49n126, 52n134
multiculturalism, 64, 91, 152, 182, 197, 197n1,
        210, 211, 213
    See also pluralism
Mumbai:
    film, radio, and song of, 202–4
    history of, 132–4, 201, 204–5
    linguistic practices of, 200, 202, 203–5
    naming of, from Bombay, 146, 147, 151
    population size of, 151, 157–8
    rent in, 139–43, 149, 158, 167
    See also capitalism; cash; cosmopolitanism;
        economy, the; finance capital; housing;
        imaginary; nationalism; New Mumbai;
        public sphere, the; scarcity; speculation;
        university system, the
Muniesa, F., 234n2, 243n14
Munn, N. D., 23, 23n44, 26, 26n55, 26n58–59,
        46, 46n112, 47, 47n117, 51

Nappi, C., 53n137
Narayan, D., 185n14
nation, the, 89–90
    as the favored space of cosmopolitanism,
        197n1
    form of, 67–8, 103–4, 111
    as the inspiration for attachment, 102–4,
        109
    and narration, 66–7, 107–11
    and the novel, 66–8
    and the problem of parts, 85–6
    See also imaginary; intimate nation, the; nation,
        my father's; sacrifice
nationalism, 64, 66–8, 88–90, 101, 197n1, 220,
        266
    as affect, 101–2, 104, 109, 111
    ethno- , 80, 90–1
    Hindu, 76, 147–8, 157, 201
    in Mumbai, 132, 146, 148,
    official and unofficial, 90, 106–10
    role of the housing Alliance in movements of,
        175
    See also anthropology; imagination, the;
        religion
National Slum Dweller's Federation (NSDF).
        See nongovernmental organizations
        (NGOs)
nation, my father's, 104, 105–11
nation-state system, 85–6, 101, 153, 175, 277
    and the crisis of redundancy, 156
    future of, 101
    See also globalization
Nef, J. U., 42, 42n103, 52n133
Negri, A., 289, 289n7
Nehru, J., 105–10
Nepal, 64, 75, 198, 202, 206, 222, 290
neoliberalism, 153, 156, 294
    See also privatization
Netaji. See C. Bose
Neuwirth, R., 120n4

New Mumbai, 157
nongovernmental organizations (NGOs), in
    India:
    Mahila Milan, 123, 128, 154, 159, 162–3, 165,
        205–8, 211
    National Slum Dweller's Federation (NSDF),
        123, 126, 128, 154, 159, 162, 164, 205,
        207–8, 211
    PUKAR (Partners for the Urban Knowledge
        Action and Research), 1, 204n5, 269,
        279–82
    Sadak Chaap (Street Imprint), 154
    Shack/Slum Dwellers International. *See* Shack/
        Slum Dwellers International (SDI)
    Society for the Protection of Area Resource
        Centres (SPARC), 123, 128, 154, 159,
        162–3, 205
    See also Alliance, the housing
Nordstrom, C., 62n1
numbers, "avalanche of," 266n7, 295, 299
    See also accounting; Appadurai, A.; statistics
Nussbaum, M. C., 197n1

objectivism, 18
object(s), 61, 65, 266, 299
    as agents, 256–8
    and contexts, 258–63
    the context as, 263–5
    grammar of, 256, 260–2
    See also commodities; demand; design
offending part, 93–9
O'Leary, T., 245n17
ontology, 73–4, 73n3, 85, 223
Orientalism, 223
Ortner, S. B., 181, 181n2
outsourcing, 61, 93, 143, 156, 220

Pagden, A., 224, 224n4
Pakistan, 82, 95, 148, 149, 151, 172, 208
Patel, R., 185n14
Patel, S., 124n8, 205n7
Patel, V., 105
patience, 190–1, 212
    meets emergency, 177, 192
    as a political virtue, 222–3
    politics of (*See also* waiting, politics of),
        159–62, 165, 173
    and risk and hope, 125–9
pavement dwellers, 117, 132, 139, 148, 154, 157,
        207, 212, 214
    See also housing; urban poor, the
Pendse, S., 121n6, 149, 158, 158n7
    See also toilers
people, the, 67–8, 104, 169, 185
    "the production of the," 89
performativity, 67, 79
    of financial devices, 233–4, 237, 243, 246, 248
Perlin, F., 13n14
Petesch, P., 185n14
philanthropy, 137, 151, 173, 193, 280, 291
Pinch, W. R., 76, 76n14

pluralism, 80, 153, 181
    See also multiculturalism
pogroms, 77, 97, 148, 201
political economy, 33–6, 41–2, 48, 57, 154, 157,
        210
    See also Marx, K.
Pollock, S., 197n1, 227n6
possibility, ethics of:
    against the ethics of probability, 1, 3, 213, 244,
        295, 298–9
potlatch, 54, 250–1
poverty. *See* citizenship; citizenship, bare; culture;
        development; urban poor, the
precedent-setting. *See* Alliance, the housing
Preda, A., 243n16
prestige, 29, 48, 51, 122, 124, 173
price, 20, 43, 46–50, 58–9, 244
    and demand, 30, 267
    negotiation of, 25, 47–8
    shifts in, 39, 47, 52–5, 132, 246
    and utility, 36
    and value, 20, 53
Price, J. A., 21n40
primordialism, 101–2, 133, 222
privacy, 116, 122, 138, 167, 169
privatization, 156, 277–8, 296
Proctor, R., 94n18
profit-making, 235–7, 240, 243–8
public sphere, the, 204n5, 295
    failure of narratives to emerge in, 107–8
    and M. Gandhi, 77–8
    in Mumbai, 137, 150, 157
    and the urban poor, 169, 171
PUKAR (Partners for the Urban Knowledge
        Action and Research) *See*
        nongovernmental organizations (NGOs);
        research
purification. *See* cleansing

Al-Qaeda, 62

racism, 104, 219, 228
Rademacher, A., 185n14
rage, surplus of, 92–3, 97–8
Rao, V., 295n17
rational choice theory, 217–18, 229, 253, 292
recognition, 128, 139, 154, 169, 206, 210, 288
    changing the terms of, 186–7, 190–2, 194, 213,
        289–90
    politics of, 170–2, 182
    and redistribution, 126, 182, 185–6, 193, 229,
        276, 289, 292
research:
    and the capacity to aspire, 282–3
    as a democratizing activity, 267, 279–83
    deparochializing the idea of, 269–70, 282
    and future making, 280, 283
    as a human right, 1–2, 269–70, 276–8, 281–3
    internationalization of, 271, 275
    modern ethic of, 271–6
    and pedagogy, 275–6, 282

See also citizenship; knowledge; nongovernmental organizations (NGOs); Weber, M.
research methods, 65–6, 274–6
Reddy, W. M., 50, 50n128
Reich, R. B., 269, 269n1
religion:
  of the market, 243
  nationalism as, 102
  and M. Weber, 74, 74n4, 230–1, 242–3, 293
  See also ahimsa; India; missionizing; nationalism; United States; violence
Renfrew, C., 40–1, 40n98
reputation, 24–7, 54, 142, 230
rights, crisis of, 276–8
  See also human right(s); research; women
Riles, A., 243n13, 294n16
risk, 3–5, 53, 61, 183, 237–51, 249n28
  anticipation, speculation and, 293–9
  collaborative, in housing activism, 128–29
  devices measuring, 238–41, 248–52, 251n29
  ethics of, 229–30
  and grace in M. Weber, 237–9
  patience, hope and, 125–9
  See also finance; speculation; uncertainty
risk society, the, 3
ritual, 81, 184, 192, 194, 287–8
  and commodities, 27, 29–30, 46, 50, 55–6
  and sacrifice, 74, 77–8, 85
  and violence, 80, 87, 98, 151
  See also Alliance, the housing; consensus; Girard, R.; *maha arati*
Robbins, B., 197n1
Roitman, J. L., 295n17
Rosenau, J., 155n2
Rothermund, I., 72n2, 79n17
Rudolph, L. I., 219
Rudolph, S. H., 219
Rwanda, 91, 92, 98, 103

Sabean, D., 18n31
sacrifice, 2, 110
  in economic life, 9–10, 20, 59
  violence of, 74–80, 82, 86–90, 94, 97–8, 102–4, 109
  See also asceticism; gift, the; ritual
Sadak Chaap (Street Imprint). *See* nongovernmental organizations (NGOs)
Sahlins, M. D., 16n24, 17n26, 18n31, 18n33, 32, 32n77, 52n134, 64n5
Said, E. W., 224, 224n3
Sarbanes-Oxley Act, 245
Sassen, S., 155n3, 181n3
Satterthwaite, D., 205n7
scapes, 68–9
scarcity, 10, 43, 267
  of housing in Mumbai, 138, 146, 151, 160
Schafft, K., 185n14
Schelling, T. C., 286n1
Schmidt, A., 11n10
Schudson, M., 52n135, 58, 58n148

Schumpeter, J. A., 234n3, 247
science and technology studies, 5, 251–2
Scott, J. C., 181, 181n2, 220n1, 265, 265n6
secularism, 226, 249, 273, 291
  See also India
Seddon, D., 13n13
semiotics, 11, 42, 43, 51, 55, 89
Sen, A. K., 183, 183n7–9, 193, 193n16, 289
sexuality, transformations of, 42
Shack/Slum Dwellers International (SDI), 123–7, 171, 192, 290
  and the circulation of internal critical debate, 173–4
  and horizontal learning and exchange, 172–3
  transnational funding of, 199
  See also Alliance, the housing; nongovernmental organizations (NGOs)
Shah, M. K., 185n14
Sharma, K., 124n8
short sellers, 239n10, 241–2, 242n12, 247–51, 249n28
Sierra Leone, 62, 95–6
Sikkink, K., 156n6, 199n2
Silverstein, M., 26on5
Simmel, G., 9–10, 9n3–5, 10n6–7, 12, 15, 19–21, 19n24, 19n36, 20n38–9, 31n76, 58, 98
Siu, L., 234n2
Smith, F. M., 74n5
social movements, 55, 125, 190, 290
  See also capacity to aspire, the
Society for the Protection of Area Resource Centres (SPARC). *See* nongovernmental organizations (NGOs)
Sombart, W., 36, 41–4, 41n101, 43n106, 52n133, 235–6
Sorkin, A.R., 241n11
South Africa, 117, 164, 171–3, 198, 209–10
South Korea, 291–2
sovereignty, 85, 91, 104, 148, 211, 277–8
spectrality. *See* housing, spectral
speculation, 1–4, 244, 272
  anticipation, risk and, 293–9
  in commodities, 28, 53–4, 57
  in housing, 124
  in Mumbai, 124, 136, 138, 143–4,
  See also commoditization; emergency; finance
Spooner, B., 33n80, 47–9, 47n114, 47n120
Sraffa, P., 13, 13n13
Srikrishna Commission, Report of the, 149n10
Stark, D., 234n2, 238n8
statistics, 3–4, 286
  disguising nature of, 119
  and the state, 166, 221, 266
  and the urban poor, 117, 119, 122–3, 167
  See also accounting; numbers
Stewart, M., 264
Stewart, S., 41n100, 51n132
Strathern, A. J., 25n53, 41n99
structuralism, 260–1
structuralism, post- , 217–18
subaltern, the, 106, 189, 218, 299

subjectivity, 9, 20, 62–4
sumptuary law, 27–8, 31, 33, 36–9, 43, 48, 60, 77, 261–2
   See also consumption; demand; fashion
surgery, political, 67, 88, 93–9
   See also amputation
Swallow, D., 47n118

tabu, 32, 37–8, 59–60
Tambiah, S. J., 17n25, 18n33
Taussig, M. T., 17n26, 46, 46n111, 56n145, 57
Taylor, C., 170n10, 182, 182n4, 186, 206, 289–90
technocratism, 111, 162, 219, 222, 299
technology:
   and the criteria of authenticity, 48–50
   and innovation, 40
   as "a plague of fantasies," 221
   revolutions in, 42, 156
   transfer, 153, 220, 222, 266
terror, 119, 199, 223, 291
   urban forms of, 62, 149–51
   "the war on," 208
Tett, G., 241n11
Thackeray, B., 147, 201
Thailand, 82, 164, 172, 198
Thapar, R., 147
therapy, 93, 98
Thirsk, J., 52n133
Thompson, M., 35, 35n87
"toilers," 121, 149, 151, 158, 207–8
toilet festivals (sandas mela). See Alliance, the housing
Tönnies, F., 17, 221
Toulmin, S., 225n5
   See also cosmopolis
trading, proprietary, 248, 249n28
trajectorism, 223–8
transparency, 128, 176, 212, 244, 273
trisula, 76–7
Turner, V., 287–8, 287n3

uncertainty, 4, 230, 294, 298
   innovative ideas in the face of, 247
   versus risk, 129, 238–9, 242, 249, 251
   social, 90–3
   spirit of, 238
   and M. Weber, 237, 246
   See also accounting; calculation; citizenship; finance; housing; identity; imaginary; Knight, F.; risk
United Nations, 63, 156, 276
   Centre for Human Settlements (UNCHS), 170–1, 199, 209–10
United States, 153
   activism in, 79, 159, 211
   capitalist development in, 52–3, 58, 238, 240, 243, 297
   and China, 277
   economy of, 248, 277
   evangelicals in, 290–2

social sciences in, 221, 266
   and M. Weber, 218, 235–6, 241
university system, the, 272–3, 275–6, 281, 282
   in Mumbai, 143, 276, 279–80
   and the rush to credentialize, 278
   in the West, 271
   See also education; research
urban poor, the:
   as an abstract political category, 184–6
   and the politics of visibility, 125, 155, 158, 167, 169, 173
   public sociality among, 169–71
   See also Alliance, the housing; citizenship; cosmopolitanism; education; expertise; housing; public sphere, the; statistics; violence
use value, 13–17
utility, economic, 10, 36–7, 202, 239–40
   See also price
utility, politics of, 162

valuation, economic, 10, 18n31, 20, 25, 29, 47, 239n10, 243, 246
value, economic, 9–60, 183, 247
   creation of, through paths and diversions, 12, 22–35
   exchange as a source of, 10
   and labor, 16, 38, 39, 46, 55
   politics of, 2, 9, 12, 26, 36, 59–60, 65
   regimes of, 2, 10, 21, 36, 59–60, 65, 257, 299
   tournaments of, 20n38, 27–8, 27n61, 53–4, 59
   See also demand; exchange value; price; use value; Weber, M.
van der Veer, P., 76–77, 76n13, 77n15, 102n2
van Gennep, A., 95
Veblen, T., 36–39, 231
victim, surrogate, 87–90, 98
violence, 2, 62–3, 66, 67, 86–99, 109, 156, 225, 299
   double geneology of non- , in India, 71, 73, 78, 79, 82
   as an exercise of male power, 77
   on a large-scale, 90–95, 103, 277
   against Muslims, 77, 96–7, 133, 146–52, 149n10, 157, 201, 208, 279
   non- , and abstention, 72–4, 75, 77–80, 86
   non- , as a form of action, 71–2, 73–5, 78–80, 82, 86
   non- , and sacrifice, 74–8, 102
   and the production of order, 80–3, 90, 91, 96, 103–4
   studies of, in the everyday, 288
   against the urban poor, 119
   See also asceticism; cleansing; ethnocide; genocide; globalization; housing; ritual; sacrifice; women
voice. See Hirschman, A.; recognition

Wallerstein, I. M., 224, 224n3
waiting, politics of, 126–9, 192
   See also patience

warfare, 20, 66, 80, 92, 102, 153, 182, 187, 225, 255, 286
and commodity flows, 32, 34, 62
in Indic thought, 71, 76–7
sociality of, 103
state-sponsored, 90
in urban housing, 115, 120, 149
waste, human:
and the politics of shit, 169–70
and waste humans, 123–5, 126
See also Alliance, the housing
Weber, M., 2–3, 217–18
and bureaucracy, 218, 242
and ethics, 74, 224, 228, 230, 234–8, 234n4, 235n5–6, 244–5, 249–50, 295, 298
and the "iron cage," 221
and methodicality, 230, 236–8, 242–4, 247
risk and grace in, 237–40, 237n7
spirit in, 228, 233–9, 251–2, 251n29, 298
and status groups, 76n31, 230–1
and human action, 235–7, 240, 243–6
and value-free research, 228, 273
and value and instrumental rationality, 229
See also accounting; asceticism; capitalism; calculation; charisma; comparative studies; consumption; economy, the; entrepreneurship; globalization; habitus; magic; magicality; Marx, K.; Mauss, M.; modernization; money; religion; uncertainty

Weiner, A. B., 26, 26n55, 26n57, 44n107
Wessel, D., 241n11
Wildavsky, A. B., 183n11, 294, 294n15
women:
activism of, among the poor See Alliance, the housing; nongovernmental organizations (NGOs) and Mahila Milan
rights of, 64, 95, 200
as sex-workers, 205, 207, 212
violence against, 92, 95–6, 171
See also gender; human right(s)
World Bank, 156, 161, 170, 173, 185, 193, 199
See also Bretton Woods
World Urban Forum, 199
Worsley, P., 55n143

xenophobia, 91, 103, 132–3, 147, 157, 220

Zaloom, C., 243n13
Žižek, S., 221, 221n2